Praise for the first editions of the Great Family Vacations series

"Stapen is a respected travel writer who has done some awfully good books on family travel. They're well researched, very well done."

—*USA Today*

"The *Great Family Vacations* series is an inspiration to parents in search of worthy destinations. Stapen is an eminently practical parent and travel expert, down to fine details. Perhaps even more important, she understands that exploring new places is a thrill that brings families closer together."

—Alexandra Kennedy, *FamilyFun Magazine*

"Stapen provides a reassuring and enthusiastic voice for families on the go."

—Christine Loomis, *Family Life Magazine*

"We found enough useful information to give these guides an A. Each section offers at-a-glance info and a What to See and Do section that includes everything from hot-air balloon rides to zoos, sports, theaters and shopping."

—Barbara Hertenstein, *St. Louis Dispatch*

"Candyce is a recognized authority on the subjects of family travel and vacations. . . . [These books] are well laid out for efficient use. The exposition is clear and friendly and kids as well as parents can read and profit from these books. Covering places all over the U.S. and Canada, it's a good set for the family to have."

—Robert Scott Milne, *Travelwriter Marketletter*

Help Us Keep This Guide Up to Date

Every effort has been made by the author and editors to make this guide as accurate and useful as possible. However, many things can change after a guide is published—establishments close, phone numbers change, facilities come under new management, housing costs fluctuate, and so on.

We would love to hear from you concerning your experiences with this guide and how you feel it could be made better and be kept up to date. While we may not be able to respond to all comments and suggestions, we'll take them to heart and we'll make certain to share them with the author. Please send your comments and suggestions to the following address:

The Globe Pequot Press
Reader Response/Editorial Department
P.O. Box 480
Guilford, CT 06437

Or you may e-mail us at:

editorial@globe-pequot.com

or the author at:

chstapen@gfvac.com

Thanks for your input, and happy travels!

Great Family Vacations

South

Third Edition

Candyce H. Stapen

Guilford, Connecticut

Cover design by Adam Schwartzman
Cover photos: Eyewire, PhotoDisc®

Library of Congress Cataloging-in-Publication Data.

Stapen, Candyce H.
    Great family vacations. South / Candyce H. Stapen.—3rd ed.
        p. cm. — (Great family vacations series)
    Includes index.
    ISBN 0-7627-0907-3
    1. Southern States—Guidebooks. 2. Family recreation—Southern States—Guidebooks. I. Title.

F207.3 .S77 2001
917.504'42—dc21

                                                2001023089

Manufactured in the United States of America
Third Edition/First Printing

To my favorite traveling companions
Alissa, Matt, and David

Acknowledgments

I want to thank Diane Ney and Chelle Koster Walton
for their contributions, and my agent, Carol Mann, for her support.

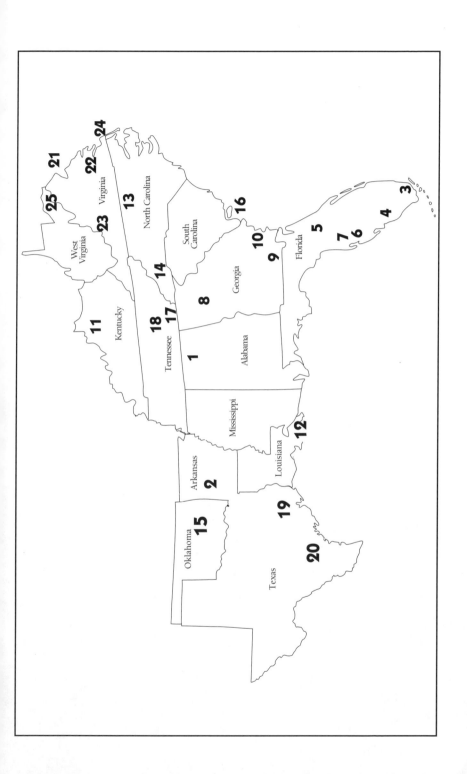

Contents

About the Author

Candyce H. Stapen is an expert on family travel. She appears on many television, cable, and radio shows, including *Today, Good Morning America,* WUSA-TV, D.C., and National Public Radio. A member of the Society of American Travel Writers and the Travel Journalists Guild, she is a contributing editor/columnist for *Expedia.com, FamilyFun,* the *Washington Times,* Familytravelnetwork.com, and *Physicians' Travel & Meeting Guide.*

In addition, her articles about family travel appear in a variety of newspapers and magazines, including *Parents, Good Housekeeping, Child, Family Circle,* USAWeekend.com, the *New York Post, National Geographic Traveler,* and *Diversion.*

Other books by Stapen are *Great Family Vacations: Northeast, Great Family Vacations: Midwest and Rocky Mountains,* and *Great Family Vacations: West* (Globe Pequot); *Family Adventure Guide: Virginia* (Globe Pequot); *National Geographic Guide to Family Adventure Vacations* (National Geographic); *Blue Guide Washington, D.C.* (W.W. Norton); and *Cruise Vacations with Kids* (Prima).

Stapen lives in Washington, D.C., and travels whenever she can with her husband and two children.

Introduction

There is a Chinese proverb that says the wise parent gives a child roots and wings. By traveling with your children, you can bestow many gifts upon them: a strong sense of family bonds, memories that last a lifetime, and a joyful vision of the world.

Traveling with your children offers many bonuses for you and your family. These days no parent or child has an excessive amount of free time. Whether you work in the home or outside it, your days are filled with meetings, deadlines, household errands, and carpool commitments. Your child most likely keeps equally busy with scouts, soccer, music lessons, computer clinics, basketball, and/or ballet. When your family stays home, your time together is likely to be limited to sharing quick dinners and overseeing homework. If there's a teen in your house, an age known for endless hours spent with friends, your encounters often shrink to swapping phone messages and car keys.

But take your child on the road with you, and both of you have plenty of time to talk and be together. Traveling together gives your family the luxury of becoming as expansive as the scenery. Over doughnuts in an airport lounge or dinner in a new hotel, you suddenly hear about that special science project or how it really felt to come in third in the swim meet. By sharing a drive along a country road or a visit to a city museum, your children get the space to view you as a person and not just as a parent.

Additionally, both you and your kids gain new perspectives on life. Children who spend time in a different locale, whether it's a national forest or a city new to them, expand their awareness. For you as a parent, traveling with your kids brings the added bonus of enabling you to see again with a child's eye. When you show a six-year-old a reconstructed Colonial village or share the stars in a Tennessee mountain night sky with a thirteen-year-old, you feel the world twinkle with as much possibility as when you first encountered these sights long ago.

Part of this excitement is a result of the exuberance kids bring, and part is from the instant friendships kids establish. Street vendors save their best deals for preschoolers, and, even on a crowded rush hour bus, a child by your side turns a fellow commuter from a stranger into a friend. Before your stop comes you'll often be advised of the best toy shop in town and directed to a local cafe with a kid-pleasing menu at prices guaranteed to put a smile on your face.

New perspectives also come from the activities you participate in with your children. Most of these activities you would probably pass up when shuttling solo. Whether it's finding all the dogs in the paintings at an art museum, playing miniature golf at a resort, or trying horseback riding in a park, you always learn more when you take your kids.

Surprisingly, traveling with your kids can also be cost-effective and practical. By combining or by extending a work-related trip into a vacation, you save money since your company picks up a good part of your expenses. Because tag-along tots on business trips are an increasing trend, several hotel chains have responded with a range of family-friendly amenities including children's programs, child-safe rooms, and milk and cookies at bedtime.

For all these reasons traveling with your children presents many wonderful opportunities. It is a great adventure to be a parent, and it is made more wondrous when you travel with your children. You will not only take pleasure in each other's company, but you will return home with memories to savor for a lifetime.

Family Travel Tips

Great family vacations require careful planning and the cooperation of all family members. Before you go you need to think about such essentials as how to keep sibling fights to a minimum and how to be prepared for medical emergencies. While en route you want to be sure to make road trips and plane rides fun, even with a toddler. You want to be certain that the room that is awaiting your family is safe and that your family makes the most of being together. When visiting relatives, you want to eliminate friction by following the house rules. These tips, gathered from a host of families, go a long way toward making your trips good ones.

General Rules

1. Meet the needs of the youngest family member. Your raft trip won't be fun if you're constantly worried about your three-year-old being bumped overboard by the white water the tour operator failed to mention or if your first-grader gets bored with the day's itinerary of art museums.
2. Underplan. Your city adventure will dissolve in tears—yours and your toddler's—if you've scheduled too many sites and not enough time for the serendipitous. If your child delights in playing with the robots at the science museum, linger there and skip the afternoon's proposed visit to the history center.
3. Go for the green spaces. Seek out an area's parks. Pack a picnic lunch and take time to throw a Frisbee, play catch, or simply enjoy relaxing in the sun and people watching.
4. Enlist the cooperation of your kids by including them in the decision making. While family vacation voting is not quite a democracy, con-

sider your kids' needs. Is there a way to combine your teen's desire to be near "the action" with your spouse's request for seclusion? Perhaps book a self-contained resort on a quiet beach that also features a nightspot.

5. Understand your rhythms of the road. Some families like traveling at night so that the kids sleep in the car or on the plane. Others avoid traveling during the evening cranky hours and prefer to leave early in the morning.

6. Plan to spend time alone with each of your children as well as with your spouse. Take a walk, write in a journal together, play ball, share ice cream in the snack shop, etc. Even the simplest things done together create valuable family memories.

7. Have a sense of humor. Attractions get crowded, cars break down, and kids spit up. Remember why you came on vacation in the first place—to have fun with your kids.

Don't Leave Home Without

1. *Emergency medical kit.* The first thing we always pack is the emergency medical kit, a bag we keep ready to go with all those things that suddenly become important at 3:00 A.M. This is no hour to be searching the streets for baby aspirin or Band-Aids. Make sure your kit includes items suitable for adults as well as children. Be sure to bring:

- aspirin or an aspirin substitute
- a thermometer
- cough syrup
- a decongestant
- medication to relieve diarrhea
- a rehydration packet which, when mixed with water, helps replenish needed electrolytes
- bandages and Band-Aids
- gauze pads
- antibiotic ointment and a physician-approved antibiotic, just in case
- a motion-sickness remedy
- sunscreen
- insect repellent
- ointments or spray to soothe sunburn, rashes, and poison ivy
- something to soothe insect stings
- a physician-approved antihistamine to reduce swelling in case of allergies to insect bites and other things
- any medications needed on a regular basis
- tweezers and a sterile needle to remove splinters

Keep this kit with you in your carry-on luggage or on the front seat of your car.

2. *Snack food.* As soon as we land somewhere or pull up to a museum for a visit, my daughter usually wants food. Instead of arguing or wasting time and money on snacks, we carry granola bars. She munches on these reasonably nutritious snacks while we continue on schedule.

3. *Inflatable pillow and travel products.* Whether on the road or in a plane, these inflatable wonders help me and the kids sleep. For travel pillows plus an excellent variety of light yet durable travel products including hair dryers, luggage straps, alarms, adaptor plugs for electrical outlets, and clothing organizers, call Magellan's (800-962-4943; www.magellans.com). TravelSmith (800-950-1600; www.travelsmith.com) carries these items as well as clothing, mostly for teens and adults.

4. *Travel toys.* Kids don't have to be bored en route to your destination. Pack books, coloring games, and quiet toys. Some kids love story tapes on their personal cassette players. For innovative, custom-tailored travel kits full of magic pencil games, puzzles, and crafts for children three and a half or older, call Sealed With A Kiss (800-888-SWAK). Surprise your kids with one of these kits once you are on the road. They'll be happy and so will you.

Flying with Tots

1. Book early for the seat you like. Whether you prefer the aisle, window, or bulkhead for extra legroom, reserve your seat well in advance of your departure date.

2. Call the airlines at least forty-eight hours ahead to order meals that you know your kids will eat: children's dinners, hamburger platters, salads, etc.

3. Bring food on board that you know your kids like even if you've ordered a special meal. If your kids won't eat what's served at mealtime, at least they won't be hungry if they munch on nutritious snacks.

4. Be sure to explain each step of the plane ride to little kids so that they will understand that the airplane's noises and shaking do not mean that a crash is imminent.

5. Stuff your carry-on with everything you might need (including medications, extra kids' clothes, diapers, baby food, formula, and bottles) to get you through a long flight and a delay of several hours . . . just in case.

6. Bring a child safety seat (a car seat) on board. Although presently the law allows children under two to fly free if they sit on a parent's lap, the Federal Aviation Administration and the Air Transport Association support legislation that would require all kids to be in child safety seats. In order to get a seat on board, the seat must have a visible label stating approval for air travel, and you must purchase a

ticket for that seat. Without a ticket you are not guaranteed a place to put this child safety seat in case the plane is full.

7. With a toddler or young child, wrap little surprises to give as "presents" throughout the flight. These work wonderfully well to keep a wee one's interest.

8. Before boarding let your kids work off energy by walking around the airport lounge. Never let your child nap just before takeoff—save the sleepy moments for the plane.

9. If you're traveling with a lot of luggage, check it curbside before parking your car. This eliminates the awkward trip from long-term parking loaded down with kids, luggage, car seats, and strollers.

10. Give infants a bottle to suck on during take-offs and landings, as this relieves pressure in the ears.

Road Rules

1. Remember that the vacation starts as soon as you leave your home. Use this time on the road to talk with your children. Tell them anecdotes about your childhood or create stories for the road together.

2. Put toys for each child in his or her own mesh bag. This way the toys are easily located and visible instead of being strewn all over the car.

3. Avoid long rides. Break the trip up by stopping every two or three hours for a snack or to find a rest room. This lets kids stretch their legs.

4. When driving for several days, plan to arrive at your destination each day by 4:00 or 5:00 P.M. so that the kids can enjoy a swim at the hotel/motel. This turns long hauls into easily realized goals that are fun.

At the Destination

1. When traveling with young children, do a safety check of the hotel room and the premises as soon as you arrive. Put matches, glasses, ashtrays, and small items out of reach. Note if stair and balcony railings are widely spaced or easily climbed by eager tots and if windows lack screens or locks. Find out where the possible dangers are, and always keep track of your kids.

2. Schedule sight-seeing for the morning, but plan to be back at the resort or hotel by early afternoon so that your child can enjoy the pool, the beach, miniature golf, or other kid-friendly facilities.

3. Plan to spend some time alone with each of your children every day. With preteens and teens, keep active by playing tennis or basketball, jogging, or doing something else to burn energy.

4. Establish an amount of money that your child can spend on souvenirs. Stick to this limit, but let your child decide what he or she wants to buy.

With Relatives

1. Find out the rules of your relatives' house before you arrive, and inform your kids of them. Let them know, for example, that food is allowed only in the kitchen or dining room so that they won't bring sandwiches into the guest bedroom or den.
2. Tell your relatives about your kids' eating preferences. Let the person doing the cooking know that fried chicken is fine, but that your kids won't touch liver even if it is prepared with the famous family recipe.
3. To lessen the extra work and expense for relatives and to help eliminate friction, bring along or offer to shop and pay for those special items that only your kids eat—a favorite brand of cereal, juice, frozen pizza, or microwave kids' meal.
4. Discuss meal hours. If you know, for example, that grandma and grandpa always dine at 7:00 P.M. but that your preschooler and first-grader can't wait that long, feed your kids earlier at their usual time, and enjoy an adult dinner with your relatives later.
5. Find something suitable for each generation that your kids and relatives will enjoy doing together. Look over old family albums, have teens tape-record oral family histories, and have grade-schoolers take instant snapshots of the clan.
6. Find some way that your kids can help with the work of visiting. Even a nursery-school-age child feels good about helping to clear a table or sweep the kitchen floor.

Family Travel Planners

These specialists can help you assess your family's needs and find the vacation that's best for you.

■ *Family Travel Network.* (FTN) at www.familytravelnetwork.com has lots of information and advice about family vacations and destinations as well as bulletin boards. Find out what other parents think of various places.

■ *Family Travel Forum.* This newsletter has information about family trips. You can contact them at 891 Amsterdam Avenue, New York, NY 10025; (212) 665-6124; www.familytravelforum.com.

■ *Rascals in Paradise.* Specializing in family and small-group tours to the Caribbean, Mexico, and the South Pacific, some of which include nannies for each family and an escort to organize activities for the kids. Call (800) U-RASCAL for more information.

■ *Grandtravel.* This company offers a variety of domestic and international trips for grandparents and grandchildren seven through seventeen. (800) 247-7651.

■ *Families Welcome!* This agency offers travel packages for families in European cities and New York. With rental of a hotel room or apartment, you receive a "Welcome Kit" of tips on sight-seeing, restaurants, and museums. (800) 326-0724.

> *The prices and rates listed in this guidebook were confirmed at press time. We recommend, however, that you call establishments before traveling to obtain current information.*

1 🐚 Alabama

HUNTSVILLE

E ver want to send your kids to the moon and back? Then come to Huntsville, where space exploration is a way of life. This small, friendly southern town has been making a name for itself as America's space capital since 1950, when Dr. Wernher von Braun and 117 German scientists arrived to develop rockets for the United States Army. The 16,000-person cotton town that von Braun joined has blossomed into a city of 180,000. The major family attractions here are the U.S. Space & Rocket Center and the living history museum, Alabama Constitution Village. Combine these educational activities with a hike or picnic at one of the beautiful surrounding parks.

GETTING THERE

Huntsville International Airport (256-772-9395; www.hsvairport.org) is serviced by seventy flights daily, operated by Delta, ComAir, American, Northwest, US Airways, and US Airways Express. The most frequent flights are to Atlanta.

Huntsville is easily reached by several highways. Take Highway 72 east from Memphis, Tennessee, or Highway 72 west from Chattanooga, Tennessee, to arrive at Huntsville, Alabama. I-65 south leads to Huntsville from Nashville, and I-65 north leads to Huntsville from Montgomery and Birmingham, Alabama. I-565 also leads here. The **Greyhound/ Trailways** downtown bus terminal is on the corner of Monroe and Holmes Streets, 1 block from the Von Braun Civic Center and the Chamber of Commerce. Huntsville does not have **Amtrak** train service. The nearest Amtrak train (800-USA-RAIL) arrives in Birmingham, about one hour and forty-five minutes away by car.

GETTING AROUND

Driving is the easiest way to get around town. **The Depot Trolley,** 320 Church Street (256-539-1860), offers a thirty-minute trolley ride through downtown Huntsville. You can get off and reboard for free.

Huntsville

▶ Go on a moon mission at Space Camp

▶ View rockets and the Hubble Telescope at the U.S. Space & Rocket Center and the Space Museum

▶ Tour the Marshall Space Flight Center and U.S. Space Camp

▶ Explore the Early Works Museum Complex

▶ Huntsville/Madison County Convention and Visitors Bureau, (800) SPACE-4U; www.huntsville.vy

WHAT TO SEE AND DO

Space Attractions

U.S. Space & Rocket Center, 1 Tranquility Base; (256) 837-3400; www.ussrc.com. The center is open daily 9:00 A.M. to 5:00 P.M., summers 9:00 A.M. to 6:00 P.M.; closed Thanksgiving Day, December 24, 25, and 31, and January 1. Dubbed the showplace of America's space program, the U.S. Space & Rocket Center is Huntsville's biggest attraction. "Awesome" is what your kids will call this vast park, which offers real-life space thrills and features more than sixty hands-on exhibits. The facility houses the NASA Visitors Center, the Space Museum, the Shuttle and Rocket Park, the U.S. Space Camp Training Center and its Space Camp Habitat, an IMAX movie theater, plus two gift shops, a cafeteria, and picnic grounds. This place offers a day or more of family fun. Begin by obtaining a map and brochure at the **NASA Visitors Center** at the entrance so that you can plan your day's activities.

The **Space Museum** chronicles space technology. One highlight is the full-scale, 43-foot Hubble Space Telescope originally constructed as NASA's major exhibit for the 1989 Paris Air Show. Other favorites are the *Apollo 16* command module, the training module of the *Skylab* space station, NASA spacesuits, the *Apollo 11* quarantine van, and a moon rock.

Outside at the **Rocket Park,** be awed by the most comprehensive collection of rocketry in the world. You can't help but see the 363-foot-tall Saturn V rocket that launched twenty-seven men to the moon, now a National Historic Landmark. Visit the simulated moonscape adjacent to the Saturn V to peer at the craters and look at the lunar module.

More than sixty hands-on exhibits will keep your kids busy at the U.S. Space & Rocket Center.

The grounds also bloom with high-tech military equipment developed by the U.S. Army Missile Command. Gawk at the Pershing II and Hawk missiles and the Patriot missile used to destroy Iraqi SCUDs in the Persian Gulf War. The United States Air Force's sleek SR-71 Blackbird draws a crowd as well. Kids will want to try out the **Space Shot,** a motion-based simulator that blasts them 150 feet in the air with 4Gs of force, duplicating the feel of a launch, and the **Mars Mission,** which takes them on a simulated ride across the Red Planet.

The **Centrifuge** exhibit, a family favorite, offers an introduction to astronaut training as it prepares you for the "G" forces of launch and reentry, three times the force of the earth's gravity.

Shuttle Park displays the only full-scale Space Shuttle exhibit in the United States, one formerly used to test procedures for the launching of the first shuttle from Florida. At the adjacent **Land the Shuttle** exhibit sit down and get ready to enact a space voyage that has you docking with an orbiting space station.

Blast off to the movies at the **Spacedome Theater,** whose 67-foot domed screen and IMAX films make you feel you're floating in space. Young children may prefer **Kids Cosmos** (for children eight and under), a play area with a Lunar Lander and a Space Station Crawl Structure.

NASA Bus Tour. Older children appreciate this ninety-minute tour, included in your admission ticket to see NASA engineers at work on the International Space Station at **Marshall Space Flight Center.** The

NASA center is actually located within an army base headquarters for the nation's missile defense program. The Patriot missile, hero of the Persian Gulf War, was created here, as was the Redstone, America's first rocket, used to launch the Explorer I satellite into the Earth's orbit in 1959. Marshall Space Flight Center is NASA's rocket base where Wernher von Braun and his team of German scientists developed the Saturn V rocket that launched three men to the moon in 1969. The tour includes a close-up view of NASA engineers at work on future sections of the space station.

Museums and Historic Sites

Sci-Quest is a hands-on science center for children and adults that's currently renovating its facility to add 150 interactive exhibits including the **Magnetic Chair,** which shows you what it feels like when two magnets pull apart instead of coming together. The **Tornado Tube** shows how a tornado is formed—with you inside it. The **Electricity Bridge** makes your hair stand up as you walk across it. Sci-Quest is located ½ mile from the Space Center, at 102D Wynn Drive, (256) 837-0606; www.sci-quest.org.

The **EarlyWorks Museum Complex,** 404 Madison Street (256-546-8100 or 800-678-1819; www.earlyworks.com, consists of four properties: EarlyWorks Children's Museum, Alabama Constitution Village, Historic Huntsville Depot, and the Humphreys-Rogers House. Admission.

EarlyWorks, 404 Madison Street (800-678-1819), part of Alabama Constitution Village, lets kids get hands-on lessons in Alabama history. Among the walk-in structures in the 49,000-square-foot facility are a log cabin, an old-fashioned drugstore, a courthouse, and a gristmill, complete with small stream. The "talking tree" is a favorite. Kids sit under the branches and listen to stories about ordinary and famous Alabamians of the past. A preschool learning gallery is scheduled to open in early 2001.

Alabama Constitution Village, 109 Gates Avenue; (800) 678-1819. Go from high-tech space back to 1819, when Alabama became the twenty-second state to join the Union.

Costumed interpreters dressed in nineteenth-century garb guide you on a ninety-minute tour of several authentically decorated Federal period buildings. Children will find more to look at than antiques. There's a whole village bustling with the activities of the season. An old-fashioned carpenter constructs furniture in Constitution Hall while a pressman generates copies of the 1819 state constitution, which was written on this site. In the nineteenth-century kitchen, visitors watch food being prepared the old-fashioned way, while outside by the vegetable garden a villager washes clothes in an iron pot. In the spring the village holds a Folk Life Festival, with candle dippers, spinners, blacksmiths, and woodworkers

U.S. Space & Rocket Center's Family Programs

- **Space Camp.** Enjoy an out-of-this-world weekend with the U.S. Space & Rocket Center's Parent and Child camp. On these three-day programs, teams of one parent (or grandparent) and one child (ages seven through eleven) train like an astronaut planning a shuttle mission. "Experience" weightlessness by strapping on the Five Degrees of Freedom Simulator that floats you above the ground, bounce as if on a moonwalk with the ⅙th Gravity Trainer, learn about space and build a rocket together. Reserve ahead.

- **Aviation Challenge.** If streaking across the skies in a bomber is more your style, sign up for the Pilot/Copilot three-day program. The Top Gun fighter pilot training, open to one parent (or grandparent) and one child (ages seven through eleven), includes lessons in a flight simulator and learning water survival tactics (just in case you are shot down).

Reserve ahead for both programs by calling the U.S. Space & Rocket Center at (800) 63-SPACE; www.spacecamp.com.

demonstrating their crafts, as well as children's games, such as hoops and sticks, plus storytellers, dancing, music, food, and appearances by historic personages such as George Washington, Ben Franklin, and Betsy Ross.

The **Humphreys-Rogers House,** 109 West Gates Avenue, has period rooms with antique furniture, including an 1850s Vose concert grand piano, plus special exhibits. Call (256) 538-1860 for information.

Huntsville Depot Museum, 320 Church Street; (256) 539-1860. At this train depot built in 1860, you'll discover the industrial history of Huntsville. Highlights include a robotic stationmaster, telegrapher, and engineer, graffiti that dates back to the Civil War and Alabama's largest public model railroad. At the Kid's Corner children can try on period costumes and play with maps and train puzzles. In September and October there's a Civil War Kids Encampment (for third-grade age and up). In this two-hour adventure, kids learn how to drill with muskets, make a poultice, and pack and unpack their own haversack.

For more backward looks peruse **Harrison Brothers Hardware Store,** Courthouse Square (256-536-3631), whose shelves simulate their 1897 look. Kids appreciate the hodgepodge array of hardware, goods, rocking chairs, and old-fashioned toys.

Older children interested in furniture might like the **Weeden House Museum,** 300 Gates Avenue (256-536-7718), a restored Federal house

Alabama's Black Heritage Trail

Along Alabama's Black Heritage Trail, the landscape comes alive with a tale of tears and triumphs. A self-guided tour, available through a brochure from the Alabama Bureau of Tourism and Travel (800-ALA-BAMA), takes you on a drive throughout the state, pointing out scenes of historic importance.

- Take a long weekend to trace African-American history from Selma to Montgomery to Tuskegee. In Selma travel along the route the freedom marchers took on March 7, 1965, to the Edmund Pettus Bridge, where armed police confronted them. Go back a century in struggle to the Old Live Oak Cemetery, where former slaves are buried.
- In Montgomery visit the moving Civil Rights Memorial, which lists the names of approximately forty people who died in the 1955-1968 struggle for racial equality. Then head to the Dexter Avenue King Memorial Baptist Church, the first pulpit for Dr. Martin Luther King, Jr., and imagine the future that Dr. King envisioned from here.
- In Tuskegee tour The Oaks, Booker T. Washington's home; the George Washington Carver Museum, which features the laboratory where Carver experimented with uses for peanuts; and the grounds of Tuskegee University, a formidable institution begun by ex-slave Booker T. Washington as a single school for thirty students.

The brochure highlights many other statewide sites, including scenes of struggle in Birmingham, black Civil War soldiers buried in Mobile, and the black infantry battles of 1864 at the Fort Morgan Historic Site in Gulf Shores.

that was home to Maria Howard Weeden, a nineteenth-century artist and poet. The **Huntsville Museum of Art,** 300 Church Street South in Big Spring International Park (256-535-4350 or 800-786-9095; www. hsvmuseum.org) houses seven galleries, which hold a permanent collection of more than 2,000 works of art, plus traveling exhibitions. Admission.

Burritt Museum and Park, U.S. 431 East; (256) 536-2882. Obtain a fuller perspective of Huntsville from the heights of Monte Sano, where a prominent physician constructed this fourteen-room mansion in the shape of an X. Inside, museum displays include local Indian artifacts. Costumed interpreters dressed in period clothing (1850 and 1900) add to the fun, especially on the second Saturday of each month when Step Back In Time occurs and interpreters invite families to join in activities. Closed

December 23 to March 1. Admission. Outdoors, the park offers 167 acres of trails to explore, some of which lead to a blacksmith shop, a smokehouse, a log cabin, and a picnic area.

Parks and Gardens

Take time out when you're downtown for a stroll through **Big Spring International Park,** between the courthouse square and the Von Braun Civic Center. Kids especially like the red Oriental bridge that spans the lagoon.

For more of the art of nature, instead of high-tech or historical happenings, walk along the grassy trails of the **Huntsville-Madison County Botanical Garden,** 4747 Bob Wallace Avenue; (256) 830-4447; www. hsvbg.org. Admission. This thirty-five-acre park offers a profusion of roses, daylilies, and dogwoods in season and more. Inside the **Center for Biospheric Education and Research,** visitors experience the multimedia show Biosphere Earth, presented on a fourteen-foot sphere. (Biospherics is a relatively new branch of science blending ecology, environmental science, biology, and physics.) Kids may also enjoy seeing the free-flying butterflies in the **Tessmann Butterfly House** and the oversized sculptures of butterflies outside. The Garden has a tea room that serves sandwiches, drinks, and snacks. Every Thanksgiving through New Year's Eve, there's a Galaxy of Lights drive-through exhibit of illuminated holiday displays. Admission. **Ditto Landing Marina,** U.S. 231 South at the Tennessee River (800-552-8769 or 256-883-9420), is a 253-acre park south of the city with picnic tables, campgrounds, and boat docks for public use.

Performing Arts

The **Von Braun Civic Center,** Clinton and Monroe Streets, is the hub of Huntsville's entertainment and houses a sports arena, concert hall, and playhouse. For information on Huntsville's cultural activities, call the Arts Council at (256) 533-1953.

SIDE TRIPS

Birmingham, Alabama's largest city, has much to see. At the **Birmingham Civil Rights Institute,** 520 Sixteenth Street North (205-328-9696; bcri.bham.al.us), teach your kids about the freedom riders. Programs include the Children's Corner every Thursday morning for children ages three to thirteen, which includes storytelling, puppetry, face painting, and magic, and Family Hour on the fourth Saturday of each month. The **Southern Museum of Flight,** at Thirty-seventh Avenue North and Seventy-third Street North (205-833-8226), has a collection of planes and an Alabama Aviation Hall of Fame. The **Birmingham Museum of Art,** 2000 Eighth Avenue North, (205-254-2566; www.artsBMA.org), has thirty galleries featuring art from the sixteenth century to the present. In the fall of 2001, a new exhibit, Town of the Creek Nation, will open, which will focus on those Native Americans who inhabited this area before their removal in the early 1800s. Hands-on activity stations throughout the exhibit will allow visitors to better understand the art of Creek beadwork and finger-weaving.

At the **McWane Center,** 200 Nineteenth Street North (205-714-8300; www.mcwane.org), a science center, little kids play at Just Mice Size, a hands-on learning area in which everything is much bigger than usual; crayons form a picket fence, and a milk carton is as big as a bus. At ScienceQuest older kids can lie on a bed of nails, build a roller coaster, and play a laser harp.

Two great places for strolling are the sixty-seven-acre **Birmingham Botanical Gardens,** 2612 Lane Park Road (205-414-3900), and the **Birmingham Zoo,** U.S. 280, Lane Park (205-879-0408 for recorded information, 205-879-0409, www.birminghamzoo.com) one of the South's largest facilities, with more than 1,000 animals, including a new Komodo dragon, on 100 acres. There are feedings, lion-training demonstrations, and a wildlife encounter show daily, and the zoo is free all day Tuesday and on Saturday mornings. Save time for **VisionLand,** I-20/59 (205-481-4750; www.visionlandpark.com), 16 miles southwest of Birmingham in Bessemer. This theme park has thrill rides, coasters, water slides, a rock climbing wall and more. Contact the Birmingham Convention and Visitors Bureau at (205) 458-8000, www.birminghamal.org.

SPECIAL EVENTS

Unless otherwise specified, call the Convention and Visitors Bureau (800-SPACE-4U) for additional information.

March. Finnegan's Parade celebrating St. Patrick's Day.

April. Panoply at Big Spring Park, a performing and visual arts fair.

May. Down Home Blues Festival, Hunt Park.

Summer Series. Monday night big-band Gazebo Concerts in Big Spring Park.

June. Black Arts Festival.

July. Fireworks Celebration at the Milton Frank Stadium.

September. Old Fashioned Trade Day.

October. At the Indian Heritage Festival, members of five native tribes demonstrate crafts and dances.

December. Holiday Parade of Lights at Ditto Landing on the Tennessee River.

WHERE TO STAY

The **Huntsville Hilton,** 401 Williams Avenue (256-533-1400 or 800-445-8667), located downtown near the train depot, offers special packages. The **Huntsville Marriott,** 5 Tranquility Base, with slightly higher rates, is located on the grounds of the U.S. Space & Rocket Center. Call (256) 830-2222 or (800) 228-9290; www.marriott.com.

Other possibilities are the **Holiday Inn—Research Park,** 5903 University Drive (256-830-0600 or 800-845-7275), or the **Hampton Inn-University,** 4815 University Drive (256-830-9400 or 800-426-7866; www.hampton-inn.com).

For a complete listing of area accommodations, call the Convention and Visitors Bureau at (800) SPACE-4U.

WHERE TO EAT

In downtown Huntsville try **Eunice's Country Kitchen** (256-534-9550), for southern country ham with biscuits and gravy. **Lofton's Huntsville Hilton** (256-533-1400) is a good dinner spot for seafood and steaks.

The **Cafe Berlin** (256-880-9920), a little farther out, serves German specialties. **Greenbrier Restaurant** (256-351-1800) features barbecued fare, plus catfish and other seafood.

There are several reasonably priced restaurants along University Drive: **Lone Star Steakhouse,** 5901 University Drive (256-837-0100; **Mr. Gratti's Pizza,** 4315 University Drive (256-830-2145); and **Waffle House,** 4896 University Drive (256-837-9781).

FOR MORE INFORMATION

Visitor Information Centers

Huntsville/Madison County Convention and Visitors Bureau Tourist Information Center, 700 Monroe Street: (800) SPACE-4U or (256) 551-2230; www.huntsville.org

Huntsville Recreation Services, (256) 532-7462

Emergency Numbers

Ambulance, fire, and police: 911

Huntsville Fire Department (general information): (256) 532-7401

Huntsville Hospital: (256) 533-8020; twenty-four-hour Emergency Room: (256) 533-5600

Huntsville Police: (256) 532-7200

Poison Control Hotline: (800) 462-0800

HOT SPRINGS NATIONAL PARK AND THE OZARKS

Hot Springs National Park, 50 miles southwest of Little Rock, is one of the only national parks in the middle of a city. At the turn of the century, the park's geothermal springs, believed to have healing powers, attracted the wealthy from around the world. While it's still possible to enjoy a soak, the Hot Springs area woos families by offering a wide variety of attractions plus recreation in the park, at nearby lakes, and in the surrounding Ouachita Mountains. An influx of $100 million worth of new attractions, new stores and new hotels, motels, and restaurants is turning Hot Springs into an up-and-coming—but still family-friendly—place.

GETTING THERE

Hot Springs has an airport, but the only commercial airline flying in is Aspen Airlines. The nearest major airport is the **Little Rock Regional Airport,** 2 miles east of downtown Little Rock on I-440, (501) 372-3430. **Hot Springs–Little Rock Airport Shuttle,** 217 Ward Street, offers regularly scheduled service by reservation from the airport to downtown Hot Springs. Call (501) 321-9911—Hot Springs; 376-4422—Little Rock; or (800) 643-1505. The drive takes one hour; kids under twelve, half price.

Amtrak's station is at Markham and Victory Streets, Little Rock; (501) 372-6841 or (800) USA-RAIL, and there's also a station at Malvern, sixteen miles from Hot Springs. **Greyhound** provides bus service to the Hot Springs' station at 229 West Grand Avenue, (800) 231-2222. By car Hot Springs can be reached from the north and south by Scenic Route 7, from the east by U.S. 70, and from the east and west by U.S. 270.

Hot Springs and the Ozarks

AT A GLANCE

- ▶ Soak in bubbling springs with a constant temperature of 143 degrees

- ▶ Watch traditional craftspeople at the Ozark Folk Center State Park

- ▶ Enjoy lake resorts and state parks

- ▶ Ride the roller coasters at Magic Springs

- ▶ Hot Springs Convention and Visitors Bureau; (800) SPA–CITY; www.hotsprings.org or www.eurekasprings.org

GETTING AROUND

Most Hot Springs attractions are within walking distance of downtown. **Hot Springs Intracity Transit,** 100 Broadway Terrace (501–321–2020), offers service throughout the historic district and to the top of Hot Springs Mountain in the park. Buses operate hourly.

WHAT TO SEE AND DO

Hot Springs National Park

As national parks go, **Hot Springs National Park**'s 5,800 acres qualifies it as rather small, although the park offers miles of scenic drives and hiking trails; www.nps.gov. Within ten acres along the west slope of Hot Springs Mountain are forty-seven streaming springs (several uncapped so that visitors can observe them). These bubble about a million gallons daily at a constant temperature of 143 degrees F. Along with bathing and hydrotherapy, these odorless waters are used in drinking and geo-thermal heating.

The park's main attractions are Bathhouse Row, Hot Springs Mountain Tower, Grand Promenade, 10 miles of good mountain roads for scenic drives, and walking trails of varying degrees of difficulty.

You can enter the park, which has no admission fee, from several points. Begin your tour on Central Avenue's **Bathhouse Row** in the heart of the compact downtown. Vintage buildings line the east side of Central Avenue, while shops, restaurants, and attractions, many housed in historic buildings, line the west side. In the 1890s twelve bathhouses operated, most of which were wooden frame Victorian buildings that soon were replaced because the hot water vapor rotted the timber. As a result, the bathhouses you see (dating from 1878 to 1923) are built of brick with iron, concrete, and marble.

Obtain information and discount coupons at the **Hot Springs Visitor Center,** 629 Central Avenue, in Hill Wheatley Plaza at the south end of Bathhouse Row.

A therapeutic and relaxing soak can still be had at several places, including **Buckstaff Bathhouse,** 509 Central Avenue (501-623-2308), where children are allowed, if they can be left on their own in the baths, and **Hot Springs Health Spa,** 500 Reserve Street (501-321-9664 or 321-1997; www.hs.com), which has coed pools where children are allowed. Massages are also offered.

Fordyce Bathhouse on Bathhouse Row, 369 Central Avenue (501-623-1433; www.nps.gov/hosp), now houses the Hot Springs National Park Visitors Center, with historical exhibits and an audiovisual presentation on the springs' early years. The Center is open year-round. In summer special family programs are offered several afternoons and evenings every week.

Built in 1915, the Fordyce Bathhouse is the largest and most ornate structure on the row. Park rangers lead guided tours of the interior and of the grounds, including the nearby exposed springs. Behind the Fordyce Bathhouse steps lead up to the **Grand Promenade,** a ¼-mile walk along a hillside, offering wonderful photo opportunities. The Promenade overlooks cascading thermal springs that flow downhill. This is the start of a number of trails that wind up **Hot Springs Mountain,** about a 2½-mile moderately strenuous hike. Dead Chief Trail, which starts at the Promenade, is one of the most popular. Other options: Drive to the mountaintop or board a motorized trolley from downtown. Once you arrive, take a glass elevator up to **The Mountain Tower** observation deck, 401 Hot Springs Mountain Drive (501-623-6035 or 800-SPA-CITY), for a panoramic view spanning 70 miles in every direction. You'll see the surrounding Ouachita Mountains, sparkling lakes, and downtown Hot Springs.

For more information contact the Superintendent, Hot Springs National Park, P.O. Box 1860, Hot Springs, AR 71902; (501) 624-3383.

Hot Springs Attractions

The town of Hot Springs is a curious blend of the historic and the tacky. You'll find the usual kitschy tourist shops right across the street from gracious buildings that recall the grandeur of days gone by. Here are some of the more popular attractions in town:

Magic Springs & Crystal Falls, 1701 Highway 70 East (501-624-0100; www.magicsprings.com), Hot Spring's newest attractions, are

Visitors of all ages enjoy testing the hot springs.

located in Hot Springs National Park in the foothills of the Ouachita Mountains and have more than seventy-five rides and attractions, plus three restaurants. At **Magic Springs,** older kids can try the Arkansas Twister, a 3,500-foot long roller coaster with drops of more than 100 feet, and Wild Thang, which suspends you 60 feet up, then twirls and spins you at the same time. Families can enjoy the Old No. 1 Logging Co. flume and the Rum Runner coaster, while younger children will be happy with the Kit n'Kaboodle Express train and the Fearless Flyers, in which they glide in a circle in their own airplane. **Crystal Falls** is a frontier-style water park with a forest setting. Crystal Cove has the big waves in its 350,000-gallon wave pool, and for younger children, there's Bear Cub Bend. Open May to mid-September. Admission.

Mid-America Science Museum, 500 Mid-America Boulevard; (501) 767-3461 or (800) 632-0583; www.midamericamuseum.com. Admission. This is a fun place. Kids can take part in enjoyable, hands-on exhibits about energy, gravity, sound waves, and perception, design a model of mountain ranges and rivers, create sparking electricity, crank up a mock tornado, and launch a hot-air balloon. A $1 million dollar renovation in the past several years has added exhibits such as an "underground" area that takes visitors on a trip through subterranean Earth, and through a very big earthworm. Take a Motion Simulator, ride to a glacier cave, a volcanic mine, or a car racetrack.

Tiny Town, 374 Whittington Avenue (501-624-4742), is a miniature city of hand-carved figurines, buildings, and landscapes. Teeny-tiny moving trains weave through little mountain ranges as animated scaled-down celebrities such as Marilyn Monroe and Clark Gable travel around town. **National Park Aquarium,** 209 Central Avenue; (501) 624-FISH; www.hotspringsusa.com/aquarium. Housing the largest exhibit of fish and reptiles in Arkansas, this aquarium lets you see how the other two-thirds of the world live. Here fish of Arkansas, such as largemouth bass, bream, and alligator gars, plus other colorful saltwater species swim in underwater scenes that re-create their natural habitats. Kids like to say "hi" to U.T. (Ugly Turtle), a 120-pound alligator snapping turtle, and there are educational (and fun) toys and games for children in the gift shop. Admission.

Kids dig for their own quartz crystals at **Ron Coleman's Mining,** 14 miles north of downtown on Highway 7 North; (501) 984-5396. The shop features such already-discovered treasures as large and small quartz, agates, whetstones, and amethysts.

Stop at **Castleberry Riding Stables,** off Highway 7 at 537 Walnut Valley Road, 8 miles north of downtown; (501) 623-6609 or 624-7291. This facility offers hayrides and mountain excursions, plus horseback riding (age six and up can ride alone) lessons, and campouts.

Green Spaces

The pine-dotted shores of 18½-mile **Lake Hamilton** hug the southwest corner of Hot Springs. From downtown follow Central Avenue (Highway 7) south, 270 West, or 70 West. The latter route leads to the free swimming area, **Hill Wheatley Park,** where you'll find a sandy beach, picnic tables, and playground, but no lifeguard. The *Belle of Hot Springs,* 5200 Central Avenue (Highway 7 South), features evening and day cruises every day from February to November; (501) 525-4438. **Salty Dog Boat and Jet Ski Rental,** 4931 Central Avenue, Highway 7 South, at the Island Complex (501-525-6400), offers miniboats, five-person wavecutters, ski boats and equipment, party barges, and parasail rides. For another lake ride try a "duck tour." **Garvan Woodland Gardens** (800-366-4664 or 501-671-2390; www.garvan.org), on 210 acres along the

Special Tours

- **President Clinton's Hot Springs.** Bill Clinton spent his boyhood in Hot Springs. Drive by such sites listed in the Convention and Visitors Bureau pamphlet as Clinton's former residence, his grade school, the site of his senior prom, and his favorite weekend hangouts.
- **Outdoor Adventure Tours,** 300 Long Island Drive (501–525-4457 or 800–489-TOUR; www.outdooradventuretours.com), has guided van tours of Clinton's haunts. The company also offers mountain biking, hiking, and canoeing excursions.
- **National Park Duck Tours,** 418 Central Avenue (501–321-2911 or 800–682-7044); and **Ducks in the Park,** 310 Central Avenue (501–624–DUCK). These tours offer combined water and land excursions aboard refurbished World War II amphibious vehicles.

Dig for Diamonds

At **Crater of Diamonds State Park,** southeast of Murfreesboro on Arkansas 301, about an hour southwest of Hot Springs (501-285-3113; www.arkansasstateparks.com), you can dig for diamonds and keep what you find (the park furnishes the tools). This is the only diamond mine in North America open to the public. You might also find jasper, agate, and amethyst. The park weighs your find and certifies whether or not it's the real thing. The park, on 888 acres along the banks of the Little Missouri River, offers orientation programs. Sixty campsites are equipped with electricity, water, laundry facilities, and an on-site restaurant; limited reservations available. In summer a daily program called Crater Minors for kids ages six to twelve is led by park interpreters, with a different theme each week.

shoreline of Lake Hamilton, is scheduled to open the spring of 2001. It will have a visitors' center and gift shop and will showcase native flowering plants and shrubs.

Theater, Music, and the Arts

On Central Avenue, between Canyon and Market Streets, dozens of renovated Victorian and early twentieth-century buildings now serve as galleries and working studios. Gallery walks the first Friday of each month explore about twenty-five galleries. While the galleries are open at other times, during these walks the hours are extended, and sometimes there are special presentations.

Bath House Show, 701 Central Avenue; (501) 623-1415. This two-hour, humorous musical includes toe-tapping fifties and sixties songs and the comedy of "Buford Presley."

For country tunes try the **Music Mountain Jamboree,** which has relocated to a new complex adjacent to Magic Springs & Crystal Falls at 1555 East Grand (501-767-3841). One of the pioneer country-music shows in the region, Jamboree offers a blend of country and comedy throughout the summer season, as well as several nights a week during the rest of the year. The new facility has indoor go-carts and an arcade.

Shopping

Thirty stores offer brand name bargains at **Hot Springs Factory Outlet,** Highway 7 South (Central Avenue just past Oaklawn); (501) 525-0888. You'll find Capezio, Book Warehouse, Fieldcrest Cannon, and more. **Hot Springs Mall,** 4501 Central Avenue, Highway 7 South (501-525-3254; www.shopmalls.com), has four large department stores, including Sears and JC Penney, plus seventy specialty shops.

SIDE TRIPS

Ouachita Foothills

Arkansas has some outstanding state parks (www.arkansasstateparks. com), most with interpretive programs. The following, in the Ouachita foothills, include rustic retreats, full-size resorts, and a park where you can dig for diamonds. All are within striking distance of Hot Springs.

- **Lake Catherine State Park,** 1200 Catherine Park Road (501-844-4176 or 800-264-2422), 10 miles southeast of Hot Springs, includes 2,180 acres of **Ouachita Mountain scenery.** The park has a playground, swimming area, and nature center with summer ranger-led interpretive programs for kids. The marina rents boats, life jackets, and fishing poles (and bait), and the park offers a **Party Barge Scenic Tour.** There's also horseback riding from Memorial Day to Labor Day. A grocery store/restaurant and laundry on premises add to the convenience. Seventeen cabins have kitchens (some with fireplaces) and access to a boat dock. Nineteen of the seventy campsites may be reserved.

- **Lake Ouachita State Park,** 5451 Mountain Pine Road; (501) 767-9366 or (800) 264-2441. About 15 miles west of the city is the state's largest man-made lake (48,000 acres with 975 miles of shoreline), considered one of the two cleanest lakes in the United States. At the eastern end visit legendary **Three Sisters' Springs,** once believed to have healing power. Enjoy scuba diving, boating (rent fishing boats or party barges at the marina), fishing, swimming, and picnicking. The visitor center has a store and snack bar. The park also has more than one hundred campsites and seven fully equipped cabins with kitchens. In summer only twenty-eight of the campsites may be reserved ahead of time; cabins can be reserved year-round. Check at the Visitor Center for ranger-led activities such as Leaf Walks and Snake Spotting during the day, and Star Tours and Sunset Lake Tours in the evening.

- **DeGray Lake Resort State Park,** off I-30 on Scenic Arkansas 7, 21 miles south of Hot Springs; (501) 865-2801 or (800) 737-8355—lodge; www.degray.com. This resort on the north shore of a 13,800-acre lake features an island lodge (accessible by a causeway) with comfortable rooms, outdoor pool, walking trails, tennis courts, eighteen-hole golf course, and a marina that rents everything from canoes and sailboats to party barges and houseboats, plus jet and water skis. There are many activities, including interpretive party barge tours, movies, outdoor workshops and special events such as fall color hayrides, fishing derbies, and moonlight cruises. There are 113 campsites; call for reservations (see Where to Stay for off-park lodging).

- **Queen Wilhelmina State Park,** west of Mena on Arkansas 88 (Tailmena Scenic Drive), 90 miles west of Hot Springs at 3877 Highway 88

Ozark Crafts

The **Ozark Folk Center State Park** (870-269-3851 or 800-264-FOLK—lodge; www.arkansasstateparks.com), a mile north of Mountain View on Spur 382 off Highways 5, 9, and 14, spreads out on eighty mountaintop acres. During the season (April through early November), craftspeople perform traditional Ozark skills such as wood carving and blacksmithing. Kids can sign up for the Young Pioneer Program. This entitles them to join a workshop or team up for a one-on-one learning experience with a particular craftsperson. Sessions are from one day to one week. Adults have similar options. In the evening, concerts are staged in the music hall, and on Sunday there is a gospel concert. Combination tickets (crafts and music) are available. The center has a lodge and two restaurants. There are festivals in the spring and fall.

West; (501) 394-2863 or (800) 264-2477. High in the sky on Rich Mountain, the state's second highest peak at 2,700 feet, and part of the Ouachita Range, this park is on the spot of an 1890s resort hostelry named in honor of the Queen of the Netherlands. The modern lodge has thirty-six guest rooms, a restaurant, a golf course, forty campsites, picnic areas, trails, an animal park, and a miniature scenic train that takes passengers on a ten- to fifteen-minute, 1½-mile trip around the grounds. The Deer Forest animal park is an "exotic" petting zoo, with llamas, pygmy goats, fallow deer, and emus. Various interpretive programs (sometimes with live animals) take place on some summer weekends. One-third of the park's campsites may be reserved.

- On the **Caddo River,** 28 miles west of Hot Springs at Caddo Gap, enjoy tubing, fishing, and canoeing. Arrowhead Cabin and Canoe Rentals, 191 Peppermint Terrace (870-356-2944), rents cabins (you supply linens and blankets) and also equipment for float trips down the Caddo River.

Eureka Springs and the Ozarks

If you have more time to explore Arkansas, head up to **Eureka Springs,** 200 miles northwest of Hot Springs, near the Missouri border. Nestled in a valley, this town and the surrounding Ozark Mountains are popular vacation destinations offering folk culture, natural beauty, and lots of recreation.

Put on your walking shoes and do some exploring. A guide that divides the city into six walking routes is available from the Chamber of Commerce office, Scenic Highway 62; (501) 253-8737 or (800) 6EUREKA—

tourist literature; www.eurekaspringschamber.com. Tours #1–5 are all under a mile; all involve "ups and downs." With young kids use the old-fashioned trolleys and open-air trams. Tour One, a popular route, begins and ends at the historic **Grand Central Hotel,** 37 North Main Street, and passes Victorian homes, limestone rock formations, and a view of West Mountain, the last home of temperance leader Carrie Nation.

Another worthwhile attraction is **Abundant Memories Heritage Village,** 2434 Highway 23 North; (501) 253-6764; www.abundantmemories.com, open April to November. Admission. In twenty-six authentically decorated buildings, the village displays toys, antiques, tools, military items, sleighs, and carriages dating from Revolutionary to Civil War times. For memories from an even earlier era, sample **Dinosaur World,** 8 miles west on Highway 287, open March–December; (501) 253-8133. This facility displays more than one hundred life-size dinosaurs—and a four-story replica of King Kong. Outside there are picnic tables and miniature golf; inside is a cafe.

There's also **Eureka Springs Gardens,** 5 ½ miles on Scenic Highway 62 West, (501) 253-9256—recording, or 253-9244; www.eurekagardens.com. Wooden walkways lead to forsythia, lilacs, wildflowers, and other flora that bloom on thirty-three acres of hillside, meadow, and woodland. Strolling is easy, with benches and pavilions along the trails. All trails are handicapped-accessible.

Onyx Cave is 3 miles east on Highway 62 (501) 253-9321. Self-guided tours lead to underground formations. This cavern is "doable" with young kids. Another plus: the free doll museum.

The **Christ of the Ozarks Statue** that overlooks the city is on the grounds of the **Great Passion Play** (501-253-9200 or 800-882-PLAY; www.greatpassionplay.com), the world's largest open-air drama. The story of Christ's resurrection takes place from late April until late October (closed Monday and Thursday) and includes a cast of 200 actors plus live camels, doves, donkeys, horses, and sheep. Several other religion-related attractions include a Bible Museum (with more than 600 bibles) and a 10-foot section of the Berlin Wall with Psalm 23 lettered in German. The Mission Buffet Restaurant is all-you-can-eat, and there's also a snack shop. Festivals are held throughout the year, including a Children's Festival in August. Admission.

About 10 miles west of Eureka Springs is 28,000-acre **Beaver Lake.** At

Scenic Train Trip

Take the **ES&NA** (Eureka Springs and North Arkansas Railway) vintage train for a 4-mile round-trip that takes about forty-five minutes. The train chugs past lush mountain scenery. Meals are available in the dining car. The Historic Depot, 229 North Main Street (Highway 23), has a display of handcars, coaches, and railway motorcars and kids can see how a turntable is used to turn engines around. Call (501) 253-9623; www.esnarailway.com. Admission.

this end there's a swimming beach with lifeguards; additional beaches and lodgings are located around the shoreline. Take a relaxing seventy-five-minute cruise aboard *Belle of the Ozarks*, which departs daily May–October, from the dock at Starkey Marina, just off Scenic Highway 62 West; (501) 253-6200. They have sunset tours, too. Admission.

SPECIAL EVENTS

Contact the Hot Springs Convention and Visitors Bureau or the individual state parks for more information on the following events.

January. Eagles Et Cetera Weekend, DeGray Lake, honors the seasonal return of bald eagles.

March. Ouachita Indians Spring Fest/Pow Wow, with traditional dances, games, arts and crafts, and children's workshops.

April. Caddo River Spring Fest, Norman, with youth fishing derby, canoe races, and more. Earth Day Weekend, DeGray Park, features environmental education, recycling demonstrations, and gardening tips. Wildflower Wanderings at various state parks.

May. Hot Springs Music Festival.

July. Independence Day festivities. Summertime in the Park Arts & Crafts Show, Hot Springs.

September. Hot Springs County Fair and Rodeo, Malvern. Hot Springs Jazz and Blues Festival.

October. Arkansas Oktoberfest, with German food, music, crafts, and more, Hot Springs. Fall Foliage Weekend, Lake Ouachita.

November. Healthfest, with races, including a kids' run, Mountain Bike Challenge, weight-lifting demonstrations, Hot Springs.

December. Hot Springs Jaycees Christmas Parade.

WHERE TO STAY

Hot Springs

The Hot Springs area has a variety of moderate-priced lodgings. Call the Convention and Visitors Bureau for package information.

Downtowner Hotel and Spa, 135 Central Avenue (501-624-5521 or 800-251-1962), has thermal baths and whirlpools, plus three-room suites, swimming pool, and restaurant. Another good choice is **Arlington Resort Hotel and Spa,** Central Avenue at Fountain Street, at the end of Bathhouse Row; (501) 623-7771 or (800) 643-1502; www.arlingtonhotel.

com. The property has 481 rooms and suites, three restaurants, in-house bathhouse, mountainside thermal water hot tub, country club privileges, game room, and twin cascading thermal pools on the lawn. **Happy Hollow Motel,** 231 Fountain Street (501-321-2230), has refrigerators in all rooms, and some kitchenettes. **Quality Inn,** 1125 East Grand Avenue (501-624-3321; www.qualityinn.com), has a game room, playground, pool, and restaurant. **The Hampton Inn,** 151 Temperance Hill Road (800-HAMPTON or 501-525-7000), offers free continental breakfast and has an outdoor pool.

The **Vintage Comfort Bed-and-Breakfast Inn,** 303 Quapaw Avenue (501-623-3258 or 800-608-4682), accepts children age six and older and promises a friendly stay in an antiques-decorated Victorian inn. **Wildwood 1884,** 808 Park Avenue (501-624-4267), a restored 1884 Victorian mansion, is within walking distance of downtown. **The Williams House Bed & Breakfast Inn,** 420 Quapaw Avenue (501-624-4275 or 800-756-4635), accepts well-behaved children. The 1890 Victorian brownstone has a carriage house that offers extra space for families.

Hot Springs Vacation Rentals, 5380 Central Avenue, Hot Springs (501-525-3500 or 888-477-2248), features furnished vacation homes around the lake available by the night, the week, or the month.

Hot Springs National Park's rustic campground **Gulpha Gorge** is 2 miles northeast of downtown and has forty-seven tent sites with concrete bases, but no electricity, showers, or water. Call the Convention and Visitors Bureau at 800-SPA-CITY.

Lake Hamilton

Try **Sunbay Resort & Condominiums,** 4810 Central Avenue; (501) 525-4691 or (800) 468-0055. They offer rooms and boat rentals, waterskiing, indoor/outdoor pools, tennis, health spa, playground, picnic tables, and outdoor grills. **The Clarion Resort on The Lake,** 4813 Central Avenue, (501-525-1391 or 800-432-5145), has a pond, playground, tennis court, and lake view. Children under nineteen sharing a room with parents stay for free. Another option is **Lake Hamilton Resort,** 2803 Albert Pike; (501) 767-5511 or (800) 426-3184. It has a private beach and lake views from each of its 104 all-suite accommodations, and features in-room refrigerators, indoor and outdoor pools, golfing privileges, private swimming beach, and marina with water sports and rentals.

DeGray Lake

DeGray Lake Resort is on Route 3, off I-30 on Scenic Arkansas 7; (501) 865-2851 or (800) 737-8355; www.degray.com. The resort, which has recently undergone a $3 million renovation, has a lodge with ninety-six rooms, plus a pool, marina, and restaurant. Kitchenette-furnished cottages with a play area are located adjacent to the State Park at DeGray Lakeview Cottages; (501) 865-3389.

Eureka Springs

Eureka Springs has the largest number of bed and breakfasts and inns in the state. The Association of Bed and Breakfasts, Cabins and Cottages of Eureka Springs, P.O. Box 13 (501-253-6657), serves as the area's largest reservation service.

Here are a few lodging choices.

Crescent Cottage Inn, 211 Spring Street; (501) 253-6022 or (800) 223-3246. Children are welcome at this Victorian inn. All rooms have private baths.

Downtown is home to several historic hotels that welcome families, including the **Grand Central Hotel,** 37 North Main; (501) 253-6756. The hotel has fourteen suites with complete kitchens. **Basin Park Hotel,** 12 Spring Street (877-643-4972; www.basinpark.com), has fifty-five units, some suites, a health spa, and a restaurant.

Contemporary choices include **Best Western Eureka Inn,** 1 Van Buren (501-253-9551 or 800-528-1234), which has a restaurant and an outdoor pool. **Ozarks Lodge,** Route 6 (junction of Highways 23 South and 62 East; 501-253-8992 or 800-321-8992), features forty-four rooms, including several oversized family rooms. There's an outdoor pool.

An Ozark family favorite, some 90 miles east of Eureka Springs: **Scott Valley Resort & Guest Ranch,** P.O. Box 1447, Mountain Home; (501) 425-5136. This guest ranch offers horseback riding, canoeing, tennis, and hayrides.

WHERE TO EAT

Hot Springs

Try some of the places in Hot Springs that Bill Clinton frequented in his youth, such as **Bailey's Dairy Treat,** 510 Park Avenue; (501) 624-4085. Enjoy the ice cream and milkshake treats, or "have what he was having" and order a chili cheeseburger. The ribs, homemade tamales, and fresh coleslaw at **McClard's Barbecue,** 505 Albert Pike (501-624-9586), continue to be as popular as they were with Clinton and his boyhood buddies. For a hot breakfast go to the **Pancake Shop,** 216 Central Avenue; (501) 624-9465. **Faded Rose,** 210 Central Avenue, serves up southern-cooked Cajun seafood dinner delicacies; (501) 624-3200. **Mrs. Miller's Chicken and Steak House,** 4723 Central Avenue (501-525-8861), is family owned and features kid's meals, fried chicken, seafood, and steak.

The **Arlington Resort Hotel and Spa** (see Where to Stay) serves up an expansive seafood buffet every Friday night and every Sunday features a brunch of smoked salmon, fresh fruit, and made-to-order omelettes.

FOR MORE INFORMATION

Hot Springs Convention and Visitors Bureau, 134 Convention Boulevard (501-321-2835 or 800-SPA-CITY), provides helpful literature and lodging information. In town, stop by the **Hot Springs Visitor Center,** Hill Wheatley Plaza, Central and Spring Streets; (501) 623-1433 or (800) 543-2284; www.hotsprings.org.

For the free *Ozark Visitors' Guide,* contact **Arkansas Ozark Mountain Region,** P.O. Box 597T, Flippin 72623; (501) 453-8563 or (800) 544-MTNS; www.ozarkmountainregion.com.

For more information on **Eureka Springs,** check their Web site at www.eurekasprings.org; **Arkansas State Parks:** (888) AT-PARKS or (501) 682-1191; www.arkansasstateparks.com.

Emergency Numbers

Ambulance, fire, police: 911

National Park Medical Center, 1910 Malvern Avenue, (501-321-1000), where there is also a poison control center (501-624-1121). Also available is St. Joseph's Regional Health Center, 300 Werner; (501) 622-1000.

Although there is no twenty-four-hour pharmacy in Hot Springs, Consumer's Discount Pharmacy, 531 West Grand Avenue, is open 7 days a week; (501) 624-2538.

Florida

MIAMI, KEY BISCAYNE, AND FORT LAUDERDALE

V isitors to Miami frequently stop in nearby Key Biscayne (both are in Dade County) before going just 30 miles north to Fort Lauderdale, in Broward County. It makes sense to discuss these destinations as a package.

The beaches in Miami and Fort Lauderdale have been attracting families for decades. But even the most avid beachcomber needs a day in the shade. Inland there's a southern Florida for families that features kid-pleasing science centers, colorful parrots, wide-grinning alligators, and vibrant modern art. Whether you need a break from the sun, a rainy-day lift, or just a follow-your-fancy day trip, here are some suggestions for indoor, off-the-shore, and "other" Florida family fun in Miami, Key Biscayne, and Fort Lauderdale.

GETTING THERE

Miami International Airport (305-876-7000), only 7 miles from downtown Miami, is served by many airlines. **Supershuttle** (305-871-2000) offers twenty-four-hour service to and from Miami International Airport.

Greyhound serves five stations in the Greater Miami Area: North Miami Beach, Miami Beach, Downtown, Miami International Airport area, and Homestead. Call Greyhound Bus Line at (800) 231-2222.

Amtrak, Miami Station, 8303 NW Thirty-seventh Avenue; (800) USA-RAIL; www.amtrak.com. **Tri-Rail** (in Florida 800-TRI-RAIL) offers commuter rail service from Miami to West Palm Beach and Fort Lauderdale. Tri-Rail connects with **Metrorail** for downtown and south Miami service. Kids under five ride for free.

The closest airport to Fort Lauderdale is the Fort Lauderdale/Hollywood International Airport, 1400 Lee Wagener Boulevard, Fort Lauderdale; (305) 359-6111.

Miami, Key Biscayne, and Fort Lauderdale

AT A GLANCE

► Play on sunny beaches

► Explore the Miami Museum of Science and Space Transit
Planetarium and Fort Lauderdale's Museum of Discovery
and Science

► Snorkel at Biscayne National Underwater Park

► Greater Miami Convention and Visitors Bureau,
(888) 766-4264; www.tropicoolmiami.com

► Greater Fort Lauderdale Convention and Visitors
Bureau; (800) 22-SUNNY or (954) 765-4466;
www.sunny.org

Arriving by cruise ship: A number of family-oriented cruise lines
embark from the Miami–Fort Lauderdale area, making it easy to explore
the region before or after you sail. Some of the family-friendly cruise lines
include Royal Caribbean (305-539-6000; www.royalcaribbean.com), Carnival (305-599-2600; www.carnival.com), Norwegian Cruise Line (NCL)
(305-436-4000; www.nci.com), Princess International (305-223-7666),
and Costa (305-358-7325; www.costacruises.com).

GETTING AROUND

Visitors to Miami have several public transportation options, although
renting a car may still be the easiest for families. **Metrorail** is an elevated
21-mile rail system serving downtown Miami, Hialeah to the west, and
Kendall to the south. Metrorail connects to **Metromover, Metrobus,
and Tri-Rail.** Metromover's individual motorized cars loop downtown
Miami atop an elevated track. Service includes Bayside Marketplace,
American Airlines Arena, the Cultural Center, and the Miami Convention
Center. Metrobus operates daily and on weekends. Call (305) 770-3131,
TDD 638-7266 (Metrobus) for information on these public transporta-
tion services. The phone number for Tri-Rail is (305) 836-0986; www.
tri-rail.com.

Rental car companies abound both at the airport and downtown.

Tri-Rail connects Fort Lauderdale with Miami and West Palm Beach

(305-836-0986 or 800-874-7245 in Florida; www.tri-rail.com). Amtrak (800-USA-RAIL) stops at Deerfield Beach, Fort Lauderdale, and Hollywood.

WHAT TO SEE AND DO

Museums

In addition to communing with nature on Miami's beaches, you can visit interesting museums that reveal the nature of art and history.

Miami Museum of Science and Space Transit Planetarium, 3280 South Miami Avenue; (305) 854-4247; www.miamisci.org. Fun at the Museum of Science includes a climbing wall, a pitching cage, and virtual basketball. With more than one hundred hands-on exhibits, this museum truly makes science fun. A new exhibit in conjunction with the Smithsonian Institution explores ancient Caribbean and Latin American cultures and settlements. Outside there is a small wildlife area. The Space Transit Planetarium also offers a variety of interesting shows for the star-struck. Allow at least two hours, or longer if you plan to see a planetarium show. For show times call the Cosmic Hotline: (305) 854-2222.

Historical Museum of Southern Florida, 101 West Flagler Street; (305) 375-1492; www.historical-museum.org. The Miami Dade Cultural Center houses the Historical Museum of Southern Florida. At the Historical Museum the tropical dreams of Miami's early days to the 1940s resort era come alive. Kids ride cannons, board trolleys, and dress up in fancy Henry Flagler–era gaiety. For an overview of the city by boat, foot, bike, metrorail, and bus, book ahead for **Miami on a Historic Tour** (305-375-1625).

Check out the changing art exhibits at the **Miami Art Museum,** 101 West Flagler Street; (305) 375-3000; www.miamiartmuseum.org. Major exhibits are showcased here. Second Saturdays are free for families from 1:00 to 4:00 P.M. and feature educational, hands-on activities.

Vizcaya Museum and Gardens, 3251 South Miami Avenue; (305) 250-9133. Built in 1916 as James Deering's winter residence, this Italian Renaissance-style villa now showcases fifteenth- to nineteenth-century furnishings and decorative arts. The antiques-filled rooms and the ten acres of formal gardens with fountains are likely to interest teens, not tots.

American Police Academy Hall of Fame, 3801 Biscayne Boulevard; (305) 573-0070; www.aphf.org. The facility displays more than 10,000 law enforcement items, including police vehicles and weapons. Visitors see what a jail cell and an electric chair really look like and can take part in solving a crime.

Someplace you may want to consider visiting with older children is the **Holocaust Memorial,** 1933–1945 Meridian Avenue; (305) 538-1663.

Miami and Key Biscayne Beaches

Miami's 10 miles of beach stretch from South Pointe Park and continue northward to Sunny Isles Beach at 192nd Street. Key Biscayne lies to the south with more wide, family-friendly beaches (listed below). For convenience, it's easiest to head for the beach nearest your lodging. Pack for the day. Kids and parents need hats, cover-ups, and sunscreen. Ask the concierge at your hotel about renting a beach umbrella for shade, or check with the local concessions.

- **Bill Baggs/Cape Florida State Recreation Area,** 1200 South Crandon Boulevard, Key Biscayne (305-361-5811), a 400-acre park on the tip of Key Biscayne, is famous for its **Cape Florida Lighthouse,** built in 1825. With a tour you can climb inside, but, beware, there are lots of stairs. The wide, long beach is inviting, and lifeguards are on duty. This is a good place for quiet beach days, and biking—bring your own bikes. But take the occasional gatehouse warnings about mosquitoes seriously.

- **Crandon Park,** 4000 Crandon Boulevard, Key Biscayne; (305) 361-5421. This public park has 3 miles of beach, a golf and tennis center, a picnic area shaded by sea-grape trees, a baseball field, and lots of green spaces.

Zoos, Animal Parks, Parks, and Green Spaces

Miami Metrozoo, 12400 SW 152nd Street (Kendall Area); (305) 251-0400; www.metro-dade.com/parks. This is one of the top zoos in the United States. The Metrozoo features animals in natural environments, confined by moats and landscaping rather than barred cages. With more than one hundred animal species on display, there's a lot to see. Highlights include the fascinating white Bengal tiger, the Caribbean flamingo lake, plus Asian River Life, an exhibit that re-creates an exotic jungle setting complete with mist, drumbeats, bamboo, and a 6½-foot Malayan water monitor, one of the world's largest lizards.

At PAWS, the children's zoo, visit the petting area, see a reptile show, and climb aboard a cement elephant or camel. New in 2000, a meerkat exhibit was added to the children's area. Playgrounds are located in a separate part of the park. Use the monorail to minimize walking, and go early to stay out of the afternoon sun.

Parrot Jungle and Gardens, presently located at 11000 Southwest Fifty-seventh Avenue (305-666-7834; www.parrotjungle.com), is scheduled to move to Watson Island near South Beach in 2001 or 2002. Take a walk on the wild side through these landscaped grounds filled with cages

Biscayne National Underwater Park

Convoy Point Visitors Center, 9770 Southwest 328th Street, Homestead, Florida; (305) 230-1100. Just a forty-five-minute drive from downtown Miami, 9 miles east of Homestead, you'll find more than 20 miles of reefs. Biscayne National Underwater Park encompasses more than 180,000 acres, only 8,800 of which are land.

You can tour this park on your own, but taking a guided boat tour is much more fun. A three-hour glass-bottom-boat tour departs daily at 10:00 A.M., or you can snorkel in the coral reefs, looking for striped, mottled, and brightly colored fish daily at 1:30 P.M.

With parental guidance and a flotation vest, kids as young as four have grabbed their first peek at sea life.

brimming with parrots. Subtropical garden paths lead you through thirteen landscaped acres, where palm, date, and cypress trees create a jungle feel for the plumed, perky, and exotically colored birds.

The regularly scheduled animal shows provide interesting facts and colorful antics. Cockatoos ride tricycles, and macaws engage in chariot races. Other shows feature monkeys, night creatures, and alligators. Be sure to stop at the posing area. Kids can't resist having their picture taken with gaily colored macaws perched atop their heads and arms. This is a great shot for the family album. The Gardens also have alligator and crocodile pools, and a new walk-through lorikeet aviary. Tots have a children's petting zoo and a playground kept cool by misting devices.

Monkey Jungle, 14805 Southwest 216th Street; (305) 235-1611. Within the safety of caged walkways, visitors view hundreds of primates roaming free in replicas of their tropical habitats. Monkey Jungle's three daily shows feature trained chimps and monkeys.

Fairchild Tropical Garden, 10901 Old Cutter Road; (305) 667-1651. A stroll through this eighty-three-acre garden, landscaped with plants and trees from around the world, is peaceful. Kids can touch and smell—but not pick—the plants. Wander through a rain forest, a sunken garden, and a rare plant house. If you tire, try the narrated tram tour.

Special Tours

Art Deco Tour, Miami; (305) 672-2014. More than 800 buildings in South Beach boast 1930s and 1940s pastel colors, neon, porthole windows, and other Art Deco adornments. Start your self-guided walking or driving tour at Ocean Drive and Fifth Street, and continue on Ocean Drive to Fifteenth Street, where it ends. Then follow Collins Avenue (one block west). This bustling area features many renovated hotels, shops, and trendy restaurants. The streets are filled with roller bladers and passersby taking in the scene. Small kids might find this noisy and crowded, whereas teens may love the "action." A visitor's guide and walking tour are available from the Welcome Center.

Shopping

In Miami head for the **Bayside Marketplace,** 401 Biscayne Boulevard; (305) 577-3344; www.baysidemarketplace.com. Located on sixteen waterfront acres, the mall offers everything from vendor stalls to boutiques, restaurants, entertainment, and classy shops. Sight-seeing cruises can be arranged from Bayside's marina, and water-taxi service is available.

Sawgrass Mills, 12801 West Sunrise Boulevard, Sunrise; (954) 846-2300 or (800) FL-MILLS. Come to this megadiscount mall, with 2½-million square feet, just 12 miles west of Fort Lauderdale. Some people dub this a shopping event. There are often good buys on school clothes as well as plenty of stores for browsing and a Game Works family entertainment center (954-845-8740; www.gameworks.com).

Performing Arts

Miami offers many cultural attractions. Among the possibilities: **Coconut Grove Playhouse,** 3500 Main Highway (305-442-4000), offers innovative productions and two stages. The **Gable Stage,** 1200 Anastasia Avenue (305-446-1116), performs classic and contemporary theater. The **Jackie Gleason Theater,** 1700 Washington Avenue, Miami Beach (305-673-7300; www.ci.miami-beach.fl.us) hosts the MasterCard Broadway series, along with other contemporary entertainment.

The **Miami City Ballet,** at the Cultural Center, 2200 Liberty Avenue; presents world-class ballet (305-532-4880; www.miamicityballet). The **Ballet Flamenco La Rosa,** 555 Seventeenth Street, (305-757-8475; www.panmiami.org), presents flamenco dance as well as ballet.

For opera there's the **Florida Grand Opera,** 1200 Coral Way; (305) 854-1643. The **Florida Philharmonic Orchestra** also performs at the Gusman and the Jackie Gleason Theater, (800-226-1812). Ask about their concerts for children. Check with the **Concert Association of Florida,** 555 Seventeenth Street, Miami Beach (305-532-3941; www.concertfla.org), for information concerning upcoming concert and performing arts events.

Visit the **Broward Center for the Performing Arts,** 201 Southwest Fifth Avenue, Fort Lauderdale (954-462-0222), a $55-million complex

Broward County Attractions and Beaches

FORT LAUDERDALE
Hollywood Beach, between Fort Lauderdale and Miami, offers a particularly nice 6-mile stretch of beach that includes the Hollywood Broadwalk, a paved walkway that extends for 2½ miles and features a bicycle lane. This is a great place for beach strolls and bicycling.

DANIA
The John U. Lloyd State Park, 3 miles south of Fort Lauderdale, is a 244-acre park with sandy beaches, nature trails, and boat rentals. Another popular park is the Hugh Taylor Birch State Recreation Area, Sunrise Boulevard and A1A, which also has nature trails, an interactive water playground, and boating.

The beautiful beaches of Miami and Fort Lauderdale offer hours of family fun and relaxation.

that opened in 1991; it features the best performances of Broadway, as well as dance and classical music. Call ahead for a schedule.

Ticketmaster (305-358-5885) has tickets to major sporting, theatrical, and concert events. Call ahead for locations.

Spectator Sports

For basketball watch the NBA's **Miami Heat,** American Airlines Arena, 601 Biscayne Boulevard, (305-577-HEAT; www.heat.com); the **University of Miami Hurricanes** (University of Miami ticket office at 305-284-2263; www.hurricanesports.com); and **Florida International University's Golden Panthers,** University Park, Southwest Eighth Street and 112th Avenue (305-FIU-GAME; www.fiu.edu/~athletic).

For football the **Miami Dolphins,** an NFL team, hold forth at Pro Player Stadium, 2269 Dan Marino Boulevard; (800) 255-3094. The **University of Miami Hurricanes** play at the Orange Bowl Stadium. For tickets contact the University of Miami ticket office at (305) 284-2263.

Baseball fans can enjoy seeing the **Florida Marlins** at Pro Player Stadium; (305) 626-7400; www.flamarlins.com.

For NHL hockey, catch the **Florida Panthers** at the National Car Rental arena in Sunrise, east of Fort Lauderdale.

For professional soccer, see the **Fusion** at Lockhart Stadium, Fort Lauderdale (954-717-2200 or 888-FUSION-4).

Participatory Sports

Fishing. **Deep sea and freshwater fishing** are year-round sports. For boat charter information contact the Greater Miami Convention and Visitors Bureau (888-766-4264) and the Greater Fort Lauderdale Convention and Visitors Bureau (954-765-4466 or 800-22-SUNNY).

Golf and Tennis. This is the land of golf and tennis. Besides the courses and courts affiliated with your hotel or resort, Miami has several public golf and tennis facilities. **Tee Time Services** offers a twenty-four-hour reservation line for golf (800-374-8633). For information about public golf and tennis, contact the Metro-Dade County Parks and Recreation Department (305-416-1308).

Kayaking. Paddle your way around Miami on a guided kayak tour or rent your own kayak with **Urban Trails Kayak** at Hanlover Park Marina (305-947-1302).

SIDE TRIPS

Fort Lauderdale

With miles of beaches and lots of attractions, Fort Lauderdale, just 30 miles north of Miami, is worth a day trip or a stay of its own. For a novel way of getting around, try **Water Taxis** (954-467-6677). The kids will love traveling on this eclectic collection of cabin cruisers and glass-bottom boats that take visitors to attractions along the Intracoastal Waterway and the New River. Hotel pickup can be arranged as well.

Here are some Fort Lauderdale attraction highlights.

- **Butterfly World,** Tradewinds Park, 3600 West Sample Road; (954) 977-4400. This three-acre park features more than 150 species of butterflies. Look through the windows of the breeding laboratory to watch the butterfly life cycle. The Insectarium displays exotic bugs, including giant beetles and tarantulas. But the highlight is the Tropical Rain Forest. Allow extra time to sample the miniature golf course and petting zoo at nearby Tradewinds Park.

- **IGFA Fishing Hall of Fame & Museum,** 300 Gulf Stream Way, Dania Beach (954-927-2628; www.igfa.org). Kids of all ages will love the hands-on stuff throughout—especially the virtual marlin or tarpon they reel in. Play the computerized "Name That Fish" game. Prize-winning fish dangle from the ceiling of this spectacularly designed, marine-influenced place. Kids ages two to seven can make fish prints and go pretend boating in the Discovery Room. Ask about summer camp, the Junior Angler Club, and educational youth programs.

- **Young at Art,** at The Fountains shopping center, 801 South University Drive, Plantation (954-424-0085; www.youngatartmuseum.org) lets kids give way to their creative tendencies. Global Village takes artistic journeys all over the planet. Raceways explores motion, and Toddler Playspace gives preschoolers a multisensory experience.

- **Museum of Discovery and Science and Blockbuster IMAX Theater,** 401 Southwest Second Street, Fort Lauderdale (954-467-6637). This science museum has seven interactive exhibit areas. Florida Ecoscapes, a "bilevel ecology mountain," re-creates such habitats as beach, living reef, underwater grotto, barrier island, mangrove estuary, and swamp. Each terrain features different animals indigenous to the particular surroundings. For children ages three to five, Kidscience offers interactive exhibits. A favorite is the climb up and the slide down the musical staircase.

  Kids also love the MMU (Man Maneuvering Unit) space jet pack, which lets them step into a simulated antigravity environment and challenges them to perform simple tasks. With Moon Voyager kids control a mock spaceship. You should also visit the Travelling Exhibit Hall to view the most recent interactive and educational exhibits on tour. The five-story-high 3D IMAX Theater shows a variety of films.

- **Museum of Art, Fort Lauderdale,** One East Las Olas Boulevard, Fort Lauderdale; (954) 763-6464 (for recorded events) or (954) 525-5500 (for more information; www.museumofart.org). Inside the Museum of Art, the colors of the CoBrA artists shine brilliantly. These canvases of a group of post–World War II painters from Copenhagen, Brussels, and Amsterdam splash the walls with vibrancy. But begin your tour at Art Amaze, a gallery geared to explaining the lines and language of twentieth-century art to children. Ask about the Kids and Family Program; call the education department at (954) 525-5500 ext. 239.

- **Children's Theater.** Both **Story Theater Productions at Parker Playhouse** (954-763-8813) and the **Fort Lauderdale Children's Theater** (954-763-8882) cater to young children. Call for a schedule.

- The Seminole Tribe of Florida has opened the **Ah-Tah-Thi-Ki Museum,** HC-61, Box 21-A, Clewiston; (941) 902-1113; www.seminoletribe.com. Through dioramas and other exhibits, the museum details the culture of the Seminoles, and there is a re-created village to tour. To see the Big Cypress Swamp, the Everglades frontier, and part of the Seminole Reservation, book the **Billie Swamp Safari;** (800) 949-6101. On this Everglades Eco-tour, opt for an airboat ride that has you "floating" above the river of grass, or sit in a swamp buggy that tours the marshy land. You might see alligators, crocodiles, southern razorback hogs, and other wildlife. The 2,000-acre site has camping for recreational vehicles and Chickees (native-style dwellings) available for rustic overnight stays; (800) 949-6101; www.seminoletribe.com/safari.

- **Davie Rodeo Arena,** 4271 Davie Road, Davie (954-384-7075), hosts a rope-'em and ride-'em rodeo every Friday and Saturday. Somehow the horse lovers settled in Davie, a town with good western wear and gear stores. At **Ft. Lauderdale Stadium,** 5301 Northwest Twelfth Avenue, Fort Lauderdale (954-776-1921), watch the **Baltimore Orioles** warm up during spring training.

Everglades National Park

Twenty miles from Miami you can experience the kind of unspoiled natural beauty that existed long before Florida's resort and condo development. These rivers of grass harbor alligators, crocodiles, and herons, all of which you can see if you hike, bike, canoe, drive, or board a guided tram or boat to tour these 1.4 million acres. The park features freshwater and saltwater areas, snaking rivers, wetlands, mangrove forests, and truly impressive expanses of tall grasses.

Bring binoculars to catch sight of osprey, herons, pelicans, eagles, and many other species of birds. Pick up a brochure at the Visitor's Center and use it as your guide to natural wonders, wildlife, and stimulating walking tours. And remember, it's hot here. Be sure to wear a hat, and use insect repellent, especially in summer when the mosquitoes are thick. Fortunately, guided boat trips do give you a breeze in addition to a water view.

Everglades National Park, Everglades National Park Boat Tours, P.O. Box 119, Everglades City; (800) 445-7724. Everglades National Park, 40001 State Road 9336, Homestead 33034; (305) 242-7700.

Special Events

January. Orange Bowl Football Classic. Art Deco Weekend Festival. Annual Key Biscayne Art Festival.

February. Black Heritage Month Celebration. The Miami Beach Festival of the Arts. Bob Marley Caribbean Festival.

March. The Carnival Miami/Calle Ocho, the nation's largest Latin-American festival, features a 23-block street party. Tennis enthusiasts like the Ericsson Open (formerly the Lipton Championships), the world's fifth-largest tournament.

May. Miami Children's Museum Film Festival.

June. Miami/Bahamas Goombay Festival, the largest black heritage festival in the United States.

July. Key Biscayne and Fort Lauderdale Fourth of July Celebrations.

September. Festival Miami offers international music in more than twenty concerts. Las Olas Art Fair, Fort Lauderdale.

November. The Junior Orange Bowl Festival has eight weeks of cultural and sporting events for kids and teens, October through March. Miami Book Fair International.

December. The Orange Bowl Festival, Miami's largest festival, runs until February and features sailing, tennis tournaments, a parade, and the Orange Bowl football classic.

WHERE TO STAY

The Miami area offers various accommodations, including motels, hotels, and resorts. Here are some picks on the following pages.

Miami Beach

The Alexander All-Suite Oceanfront Resort, 5225 Collins Avenue, Miami Beach (305-865-6500 or 800-327-6121; www.alexanderhotel. com), offers families suite space on the ocean. In the Deco District, but removed from the fracas and with suites and a small pool, **Essex House,** 1001 Collins Avenue (305-534-2700 or 800-553-7739; www. southbeachresorts.com) is set up for children. The **Days Inn—Ocean-side,** 4299 Collins Avenue, Miami Beach (305-673-1513 or 800-356-3017), has an oceanfront location and reasonable rates. See "Great Family Resorts" on page 36.

Key Biscayne

Low-key and on the beach, the **Silver Sands Beach Resort,** 301 Ocean Drive, Key Biscayne (305-361-5441) is convenient for families, with affordable mini-suites and cottages with kitchenettes, facing the pool or ocean.

Sunny Isles Beach

Farther north in the Sunny Isles Beach area, try the **Beacharbour Resort Hotel,** 18925 Collins Avenue; (305) 931-8900 or (800) 643-0807. This oceanfront resort attracts families as does the **Best Western Surf Vista Beach Hotel,** an oceanfront property, 18001 Collins Avenue, Sunny Isles Beach; (305) 932-1800 or 800-992-4786.

Fort Lauderdale

One choice is **Doubletree Guest Quarters Suites,** 2670 East Sunrise Boulevard; (305) 565-3800. Many of these suites have balconies overlooking the Intracoastal Waterway. The **Howard Johnson Oceans Edge Resort,** 700 North Fort Lauderdale Beach Boulevard (954-563-2451), is

Great Family Resorts in the Miami Area

Families have been coming to the Miami area for sun, sand, and fun for decades. Favorite family-friendly resorts include:

- **Sonesta Beach Hotel Key Biscayne,** 350 Ocean Drive, Key Biscayne; (305) 361-2021 or (800) 766-3782; www.sonesta.com. This beachfront property, known for its comprehensive and innovative kids' program, is our favorite Miami area resort. The complimentary kids' program for ages three to thirteen operates from 10:00 A.M. to 10:00 P.M. year-round. Besides beach games and arts and crafts, the program takes kids to such attractions as the Zoo and science museum. The teens' program, Thursday through Saturday, runs from 5:30 P.M. to 10:00 P.M.

- **Fountainebleau Hilton Resort,** 4441 Collins Avenue, Miami Beach; (305) 538-2000 or (800) 548-8886; www.hilton.com. An Octopus Pool water playland with a 23-foot slide opened in late 2000. Kids Korner keeps kids ages five through twelve busy from 9:00 A.M. to 5:00 P.M. daily. The Night Owls program, available Friday and Saturday from 6:00 to 10:00 P.M., features dinner, activities, and a movie. Families can borrow complimentary games and toys.

- **Wyndham Miami Beach Resort,** 4833 Collins Avenue (305-532-3600 or 800-20-EVENT; www.wyndham.com) recently implemented Wyndham's new Family Retreat program. The program provides activities that bring the family together—such as pool and beach games, and "Cooking with the Chef," where children prepare dinner for their parents—and Wyndham Kids Retreat, where children ages four to twelve take part in supervised, kids-only activities from 9:00 A.M. to 5:00 P.M. daily.

- **Doral Golf Resort & Spa,** 4000 NW Eighty-seventh Avenue, Miami (305-592-2000) is known for its golfing and spa, but with its new Blue Monster fantasy pool complex, and top-rated kids program, Doral is the place for quality family time—together and apart. Camp Doral gets kids involved in golf, tennis, basketball, arts and crafts, fishing, and Sega Dreamcast Games.

- **Boca Raton Resort & Club,** 501 East Camino Real, Boca Raton; (561) 447-3000 or (800) 327-0101. This resort offers a daily, extensive kids' program as well as many scheduled family events. The program features age-appropriate groupings for kids ages three to seventeen.

across the street from the beach. **Marriott's Harbor Beach Resort,** 3030 Holiday Drive (954–525–4000 or 800–831–4004; www.marriottharbor-beach.com), sits beachfront and offers in-season children's programs. **Embassy Suite Fort Lauderdale,** 1100 Southeast Seventeenth Street (954–527–2700 or 800–EMBASSY), offers families extra space.

WHERE TO EAT

Miami

Miami's cuisine rivals that of such cities as San Francisco, Chicago, and New York. Caribbean and Latin American influences add spice to south Florida cuisine. The following is a partial list of inexpensive, family oriented restaurants.

Fuddruckers serves up "the world's greatest hamburgers" along with sandwiches, chicken, fish, hot dogs, and taco salads. You'll find them at 3444 Main Highway, Coconut Grove (305–442–8164); 7800 Southwest 104th Street, Kendall (305–274–1228); and 17985 Biscayne Boulevard, Aventura (305–933–3572). Teens like **Harry's Bar,** at the Ritz Plaza Hotel, 1701 Collins Avenue in the Art Deco district; (305) 534–3500. This 1950s-style diner has a soda fountain and Wurlitzer jukebox.

For new Cuban fare try **Yuca Restaurant,** 501 Lincoln Road; (305) 532–9822. Baby back ribs in spicy guava sauce and pan-seared grouper fillet touched with cumin, pumpkin seeds, and orange sauce are two favorite dishes.

Puerto Sagua, 700 Collins Avenue, Miami Beach (305–673–1115), also serves Cuban cuisine, but more of a folk version and at more afford-able prices. Its extensive menu offers Cuban sandwiches, seafood, and traditional specialties such as *ropa vieja, picadillo,* and black beans and rice.

The boldly colorful murals and wholesome, home-cooked specialties appeal to adventurous families at **Tap Tap Haitian Restaurant** 819 Fifth Street, Miami Beach (305) 672–2898. Authentic Haitian meals of stewed chicken, grilled conch, and fish are sumptuous and filling.

Wolfie's Gourmet Deli Restaurant, 2038 Collins Avenue, Art Deco district (305–538–6626), has been serving pastrami and other deli delights since 1947; open twenty-four hours. **Cafe Tu Tu Tango,** CocoWalk, 3015 Grand Avenue, Coconut Grove (305–529–2222), is fashioned after an artist's loft and serves a wide variety of dishes, from pizza to lobster quesadilla and Jamaican spiced chicken wings.

The **Mambo Cafe** advertises "original and traditional Cuban cuisine" and has a deli and take-out counter and seating indoors and out. Original would be the roast turkey sandwich with cream cheese and strawberry marmalade. Traditional dishes include *calamari creole,* paella, and roast pork. The desserts, shakes, and ice cream are a hit with kids. Its Coconut

Grove location is on the sidewalk at 3105 Commodore Plaza (305-441-6655). There's another Mambo at Bayside Marketplace (305-374-7417). The **Hard Rock Cafe,** 401 Biscayne Boulevard, Bayside Marketplace (305-377-3110), lures 'tweens and teens with music memorabilia, burgers, pastas, salads, and basic fare.

Fort Lauderdale

Fort Lauderdale has an array of restaurants. Besides the chain restaurants, here are some local favorites to try.

Fisherman's Wharf, 222 Pompano Beach Boulevard, Pompano Beach (954-941-5522), offers seafood and grilled hamburgers served on the pier.

Two places vie for the title of best barbecue. Some prefer **Ernie's Bar-B-Que,** 1843 South Federal Highway (954-523-8636), whose specialties include conch chowder and barbecue on Bimini bread. Others vote for **Georgia Pig Bar-B-Q,** 1285 South State Road (954-587-4420).

A popular twenty-four-hour eatery is **Lester's Diner,** 250 State Road 84, Fort Lauderdale; (954) 525-5641. It's famed for its 14-ounce cup of coffee, which parents on a long drive might appreciate.

Las Olas Riverfront at 300 Southwest First Avenue, has open-air restaurants overlooking the New River and Riverwalk park, including **Dan Marino's Town Tavern** (954-522-1313) and **Ugly Tuna Saloon** (954-467-TUNA). Both also have indoor seating. At Dan Marino's kids can choose from the regular menu of steaks, pasta, meatloaf, and tuna, or from the kids' menu, where they learn all about Marino's football career. Fun and casual Ugly Tuna serves sandwiches, pasta, and seafood (but no tuna).

For kicks take the kids somewhere fun to eat, such as **The Caves** 2205 North Federal Highway (954-561-4622), where they can make like the Flintstones and munch on ribs or seafood in their own private cave; or **Mai-Kai,** 3599 North Federal Highway (954-563-3272), where they can watch hula dancers while they eat. Sundays are especially for kids, and children under age twelve are admitted free to the show every night.

Grade-schoolers who like video games with their burgers and pizza will like **Dave & Buster's Restaurant,** 3000 Oakwood Boulevard, Hollywood; (954) 923-5505. For a change of pace, try one of the many sidewalk cafes along Hollywood Beach's Boardwalk. They have a distinctly French-Canadian flavor.

FOR MORE INFORMATION

For more information contact the **Greater Miami Convention and Visitors Bureau,** 701 Brickell Avenue, Suite 2700, Miami, Florida 33131; (888) 766-4264; www.tropicalmiami.com. The Activity Line (305-557-5600) features information on dining, special events, and attractions and is available twenty-four hours a day in English, Spanish, German, French, Swedish, and Portuguese. For Fort Lauderdale information contact the **Greater Fort Lauderdale Convention and Visitors Bureau,** 1850 Eller Drive, Suite 303, Fort Lauderdale, Florida 33316; (800) 22-SUNNY or (954) 765-4466; www.sunny.org.

Emergency Numbers

Ambulance, fire, and police: 911

Emergency medical care in Miami: Jackson Memorial Hospital, 1611 Northwest Twelfth Avenue; (305) 585-1111

Twenty-four-hour pharmacy in southern Miami: Walgreens, 5731 Southwest Bird Road; (305) 666-0757. In northern Miami: Walgreens, 12295 Biscayne Boulevard; (305) 893-6860

Emergency medical care in Fort Lauderdale: North Broward General Hospital, 303 Southeast Seventeenth Street, Fort Lauderdale; (800) 528-4888

Pharmacy in Fort Lauderdale: Eckerd Pharmacy, 1711 South Andrews Avenue, Fort Lauderdale; (954) 462-8185

Poison Control: Call the local hospital emergency rooms or Tampa Bay General Hospital; (800) 282-3171

NAPLES

L ocated on the southwest coast of Florida, Naples has a less crowded feel than Miami's hotel-to-hotel beachfront. Naples offers 41 miles of Gulf Coast public beaches, some great family resorts, plus easy access to wilderness areas and wildlife. From Naples three of the region's defining ecosystems are a day trip away. Explore the coastline with its barrier islands, estuaries, and salt marshes; boat through cypress swamps; and discover the Everglades, the third-largest national park in the United States. On these wilderness forays peer at alligators, and look at endangered Florida panthers, Southern bald eagles, West Indian manatees, wood storks, and peregrine falcons, then come back to some fine family resorts.

GETTING THERE

Southwest Florida International Airport, exit 21 on I-75 (RSW) in Fort Myers, is the largest airfield serving the area. The airport is 38 miles north of Naples and serves American Airlines, Continental, Delta, Midway, Northwest, TWA, United, and USAirways. **Naples Municipal Airport,** 160 Aviation Drive, next to Airport Road (941-643-0733), serves American Eagle, Cape Air, United Express, and USAir Express.

I-75 offers easy access into the Naples area. For Audubon's Corkscrew Swamp Sanctuary, use exit 17; for Naples use exits 15 and 16; for Marco Island, and the Briggs Nature Center, use exit 15.

GETTING AROUND

Rental cars are available at both airports. **Naples Trolley Tours** is a good way to see the sights, with ten tours daily; call (941) 262-7300.

WHAT TO SEE AND DO

Nature and Wilderness
Start your wildlife tour in town at the **The Conservancy of Southwest Florida,** 1450 Merrihue Drive; (941) 262-0304. Exhibits describe

Naples

AT A GLANCE

▶ Enjoy glorious Gulf Coast beaches

▶ Stay at great family resorts

▶ Explore Ten Thousand Islands and other wilderness areas

▶ Visit the Teddy Bear Museum

▶ Visit Naples, Inc: (800) 605-7878; www.naples-online.com

Florida's wildlife and include snake and sea turtle presentations, a comprehensive exhibit on shells, and a rehabilitation area for eagles, hawks, and owls. There are nature trails to stroll along, as well as a boat tour along a tidal lagoon through a mangrove forest.

Naples Aquarium at Old Naples Seaport, 1001 Tenth Avenue South (941-403-7300), focuses on education during its forty-minute guided tours of an aquarium-lined room. The 7,000-gallon tank holds local species of fish, including sting rays, flounder, and shrimp that kids can stroke in the touch tank. You'll learn about the unusual characteristics and habits of the tamk's denizens, and little ones are invited to feed the snook, sheepshead, nurse sharks, and other creatures. Guests wait for their tours to start in a room that holds a sand touch table and small touch tank. Displays and guides educate the public about pollution, water management, and the importance of mangroves and sea grass.

Two must-dos: Tour the **Conservancy's Briggs Nature Center,** Rookery Bay National Estuarine Research Reserve, Shell Island, off State Route 951 (941-775-8569), and explore the **Everglades National Park** (see Side Trips).

Drive south along the coast, about 30 miles (45 from town) to the Conservancy's Briggs Nature Center. This area forms part of a maze of mangrove islands on the edge of the Everglades called **Ten Thousand Islands.** Explore the self-guided nature trail, and, December through April, board the *Sea Queen,* a 33-foot pontoon boat, for a shelling trip to Key Island (minimum age is six). Your kids won't soon forget this boat ride through the bays and inlets where the reddish, fingered roots of the mangroves reach down into the shallows. Dolphins often breach the greenish water, and follow the boat, swimming in circles, diving, and arcing to the delight of the kids—and adults—on board.

Pelicans roost on the pilings at Key Island. The path to the wonderfully deserted beach is lined with Brazilian pepper trees, cabbage palms,

Great Beaches

Naples resorts and hotels are either on or near the beach. In addition to enjoying these resort beaches, you and your children should take time to explore the region's other beaches. On some of these beaches in the summer months, the endangered loggerhead turtles deposit their eggs. Advise your kids not to disturb these nests.

- **Delnor-Wiggins Pass State Recreation Area,** off Vanderbilt Drive in North Naples, 11 miles northwest of town; (941) 597-6196. Besides a beautiful swimming beach, the park offers such family-friendly features as lifeguards, a boat launch, an observation tower, showers, and turtle walk educational beach programs in summer.
- **Barefoot Beach Preserve County Park,** 3300 Santa Barbara Boulevard, north of Delnor-Wiggins (941-353-0404), is pretty and often relatively uncrowded. The facility has restrooms and a snack bar, but no lifeguards.
- **Clam Pass County Park,** Seagate Drive (941-597-6196), which in the past has been listed as among the nation's twenty most pristine beaches. Kids like strolling along the boardwalk or riding the tram through the mangrove forest.
- **Tigertail Beach,** on Marco Island (941-597-6196), combines sandy shores with lots to do. A boardwalk leads through a mangrove preserve, and there are boat rentals, a Tot Lot play area, and concession stands.

and Norfolk pines. This is the place to walk hand in hand with your child, examining the myriad shells and building sand castles as you watch the pelicans dive-bomb into the water to come up with gullets bulging with fish. Remember to bring your own picnic lunch and lots of water and juice to drink, as there are no services on the island. See Tours for other pontoon tours departing from Briggs.

The **Corkscrew Swamp Sanctuary,** 375 Sanctuary Road, about 20 miles north of Naples (941-348-9151; www.audubon.org), is an 11,000-acre preserve that belongs to the National Audubon Society. The sanctuary is famous as a nesting spot for North American wood storks and as the largest stand of bald cypress trees in the south. Enjoy a stroll along a boardwalk that cuts through a towering bald-cypress forest.

Boat and Buggy Tours

An organized boat or buggy tour is a great way to become familiar with this region's interesting ecosystems. **Babcock Wilderness Adventures,** 8000 State Road 31, Punta Gorda (800-500-5583), provides a swamp-buggy tour of the 9,000-acre Crescent B Ranch, which features alligators, Florida panthers, and herds of bison in their natural habitats; **Estero Bay Tours,** 5231 Mamie Street, at the end of Coconut Road (941-992-2200), has a narrated boat tour of the mangrove islands, rookeries, and a Calusa Indian mound.

Collier-Seminole State Park Boat Tours, 20200 East Tamiami Trail, 17 miles south on U.S. 41 (941-642-8898), take passengers on the Beachwater River, which runs through Collier-Seminole State Park. The one-hour tours include narrations about the area's early settlements and the various plants and animals throughout the Everglades. Tours operate daily.

To get a naturalist's view of J. N. "Ding" Darling National Wildlife Refuge, board the tram tour from **Tarpon Bay Recreation,** 900 Tarpon Bay Road, Sanibel Island (914-472-8900). Learn about creatures as small as the barnacle and mangrove crab and as large as the manatee.

Most famous for its dolphin-watching tours, *Double Sunshine* at Tin City on Highway 41 (941-263-4949) departs five times daily for 1½-hour narrated sightseeing, sunset, and dolphin cruises. Call ahead to reserve.

The *Naples Princess* at Old Naples Seaport, 1001 Tenth Avenue South, offers themed meal cruises: Conservancy-Narrated Nature Cruise with continental breakfast, Naples Bay buffet lunch, Midafternoon Sightseeing, Sunset Hors d'Oeuvres, Sunset Dinner Buffet on the Gulf, and Sunday Brunch. Call ahead for times and to make reservations.

For a naturalist-guided tour, book one of **Brigg's Nature Center's** (941-775-8569; see above) two-hour pontoon tours Tuesday through Saturday. The morning tour studies the ecology of Rookery Bay's fertile mangroves; in the afternoon go shelling and explore nature on Key Island; at sunset, get a birding tour. Children must be six or older. The Nature Center also conducts informative muck-about and seining tours on Marco Island's mudflats and Tigertail Beach.

Factory Bay Marina, 1079 Bald Eagle Drive, Marco (941-642-6717 or 888-642-6717; www.FactoryBayMarina.com) conducts daily shelling and sightseeing charters to local islands and sights. Airboat tours into Ten Thousand Islands leave mornings and afternoons every day except Wednesday.

Combine land and water exploration with the **Everglades Tram Ride,** located ½ mile west of Route 29 on Highway 41 (877-695-2820). To experience the raw water-world nature of Ten Thousand Islands and Everglades National Park, choose from a large or small airboat-only tour, or a combination pontoon boat, airboat, tram, and foot excursion. The airboats are noisy, but as they glide above water they give you a feeling of being on a magic-carpet ride.

Wooten's Everglades Tours, 32330 Tamiami Trail, Ochopee, 35 miles south of Naples (800-282-2781) is one of the oldest and largest airboat and swamp buggy tour operators in the 'Glades. Follow ancient Native American trails through the mysterious "River of Grass." For other Everglades tours, see Side Trips.

Parks and Zoos

Instead of lions and tigers, **Caribbean Gardens,** 1590 Goodlette Road (941-262-5409; www.caribbeangardens.com), brings you face to face with wild birds and monkeys. The fifty-two-acre park combines a preserve and botanical garden in an ersatz jungle setting. Take a self-guided tour, or hop aboard the island boat for a cruise through this habitat, where primates roam freely. Young children also enjoy the animal shows and the petting farm.

A popular urban park for family picnics or some outdoor fun is the **Lowdermilk Park** (914-434-4698), at Gulf Shore and Banyan Boulevards. The park has open spaces and beach for sports and romping, gazebos for picnics, and a playground area for younger children.

Museums

The Teddy Bear Museum, 2511 Pine Ridge Road (941-598-2711; www.teddymuseum.com), is a great place to visit with younger children. This unique museum houses more than 3,000 teddy bears in rooms that contain static as well as mechanical displays. Preschoolers will especially like playing in the Three Little Bears' house. Read about real and make-believe bears in the "Li-bear-y," which contains more than 400 books.

Performing Arts

Naples' premier performance center, featuring symphonies, theater productions, concerts, and children's performances, is the **Philharmonic Center for the Arts,** 5833 Pelican Bay Boulevard; (941) 597-1900. Call for a schedule of performances. The oldest community theater group, The Naples Players, performs at the new **Sugden Community Theater,** 701 Fifth Avenue South, (941-263-7990), and sometimes offers children's plays in its season's offerings of comedy and drama.

Shopping

Stroll around **Third Street and the Avenues** (941-649-6707), a shopping district at Twelfth, Thirteenth, and Fourteenth Avenues, which intersect with Third Street South; and newly revitalized **Fifth Avenue South,** with its lively sidewalk cafes and mix of shops and boutiques. For family budgets try **Tin City,** 1200 Fifth Avenue South.

Sporting Events

The **Florida Sports Park,** off Highway 951 near Rattlesnake Hammock Road, Golden Gate (941-774-2701 or 800-897-2701), features various sporting events as well as, occasionally, country line dancing or flea markets. In March, May, and October, the park has swamp-buggy races.

SIDE TRIPS

Everglades National Park

For more of this alluring tropical topography, drive about 25 miles east (about forty-five minutes) to **Everglades City,** the northwestern entrance to the **Everglades National Park.** Stop by the Everglades National Park Visitor's Center, 1 mile south of Everglades City (941-695-3311), for information and brochures. The Everglades, the third-largest national park in the United States, is spread over 1.5 million acres. You can hike, bike, canoe, drive, or take a guided tram or boat through these 1.5 million acres. Bring binoculars. A fun way to explore this section of the Everglades is to take a boat tour through the park. **Everglades National Park Boat Tours,** P.O. Box 119, Everglades City; (941) 695-2591 or (800) 445-7724.

Sanibel-Captiva

A short drive from downtown Naples is the resort area and islands of Sanibel-Captiva. **The Bailey-Matthews Shell Museum,** 3075 Sanibel-Captiva Road, Sanibel (941-395-2233), is an interesting place for children who are in the beachcombing business. The museum has a hands-on exhibit with specimens from the area, and more than thirty displays with more than a million shells from around the world

SPECIAL EVENTS

February. Everglades City hosts three days of fresh seafood, country music, and Native American and other arts and crafts at **Everglades Seafood Festival.**

May. The **Great Dock Canoe Race** is popular event involving 200 canoe teams and crazy costumes.

November. Early in the month Naples's Teddy Bear Museum holds its **Bear Fair,** with pony rides, kids' games, and other activities for the family. Later in the month the **Festival of Lights** kicks off holiday decorating and festivities.

Great Family Resorts

Naples has several great family resorts.

- **The Registry Resort,** 475 Seagate Drive; (941-597-3232 or 800-247-9810). This 4-diamond, 3-star resort, set on 23 acres with 3 miles of beachfront and mangrove forests, offers a daily year-round children's program, Camp Registry, in which kids learn about the beach and its wildlife. Three nights weekly, counselors throw a movie and dinner party just for kids. Kids under nineteen stay free when sharing a room with parents.

- **Ritz-Carlton Resort,** 280 Vanderbilt Beach Road; (941) 598-3300 or (800) 241-3333. This 5-star and 5-diamond resort offers a pampered stay. There is no kids pool. The resort offers a supervised Children's Dinner Theater on Friday and Saturday nights (with a nominal fee) and a year-round Ritz Kids Day Camp.

- **Naples Beach Hotel and Golf Club,** 851 Gulf Shores Boulevard North; (941) 261-2222 or (800) 237-7600; www.NaplesBeachHotel.com. Located beachfront, this family-friendly resort offers Beach Club 4 Kids, a daily complimentary children's program (charge for lunch only) for ages five to twelve from 9:00 A.M. to 3:00 P.M. For a nominal charge kids enjoy dinner and a movie Friday and Saturday nights from 6:30 to 9:00 P.M. The resort has golf, tennis, and a new spa as well.

Not too far away from Naples are Sanibel and Captiva Islands and Fort Myers. Consider staying here as add-ons to your Naples trip.

- **Best Western Pink Shell Beach Resort,** 275 Estero Boulevard on Fort Myers Beach (941-463-6181 or 800-237-5786), is located on twelve acres between bay waters and a 1,500-foot beach along a secluded two-lane island road. This resort offers hotel rooms, suites, and efficiencies. Families enjoy the three heated swimming pools, tennis, beach volleyball, water-sport rentals, and more. A day-long children's program, Fun Factory, is available, and there are evening activities for children as well.

- **The Sundial Beach Resort,** 863 East Gulf Drive on Sanibel Island (941-472-4151 or 800-237-4184), offers a daily, year-round children's program for ages three to eleven, with half-day or full-day programs. Activities include

(continued)

Great Family Resorts *(continued)*

nature walks, arts and crafts, scavenger hunts, and the like. Teen programs are offered as well. The resort features suites with full kitchens, including a dishwasher and microwave, as well as a living area. The Sundial stresses environmental awareness in its children's pro-gram and has an on-site ecocenter. Sundial Beach Resort's sister property, **Sanibel Inn,** Sanibel Island (800-237-1491 or 941-472-3181), also has environmentally focused children's programs.

- **South Seas Plantation,** P.O. Box 194, Captiva Island; (941) 472-5111 or (800) 237-3102; www.southseas.com. Situated on a barrier island, this low-key resort has a first-rate beach for shelling. Guests can stay in hotel rooms or houses. This resort also offers Fun Factory year-round for ages three to

eleven. Among the activities: children three to five enjoy arts and crafts, ages six to eight become "certified" scavenger hunters; and ages nine to eleven get tips from their personal fitness trainer. The program runs from 9:00 A.M. to 1:00 P.M. and includes lunch, and from 5:00 to 8:00 P.M. and includes dinner.

- **Sanibel Harbour Resort and Spa,** 17260 Harbour Pointe Drive, Fort Myers (941-466-4000 or 800-767-7777), offers Kids' Klub for children ages five to twelve. Activities include sand-castle building, pool games, picnics, treasure hunts, and more. The program is offered Monday through Sunday from 10:00 A.M. to 4:00 P.M., with additional activities on Friday and Saturday from 6:00 to 8:00 P.M. The resort features a top-rated spa.

WHERE TO STAY

The **Park Shore Resort,** 600 Neapolitan Way (941-263-2222), is located behind Neapolitan Shopping Plaza and overlooks a small lake. The one- and two-bedroom apartments are equipped with full kitchen and patio or balcony. The complex features a heated pool, four tennis courts, racquetball, and volleyball facilities. A children's program is available in season.

Vanderbilt Inn, 11000 Gulf Shore Drive North, Vanderbilt Beach (941-597-3151 or 800-643-8654) is casual and beachside, with a pool and restaurant for family convenience.

For private condo, cottage, or home rentals, request a catalog from Bluebill Vacation Properties, 4628 Tamiami Trail (800-237-2010;

www.bluebill.com). Weekly and monthly rentals are available in the Naples area.

WHERE TO EAT

Naples is known for its fine and trendy restaurants and bistros, many of which do not make any pretense of being family friendly. One family favorite on the water is **Riverwalk Fish & Ale House** at Tin City off Highway 41 at Fifth Avenue South (941-263-2734). It offers seafood and sandwiches with a Cajun flair, and a kid's menu. **The Dock at Crayton Cove,** at Twelfth Avenue South (941-263-9940), is casual, with indoor and outdoor seating on Naples Bay and enough variety to please everyone. Kids will like the caboose out back and the railroad theme throughout the **Whistle Stop Steakhouse,** 200 Goodlette Road (941-263-8440). It offers an extensive lunchtime salad bar, steaks, and a kids' menu.

For a more formal occasion, try **Terra,** 1300 Third Street (941-262-5500), which serves Mediterranean-style cuisine. A children's menu is available.

FOR MORE INFORMATION

Contact Visit Naples, P.O. Box 10129, Naples 34101 (800-605-7878; www.naples-online.com), or stop by the **Naples Chamber of Commerce/Visitors Center** at 895 Fifth Avenue South for brochures and information.

Emergency Numbers

Ambulance, fire, and police: 911

Naples Community Hospital, 350 Seventh Street North: (941) 436-5000

For poison control: (800) 282-3171

For twenty-four-hour home health care, during business hours, Dial-A-Nurse: (941) 434-8000

5 🌐 Florida

ORLANDO

O rlando is a family travel mecca. Traditionally Walt Disney World has been the reason most families have headed here, but Universal Studios' mega-expansion makes this theme park as exciting— some feel more exciting—than Walt Disney World. Universal's five new themed areas offer state-of-the-art roller coasters, imaginative rides, plus a Dr. Seuss play area for young children. SeaWorld Adventure Park Orlando, another attraction not to miss, offers the adventure of animal encounters. Orlando also features other exceptional attractions, so allow plenty of time to visit.

GETTING THERE

Orlando International Airport (407-825-2001) is served by numerous domestic and international airlines. Car rentals, van and bus service, and taxis are available. Many hotels also operate shuttles.

Amtrak (800-USA-RAIL) has four trains to the Orlando area; two trains from New York that come into Orlando/Miami, one from Los Angeles that arrives in Orlando, and the Auto Train from Lorton, Virginia, that comes into Sanford. **Greyhound** buses arrive at the terminal at 555 Magruder Boulevard. Call (407) 292-3422 or (800) 231-2222.

Orlando may be reached by major highways including I-75 from the Midwest connecting with the Florida Turnpike, I-95 from the Atlantic Coast states, and I-4 running east-west through Orlando and connecting Daytona and Tampa.

GETTING AROUND

A car is extremely helpful in Orlando. The many attractions are spread out, and it's often easiest to reach them by car. If you stick to the major attractions, however, it is possible to rely on van transportation and hotel shuttles. Check with the concierge at your hotel. **Mears Transportation Group** (407-839-1570; www.mears-net.com) is a popular choice; **Culture Quest** (800-327-5254 or 407-855-6434) provides shut-

Orlando

AT A GLANCE

▶ Get tossed, twirled, and thrilled at Universal Studios' Islands of Adventure

▶ Visit Walt Disney World, MGM Studios, Animal Kingdom, and Epcot

▶ Encounter sharks, penguins, and whales at SeaWorld Adventure Park Orlando and swim with dolphins at Discovery Cove

▶ Have hands-on fun at the Orlando Science Center

▶ Learn quirky facts at the interactive Guinness World of Records Experience

▶ Orlando/Orange County Convention and Visitors Bureau: (407) 363-5872 or (800) 643-9492; www.Go2orlando.com

tles to fifteen of the area's cultural attractions. When using a taxi, always heed the advice of the Convention and Visitors Bureau: Use only metered cabs and confirm the cost of the trip with the driver before departing. The **I-Ride Trolley** shuttles guests from SeaWorld. Call (407) 248-9590.

WHAT TO SEE AND DO

Walt Disney World Vacation Kingdom
Situated on 28,000 acres in Lake Buena Vista, **Walt Disney World Vacation Kingdom** is the number-one attraction. Walt Disney World comprises the Magic Kingdom, Epcot Center, Disney-MGM Studios, and Disney's Animal Kingdom.

A world unto itself, Walt Disney World deserves a guidebook of its own and several good ones are available at bookstores. For Walt Disney World reservations and information, call (407) W-DISNEY.

Animal Kingdom. (407-824-4321). With Animal Kingdom Walt Disney World adds animals—some real and some fake—to its winning formula of rides, shows, and fantasy. More than 1,000 critters live in, or at least roam in re-created habitats.

The park is a success, particularly with younger kids, grade-schoolers,

Zip through the Theme Parks

Use these tips to save time when touring Orlando's theme parks:

- **Walt Disney World.** FAST-PASS, a free timed ticket option, allows you to cut out long waiting lines at Magic Kingdom's Splash Mountain and Space Mountain; Epcot's Test Track and "Honey, I Shrunk the Audience"; Disney-MGM Studios Rock 'n' Roller Coaster, Tower of Terror II, and "Voyage of the Little Mermaid"; Disney's Animal Kingdom's DINOSAUR; and Kilimanjaro Safaris, as well as other attractions. With FASTPASS you put your ticket into a turnstile and receive a one-hour window for your return.

- **Universal Studios.** Beat the crowds by booking a VIP tour. This three-hour group tour gets you to the front of the lines and guarantees you'll see several preselected attractions.

- **SeaWorld Adventure Park Orlando.** Adventure Express is a five-hour guide-escorted program. You go to the front of the line for attractions, get reserved seating for shows, and go on a behind-the-scenes tour that often includes petting a penguin.

and parents looking for an Orlando outing with a less frenetic pace. But most teens and preteens, despite **Dinosaurs** (formerly Countdown to Extinction, a jerky, dark, and sometimes scary ride in which Jurassic Park–like dinosaurs attack guests) are likely to be bored by the sometimes elusive herd of big game and the tame, sweet shows.

Kilimanjaro Safaris is an eighteen-minute jeeplike ride through a re-created landscape surprisingly like the savannas and waterholes of Kenya. Unlike in a real safari, the Harambe Wildlife Reserve's lorry doesn't stop for photo opportunities or extended viewing.

At the **Conservation Station,** an interactive research area, touch-screen computers inform you about the animals, some of which can be seen "live" on the "animalcam," a video camera. Don't miss the bathrooms here, which are definitely the potties with the most personality. Recorded animal grunts, snorts, twitters, and roars echo throughout the room, and each stall has a well-placed sign asking HOW DO SCIENTISTS KNOW WHAT DINOSAURS ATE? The answer: BY STUDYING FOSSILIZED POOP.

Except for an aviary and some decorative flocks of flamingos, the rest of the park concentrates on extinct or fanciful animals, one of the ways the Walt Disney Company distinguishes this park from zoos or other animal-oriented theme parks. In **DinoLand U.S.A., Dinosaur Jubilee,** a hangarlike hall displaying the re-created skeletons of dinosaur and amphibious creatures is home to Sue, a 67-million-year-old *Tyrannosaurus*

SeaWorld and Discovery Cove

SeaWorld Adventure Park Orlando combines entertainment and recreation with education and conservation. Park highlights:

- **Journey to Atlantis.** Combining roller-coaster thrills with get-wet fun, this water coaster plunges you eight stories.
- **Key West.** Feed the stingrays at Stingray Lagoon, watch Atlantic bottle-nose dolphins swim at Dolphin Cove, and learn about endangered sea turtles at Sea Turtle Point.
- **Wild Arctic.** Become a polar explorer on a simulated helicopter ride. Afterward see real polar bears, beluga whales, and walruses.
- **Penguin Encounter.** View a colony of these aquatic birds.
- **Terrors of the Deep.** Encounter the world's largest collection of dangerous sea creatures. Get an up-close look at eels, barracudas, and sharks.
- **Shamu's Happy Harbor.** Splash through water areas with pirate nets and down slides in this kids-only play area.
- **Shamu.** Watch Shamu jump, fluke-hop, and do other tricks.
- **Dolphin Interaction Program.** Get in the tank with these gentle animals. Learn about their physiology and habitat.

SeaWorld Adventure Park Orlando, 7007 SeaWorld Drive; (407) 351–3600; www. seaworld.com.

Discovery Cove, SeaWorld Orlando's sister park, delivers the best of the marine park's animal encounters in a relaxing resortlike setting of river pools and sandy beaches. By limiting attendance to 1,000 guests, Discovery Cove promises no crowds and offers exciting swims with dolphins as well as snorkeling and bird adventures.

The park's swim-with-dolphins experience is one of the best such programs around. It's carefully controlled, safe, educational, and fun. In the snorkeling lagoon you can wriggle through schools of tropical fish and come safely face to face with barracudas and sharks on the other side of the clear acrylic partition.

Allow time to meander through the aviary, where three hundred exotic birds reside. These people-friendly creatures will eat right from your hand.

Discovery Cove, 6000 Discovery Cove Way, (877) 4–DISCOVERY; www.discoverycove.com is adjacent to SeaWorld. The minimum age for the dolphin swim is six. Regular admission includes a dolphin-swim experience plus a seven-day pass to SeaWorld Adventure Park. For those who don't want to swim with the dolphins, as well as for children ages three to five, there's a reduced admission.

Families can swim and play with dolphins at Discovery Cove.

rex. Sue is one of the largest and most complete T-rexs ever discovered. At 45-feet long, 13-feet high at the hip, and weighing 14,000 pounds when alive, Sue must have been a formidable foe.

The **Boneyard,** a fossil-themed playground, impresses preschoolers. Along with dino skeletons and a jeep to climb on, there are rope bridges and slides, some of which are thoughtfully sized for very young kids. Little ones will also like **Camp Minnie-Mickey,** whose short trails lead to meet and greet areas where such beloved characters as Minnie, Mickey, and Winnie the Pooh await.

Of the Animal Kingdom's several shows, the blockbuster best is Camp Minnie-Mickey's **Festival of the Lion King,** a mélange of floats, dancers, acrobats, singers, and stilt walkers, all wearing fanciful and colorful costumes. By the end of this thirty-minute, feel-good fest, you'll be singing along with the cast.

Another don't miss is **It's Tough to Be a Bug,** the 3-D film shown inside the Tree of Life. The feature is pure fun, with 3-D effects and a special seat-of-your-pants insect exit that gets the whole theater squealing.

Alas, **The Disney Institute,** is no longer open to individual families. As of June 2000 the learning vacations offered are only available to corporate groups.

Downtown Disney

To **Pleasure Island,** a nighttime club and a restaurant area, Disney has added **Downtown Disney** (407–828–3058), a shopping, dining, and

Universal Studios' Islands of Adventure

Using technologically advanced rides and attractions, **Islands of Adventure,** combined with Universal's already existing "ride the movies," rivals, and some say surpasses, the excitement of Walt Disney World. Note: the thrill coasters and many of the action rides, including the Amazing Adventures of Spider-Man, require guests to be at least fifty-four inches tall, but not the Flying Unicorn. This coaster takes kids as short as thirty-six inches.

- **Marvel Super Hero Island.** The park's signature action ride, the Adventures of Spider-Man, combines 3-D action, live action, and special effects with a moving ride that drops you 400 feet into darkness. The Incredible Hulk Coaster shoots riders out of an emerald gamma ray booster with the same thrust as a U.S. Air Force F-16 fighter attack jet (not a ride for the faint-hearted). On Dr. Doom's Fearfall get dropped 200 feet. Popular with the younger set is the parade of comic book characters.

- **Seuss Landing.** Lots of irregular angles and spiral-shaped trees re-create the whimsical feel of a Dr. Seuss landscape for this ten-acre island aimed at younger kids. On the Cat in the Hat Ride, animatronics and special effects take guests through scenes from the much-loved story. One Fish, Two Fish, Red Fish, Blue Fish lets kids steer a Seussian-inspired fish through spouting fountains and other water obstacles, and in If I Ran the Zoo, an interactive playland, kids play with water elements and strange animals.

- **Lost Continent.** Battle through water and flames on Escape From the Lost City and watch pyrotechnics at the stunt show The Eighth Voyage of Sinbad. On Dueling Dragons, one of the park's signature roller coasters, sit in one high-speed coaster while the other appears to be hurtling at you.

- **Jurassic Park.** Jurassic Park River Adventure features an 85-foot plunge and attacks by animatronic dinosaurs based on the Steven Spielberg movie. Touch these real-looking creatures at Triceratops Encounter.

- **Toon Lagoon.** See some of your favorite cartoon characters, including Popeye, Bluto, Betty Boop, and Beetle Bailey. Kids scamper around on Me Ship, the Olive, a three-story play boat, and tots can crawl around in Swee' Pea's Playpen. Get wet on Dudley Do-right's Ripsaw Falls, a flume ride, and on Popeye & Bluto's Bilge-Rat Barges, a whitewater raft ride. Kids also like the street show. For more info, (800)–U-ESCAPE; www.uescape.com.

Halloween at Universal Studios Escape

It's Halloween, but your kids have gotten to that scary stage—they wear rings through their noses, spiked dog collars, and belly chains all year long. The thought of your child's unsupervised hanging about on the streets and at parties fills you with horror, but your teen wants to roam and prowl.

What to do? Take your kids—preteens and older—to **Universal Studios Florida Halloween Horror Nights: Frightmares.** The nocturnal festivities have become the preeminent place to celebrate the season in a safe but sufficiently spooky atmosphere, one that will thrill even the most blasé of teens. Universal Studios' celebration isn't just on Halloween night; the scary party goes on for about seventeen nights in October after the regular park closes.

The park is transformed. Universal uses its highly skilled creators, make-up artists, and technicians to deliver creepy critters and well-timed surprises. Because the after-dark chills pack a wallop, Universal Studios recommends that children be at least ten years old.

Fog envelopes the section near the Jaws attraction, creating a suitably mysterious aura for the Midway of the Bizarre, where you encounter such "scare-actors" as ghouls, vampires, witches, and other weird fiends.

Several specially created haunted houses deliver chills. The timing and the technical savvy make these walk-through places scary; even my you-can't-scare-me teen was shriekingly impressed. Since most of Universal Studios' attractions are open, you can enjoy the rides—often the lines are shorter than in the day—and the frights. (A Day in the Park with Barney and a few others aimed at younger kids are closed.)

For Halloween Horror Nights call (407) 22-HORROR. For park information call (407) 363-8000 or (800)-U-ESCAPE.

entertainment complex. **Cirque du Soleil,** the wonderful acrobatic circus without animals, performs in a permanent new home. At **DisneyQuest** indulge in virtual adventures and arcade games, and dine and listen to blues and gospel music at **House of Blues.** Other popular restaurants are **Wolfgang Puck's Cafe** and **Bongos Cuban Café.** Teens keep busy browsing through the **Virgin Megastore,** and moviegoers can pick from twenty-four **AMC Theaters.**

There's traffic and not enough parking. If you're staying on Disney property, the best way to get here is to take a water taxi from Disney's Port Orleans Resort, Dixie Landings Resort, or from Old Key West Resort.

Universal Studios Escape

With the opening of Universal Studios Islands of Adventure, a 110-acre, five-area theme park; Universal Studios CityWalk, an entertainment complex; and the Portofino Bay Hotel, Universal Studios' new name emphasizes its all-encompassing experience. Call (800)-U-ESCAPE or www. escape.com.

Universal Studios CityWalk, like Downtown Disney, features live music, dance clubs, and other evening entertainment. CityWalk has a twenty-screen Universal Cineplex, E! Entertainment Television, television studios, and themed eateries, including a Hard Rock Cafe, Jimmy Buffett's Margaritaville, and Motown Cafe.

You can zap extraterrestrials as you career through **Men in Black Alien Attack.** Based on the movie, the ride uses state-of-the-art technology to keep score.

Twister is a walk through a tornado. See the skies darken, feel the room shake, and endure the blasts of 35 mph winds.

Some of the rides in the new Islands of Adventure, as well as some of the top rides in the older portion of the park, might scare little kids but will surely delight most children ages eight and older; some of Universal's rides may be unsettling to those with queasy stomachs.

With **Terminator 2 3-D,** a "virtual adventure" based on Arnold Schwarzenegger's movie *Terminator 2,* you time travel via 3-D movie images projected onto multiple screens. This high-tech happening mixes robotic characters and live-action stunt work on 3-D film images to blur reality and fantasy. At one point, the Fat Boy, a specially made Harley motorcycle, appears to roar out of the screen onto the stage.

At **Jaws,** get (safely) attacked by the Great White Shark and survive the explosion of Amity harbor. During **Kongfrontation,** watch the giant ape destroy a helicopter and get so close he can blow banana breath on you. With **Earthquake, the Big One,** survive the crash of your subway train and the city's floods and fires. Find stunt thrills at **Dynamyte Nights Stuntacular.** Updated tricks include a motorboat that jumps through 30 feet of flame.

If jostling nauseates you, consider skipping **Back to the Future,** where kids under 40 inches tall aren't allowed. But if being shaken up adds to your fun, come here and board your DeLorean. Experience old-fashioned thrills while a clever high-tech video whizzes you on a time chase that propels you past ice-age glaciers, volcanoes, dinosaurs, and into the twenty-first century.

Those with flighty stomachs don't have to skip the **Futuristic World of Hanna-Barbera.** Even little tykes and pregnant women can enjoy this go-round with Yogi and pals by sitting in the front row's stationary seats. Similarly, don't forgo E.T., which doesn't jostle you and is mostly a tame

Orlando Science Center

Orlando Science Center is a kid-pleaser; don't miss it. The 193,000-square-foot museum houses ten themed exhibit halls with hundreds of hands-on interactive exhibits, an Adventure Theater, five Discovery Laboratories, an observatory, the Cine-Dome (images projected onto ceiling), a restaurant, and two science stores. At KidsTown, creative play for preschoolers includes a Science Story tree, with resident birds and animals as well as tunnels and kid-size shops and exhibits. NatureWorks focuses on the diverse ecosystems of central Florida, such as coral reefs, salt marshes, and mango swamps; the exhibit also includes miniature insect zoos. Science City, which explores physical science and mathematics, has arches and bridges, pendulums, and spinning chairs to demonstrate how science is a basic part of life. The Puzzle House, the centerpiece of 123 Math Avenue, features math concepts in our everyday lives.

At Techworks, kids can try out high-tech careers in computers, simulation, lasers, and optics. ShowBiz Science is sure to be an eye-opener, detailing how technology and science produce theme-park magic and other memorable adventures. Admission.

Check the schedule for family workshops and family camping overnights at the Science Center, which are scheduled throughout the year.

The Orlando Science Center is at 777 East Princeton Street (407-514-2000 or 888-672-4386; www.osc.org).

ride but does have moments of darkness and noise that could scare younger children; just opt for riding a spaceship, not a bike. Listen carefully to E.T.'s good-by; he wows kids by saying their names.

Preschoolers especially love **A Day in the Park with Barney.** Dedicated to the popular purple dinosaur, this park sports a theater where Barney performs with his playmates Baby Bop and BJ while kids sing along. At the interactive play area kids can explore Barney's tree house and sandbox.

Nickelodeon's studios are a treat for your grade-schoolers. They can ogle the Slime Geyser as it erupts and taste gak. If they're very lucky, they might participate in a routine for such popular Nickelodeon cable network kid shows as *Think Fast* and *Super Sloppy Double Dare.*

Fabulous **Fievel's Playland,** near the E.T. ride, delights young kids; everything is oversize—as it would be from a mouse's perspective. Tots giggle as they climb up the 30-foot spider web or bounce under a thousand-gallon cowboy hat.

Water Parks

Aside from Walt Disney World's water parks, the Orlando area has **Wet 'N Wild,** 6200 International Drive; (407) 351-1800, (800) 992-WILD, or (407) 351-9453 (recorded information about hours, admission, and rides); www.wetnwild.com. **Children's Playground,** a water park for ages one to ten, features miniature versions of popular adult attractions, such as a Miniature Raging Rapids, Children's Lazy River, and a one-of-a-kind Children's Wave Pool. There are even kid-size beach chairs and lounges, plus a food kiosk. (Adult-size seating encircles the area.) **Bubble Up** lets kids climb to the top of a slippery surface and then bounce down into a kiddie pool.

For older kids, thrills and chills include Hydra Fighter, the Bubba Tub, a triple-dip thrill ride, which holds up to five (brave) family members at a time; the Fuji Flyer, which shoots the willing in four-passenger toboggans along banked curves and winding tracks; and the Black Hole, that slides you through 500 feet of twisting darkness. Newer rides include the **Blue Niagra,** 300 feet of intertwined looping tubes that twist from six stories above the park, and **Bomb Bay,** which drops you (like a bomb out of a plane's bay) from a ledge hanging over a six-story water slide. Open year-round, with heated pools in winter. Admission.

Parks and Beaches

See Side Trips for the closest ocean or Gulf beaches. If you want a break from Orlando's fantasy-world attractions, head to **Turkey Lake Park,** 3401 Hiawassee Road; (407) 299-5594. This recreational haven has a swimming pool, picnic tables, a 3-mile bicycle trail, numerous hiking trails, a fishing pier, a petting farm, and an "All Children's Park." There are also picnic areas with grills, RV sites, and five cabins for rent that accommodate ten people each.

Shopping and More Attractions

All the major theme parks have shops where you will undoubtedly spend a sizable portion of your money. If there's anything left, however, you'll have fun strolling through **Church Street Station** (407-422-2434) in downtown Orlando, an all-in-one shopping, entertainment, and dining complex. **The Mercado, A Festive World Marketplace,** (407-345-9337), 8445 South International Drive, offers seventy-five specialty shops, free nightly entertainment, a food court, bird shows, and colorful continental atmosphere. The **Guinness World of Records Experience** (407-248-8891) is an interactive museum featuring games, music, simulated trips in the Space Shuttle, and a chance to explore the inside of a computer, plus presentations of many of the quirky facts and records for which Guinness is famous. **Titanic—The Exhibition**

(407-248-1166; www.titanicshipofdreams.com), permanently docked at The Mercado, uses state-of-the-art sound and visual effects to transport visitors into the story of that fated ship. **Orlando Premium Outlets,** 8200 Vineland Avenue (407-238-7787; www.premiumoutlets.com), which opened in June 2000, has more than 110 stores, a food court, and such child-friendly places as Carter's, Disney, Oshkosh B'Gosh, and Toyco.

Spectator Sports

The **Orlando Magic** NBA basketball team plays at the downtown Orlando arena; (407) 89-MAGIC. The arena is also home to the **Orlando Predators** football team (407-872-7362). Check with the Convention and Visitors Bureau about baseball spring training teams and locations.

The **Orlando Rays,** the Tampa Bay Devil Rays' AA baseball team, plays at Walt Disney World's Wide World of Sports (407-649-7297).

Special Events

In addition to the special events scheduled at Orlando's main attractions throughout the year, there are a number of other events your family will enjoy:

March. Central Florida Fair, featuring more than ninety rides and exhibits.

May. More than 25,000 people come each year to the Zellwood Sweet Corn Festival, which offers (besides corn-eating contests) carnival rides, games, arts, and crafts.

October. Silver Spurs Rodeo and Kissimmee RibFest, the largest rodeo in the eastern United States (since 1944), features the world's best rodeo athletes.

November. Silver Springs' Annual Native American Festival.

SIDE TRIPS

- **Beaches.** Orlando is convenient to both the Atlantic Ocean east coast or Gulf of Mexico west coast beaches. The closest beaches—**Cocoa, New Smyrna,** and **Daytona Beach**—are about an hour's drive to the east.
- **Space Attractions.** At the new **Astronaut Hall of Fame,** in Titusville, just west of Kennedy Space Center and about 60 miles from Orlando (407-269-6100; www.astronauthalloffame.com), more than twenty-five simulators and hands-on activities, coupled with memorabilia and actual hardware from the astronaut program make this a must see for anyone interested in space travel. Special shuttle-launch viewing activ-

ities are offered on launch days, and astronauts periodically are onsite to make presentations about their experiences and about the space program. In the **Astronaut Adventure** area, kids can experience up to four times the force of gravity on the G-Force Trainer; see the view from a space shuttle window heading into space; and steer a lunar rover on the moon. There's also a gift shop (the Right Stuff), and at the Cosmic Cafe you can get sandwiches and salads. Admission.

The **Kennedy Space Center,** on State Road 405, North Merritt Island (321-452-2121 or 800-SHUTTLE; www.kennedyspacecenter. com) also has much to offer. At the Kennedy Center Visitor Complex, guests can meet an astronaut for a question-and-answer session. (The Visitor Complex may be a little tough on toddlers, although school-age and older kids will find it fascinating.) Exploration in the New Millennium takes visitors on a journey from the Vikings' discovery of Greenland to the Mars Viking Lander. Kids can submit their names for a chance to fly in a future space mission. At the International Space Station Center, visitors walk through a full-scale mockup of space station modules, and two IMAX Theaters provide larger-than-life films on space travel. There's also a two-hour bus tour of the center and a two-hour bus tour of the Merritt Island National Wildlife Refuge. (The Kennedy Center is also a National Wildlife Refuge, with more than twenty-five endangered species calling it home.) Three restaurants and a gift shop with more than 8,000 space-related items are also on site.

■ **Cypress Gardens,** in Winter Haven, is forty minutes from Walt Disney World. Cypress Gardens has gorgeous botanical gardens; waterski, circus, and exotic bird shows; high divers; synchronized swimmers; and special events throughout the year. Call (800) 282-2123 or (800) 237-4826 elsewhere in the United States.

Where to Stay

The Kissimmee-St. Cloud area offers reasonably priced accommodations close to the area's major attractions; you can book many by calling (800) 333-KISS. Since Orlando is a family-vacation destination, most hotels and resorts offer appealing features for kids. Here's a sampling of what you'll find.

With so many on-site choices at Walt Disney World, it makes sense to stay on property, particularly if you plan to spend most of your time at the Disney parks. The buses and monorail provide easy access to the parks, and when you are close to your hotel, you can come back for an afternoon swim and nap, something we highly recommend. The moderately priced Disney resorts are **All-Star Sports, All-Star Music,** and **All-Star Movies Resort.** The rooms, while smaller than at most hotels, are

Disney Cruise Line

The Disney *Magic* and the *Wonder* are beautiful ships with terrific cabins, creative children's programming, and some interesting adult entertainment. The cabins (all except inside cabins) are spacious (about 25 percent bigger than the industry standard) and have two bathrooms—one has a toilet and sink, and the other has a shower/tub combo with another sink.

The kids' facilities, at 15,000 square feet, are the largest at sea. Oceaneer's Club is a pirate-themed play space for ages three to eight; Oceaneer's Lab, with its computers and science lab, is designed for ages nine to twelve, and Common Grounds, designed to look like a New York coffee bar, has magazines, music, comfy couches, and flavored sodas and coffees to lure teens.

The *Magic* does seven-day Caribbean trips that include a stop at Disney's private Bahamian island, and the *Wonder* does three- or four-day trips in the Bahamas. Most families spend three or four days at Walt Disney World, then book the rest of the week at sea.

For more information call Disney Cruise Line (407-566-7000 or 800-WDW-CRUI; www.disney.com/DisneyCruise).

serviceable, and the cafeteria serves inexpensive (if not good) meals. Disney's **Port Orleans Resort** and **Dixie Landings Resort** are in the next-higher price range. Each has a themed pool and rooms that can accommodate four.

Other good family choices include **Disney's Boardwalk Villas,** nicely located on a boardwalk and near an ersatz sand beach; **Disney's Yacht Club** and **Disney's Beach Club** are within walking distance to Epcot and share a heated three-acre pool; the **Walt Disney World Swan** and the **Walt Disney World Dolphin** are well-located, feature several pools and miniature golf courses, and offer Camp Dolphin Youth programs; **Animal Kingdom Lodge,** a new upscale property in Animal Kingdom; and **Disney's Old Key West Resort** offers the convenience of studios to three-bedroom homes complete with kitchens.

Disney's Fort Wilderness Resort and Campground has campsites and recreational vehicle hookups. Contact (407) W-DISNEY for information; www.disneyworld.com.

If you are visiting **Universal Studios** and need on-site lodgings, try the **Portofino Bay Hotel,** 5601 Universal Boulevard, (407-224-7117 or 888-837-2273; www.loewshotels.com), an upscale property with an Italian seaside village theme. Also on site is the slightly less expensive 654-

room **Hard Rock Hotel,** which opened in early 2001, and a 1,000-room **Royal Pacific Resort,** which will open later in 2001. Stay at these properties and receive early admission to Universal's theme parks and priority seating at restaurants at Universal Studios Escape.

Near SeaWorld and Discovery Cove, try **Marriott's Renaissance Orlando Resort,** 6677 Sea Harbor Drive (407-351-5555 or 800-228-9292; www.renaissancehotels.com). The property features a larger outdoor pool, a children's pool, and a playground, plus restaurants.

The $80 million **Holiday Inn Family Suites Resort,** located approximately 1 mile from the Walt Disney World Resort, 14500 Continental Gateway (407-387-5437 or 877-387-5437; www.hifamilysuites.com), includes parlors with a pull-out sofa, a kitchenette, two or three televisions, and a second room suited to your clan.

The CinemaSuites, among the most popular, turns the extra space into a red-velvet-draped home theater with a sixty-inch television, surround-sound stereo system, dual recliners, and two bean bag chairs. Fitness Suites feature recumbent bicycles and free weights. The corporate sponsored, bunk-bedded Kidsuites, come with outerspace designs, ice cream logos, cartoon characters, Coca-Cola polar bears, and other corporate—but kid-friendly—icons. The resort provides complimentary shuttles to the four Walt Disney World theme parks, as well as kids-only check-in desk and an 1,800-square-foot game room. Kids twelve and under eat free at the food court or restaurant when accompanied by a dining adult.

An older property, the **Holiday Inn Hotel and Suites Main Gate East,** 5678 Irlo Bronson Memorial Highway (U.S. 192), Kissimmee (407-396-4488 or 800-366-5437; www.familyfunhotel.com), offers similar amenities and services, with a Camp Holiday Entertainment Center.

Summerfield Suites Hotels offers two properties in Orlando, each featuring suites with a living area plus two bedrooms. **Summerfield Suites Orlando–International Drive,** 8480 International Drive (407-352-2400 or 800-830-4964), is about fifteen minutes from Walt Disney World. **Summerfield Suites Lake Buena Vista,** 8751 Suiteside Drive (407-238-0777 or 800-830-4964), is a chain that offers kitchen facilities and a daily continental plus buffet breakfast. There are also children's videos to rent (the two-bedroom units have three televisions and a VCR) and a twenty-four-hour convenience store on-site. Ask about special weekend rates.

WHERE TO EAT

At Universal Studios CityWalk and Downtown Disney, dining options and theme eateries abound. If those choices aren't enough, Orlando offers more.

Medieval Times, 4150 West Irlo Bronson Memorial Highway West, is a kid's dream come true. As you dine stadium-style, knights atop horses joust for a fair maiden, who is plucked from the audience. Call (407) 396-1518 or (800) 327-4024. **Arabian Nights,** in the 1,200-seat Palace of the Horses (407-239-9223), offers a two-hour prime-rib dinner show that features twenty-five horse acts and thrill rides, plus chariot races.

Racing enthusiasts can choose between **NASCAR Cafe Orlando,** CityWalk (407-224-7223), which combines eating from a racing-theme menu with viewing rare artifacts and collectibles on display throughout the cafe and **Race Rock Supercharged Restaurant** (407-248-9876), whose owners include the legendary Richard Petty and Mario Andretti.

For preteens and teens, a meal at the **Hard Rock Cafe,** CityWalk (407-351-7625), is a must. This guitar-shaped eatery, with its rock-legend memorabilia, is the largest restaurant in the Hard Rock Cafe chain. At selected intervals the serving staff breaks into song, encouraging diners to dance.

FOR MORE INFORMATION

Orlando/Orange County Convention and Visitors Bureau has a Visitor Center at 8723 International Drive; (407) 363-5872 or (800) 643-9492, open daily 8:00 A.M.–7:00 P.M. Call or stop by for their *Official Visitors Guide,* with information about accommodations, attractions, restaurants, shopping, and transportation. Also ask about the Orlando Magicard that offers discounts on hotels, attractions, and restaurants. The Flexiticket also offers savings at Universal Studios, SeaWorld, Wet 'N Wild, and other attractions.

Kissimmee–St. Cloud Convention and Visitors Bureau can provide maps, brochures, directions, and discount coupons: P.O. Box 422007, Kissimmee, Florida 34742-2007; (800) 327-9159 or (407) 847-5000. Accommodations reservations number: (800) 333-KISS.

Emergency Numbers

Ambulance, fire, and police: 911

Non-emergency police: (407) 246-2414

Non-emergency fire: (407) 246-2141

Emergency room (twenty-four hour): Orlando Regional Medical Center, 1414 Kuhl Avenue; (407) 841-5111

Poison Control: (407) 841-5222

Twenty-four-hour pharmacy: Walgreen's, 1003 West Vine Street, Kissimmee; (407) 847-5252

St. Petersburg and Clearwater

The St. Petersburg/Clearwater area is located on Florida's west coast; the region is bordered by Tampa Bay to the east and the Gulf of Mexico to the west. Nicknamed the Pinellas Suncoast, the region boasts 35 miles of beaches, part of the area's 400 miles of shoreline. The Pinellas Suncoast includes Clearwater Beach, St. Petersburg, St. Pete Beach, Treasure Island, Madeira Beach, Indian Rocks Beach, Dunedin, and Tarpon Springs.

Much of what you'll want to do here is outside. Explore parks and preserves to experience the "natural Florida," the land before theme parks and condominiums. And of course, make lots of time for the beach. St. Petersburg brags about its place in *The Guinness Book of Records* for 768 consecutive days of sunshine (from February 9, 1967 to March 17, 1969).

GETTING THERE

There are two airports in the Tampa/St. Petersburg area. Among the carriers serving the **Tampa International Airport,** P.O. Box 22287, Tampa (813-870-8700 or 800-767-8882; www.tampaairport.com), are America West, American, British Airways, Carnival, Continental, Delta, Northwest, TWA, United, and USAirways. The **St. Petersburg–Clearwater International Airport,** 3800 Roosevelt Boulevard in Clearwater (727-535-7600), is served by Air Transat, ATA, Canada 3000, Nations Air Royal Airlines, and Sun Jet.

The St. Pete/Clearwater area is linked to the interstate system and is accessible by I-75, I-4, U.S. 19, and state road 60.

GETTING AROUND

Unless you plan to stay pretty much plastered to your hotel's beach, you'll need to hire a taxi for excursions or rent a car if you plan much off-property sight-seeing. Car-rental agencies are at both airports.

St. Petersburg and Clearwater

AT A GLANCE

▶ Enjoy 35 miles of sandy beaches and lots of sunshine

▶ Splash in calm Gulf waters

▶ Go on dolphin, manatee, and shelling excursions

▶ St. Petersburg/Clearwater Area Convention and Visitors Bureau: (877) 352-3224; www.stpete-clearwater.com

The **PSTA** offers transportation by bus; call (727) 530-9911 for schedules and rates. The **Clearwater Ferry Service,** P.O. Box 335, Clearwater (727-442-7433), offers such boat trips as the Tarpon Springs Excursion and the Dolphin Encounter. The company also provides a water taxi to certain beaches. Call for the rates and hours of operation for the Clearwater Beach Water Taxi.

The **Looper** makes checking out the downtown museums and other sites hassle-free. Every twenty minutes, from 11:00 A.M. to 5:00 P.M., the shuttle, which costs about 50 cents, stops at the Dali Museum, Tropicana Field, the Museum of Fine Arts, and the Pier.

WHAT TO SEE AND DO

Beaches, Parks and Green Spaces

The beaches are the area's treasure. **St. Pete Beach** sports fine sands with calm Gulf waters. Connected to the mainland by the St. Pete Beach Causeway and the Pinellas Bayway, St. Pete Beach is the place to head with your children for fun and sun. **Sand Key Park,** Clearwater, is an especially nice wide, white-sand public beach.

For relatively isolated beaches on the Gulf coast, visit some of the undeveloped barrier islands such as **Caladesi Island State Park,** 1 Causeway Boulevard, Dunedin; (727) 469-5918. The swimming and shelling are fine here, and a 3-mile nature trail winds through the island's interior. A 1995 survey by the University of Maryland rated this beach as being the second-best in the United States. **Honeymoon Island Recreation Area,** 1 Causeway Boulevard, Dunedin (727-469-5942), is also an undeveloped barrier island with interesting topography. Both islands, which are north of Clearwater, are accessible by ferry from the Dunedin Causeway or from downtown Clearwater. At low tide you can actually walk from north Clearwater Beach to Caladesi, about a 1-mile

Parks and Preserves

Outdoor life here isn't just the beach. Among the St. Pete/Clearwater region's nineteen county parks and preserves:

- In St. Petersburg **Sawgrass Lake Park,** 7400 Twenty-fifth Street North (727-217-7256), and in Clearwater, **Moccasin Lake Nature Park,** 2750 Park Trail Lane (727-462-6024), sport lakes, interpretive centers, and trails where you can view snakes, alligators, turtles, armadillos, and opossum.
- Children enjoy **Weedon Island,** 1500 Weedon Island (727-217-7208; www.stpete.org/weedon.htm), a 1,500-acre nature preserve of sea-grass beds and mangrove stands, northeast of St. Petersburg on the edge of Tampa Bay. A Native American Cultural Center focusing on the Timucuan Indians is planned for the future, in conjunction with the Smithsonian Institution. Canoe rentals are nearby.
- **Boyd Hill Nature Park,** 1101 Country Club Way South, St. Petersburg (727-893-7326),

has 250 acres and six trails that lead through Florida upland habitats where the "locals" include gopher tortoises and eastern indigo snakes. Younger kids will like the playground and butterfly gardens. Nature hikes are conducted on the third Wednesday night of every month. A tram tour takes place daily at 1:00 P.M.

- Located south of St. Petersburg, **Fort DeSoto Park,** off I-275, exit 4, at Pinellas Bayway (727-866-2484), comprises five islands: Madeleine, St. Jean, St. Christopher, Bonne Fortune, and Mullet. The park offers 900 acres, including 7 miles of undeveloped beaches and a clean campground with playground equipment. Some children like exploring Fort DeSoto, an unfinished artillery installation built in 1898 to protect Tampa Bay during the Spanish-American War.

hike. A passenger ferry (no cars allowed) operates from Honeymoon Island to Caladesi Island. Both islands offer great shelling and birding. Look for ospreys, eagles, herons, and ibis.

Boat Excursions

Spending time on the water is easily accomplished here, as St. Petersburg/Clearwater, between Tampa Bay and the Gulf of Mexico, is a boating mecca, laced with creeks, canals, bayous, and an intracoastal waterway. If you know what you're doing, you can rent your own boat and head to such popular destinations as **Anclote Key, Three Rooker Bar, Caladesi**

Island, and **Egmont Key,** all accessible only by boat. There are many powerboat and sailboat rental shops, including **Bayway Adventures,** 17811 Gulf Boulevard, Indian Shores (727-397-5171), and **Tierra Verde Boat Rentals,** 100 Pinellas Bayway (727-867-0077). Sea kayaks and canoes are popular, too.

Several companies offer **dolphin, manatee,** and **shelling excursions.** Among them are **Aquatic Obsession,** 980 Fifty-eighth Street North, St. Petersburg (727-344-3483), and **St. Croix Custom Cruises,** John's Pass Boardwalk, Madeira Beach (727-866-1900). In Clearwater Beach the *Show Queen,* Clearwater Beach Marina, 25 Causeway Boulevard (727-461-3113 or 800-772-4479) offers two-hour narrated scenic cruises.

Team with a marine biologist to study endangered animals and, if necessary, help with an animal rescue at **Marine Life Adventures.** On these one- to four-day outings, there's also time to snorkel and beachcomb. Contact the **Clearwater Marine Aquarium** at (727) 441-1790. Two-hour **Sea Life Safari Cruises** (727-462-2628 or 800-444-4814) include trawl netting, encounters with marine life, and a visit to a bird sanctuary.

For families the best water tour is **Captain Memo's Pirate Cruise** at the Clearwater Beach Marina, Dock 3, (727-446-2587; www.pirateflorida. com). Kids wear pirate hats, get their faces painted, hear swashbuckling tales, and engage in watergun battles.

Captain Anderson Cruises, St. Pete Beach, and the **Starlite Majesty Dining Yacht,** Clearwater, offer sight-seeing and meal cruises.

Bicycling and Inline Skating

The **Pinellas Trail** winds for 47 miles, north to south, through Pinellas County from Tarpon Springs to downtown St. Petersburg, providing a great place for jogging, hiking, cycling, and in-line skating. The 15-foot-wide paths are divided into a lane for cyclists and skaters and a lane designated for walkers and joggers. There are a few traffic intersections that must be crossed, but a good deal of the trail circumvents busy roads. For a free guidebook to the trail, call (727) 464-4751. These specialists can also tell you about local bicycle clubs so that you can pedal with some newfound friends. For nearby bicycle-rental places, ask your hotel's concierge. Some rental shops include **Transportation Station,** 652 Gulfview Boulevard (727-443-3188), and **Mike's Cycle City,** 1799 Clearwater Largo Road, Clearwater (727-585-1449).

The Pinellas Trail also attracts in-line skaters. Skate-rental places include **Transportation Station** (see above) as well as **Trailways,** 611 Palm Bluff, Clearwater (727-461-9736).

Suncoast Seabird Sanctuary

Especially with young children, don't miss the **Suncoast Seabird Sanctuary,** 18328 Gulf Boulevard, Indian Shores; (727) 391-6211; www.webcoast. com/seabird. Although this facility occupies only one and a half acres and is sandwiched between apartment and office buildings, the Sanctuary is the largest treatment facility for injured birds based on the number of birds treated daily, which ranges from fifteen to twenty. At any one time the resident population hovers around 500 to 600 birds. About 90 percent of all the birds are able, after care, to be released back into the wild.

Kids are intrigued by this facility. Those birds that can't be turned free because they cannot fend for themselves are on permanent display in cages, providing children with a rare opportunity to see raptors and other wild creatures up close. Free-flying pelicans come here to nest on top of nets, attracted by the comfortable ambience and the hope of stealing food from some of the recuperating birds.

More Wildlife

At the **Clearwater Marine Aquarium,** 249 Windward Passage, Clearwater (727-447-0980; www.cmaquarium.com), a research and rehabilitation facility, children see bottle-nosed dolphins, baby sea turtles, and various fish and other mammals. Children also learn about how the facility rescues and nurtures injured marine mammals.

Museums

Even in the sun-kissed coast, you need to be off the beach sometimes. These are some good choices.

Great Explorations, 800 Second Avenue Northeast, The Pier, Third Floor; (727) 821-8992. This facility, though not large, packs plenty of fun. Geared for elementary-age kids and younger ones, this museum focuses on the arts, sciences, and the body. A highlight is the Touch Tunnel. Test your sense of touch by crawling through a 96-foot dark maze with tactile surfaces (for ages seven and older). At the Power Plant produce electricity with a potato and play mind games in the Experimental Gallery.

The Explore Gallery is a special section catering to ages six and younger. There are fire boots to try on and fire engines to climb on, as well as a wall of gears to turn and balls to roll through mazes. A padded area is cushy enough for crawling infants.

Captain Dave Zelewski of the Lucky Too *helps visitors to St. Petersburg/Clearwater find king mackerel, barracuda, amberjack, grouper, and other game fish.*

The **Salvador Dalí Museum,** 1000 Third Street South, St. Petersburg (727-823-3767; www.daliweb.com), exhibits the work of Dalí. Don't shy away from visiting this place. The unusual perspective of this artist often appeals to grade-school children and teens, many of whom are fascinated with Dalí's use of strange forms and odd combinations. The gift shop offers great Dalí souvenirs, from his wiggly watches to coloring books.

Florida International Museum, 100 Second Street North, St. Petersburg; (727) 822-3693 or (800) 777-9882; www.floridamuseum.org. At selected times this museum houses special exhibits of traveling art and cultural shows. The 1999 "John F. Kennedy: The Exhibition" has become a permanent part of the museum.

The **Tampa Bay Holocaust Memorial Museum,** 55 Fifth Street South, St. Petersburg (727-821-8261; www.tampabayholocaust.org), is the fourth-largest facility in the United States devoted to the Holocaust. Among the collections is an actual boxcar used to transport people to the Nazi concentration camps.

The Museum of Fine Arts, 255 Beach Drive Northeast, St. Petersburg (727-896-2667; www.fine-arts.org), might not impress children used to large collections, but this museum is noted for its French Impressionist paintings and works by American photographers. The museum also exhibits European, American pre-Columbian, and Far Eastern art.

The **Pinellas County Historical Museum** displays vintage toys and lays down a timeline from Native American to modern times using vignettes.

Pinewood Cultural Park is developing next door to Heritage Village at 12175 125th Street North, Largo (727-582-2100). It has eighteen gardens that opened in October 2000 and grows everything from roses to kitchen vegetables. It is also home to the new **Gulf Coast Museum of Art** (727-518-6833), featuring Florida artists on a permanent basis as well as temporary exhibits.

Just a short drive from St. Petersburg and Clearwater, the **Florida Aquarium** is worth a visit. (See Tampa chapter.)

More Attractions

A landmark in St. Petersburg, **the Pier,** 800 Second Avenue Northeast, St. Petersburg (727-821-6164; www.stpete-pier.com), is an ochre-and-turquoise inverted pyramid that juts out 2,400 feet into Tampa Bay. The facility houses an aquarium, a miniature golf range, the children's museum Great Explorations, restaurants, bicycle, in-line skates, and water sports rentals and specialty shops. This is a lively spot for people and pelican watching. Teens rollerblade along the straightaway, and birds roost on the pilings, hoping to be fed or at the very least to share some of the catch of the local anglers. The boutiques offer just the kinds of stuff that intrigues children longing to spend their allowance. A trip to the fifth floor observatory is a must, as is lunch at the **Columbia Restaurant,** on the fourth floor. (See Where to Eat.)

Performing Arts

The **Mahaffey Theater** in the **BayFront Center,** 400 First Street South, St. Petersburg (727-892-5767), and **Ruth Eckerd Hall,** 1111 McMullen Booth Road, Clearwater (727-791-7400), offer traveling Broadway shows and performances by the Florida Orchestra, Florida Ballet, and Florida Opera. Call for a schedule of performances and events.

Shopping

Beach Drive in downtown St. Petersburg, part of "The QuARTer" district, hosts a number of antiques shops and boutiques. **Dolphin Village,** in Clearwater, is a similar district. There are also a number of shopping malls located throughout the county, but none in town.

Spectator Sports

The **Tampa Bay Devil Rays** play in Tropicana Field, 1 Tropicana Drive, St. Petersburg; (727) 825-3250 or (888) FAN-RAYS. The indoor, air-conditioned field features a kids' interactive area and a climbing wall. The **Philadelphia Phillies** train in Clearwater, and the **Toronto Blue Jays** train in Dunedin.

College football comes to town for the **Outback Bowl** every New Year's Day.

SIDE TRIPS

- **Tarpon Springs,** about 45 miles from downtown St. Petersburg, is worth a drive just for the food, but this is the heartland of sponges—real sponges. This tight-knit Greek community is the center of the sponge industry in the United States. For a nominal fee you can take an outing on the **St. Nicholas Boat Line,** at the dock along Dodecanese Boulevard, to see how traditional sponge diving is done. Shops sell real sponges, which your children will probably recognize as the kind that are sold at such trendy chain stores as the Body Shop. Here the sponges are bigger, better quality, and much cheaper.
- Take some time to snack on such Greek treats as *baklava* (a walnut and honey pastry) or *spanakopita* (spinach pie), available at the many bakeries and Greek restaurants. **Mykonos Restaurant,** 628 Dodecanese Boulevard (727-934-4306), offers large portions of tasty traditional Greek fare at moderate prices.
- **Tampa,** with Busch Gardens Tampa, the Florida Aquarium, plus many other attractions, is just thirty minutes away (see Tampa). **Orlando,** with Walt Disney World plus SeaWorld and Universal Studios Escape, is about ninety minutes away (see Orlando).

SPECIAL EVENTS

In **March** St. Petersburg hosts the two-week-long **Festival of States,** an event in which bands from all over the country compete. Parades, sporting events, a clown school, fireworks, and concerts are held during this annual celebration. In **May** there's a triathlon along the beach.

Children are the focus of a week-long series of events in **June.** Programs during **Kid's Week** include a variety show, environmental programs, a fishing tournament, and arts and crafts.

During **October's Annual John's Pass Seafood Festival,** the food is fresh from the sea and very tasty. October also brings the annual free **Clearwater Jazz Holiday,** known for its top-name jazz musicians.

WHERE TO STAY

More moderate choices include the **St. Petersburg Bayfront Hilton,** 333 First Street South (727-894-5000); the **Holiday Inn SunSpree Resort,** 6800 Sunshine Skyway Lane (727-867-1151); children's programs offered in season; and the **Hampton Inn, Clearwater/St. Pete,** 3655 Hospitality Road (727-577-9200 or 800-HAMPTON), where rates include free continental breakfast.

Hilton Clearwater Beach Resort, 400 Mandalay Avenue (727-

Great Family Resorts

Staying right on the beach is the best for families. TradeWinds and Don Cesar are two beachfront options and The Westin is a good off-the-beach family resort.

■ **TradeWinds Island Grand,** 5500 Gulf Boulevard (800–808–9821; www.tradewinds resort. com).With several oddly placed buildings it's a little bit confusing at first, but this property is family-friendly. All rooms have refrigerators and coffeemakers. The larger rooms include a microwave. Suites feature living areas and full kitchens. The Konk Club offers selected activities for children, including swimming lessons Monday through Friday and Club Teen three days a week. Morning might include beach play and arts and crafts. An evening activity that's popular is the family movie.

■ The historic **Don Cesar Beach Resort,** 3400 Gulf Boulevard (800–282–1116), is a more

upscale resort located on the beach. The hotel features a children's playroom and a supervised children's program year-round for ages four to twelve from about 10:00 A.M. to 4:00 P.M. In addition, sometimes there are Friday- and Saturday-night pizza parties for kids.

■ **The Westin Innisbrook Resort,** Tarpon Springs; (727) 942–2000 or (800) 456–2000; www.westin-innisbrook.com. Too far from St. Pete's beaches for a daily trek, this upscale property offers a kids' program for ages four to twelve, a Junior Golf Institute, a Junior Tennis Camp, and six pools, including the three-acre Loch Ness monster pool featuring two water slides and a waterfall.

461–3222 or 800–753–3954; www.hilton.com) is handily located next to Pier 60, with its family facilities and activities. Besides beachfront recreation, its amenities include two pools, restaurants, bars, and the Fun Factory, an innovative kids' program.

Stay in grand style at **Belleview Biltmore Resort & Spa,** 25 Belleview Boulevard, Clearwater (727–442–6171 or 800–237–8947; www.belleview biltmore.com). It was built in the 1890s with wide verandas, gables, and Victorian flair. Recent renovations have modernized its 292 rooms, swimming pool with waterfalls, spa, and gracious lobby/dining areas.

The region has more than thirty county, state, and private campgrounds. Many accept recreational vehicles as well as tent camping. Among these are **Fort DeSoto Park Campgrounds,** Tierra Verde (727–582–2267); **Caladesi Island State Park,** Clearwater, (727–469–

5918), which has only boat camping; and, for boat camping, **Egmont Key State Park,** Egmont Key (727-893-2627).

WHERE TO EAT

A longtime area tradition (from 1905) is the **Columbia Restaurant,** with a spin-off located at the Pier, 800 Second Avenue Northeast (727-596-8400), a Spanish/Cuban restaurant. Stick to the traditional favorites. This is the place to introduce your children to black bean soup and *tostones* (fried plantains). Just in case, the restaurant serves cheeseburgers, too.

Also at the Pier **ChaCha Coconuts** (727-822-6655) is fun—it's situated sky-high, with a panoramic view, and is brightly decorated. The decor and menu have a Caribbean flair. The kids' menu offers "chicken thumbs," quesadillas, and other standards.

Leverock's, a local chain of seafood restaurants, has several locations, including 4801 Thirty-seventh Street South, St. Petersburg (727-864-3883); 10 Corey Avenue, St. Pete Beach (727-367-4588); and 7000 U.S. Highway 19 North, Pinellas Park (727-526-9188).

For moderately priced fresh seafood in an informal setting, try the **Hurricane Seafood Restaurant,** 807 Gulf Way, South Street; (727-360-9558). Besides grouper, the house specialty, the restaurant serves stone crabs and a well-known Key lime pie. Get some gator bites to start off. These bits of deep-fried alligator with barbecue sauce should amuse the kids. See if they can tell these from chicken nuggets.

For the breakfast of champions or the just plain famished, head for **Skyway Jack's,** 2795 Thirty-fourth Street South, Pinellas Point Drive, 1 block south of exit 3, St. Petersburg; (727-866-3217). This roadside eatery is down-home, and the food is dirt cheap and delightful. Children should gobble such goodies as the chocolate chip and banana pancakes plus the southern French toast, a powerhouse plate laced with marmalade, cream cheese, and honey.

At Clearwater Beach **Frenchy's Rockaway Grill,** 7 Rockaway Street, (727-446-4844) is convenient and lively. Seating is outdoors on the beach, with a view of waves or a volleyball game, or inside, where it's cooler and equally colorful. Seafood dominates the menu, which has plenty of offerings that kids will like but no kid portions for little ones.

At **Woody's Waterfront Cafe & Beach Bar** at Corey Ave and Sunset Way (727-360-9165), you can dine in the open air, beneath a ceiling of hanging surfboards, or under umbrellas on the patio, overlooking the pass between Treasure Island and Sand Key. The fare is burgers and seafood baskets.

FOR MORE INFORMATION

For additional information on the area's beaches, call the Gulf Beaches Chamber of Commerce, 6990 Gulf Boulevard, St. Pete Beach, FL 33706; (727) 360-6957 or (800) 944-1847; www.gulfbeaches-tampabay.com.

For general information contact the St. Petersburg/Clearwater Area Convention and Visitors Bureau; (877) FL-BEACH; www.stpete-clearwater.com. For county park information contact Pinellas County Parks, Clearwater; (727) 464-3347.

Emergency Numbers

Ambulance, fire, and police: 911

Palms Pasadena Hospital, 1501 Pasadena Avenue South, South Pasadena; (727) 381-1000

Florida Poison Information Center: (800) 282-3171

A pharmacy is located in Walgreens, 337 Seventy-fifth Avenue, St. Pete Beach; (727) 367-7657

Florida

TAMPA

Tampa, which began as a Native American fishing village, has been luring adventurers for centuries. Ponce de León, the first recorded European visitor, came here in 1513 in search of gold. So did explorers Hernando de Soto in 1539 and Pedro Menéndez in 1565. Situated on Florida's west coast, Tampa is on Hillsborough Bay, which opens into Tampa Bay and the Gulf of Mexico. Tampa served as a military post in 1824, when Fort Brooke was established to monitor the Seminole Indians. In 1885 Don Vincente Martinez Ybor developed a cigar manufacturing center here. But since 1891, when railroad and steamship magnate Henry Plant opened the Tampa Bay Hotel, now a landmark building, Tampa has been a tourist area.

Only a short drive from some fine west coast beaches, Tampa offers sophisticated city attractions, an interesting aquarium, and kid-pleasing adventures such as Busch Gardens Tampa and Adventure Island.

GETTING THERE

Tampa International Airport (TPA) (813-870-8700 or 800-767-8882; www.tampaairport.com) is just 7 miles from downtown Tampa and serves twenty airlines.

Amtrak arrives at Union Station, 601 North Nebraska Avenue; (800) 872-7245. The **Greyhound Bus** terminal is at 610 East Polk Street; (813) 229-2112. Among the major highways leading to Tampa, I-75 provides access from the north and south.

Several ships take advantage of Tampa's port location, including Carnival Cruise Lines' *Sensation* and *Tropicale* and Holland America's *Nieuw Amsterdam*. For cruise information call the Tampa Port Authority at (800) 741-2297.

GETTING AROUND

With its streets laid out in a geometric grid, Tampa is a fairly simple city to navigate. Most Tampa attractions are near I-275 or I-4. An express-

Tampa

AT A GLANCE

▶ Explore Busch Gardens: 300 acres of family fun including rides and animals

▶ See 4,300 animals and plants at the Florida Aquarium

▶ Try the interactive exhibits at the Museum of Science and Industry

▶ Splash at Adventure Island water park

▶ Tampa Bay Convention and Visitors Bureau, (800) 826-8358; www.gotampa.com

way, with tolls, takes you across town. The **HARTline** is Tampa's public transportation bus system. Call (813) 254-HART for fare and route information. The **Tampa-Ybor Trolley** (813-254-4278) connects downtown hotels, shops, museums, and restaurants with Harbour Island, Ybor City, the Florida Aquarium, and the Garrison Seaport Center.

A car, however, may still be the best way to get around.

WHAT TO SEE AND DO

Busch Gardens Tampa Bay
Busch Gardens Tampa Bay, 3605 Bougainvillea Avenue; (813) 987-5082 or (800) 4-ADVENTURE; www.buschgardens.com. Busch Gardens, the area's biggest family draw, is a thirty-five-acre theme park with rides, live performances, shops, restaurants, and a top-notch eighty-acre African zoo. When you purchase your admission, consider a combined ticket for Busch Gardens and the nearby Adventure Island, a water theme park.

Rides. Busch Gardens is one of those places you could explore all day, or for several days, depending on your family's exuberance for rides and tolerance for lines. Come early, wear a bathing suit with shorts or a T-shirt for the water rides, and bring some travel toys for kids to play with while waiting in lines. (Water bottles help, too.) The wait can be long, and hot, depending on the season. Go on the water rides fairly early. Being wet helps keep you cool as you stand in line; by the time you leave the park, you're likely to be dry for the ride back to your hotel. If cool weather makes drenching uncomfortable, bring a change of clothes and rent a locker.

What's fun here? Most things will interest somebody in your clan. Little kids love **Land of the Dragons,** a dragon-themed playland whose pint-sized attractions pack a lot of fun. Tykes like riding the mini–Ferris wheel, splashing down a mini-flume ride, and climbing the tree house, a three-story structure with a bridge, waterfall, and slide.

Egypt, a seven-acre themed area, features a walk-through of a replicated King Tut's tomb, a Sand Dig where youngsters unearth buried antiquities, a shopping bazaar that offers cartouche paintings and other handicrafts, and, its crown jewel, a mega-coaster. **Montu** is one of the world's tallest and largest inverted (your legs dangle) roller coasters. This beast moves along 4,000 feet of track at speeds topping 60 miles per hour. Two sandboxes are nearby, good places for little kids and parents to wait while older siblings and others ride. Sifting Sands, the quieter, well-shaded play area, is to the right of the entrance to Montu.

Another roller coaster, **Kumba,** is one of the fastest steel coasters in the southeastern United States. Kumba screams around its turquoise tracks, turning riders upside down seven times and reaching speeds of more than 60 mph. If you're brave enough to hop on, Kumba swirls you around three first-of-a-kinds for coasters: an innovative diving loop, a camelback featuring a 360-degree spiral, and the world's largest loop. **Tanganyika Tidal Wave,** one of the reasons you brought your bathing suit, takes you on a water "safari" that ends with a dousing by a big wave. Other watery wonders include the **Stanley Falls log flume** and the **Congo River Rapids raft ride.**

Animals. To its credit Busch Gardens is more than just a place for amusement rides. The park features cleverly presented animals and habitats. On-site are more than 2,700 animals representing 340 species. The TransVeldt Railway takes you through the Serengeti Plain, an area loosely representing the African savanna. Young kids especially like this easy way to sit back and see giraffes, gazelles, flamingos, and ostriches. Newly restored, the Serengeti now grows 150 species of African trees, shrubs, grasses, and aquatic plants.

Don't miss **Edge of Africa,** a fifteen-acre walk-through safari habitat. On the way in pick up a Jack Hanna field guide. In several places only a thin (but strong) wall of glass separates you from the animals, thereby allowing you to get amazingly close to these creatures. The glass-walled hippo pond gives you a great below-water look at these rotund bathers, and the thin partition in the lion area—if the lion's sitting there—puts you within inches of these kings of the jungle. Kids and adults are fascinated by the proximity. Other wildlife in this area are baboons, spotted hyenas, zebras, and a pond of flamingos.

Myombe Reserve, the Great Ape Domain, another major wildlife area, features gorillas and chimpanzees in a three-acre rain-forest habitat. A video camera brings you close-ups, just in case the resident group is relaxing in a far corner of the habitat. The many shaded areas and benches make viewing pleasant—no standing in the hot summer sun unless you want to.

Take your kids by the **petting zoo,** the **elephant habitat,** and the **Nairobi Field Station,** where you can admire some interesting newborns. Walk through **Lory Landing,** a free-flight aviary, and a lorikeet or two may land on you, especially if you are carrying nectar. Kids also like admiring the Clydesdales in the white barn. Check the board for times for photo opportunities.

Shows. Busch Gardens Tampa Bay also has several shows. *Hollywood Live on Ice's* skating segments look at movie history from silent films to today's special effects. You'll find it "horribly" entertaining when a 17-foot-tall dinosaur, a werewolf, and a gang of skeletons rise out of the fog to cavort in a graveyard. *American Jukebox* is a tribute to rock 'n' roll and country music. The newest show is *World Rhythms on Ice* at the Moroccan Palace.

When you enter the park, obtain a schedule of the daily shows. The variety acts—juggling, dancing, and magic—may appeal more to little kids than older ones, but try these as a way to rest a bit between the hustle and bustle of the rides and the roller coasters, especially at midday, when lines are longest.

Adventure Island

Adventure Island, 4500 Bougainvillea Avenue (813-987-5600) www.adventureisland.com, open mid-February to October (weekends only mid-September through October), is located just ¼ mile from Busch Gardens Tampa Bay. Cool off at this all-play park replete with twenty-two acres of water rides and sunbathing areas. Come early, though, perhaps an hour before the park opens. The lounge chairs and picnic tables are grabbed on busy days by 10:30 A.M. Bring towels, and a picnic lunch if you like. "Water socks" are a good idea as well since you and your kids will be dashing across paved areas to jump in and out of the water.

Busch Gardens' Serengeti Safari

Serengeti Safari is a must for animal lovers. On this forty-five-minute ride through the Serengeti Plain on a flatbed truck, ostrich and bongo stroll over to check out the people. You get to feed carrot slices and lettuce to Claudia and Tango, 14-foot-tall. These long-necked beauties welcome being touched, an experience your kids will long remember. The naturalist guide tells you about the animals and has things such as real ostrich eggs to handle.

Book this adventure in the morning (813-987-5212), as soon as you arrive in the park. For ages five and older. There is an extra charge for the safari. Watch for a new off-road Rhino Rally, opening in 2001.

Splash Attack's fifty water elements give you lots of play. Cross bridges, crawl through webs, twist down slides, squirt each other with water jets, and get dumped on with 1,000 gallons of water. Your clan can get wet together at the park's **Key West Rapids.** Interlock your inner tubes for the nearly five-story downhill ride that slides you by water geysers, jets, and sprays.

Aruba Tuba twists under, over, and around the park's other water slides. You probably won't notice the other slides, though, as you rush through light into dark in this alternately open and closed tube. **Fabian's Funport** offers water thrills scaled for young children. There are kiddie slides, a maze of water jets, a wave pool with gentle, rolling surf, and a spring that blows bubbles, sure to elicit giggles from even the most timid tot.

School-age kids and teens can ride down a four-story tower on the **Caribbean Corkscrew;** careen down the **Gulf Scream Slide;** splash into the **Everglides,** a 72-foot-high water sled ride; and twist down the **Runaway Rapids,** a 34-foot-high series of water flumes. Nobody will be bored at Adventure Island.

Aquarium and Zoo
Don't miss the **Florida Aquarium,** 701 Channelside Drive (813-273-4020; www.flaquarium.net). With more than 4,300 animals and plants that represent 550 species native to Florida, this aquarium is a big fish story. The facility focuses on Florida's waters from origins in underground springs through wetlands, bays, coral reefs, and out to the open sea. Walk through a re-created wetland with real wood ducks, stilt birds, and alligator hatchlings and grow wide-eyed at the panoramic Coral Reef gallery, with its myriad schools of rainbow-colored fish. Wetlands Lookout houses Fright of the Forest, presenting such Amazon creatures as electric eels, poison arrow frogs, vultures, and vampire bats. To supplement the vivid show, the galleries feature hands-on exhibits.

Lowry Park Zoo, 7530 North Boulevard (813-935-8552; www.lowryparkzoo.com), features a variety of animals from birds to alligators in twenty-four acres of natural habitats. Be sure to visit the Manatee and Aquatic Center. Here you gaze upon lumbering masses of manatees. Lowry Park rehabilitates and studies these sea animals, which are frequently found injured along Florida's west coast. Learn about the plight of these critters and watch as the scientists go about their research in a laboratory open to public view.

Other attractions include an exhibit of Komodo dragons, the world's largest lizards; a Florida aquatic and wetland animal exhibit, with coral, lobster, river otters, and Florida's most famous inhabitant—the alligator. With young children visit the petting zoo, splash fountains (dress them in swimsuits), the carousel ride, and discovery center.

Outdoor Adventures

- **Hillsborough River State Park.** Families will have fun exploring one of Florida's oldest and loveliest state parks, situated northeast of Tampa along the Hillsborough River. A reconstructed Seminole War historic site, **Fort Foster** is open for touring four times daily on Saturday and Sunday in season and twice daily the third Sunday of the month in summer. The park features two campgrounds, a big swimming pool, a playground, canoe rentals, nature trails, and oak-shaded picnic grounds. Contact the park at 15402 Highway 301 North, east of Interstate 75 exit 35; (813) 987-6771.

- **Canoe Tour.** Paddle along the Hillsborough River, where alligators lurk and ibises and ospreys provide the sound track. Call Canoe Escape, 9335 East Fowler Avenue; (813) 986-2067; www.canoeescape.com.

- **Hot Air Balloon Ride.** Leave earth on a big red balloon as you float over the city and its surrounding waterways. Call Big Red Balloon, 16302 East Course Drive; (813) 969-1518; www.bigredballoon.com.

- **Horseback rides.** See wetlands from astride a horse with Horseback River Safaris; (813) 659-0743.

Museums

Museum of Science and Industry (MOSI), 4801 East Fowler Avenue; (813) 987-6300 or (800) 995-MOSI; www.mosi.org. Mosey on down to MOSI for at least half a day. MOSIMAX is an IMAX Dome theater that wraps you in the action by projecting movies onto an 85-foot-high domed screen. Also notable are two giant, 85-foot-long, six-story high *diplodocus* dinosaur skeletons in the lobby.

With more than 450 hands-on exhibits, science is fun here. Ever wonder what a hurricane feels like? Then get blown away by sitting through a simulated Gulf Coast storm with powerful 75-mph winds. Listen to Dr. Thunder explain thunder and create some lightning. At Electric Plaza learn why static electricity makes your hair stand on end. At the Florida Fossil Gallery, walk through a cavern filled with crystal-lined fissures and fossil impressions. Two areas please little ones. At Kids-in-Charge, a discovery area for ages five and under, preschoolers explore science concepts with an adult. Tykes build their own houses, dress up like cowboys, and journey into a forest filled with stuffed animals; and at the Butterfly Encounter, kids are charmed when free-flying butterflies alight on their shoulders.

There's even a Tot Lot so that curious toddlers can climb, build, bounce, and touch objects. This area is open at selected times to MOSI members and their guests.

MOSI offers a wide variety of fun-filled educational programs that require prior registration but are worth the planning. **PAACT** (Parents and Children as Co-Travelers in a World of Ideas) courses take place at MOSI, one of eleven Challenger Learning Centers across the country and the only one in Florida. Four different space-age programs range from the thirty-minute Crew Training add-on; to the two-hour Visit the Future scientist role-playing; to four-hour Discovery Missions (where participants simulate NASA shuttle missions); and the eight-hour Lunar Challenge (where you design and build models of a working lunar habitat).

Family Camp-Ins revolve around themes such as dolphins and Egyptian Wonders for a night of activities and fun, usually in the summer. For information on the PAACT programming, which began in October 2000, call (813) 987-6338.

The **Tampa Museum of Art,** 600 North Ashley Drive; (813) 274-8130), specializes in classical antiquities and twentieth-century American art. Kids will like browsing through the Egyptian, Greek, and Roman antiquities collection. The museum also features up to twenty temporary exhibitions per year in addition to its permanent collection of more than 7,000 pieces.

Performing Arts

The **Tampa Bay Performing Arts Center** is at 1010 North MacInnes Place; (813) 222-1000/Box Office (800) 955-1045; www.tampacenter. com. This facility includes a concert hall, festival hall, playhouse, and the intimate Jaeb Theater. This is the largest performing arts center south of the Kennedy Center in Washington, D.C.

Check out what's playing at the **Tampa Theatre,** 711 Franklin Street Mall; (813) 274-8981; www.tampatheatre.org. This fanciful theater, an attraction in itself, is housed in a restored 1926 movie palace ornately decorated with colonnades, balconies, and replicas of Greek and Roman sculpture. Attend a film or concert, to take a guided tour and learn about the resident ghost.

Tours

Ybor City Walking Tour. Don't forget that Tampa was once the "Cigar Capital of the World," populated by thousands of immigrants working in cigar factories. Stop in the Chamber of Commerce for a map and take a self-guided walking tour of Ybor City, Tampa's historic Latin Quarter, where more than 1,300 cigar factories were once concentrated. The map focuses on historic sites in the neighborhood, now transformed into an artist's and commercial community filled with shops, restaurants, and night spots. Older kids might like the **Ybor City Ghost Walk** tour (813-242-9255). **Historic Tours and Events,** 1320 East Eighth Avenue (813-247-6692) offers custom tours of Ybor City, led by a resident whose mother once worked as a cigar roller. Visit Ybor Square, a Cuban bread bakery, Ybor City State Museum, and the Columbia Restaurant.

Spectator Sports

Tampa offers a wide variety of sports events. The **Tampa Bay Lightning** national hockey team (813-229-8800) plays in the Ice Palace. The **Tampa Bay Buccaneers** football team (813-879-BUCS) plays at the Raymond James Stadium August through December. When the Bucs score, cannons shoot flares from the deck of a 103-foot-long pirate ship. College football fans like the **Outback Bowl** (813-874-BOWL; www. outbackbowl.com), usually held on New Year's Day. Soccer fans can root for the **Tampa Bay Mutiny** team. Home games are at the Raymond James Stadium. Call (813) 289-6811 for information. The New York Yankees' minor league team (813-875-7753 or 800-96-YANKS) plays at Legends Field, Dale Mabry Highway and Dr. Martin Luther King Jr. Boulevard. This 10,000-seat stadium is modeled after the original Yankee Stadium in the Bronx, New York. The major league Yankees practice at Legends Field during spring training. For tickets call (813) 875-7753 or 800-96-YANKS

SIDE TRIPS

- A mere 18 miles to the west, **St. Petersburg** features the Salvador Dalí Museum, Great Explorations Hands-On Museum, and the Suncoast Seabird Sanctuary, not to mention the 35 miles of beaches. (See St. Petersburg and Clearwater chapter.)

- **Sarasota,** approximately 100 miles to Tampa's south, is home to the **Ringling Estate,** 5401 Bay Shore Road; (941) 355-5101. At this combination history-and-art museum created by one of the famous circus brothers, older children will appreciate the Circus Gallery, filled with authentic circus posters, costumes, clown props, and calliopes. But there's more than the big-top hoopla: The **John and Mable Ringling Museum of Art** is renowned for its fine collection of baroque art, including masterworks by Rubens. Upstairs, you'll find a small room with a Scribble Pad and other items so little kids can have fun creating their own art. The Ringling mansion, Ca'd'Zan, is a separate thirty-room Venetian Renaissance palace of marble arches, ballrooms, and balconies built with a 1920s flair.

Special Events

Winter is festival time in Tampa Bay. The most exciting is the **Gasparilla Pirate Fest** in February, when the legendary pirate Jose Gaspar and his rowdy crew invade the city from a fully rigged pirate ship during month-long antics. For a good view of the invasion and parade, it's best to call ahead for reservations; (813) 353-8108.

March. Florida Strawberry Festival, Plant City. Gasparilla Festival of the Arts.

April. Brandon Balloon Classic.

August. WAZOO! Lowry Park Zoo.

October. Fall Zoo Boo, Lowry Park Zoo. Guavaween, Tampa's Halloween Celebration, Ybor City.

Call the Tampa/Hillsborough Convention and Visitors Association at (800) 826-8358 or (813) 223-1111; www.gotampa.com; or call the Arts Council at (813) 229-6547 for more information.

Where to Stay

Since the majority of the area's attractions are not near one another (with the exception of Busch Gardens, Adventure Island, and MOSI, almost any hotel location within Tampa is acceptable. Be sure to ask hotels about family and weekend packages, and deals in conjunction with Busch Gardens. These often include complimentary shuttle service to the park.

Embassy Suites, 3705 Spectrum Boulevard (813-977-7066 or 800-EMBASSY), offers free-on-demand shuttle service to anywhere within a 5-mile radius of the hotel. That includes Busch Gardens Tampa, Adventure Island, and MOSI, as well as malls and restaurants.

Other hotels situated near Busch Gardens include **Crown Doubletree Guest Suites Tampa/Busch Gardens,** 11310 North Thirtieth Street (813-971-7690), and **Quality Suites Hotel USF,** 3001 University Center Drive (813-971-8930 or 800-786-7446).

Both the **Holiday Inn Tampa-Busch Gardens,** 2701 East Fowler Avenue (813-971-4710 or 800-29-OASIS), and **Howard Johnson's Busch Gardens Main Gate,** 4139 East Busch Boulevard (813-988-9191 or 800-874-1768), are moderately priced and sometimes offer child-care services. Holiday Inn recently added Kidsuites (kid-equipped cubbies within the room) and a pirate-themed water playground that's great for toddlers and gradeschoolers.

The Wyndham Harbour Island Hotel, 725 South Harbour Island

Boulevard (813-229-5000 or 800-822-4200), features deluxe accommodations on the waterfront at Harbour Island. If you prefer to be near the
airport, the **Hyatt Regency Tampa,** 6200 Courtney Campbell Conservancy (813-874-1234 or 800-233-1234), sometimes has a children's program and child-friendly services. Other possibilities include the **Chase
Suite Hotel,** 3035 North Rocky Point Drive West (813-281-5677 or 800-
287-0778), and the **Hampton Inn,** 4817 West Laurel Street (813-
800-WOODFIN or 800-426-7866).

For a more complete listing of accommodations, call (800)44-TAMPA
or take advantage of Discover Tampa (800-284-0404), a vacation information and planning hotline visitors can use to book complete vacation
packages to Tampa and Central Florida, including hotels, car rentals, and
tickets to attractions.

WHERE TO EAT

Tampa has a wide range of cuisine from fresh seafood catches straight
out of the Gulf of Mexico to authentic Spanish and Cuban dishes in the
city's ethnic neighborhoods. Red snapper, grouper, and shrimp are some
regional favorites. Ybor City and South Howard Avenue (dubbed the
SoHo District) are the places to go for a large selection of eclectic restaurants, and Cuban cuisine and music.

Bern's Steak House, 1208 South Howard Avenue (813-251-2421),
has an astounding collection of more than seven *thousand* wines. Kids will
love it for the juicy steaks and hamburgers. Ask for a kitchen tour and
don't miss the dessert room upstairs.

SideBern's, 1002 Howard Avenue South (813-258-2233), began as
overflow seating for Bern's, down the street. Since then it has created its
own brand of "one world" fusion cuisine, featuring Szechuan glazed
grouper, chorizo-scaled sea bass with truffled plantain puree, and grilled
golden oyster mushrooms with blue-corn tamales and green chile chut-
ney. Teens should like this trendy place.

In Olde Hyde Park Village, **Cactus Club,** 1601 Snow Avenue (813-
251-4089) is casual, with indoor or outdoor seating under umbrellas,
and creative Southwestern specialties such as Texas pizza, scallop
chimichanga, and moo shu quesadillas. It's also known for its burgers
and margaritas.

For a taste of Tampa's Spanish heritage, try the **Columbia Restaurant,** 2117 East Seventh Avenue in Ybor City (813-248-4961). Kids like
the Spanish decor and the flamenco dancing. Adventurous children will
want to try some of the classic Spanish dishes, including seafood with
saffron rice, and black bean soup with crusty Cuban bread. Although
Ybor City becomes more yuppified by the day, it still retains its small,

Family Resort: Saddlebrook

Saddlebrook Resort, about forty minutes north of Tampa International Airport, offers a relaxing respite on 480 acres featuring two golf courses, a tennis academy, and a spa. Kids can have golf and tennis lessons, meet friends at the S'Kids Club for ages four to twelve, and splash in the Super-pool that's as big as a football field. Call for packages; (813) 973-1111 or (800) 729-8383; www.saddlebrookresort.com.

ethnic eateries. Two survivors: **La Tropicana,** 1822 East Seventh Avenue (813-247-4040) and, across the street, **Cajun Cuban Seafood Grille,** 1831 East Seventh Avenue (813-247-3593), where genuine Cajun specialties augment Cuban favorites. For something more trendy, try **Ovo Cafe** at 1901 East Seventh Avenue (813-248-6979), for peanut butter waffles, salads, sandwiches, pizzas, and stuffed "pasta pillows."

Ybor Square Ltd, 1901 North Thirteenth Street (813-247-4497), is a fun place to stop for lunch on your tour of Ybor City. Choose from a variety of ethnic cuisines all under the roof of this old cigar factory. Or, pop into one of the Cuban luncheonettes or creative cafes in Ybor City for a healthful and hefty sandwich. Taste some seafood gumbo or jambalaya at **Cafe Creole,** 1330 East Ninth Avenue (813-247-6283) in Ybor City, where there's live jazz and New Orleans-style cuisine. **Cafe Pepe,** 2006 West Kennedy Boulevard (813-253-6501), is a good place to try Spanish dishes in a casual, family atmosphere.

At **Mel's Hot Dogs,** near Busch Gardens, 4136 East Busch Boulevard (813-985-8000), you can choose from a classic Chicago-style dog, a bagel dog, bacon dog, corn dog, and others. For something in junkyard funk, head for **Skipper's Smoke House** at Skipper Road and Nebraska Avenue (813-971-0666). Specialties include smoked fish, raw oysters, Black Bean Gator Chili, and crab cakes with black bean salsa. Kids will enjoy the casual, graffitied setting.

FOR MORE INFORMATION

Visitor Information Centers
The Tampa Bay Convention and Visitors Bureau, 400 North Tampa Street, Suite 1010, (800-826-8358 or 813-223-1111; www.gotampa.com), has brochures on attractions, hotels, and restaurants. Other visitor centers are located at Ybor Square and at the Tampa Convention Center.

Other Useful Information and Numbers
The public transit system, HARTline Information for Hearing Impaired: (813) 626-9158.

TDD Florida Relay Station: (800) 955-8771.

North Tampa Chamber of Commerce: (813) 980-6966.

Ybor City Chamber of Commerce: (813) 248-3712.

Greater Tampa Chamber of Commerce: (813) 228-7777.

Emergency Numbers

Ambulance, fire, and police: 911

Tampa General Hospital Emergency Room: (813) 251-7100

Poison Hotline: (813) 253-4444

Free medical information twenty-four hours a day: Ask-a-Nurse; (813) 870-4444

Pharmacy open 7:00 A.M. to midnight: Eckerd Drugs, 3714 Henderson Boulevard; (813) 876-2485

ATLANTA

A tlanta, often referred to as the city of the new South, typifies a twenty-first-century blend of sophistication and southern charm. This family-friendly city offers lots of hands-on educational fun for kids. Atlanta is rich in African-American heritage and Civil War attractions, and for pure fun, head for the nearby theme parks.

The legacy of the 1996 Olympics is a renovated renewed city.

GETTING THERE

The **Hartsfield Atlanta International Airport** (404-765-1300), just south of the city, is Atlanta's main airport and is served by several national and international airlines. **MARTA** (Metropolitan Atlanta Rapid Transit Authority), Atlanta's rapid rail system, provides an inexpensive fifteen-minute connection to the airport. Call (404) 848-4711 for more information. **Atlanta Airport Shuttle** (404-524-3400) provides service to and from the airport.

Amtrak, 1688 Peachtree Street, N.W. (800-872-1477 or 404-881-3062) has service to Atlanta. The **Greyhound Bus** terminal is at 232 Forsyth Street (404-584-1731 or 800-231-2222). Several major highways, including 1-85/75/20 and U.S. 78, intersect with roads leading into the city.

GETTING AROUND

You need a car to get to several of the attractions in the Atlanta metro region; however, for your downtown adventures simplify life and take MARTA; (404) 848-4711. MARTA is visitor friendly and a snap to decode. Five Points is the central station; all other stations are identified by a name, the direction, and the number of stops away from Five Points. For example, Midtown N4 means four stops north. For schedules and handicapped services, call (404) 848-4711. Car rentals are available at the Atlanta airport and throughout metro Atlanta.

Atlanta

AT A GLANCE

▶ Try hands-on experiments at SciTrek and the Fernbank Science Center

▶ Ride the skylift to the top of Stone Mountain

▶ Explore Sweet Auburn and the Martin Luther King Jr. National Historic Site, and many Civil War sites

▶ Tour CNN's high-tech headquarters

▶ Atlanta Convention & Visitors Bureau: (404) 521-6600 or (800) ATLANTA; www.atlanta.com

▶ DeKalb Convention & Visitors Bureau: (404) 378-2525 or (800) 999-6055; www.atlantadekalb.org

WHAT TO SEE AND DO

Museums

Fernbank Museum of Natural History, 767 Clifton Road, NE; (404-370-0960; www.fernbank.edu/museum). This hands-on museum is not to be missed. The permanent exhibit, A Walk Through Time in Georgia, dazzles visitors with fifteen galleries leading from a high-definition video of the Big Bang to a spectacular hall overrun with seven life-size dinosaurs to an Okefenokee Swamp display filled with sounds and sights. In June 2000 the museum unveiled its latest acquisition; The world's largest carnivore ever documented, *Gigantosaurus,* was added to the "Giants of the Mesozoic" exhibition, and the first fully mounted *Argentinosaurus* in any museum in the world was scheduled to be added to the exhibit in December.

Kids are catered to in the Martha Ellis Discovery Rooms. In the Fantasy Forest, three- to-five-year-olds put on bee gloves, collect pollen balls, and pollinate Crayola-colored flowers. In a hide-and-seek maze, kids discover how nature protects plants and animals by donning a camouflage smock and finding the environment in which they blend in best. Coca-Cola Georgia Adventure, for six- to ten-year-olds, is a "state of adventure" with five theme areas. After picking up a map at the ranger station, kids are on their way to Jekyll Island to drag for shellfish from a shrimp boat, to Cohutta Cave to learn about hibernation, and to Atlanta to construct their own cityscape.

Sensing Nature has dozens of interactive exhibits that literally illuminate the physical laws of sight and sound. Computer-age kids won't be bored by these galleries filled with lights, videos, and lasers. There's even an IMAX theater with a five-story screen. A dining room (with moderate prices) is open Monday to Saturday, 11:00 A.M. to 4:00 P.M. and Sunday from noon to 4:00 P.M. Admission.

The **Fernbank Science Center,** 156 Heaton Park Drive, NE (404–378-4311; fsc.fernbank.edu), features an exhibition hall, a planetarium, an observatory, two greenhouses, and sixty-five acres of forest. Catch a creative show at the planetarium, evenings from Tuesday through Friday. Get an up-close perspective of the night sky and learn to spot star clusters and galaxies. Children under five aren't allowed into the nightly shows, so there's a program just for them on Saturday and Sunday at 1:30 P.M. and on weekday afternoons during the summer, to explore the stars, planets, and other objects in the sky. Call in advance for a schedule.

On Saturday mornings at 11:00 A.M. (except in December), "The Sky Tonight" is presented by a Fernbank astronomer, who takes you on a tour of the constellations, planets, and events of the current night sky.

Nature lovers will enjoy the 1½-mile walk through Fernbank Forest, open daily. Pick up a seasonal guide sheet and search for the Georgian flora and fauna in this nature reserve.

For more flowers visit the **Botanical Garden and Greenhouse** at 765 Clifton Road, which is open to the public on Sunday afternoons. Adults appreciate the guided tour of the extensive herb and rose garden while kids get a kick out of potting their own plants to take home.

SciTrek, 395 Piedmont Avenue, NE (404-522-5500; www.scitrek. org), is Atlanta's Science and Technology Museum. This colorful facility features ten theme halls filled with more than one hundred and fifty hands-on exhibits. Alter your image without plastic surgery in Perception and Illusions. The littlest ones can get their hands wet in Kidspace, a water playground with dams and waterfalls. Kids ages two to seven can see themselves on TV, build a kid-size house, and draw pictures on a computer.

For an extended museum adventure, children between the ages of five and twelve can participate in the SciTrek Overnight Program in spring and fall. They explore the museum, take a workshop, wind down with a bedtime video, then wake to breakfast and a science demonstration. The one-week Aviation Camp for children nine to twelve and the SciTrek Summer Camp for five- to twelve-year-olds enable kids to awaken and

Black Heritage

- **Sweet Auburn,** known as the birthplace and home of the young Martin Luther King, Jr., has been preserved as a historic district, symbolizing African-American achievement in America after the Civil War. Walk through history in this neighborhood of businesses, churches, community organizations, and private homes.
- **The Freedom Walk,** a self-guided tour of the Sweet Auburn district, begins at the information center, Underground Atlanta, Peachtree and Alabama Streets; (404) 523-2311. Pick up this colorful, illustrated map and follow it through 16 blocks (1.2 miles) of civil rights history. Highlights include the major sites described next.
- **Martin Luther King, Jr. National Historic Site,** (404) 331-3920; www.nps.gov/malu, within the Sweet Auburn District, encompasses Martin Luther King, Jr.'s restored Birth Home, 501 Auburn, the Martin Luther King Jr. Center for Non-Violent Social Change, and the Ebenezer Baptist Church. King's white marble crypt in Freedom Plaza is perhaps the most moving site. The home's photographs, clothing, and memorabilia enable children

to envision the respected world leader as a child. The National Park Service provides information and free tours of these sites at the Interpretation and Visitor Services Office, 450 Auburn Avenue, N.E. (404-331-5198, extension 3017). The Center has videos about the Civil Rights movement and the life of Dr. King as well as a fifteen-minute video about children who were involved in the movement in the 1950s and 1960s.

- **APEX Museum** at 135 Auburn Avenue, NE; (404) 521-2739. (APEX stands for African American Panoramic Experience.) The museum portrays the story of African Americans in Atlanta. Along with a video, exhibits include a replica of the first black-owned drugstore, as well as a vintage trolley. Sankofa!, an African artwork exhibit, is accompanied by African music and photography. Admission.
- **Hammonds House Gallery,** 503 Peeples Street, SW (404-752-8730), offers a broad view of African-American art and artists from the nineteenth century to the present in this gallery and national research center. Tours are available with prior reservations. Open Tuesday through Sunday.

The wonders of science and technology come to life at Atlanta's SciTrek Museum.

expand their scientific curiosity. Call (404) 522-5500, ext. 217, for more information. Admission.

The **World of Coca-Cola** is at 55 Martin Luther King, Jr. Drive (adjacent to Underground Atlanta); (404) 676-5151. Trace the history of Coca-Cola from its birth in Atlanta in 1886 to the present day with interactive exhibits, videos, and enough commercials to leave visions of Coke bottles dancing in your head. You get a view of the bottling process in the imaginative Bottle Fantasy kinetic sculpture, witness a "soda jerk" prepare a soft drink at a 1930s soda fountain, and finally quench your thirst at a spectacular soda fountain that features neon lights and sound effects. The self-guided tour takes about one and a half hours. Reservations are strongly recommended. The Everything Coca-Cola store lives up to its name. Admission.

Atlanta's major visual arts museum is the **High Museum of Art.** Its midtown facility is at 1280 Peachtree Street NE, and its Folk Art and Photography Galleries are at 133 Peachtree Street NE (404-733-4400 or 404-733-HIGH for twenty-four-hour recorded information; www.high. org). This museum's main center focuses on nineteenth-, twentieth-, and twenty-first-century art, including decorative and contemporary art. The museum's downtown facility focuses on folk art and photography. Family Fun Days, scheduled throughout the year, feature storytellers, art projects, live jazz, and tours. Admission.

At the **Monetary Museum,** Federal Reserve Bank, 104 Marietta Street (404-521-8764), kids learn what it literally takes to make money. The

Nearby Parks and Green Spaces

■ **Stone Mountain Park,** Highway 78, Stone Mountain; (770-498-5690; www.stonemountainpark.org) 16 miles east of the city has 3,200 acres of swimming, fishing, tennis, and golf, a sky lift to the top of the mountain, a 5-mile scenic railroad tour, and a paddle-wheel riverboat adventure. Tiny tots enjoy the playground and petting zoo.

Don't miss the skylift ride to the top of the world's largest mass of exposed granite, or the nightly laser show. The mountain's monumental granite carving of southern heroes President Jefferson Davis, General Robert E. Lee, and General "Stonewall" Jackson is sure to impress. Several restaurants, a campground, and two hotels are also located here.

Plans for future expansion include a Main Street with shops and a 4-D theater.

■ **The Yellow River Wildlife Game Ranch,** 4525 Highway 78, Liburn (770-972-6643), is situated 2½ miles past Stone Mountain (about thirty minutes from Atlanta). This unique place is a must-see for animal-loving kids and parents. Yellow River allows visitors to get "up close and personal" with animals.

Stock up on animal food that the ranch supplies, then follow a mile-long path to befriend the wildlife. Yellow River has more than 600 animals, most indigenous to Georgia, including a hundred white-tail deer and the area's only buffalo herd. General Lee the groundhog issues his springtime weather prediction on Groundhog Day, February 2. In mid-May on Sheep Shearing Saturday, everyone can help clip and snip. Springtime means baby animals, in fall there are hayrides and hot-dog roasts.

Strollers and picnic tables are available at the ranch.

gold coins on display are eye-catchers. There's a fifteen-minute video and a self-guided tour.

At the **Jimmy Carter Library and Museum,** One Cleburne Avenue, NE (404-331-0296 or 404-331-3942; www.cartercenter.org), trace Jimmy Carter's life and actions at the White House, see the Oval Office replica, and review modern-day issues and events in display stalls. Highlights include a town hall where visitors can pose questions to the former president, such as "What did Amy do all day at the White House?"

Other Family Attractions

Center for Puppetry Arts is at 1404 Spring Street at Eighteenth; call (404) 873-3089 for recorded information or (404) 873-3391 for tickets; www.puppet.org. Call ahead and get tickets for a Family Series presentation. In the past they've done *Winnie the Pooh* and *Hansel and Gretel*, but each year brings new adaptations of classic stories.

Tots four and up can try their hand at creating their own puppets in **Create a Puppet workshops,** Monday through Saturday, while older children learn how to manipulate puppets in scheduled Saturday workshops. Advance reservations are necessary.

At the center's museum you soon discover that puppets aren't only the Muppets and Punch and Judy (although they're here, too). Take a free guided tour and discover how puppets are used in entertainment, rituals, and sociopolitical satire across the globe. Three temporary exhibitions focus on a specific artist or cultural use.

Summer Festival presents six different productions. Call for schedules and reservations.

The cable generation will appreciate a **CNN Studio Tour,** 1 CNN Center, (404) 827-2300. The forty-five-minute tour gives you a behind-the-scenes look at the production of CNN and *Headline News.*

By walking along an elevated glass tour route, visitors watch technicians, writers, and on-air journalists in the act. Tours begin on the half hour, Monday through Saturday. Get your tickets an hour or two in advance since tours sell out quickly. Tickets are valid only on the day of purchase. Children under six are not permitted.

Wren's Nest, 1050 Ralph David Abernathy Boulevard, SW (404-753-8535), is the home of nineteenth-century author Joel Chandler Harris, creator of the Uncle Remus characters including Br'er Rabbit and Fox. Take a trip to Atlanta's oldest neighborhood to tour this 1870s house decorated with authentic furniture, photos, and family artifacts. There's a slide show of the author's life and works. The best time to come with children is in summer, when a storyteller enacts one of Harris's classic stories on selected days.

Green Spaces and Downtown Areas

Zoo Atlanta, Grant Park, 800 Cherokee Avenue, SE; (404) 624-5600; www.zooatlanta.org. The coming of the Giant Pandas Lun Lun (the female) and Yang Yang (the male) has brought huge crowds to Zoo Atlanta. Visitors are given a timed ticket to the panda exhibit and are admitted on a first-come basis. Happily, there's a lot to see and do on this forty-acre facility with its natural habitats for the nearly 1,000 specimens representing 250 species. Visits to the orangutans, the Sumatran Tiger Forest, one of the country's largest reptile collections, and the Public Petting Zoo easily pass the time. The Children's Playground has an ark with steering wheels, compasses, binoculars, climbing nets, and a slide. The Norfolk Southern Zoo Express Train, a replica of an original 1863 locomotive, takes families around the zoo, and there's a carousel with reproductions of some of the world's endangered species. Little ones can also pet and feed the animals at the OK-To-Touch corral open daily. A variety of family programs throughout the year let children and parents explore the worlds of pandas, reptiles, birds, and marine animals. Family Overnights include a nocturnal tour of the zoo, an up-close encounter with animals, food, and fun. Call for schedule and prices.

The **Atlanta Botanical Garden,** Piedmont Avenue at the Prado; (404) 876-5859. Enjoy flowers and plants just 3 miles from downtown Atlanta. Situated on thirty acres of preserved land in midtown Piedmont Park, the Botanical Garden features a variety of gardens including rock, rose, Japanese, and herb. If you're looking to beat the heat, stroll among the hardwood trees in the fifteen-acre Storza Woods. The Scottish Rite Children's Medical Center Children's Garden, which opened in 1999, is a two-acre garden with a child-size amphitheater, a maze, Peter Rabbit's den, and a butterfly garden, plus special areas set aside for quiet play. The Botanical Gardens are open Tuesday through Sunday.

At the **Chattahoochee Nature Center,** 9135 Willeo Road, Roswell (770-992-2055), go on a guided nature hike to discover native Georgian plants and animals. This environmental education center, situated on 127 acres, features exhibits on nature and one-hour learning programs, including talks on forest and river ecology. Afternoon sessions are geared toward children; call for more information.

Part of the legacy of the 1996 Summer Olympics is **Centennial Olympic Park** (401-222-PARK), the twenty-one-acre downtown site located between the Georgia World Congress Center and the hotel district. During the Olympic Games, this area served as the Olympic hub and gathering place. The Fountain of Rings, a water fountain with the Olympic rings, is a kid-pleaser. Another legacy is the rejuvenated **Woodruff Park,** between Edgewood and Auburn Avenues along Peachtree Street. Both the 30-foot fountain and the impressive, bronze sculpture *Phoenix Rising from the Ashes* (a woman and a bird represent the city's comeback after the Civil War) help make this park a more pleasant place to be.

Civil War and Other Historic Attractions
The **Atlanta Cyclorama,** Grant Park, Georgia and Cherokee avenues, SE, next to the zoo, (404-658-7625), starts off with a short movie, *The Atlanta Campaign,* which relates background, then depicts the warfare. The *Cyclorama,* a century-old oil painting, has lights that depict the Battle of

Atlanta in 1864. Hour-long tours—including the movie, *Cyclorama*, and a visit to the museum—depart every thirty minutes.

At the **Atlanta History Center,** 130 West Paces Ferry Road, NW; (404-814-4000; www.atlhist.org), find out what happened to Atlanta in the aftermath of the Civil War. Learn how the city rebuilt itself from rubble at the Atlanta Resurgence exhibit. A folk art exhibit features handcrafted pottery, quilting, and more, with video monitors illustrating folk art processes complemented by touchable examples. Two enclosures provide space for folk storytelling, singing, and instrumental music. For those addicted to the green, there's an exhibit on the life and sport of Atlanta native and golfing great Bobby Jones. Kids like the History Center's Coca-Cola Cafe with its re-created fifties atmosphere. Try the shakes and forgo the sandwiches. Family Fun Programs are held throughout the year: African Rhythms during Black History Month in February explores traditional African music and dance, and children can create and play African instruments and make colorful dance masks. In summer there's a Civil War Encampment, and also week-long summer camps for kids, where they do crafts, keep a daily journal, and enjoy games and other activities.

At **Kennesaw Mountain National Battlefield Park,** Old Highway 41 and Stilesboro Road, Marietta (770-427-4686; www.nps.gov/kemo), relive the 1864 Battle of Kennesaw Mountain, where Sherman's 100,000 Union troops faced the lesser 65,000 Confederate troops at this 3,000-acre preserved park and battlefield. Walk through 16 miles of trails, and stop for a picnic. Living-history programs on Sunday afternoons in summer bring the Civil War to life for the whole family.

Amusement Parks and Interactive Entertainment

Six Flags Over Georgia, 7561 Six Flags Road, SW, at I-20 West in Mableton (770-948-9290 or 770-739-3440; www.sixflags.com), is 12 miles west of Atlanta. Here tour-weary kids find plenty of fun. They can meet their favorite cartoon characters in a Bugs Bunny World Theater Show, take a twisted ride on the Ninja, and cool off in the Thunder River. This amusement park includes restaurants, a Looney Tunes shop, live performances, and a nightly Batman Fireworks and Laser Show. Recent additions include the Georgia Scorcher, one of the Southeast's tallest and fastest stand-up rollercoasters, with lots of twists and loops. Six Flags Over Georgia is open from March to October. Be sure to call ahead for hours of operation since these vary.

White Water, 250 North Cobb Parkway, Marietta (770-424-WAVE), offers wicked water chutes and lazy river rafting. This thirty-five-acre water park's Captain Kid's Cove is a wet-and-wild jungle gym just for the preschool crowd. Tree House Island has tot-size slides and pumping station. Parents can sunbathe in peace since Red Cross-certified lifeguards are on duty. Bigger kids can plunge 90 feet down the Cliffhanger, a free-fall flume. The park also includes six restaurants and shopping. There's a stunt-filled Pirate Invasion Dive show three times a day. On Fridays enjoy the Dive-In movies; you watch while staying wet. Open from May through August. Call in advance for hours of operation.

American Adventures, 250 North Cobb Parkway (404-424-9283), next door to White Water, caters more to the young children. Here there's an easier-paced Ridgeline Roller Coaster, a Timber Line Truckers convoy for toddlers, and the Foam Factory, a play area with bridges, tubeslides, and a playing field with balls. Tiny tots can also ride on planes, trains, and a Ferris wheel that are just their size.

If you plan to visit White Water, too, look into a money-saving joint ticket to both parks. American Adventures is open year-round.

Performing Arts

Ticketplace (404-249-6400) sells tickets to most arts and sports events. **Woodruff Arts Center,** at 1280 Peachtree Street, NE (404-733-5000), is Atlanta's major arts center, housing the Atlanta Symphony Orchestra, Alliance Theatre Company, and the High Museum of Art.

The Alliance Children's Theatre (404-733-4650) at Woodruff Arts Center presents classics and new children's productions twice a year in the fall and spring. Special workshops and study guides make this entertaining experience educational as well. Enjoy the great acoustics at **Fox Theatre,** 660 Peachtree Street, NE; (404) 881-2100. Built in 1929, this Byzantine-style theater stands as one of Atlanta's landmarks. The Fox's summertime program features a film festival. Same-day, half-price theater tickets are available through AtlanTIX, located at the Atlanta Convention & Visitors Bureau's Visitor Center at Underground Atlanta, 65 Upper Alabama Street.

Spectator Sports

Atlanta's best-known team, the **Atlanta Braves,** plays ball at **Turner Field** (formerly the Olympic Stadium); (404) 249-6400 or (800) 326-4000. In football season the **Atlanta Falcons** take to the field at the Georgia Dome. For tickets call (404) 223-5444. Other professional sports teams include the **Atlanta Hawks** basketball team (404-249-6400), which plays in the new Philips Arena, as do the **Atlanta Thrashers** NHL hockey team (404-584-PUCK), and the **Atlanta Attack** soccer team (770-431-6111). An Olympic legacy worth seeing is the **Georgia Tech Aquatic Center** (404-894-8825).

SIDE TRIPS

- Where do Cabbage Patch dolls come from? Find out at **Babyland General Hospital,** 19 Underwood Street, Cleveland; (706) 865-2171. About ninety minutes north of Atlanta, discover the doctors and nurses who deliver Cabbage Patch Kids.
- Strike it rich in **Dahlonega,** where gold rushing took place in Georgia long before 1849. Pan for gold in the area mines and visit the **Gold Museum.** While you're at it, tour the nearby Chattahoochee National Forest. For more information call the Chamber of Commerce at (706) 864-2257.
- An hour east of Atlanta, tour the antebellum mansions of **Madison** and get a glimpse of the pre-Civil War South. Call the Chamber of Commerce at (706) 342-4454 or (800) 709-7406 for more information. To see the largest glass-enclosed butterfly conservatory in North America or explore more than 2,500 acres of woodlands, visit **Callaway Gardens,** Pine Mountain, ninety minutes southwest of Atlanta. Call (800) 225-5292 for more information. **Warm Springs,** the home of President Franklin D. Roosevelt, is an hour and forty-five minutes southwest of Atlanta. For information on a house and museum tour, call (706) 655-2588.

SPECIAL EVENTS

Unless otherwise stated, further event information can be obtained from the Atlanta Convention & Visitors Bureau by calling (800) ATLANTA or on the Web site at www.atlanta.com.

January. During Martin Luther King, Jr., Week, special events all over the city celebrate the civil rights leader. Atlanta Boat Show.

February. Mardi Gras Atlanta, parade and celebration. Atlanta Flower Show, featuring landscaped gardens and free seminars.

May. Storytelling festival, Atlanta History Center. Music Midtown: An Atlanta Festival. Atlanta Jazz Festival. Black Expo Atlanta.

June. Gorilla Willie B's Birthday, Zoo Atlanta. Taste of Virginia-Highland & Kidsfest.

June–August. Arts Festival of Atlanta, downtown.

July. KidsFest, Six Flags. Civil War Encampment, Atlanta History Center. Independence Day Celebrations downtown.

August. Folk Fest, Atlanta Trade Center. Vineyard Fest.

September. Country Star Jamboree at Six Flags. Yellow Daisy Arts & Crafts Festival, Stone Mountain Park. Gwinnett County Fair.

October. At Fright Fest, Six Flags, spookiness prevails in a haunted park. Great Miller Lite Chili Cookoff, Stone Mountain Park.

November. Folklife Festival, Atlanta History Center. Steeplechase at Calloway Gardens. Veterans Day Parade.

December. Santa's Zoo Review, at the zoo. Candlelight Tours, Atlanta History Center. Holdiays Around the World, Zoo Atlanta.

WHERE TO STAY

Kids under seventeen stay free, and those under twelve generally eat for free at three Days Inn locations in Atlanta. **Days Inn—Atlanta/Downtown,** 300 Spring Street (404-523-1144) or (900-942-PKGE). Other major hotel chains that organize family packages and special children's services include the **Hyatt Regency Atlanta,** located downtown at 265 Peachtree Street (404-577-1234 or 800-233-1234), which has completed a $10.5 million renovation of its guest rooms; the **Ritz-Carlton,** 181 Peachtree Street, NE (404-659-0400); the **Omni Hotel at CNN Center,** 100 CNN Center (404-659-0000), which is completing a $9 million renovation that includes a new restaurant, the Prime Meridian; and the **Westin Peachtree Plaza,** 210 Peachtree Street, NW; (404-659-1400). At this upscale property kids like the seventy-two-story elevator ride to the observation deck, as well as the heated indoor/outdoor pool. The hotel is undergoing a $25 million refurbishment of its guest rooms and suites. **Atlanta Marriott Suites Midtown** (404-876-8888 or 800-228-9290) offers discounts to families—occasionally during summer—visiting Six Flags Over Georgia.

Summerfield Suites Atlanta, 760 Mount Vernon Highway (404-250-0110). This chain offers one- or two-bedroom suites with kitchen facilities and a daily continental breakfast plus buffet.

For a homey feel try a bed and breakfast. **Atlanta International Bed & Breakfast Reservation Service,** 223 Ponce de Leon Avenue (408-875-2882), or **Bed & Breakfast Atlanta,** 1801 Piedmont Avenue, Suite 208 (404-875-0525 or 800-967-3224), will help you find a place to suit your family. Be sure to ask if children are welcome.

Atlanta also offers a free travel service that will book reservations for your stay. Call (800) ATL-TOUR.

WHERE TO EAT

Underground Atlanta, Peachtree at Alabama Street; (404) 523-2311. With twenty restaurants, this restored market in the heart of downtown has something to appeal to everyone's taste. Open Monday through Saturday from 10:00 A.M. to 9:30 P.M., Sundays from 11:00 A.M. to 7:00 P.M.

The Old Spaghetti Factory, 249 Ponce de Leon Avenue, NE (404-872-2841), is a good dinner spot with inexpensive eats and an easy atmosphere. **Johnny Rockets,** 50 Upper Alabama Street (404-525-7117), brings you back to the 1950s with a burger, fries, and a cold shake.

Steak lovers probably know that the eleven-state chain restaurant, **Longhorn Steakhouse,** was born in Buckhead in 1981. The restaurant serves steaks, chicken, and buffalo wings at moderate prices; 2151 Peachtree Road (404-351-6086). Other moderately priced restaurants: **Thelma's Kitchen,** 786 Marietta Street (404-688-5855), serves southern staples such as fried chicken, twice-baked potatoes, and pork chops. **OK Café,** 1284 West Paces Ferry Road (404-233-2888), a fifties-themed diner, serves such retro kid-comfort food as Six-Cheese Macaroni, Coke floats, and banana splits.

In midtown near Georgia Tech, **The Varsity,** 61 North Avenue (404-881-1706), is an Atlanta institution. This big, fast-food place serves 2 miles of hot dogs and 2,500 pounds of potatoes each day. Kids like the lingo. When a server at the counter shouts, "Walk a dog sideways, bag of rags," he's just placed your order for a hot dog and fries to go.

'Tweens and teens like the Atlanta branch of the **Hard Rock Cafe,** 215 Peachtree Street (404-688-7625). Arrive early or be prepared to wait in line. At **R.W. GoodTimes,** Jimmy Carter Boulevard at I-85, Norcross (770-248-9400), part entertainment complex, part restaurant, kids won't be bored. The 55,000-square-foot facility has high-tech games such as simulated skateboarding, baseball, car racing, and lots more. In between asking you for more money, your kids can eat burgers, pizza, chicken fajitas, and pasta. **Disney's ESPN Zone,** 3030 Peachtree Road, N.E. (404-682-ESPN) is a sports-themed eatery with state-of-the-art games and TV sports broadcasts. **Jocks & Jills** has six locations around town, all of them full of sports memorabilia and televisions, plus pizza, nachos, burgers, and grilled salmon; try the one at One CNN Center (404-688-4425).

If you want good food in a beautiful setting, try **Canoe,** 4199 Paces Ferry Road (770-432-2663), set on the banks of the Chattahoochee River among lovely gardens.

FOR MORE INFORMATION

Atlanta Convention & Visitors Bureau (ACVB), 233 Peachtree Street, Suite 100, Atlanta (404-521-6600), publishes *Atlanta Now,* a free bimonthly visitor's guide. ACVB Visitor Information Centers are located at Underground Atlanta, 65 Upper Alabama Street; Georgia World Congress Center, 285 International Boulevard (during GWCC conventions); Hartsfield Atlanta International Airport, and Lenox Square, 3393 Peachtree Road. Call (404) 222-6688 or 800-ATLANTA; www.atlanta.com.

Other sources of information are the **DeKalb County Convention and Visitors Bureau,** 750 Commerce Drive, Suite 200, Decatur (404-378-2525 or 800-999-6055).

Emergency Numbers

Ambulance, fire, and police: 911

Atlanta Police: (404) 658-6600

Piedmont Hospital: (404) 605-5000

Poison Hotline: (404) 589-4400

Twenty-four-hour pharmacy: CVS Drugs, 1061 Ponce de Leon Avenue; (404) 876-0381

Georgia

THE OKEFENOKEE

The Okefenokee National Wildlife Refuge, mostly in Georgia, is the largest national wildlife refuge in the eastern United States. Occupying 396,000 acres, this is one of America's great unspoiled places. This slow-moving body of water, which comprises lakes, marshlike prairies, and islands, is a habitat where alligators bask on logs, white ibis roost on gum trees, and turtles slide into the dark brown waters.

The Okefenokee was established as a refuge in 1937 to preserve the unique ecosystem of the swamp; in 1974, to further protect the area, 353,981 acres of the refuge's interior were designated a National Wilderness area. The Okefenokee serves as an important habitat for waterfowl, wading birds, alligators, and river otters. In these headwaters of the Suwannee River, cypress trees rise up in thickets that float almost magically on dense beds of peat, called "houses." Walk on them, and the land quivers, a phenomenon that led the Indians to call this place *Okefenokee,* or "the land of the trembling earth."

Your kids can't help but come away with an appreciation of the land and the wildlife. Another plus: A trip here is low-budget. Cabin rentals and campsites are inexpensive, and a guided trip is moderately priced. Although you can drive from Savannah or Jacksonville for a day trip, your time in the national wildlife refuge will be limited without sleeping on-property, as all canoers must leave the water before dark. On a cross-swamp canoe trip, camping on raised platforms, where alligators grumble below you, adds an unusual element of excitement, but do this by yourselves only if you are experienced.

We recommend staying overnight in one of the state park cabins, which are modern, heated, and come with two bathrooms, two bedrooms, and a kitchen. This location offers you ample opportunity for paddling on different trails; at night come back to the sure comforts of hot chocolate, hot food, and hot showers. Such civilized touches make it easy to take even first graders into this wilderness. Even if you're an experienced camper, consider going with a guide. You'll enjoy less work and more learning.

The Okefenokee

AT A GLANCE

▶ Visit "the land of the trembling earth"

▶ Explore the largest national wildlife refuge in the eastern United States

▶ Paddle cross-swamp on a canoe trip

▶ See sunbathing alligators, slider turtles, and wading birds

▶ Okefenokee National Wildlife Refuge: (912) 496–7836 (reservations) or (912) 496–7836 (general information); http://okefenokee.fws.gov

GETTING THERE

Traveling to Okefenokee by airplane, you can fly to **Savannah International Airport,** Davidson Drive (912-964-0514), which serves numerous national and international airlines. The drive from Savannah to the swamp is approximately two hours. To access **Stephen C. Foster State Park** on the western side of the park, take I-95 from Savannah, exit onto Route 84, then follow Route 441 South to Georgia Highway 177, and follow the signs to the park.

Coming from **Jacksonville International Airport** (904-741-4902); it's an 80-mile drive to the Okefenokee National Wildlife Refuge's east entrance. Jacksonville International Airport also serves several national and international airlines daily. From Jacksonville follow I-95 North to the Kingsland exit, to Georgia State Highway 40 West, to Folkston. In Folkston take Georgia State Highway 23/121 southwest for 11 miles, following the brown-and-white signs to the Okefenokee National Wildlife Refuge's east entrance.

Rental cars are available at the Savannah and Jacksonville airports.

Don't be fooled by the north entrance, 8 miles south of Waycross, Georgia, off U.S. Highway 1. This entrance does not offer access to the Okefenokee National Wildlife Refuge itself, but to the **Okefenokee Swamp Park** (912-283-0583), a privately administered commercial park.

The refuge has two primary entrances. The more frequently used **Okefenokee East Entrance** (912-496-7836), is 8 miles southwest of Folkston, Georgia, off Georgia State Highway 23/121. The more remote **west**

entrance, which leads to the **Stephen C. Foster State Park** (912-637-5274), is 17 miles from Fargo, Georgia, along State Highway Spur 177. Both these entrances lead to visitor's centers, which feature exhibits, guided boat tours, canoes, and boat rentals. The west entrance also has campgrounds and cabin rentals. There is a $5.00 entrance fee per vehicle. Additional access to the refuge is via Kingfisher Landing, off U.S. 1 between Waycross and Folkston, Georgia. This unstaffed entrance has a public boat ramp, parking lots, and a composting toilet.

GETTING AROUND

The best and only way to see the Okefenokee up close is by boat. Bring your own canoe, or rent a canoe, motorboat, or kayak at **Okefenokee Adventures** at the **Okefenokee East Entrance,** Folkston; (912) 496-7836. You can also rent from the **Stephen C. Foster State Park,** on the west side; (912) 637-5274. The park also offers bicycle rentals at hourly rates for use within the Foster State Park only.

WHAT TO SEE AND DO

Okefenokee National Wildlife Refuge

The best time to visit the refuge is spring. Come March, April, and May, long stretches of white and yellow water lilies carpet the refuge waters. Hundreds of slider turtles live up to their names, splashing from the shore into the water, and thousands of alligators bask on logs along the 107 miles of canoe trails. In spring, too, the swamp resounds with the bellowing of breeding gators and the exuberant trilling of frogs. By late June the temperatures and the bugs (primarily after dark) could make a visit uncomfortable. Local experts also like to visit in fall, when some of the foliage turns russet and the swamp is less crowded, but the weather still pleasant. June through September brings the rainy season, humid temperatures, wet afternoons, and frequent thunder and lightning storms. Avoid visiting during these months.

The rules and regulations of the Okefenokee swamp vary somewhat depending on whether you stay overnight. If you do, you need a permit; you don't need one for other activities in the refuge or the park.

If your time is limited, book a cabin at Stephen C. Foster State Park and explore from this area.

Stephen C. Foster State Park

The Visitor's Center at the **Stephen C. Foster State Park** (912-637-5274) has a store that sells basic groceries—some canned goods and microwave popcorn—and books, including a surprisingly good selection of chil-

Great Swamp Canoe Trails

You won't be bored paddling for several days, as the swamp offers diverse stretches and subtle differences.

- **Billy's Lake** leads you to Billy's Island, 15 miles into the heart of the swamp and about 2 miles from the put-in site at Stephen C. Foster State Park. Come ashore here for a picnic lunch and to explore. Hike through the island's pine forest, where through the 1920s loggers attempted to tame the swamp. Now there is just a small, family graveyard, a rusty steam-train boiler, and the remains of a rail handcar.
- **Minnie's Lake Run.** This popular canoe trail feels like a real-life Disney World river ride. On this curvy, narrow trail, paddle by dense stands of cypress and maneuver around knobby cypress stumps, called "knees," as you delight in the peacefulness.
- **River Narrows** trail. This winding stretch of cypress trees gives way to a forest of gum trees that have clusters of mistletoe growing in the crook of their trunks. The wispy lichen, aptly named old man's beard, hangs from their branches like tinsel, lending a green feathery quality. In March pass by clusters of golden club, a spiky yellow flower, a harbinger of spring. In spring the sky fills with scores of ibis, fluttering back to their roosts like hovering white angels.

dren's wildlife educational materials, including mazes, dot games, and naturalist guides. Whether you're camping or lodging at a cabin, bring your supplies. Although it's nice to know there's a store nearby, you'll be a lot happier bringing your own food.

At Stephen C. Foster State Park, 25 miles of waterway trails are open to the public, canoe and motorboat rentals are available (reserve ahead), and park rangers lead ninety-minute guided tours on a pontoon boat. Depending on your endurance, you can paddle to some of the swamp's most magical sites on a day trip. **Billy's Island** is the closest point, a 2-mile one-way trip (4 miles round trip) from your put-in spot, and **Minnie's Lake** is a 10-mile round trip that should take about five hours.

As soon as you paddle out of the channel from the dock, the spell of the Okefenokee takes over.

Once in the swamp you'll be on a photo hunt for the critters. Seeing your first gator up close, on his turf, is dazzling. Sighting a half-submerged barklike snout and two bulging eyes peering at you from the reeds is unforgettable. Paddling along on a warm day, you'll pass by hundreds of these creatures.

Alligator Savvy

The first time you see a pair of bulging eyes staring at you, you'll be amazed. But how do you calm a frightened child? First of all, paddled correctly, canoes rarely tip, and if they did, the great splash you would make would most likely frighten away the alligators.

Still, use common sense. Teach your kids to sit still in the canoe (this is actually easy since they will like the scenery and be busy paddling), and make sure they wear properly sized life jackets. Call ahead to find out if the rental facility has child-size jackets, or bring your own.

Rangers at the refuge will tell you that the two biggest problems they have are people trying to feed the alligators and people thinking the alligators aren't real because they're lying so still on the riverbank. You should NEVER try to feed alligators. Feeding them makes them aggressive, and they may actually tip your canoe trying to get more food. And there are no fake alligators along the riverbank. Those are all *real* alligators and should be left in peace.

The sun transforms the swamp. Not only do the alligators appear, but so do the birds. You'll see hawks, herons, woodpeckers, and lots more. The sun's effect on the dark water is magical as well, creating perfect, mirror-like reflections that shoot into the depths. In fall and February and March, there tend to be more river otters since the gators are less active. Look sharp at the shoreline to find a family of otters catching a fish dinner.

Wherever your paddles take you, don't forget your fishing gear. **Anglers** are welcome year-round at Stephen C. Foster State Park, but those sixteen years or older must have a fishing license. Pick one up in the Trading Post, at the park's entrance.

Suwannee Canal Recreation Area

The **Okefenokee East Entrance Visitor's Center,** (912–496–7836), has been renovated to include several interactive exhibits for children. One allows them to walk on simulated trembling earth, another to see what lives in a cyprus canopy. There's a new audiovisual program that helps parents plan their trip around the refuge and state park. Obtain information on the area's attractions, a wildlife observation drive, hiking trails, and photo blinds. Concession stands offer guided boat tours, boat and bicycle rentals, snacks, and souvenirs, plus camping and fishing supplies.

Since the trails branching off from the **Suwannee Canal** are wildlife refuge property, strict rules apply. Overnight visitors may stay for no more than five days and must apply for a canoe trail permit. Make reservations for the canoe trails by calling (912) 496-3331; you can book no sooner than two months prior to your trip.

If visiting for the day, you do not need permits, but you are restricted to day trails that access only a small portion of the swamp. Even so, you can head into the heart of the swamp, known for its vast open areas, called prairies, by way of the man-made Suwannee Canal.

Of three routes the most popular is the **Cedar Hammock trail.** Paddle 2 miles up the canal, then cut off to the right near **Mizell Prairie**—stop awhile for the exceptional bird-watching—then continue to a raised platform another 2½ miles north. You can dock there, stretch your legs, and have a picnic lunch (there's also a compost toilet there), and then return for a 9-mile round-trip. This trail offers a good view of the swamp. Another picnic spot, 4 miles further on, is **Coffee Bay,** where there's also a platform to spread out on. The easiest route is to paddle 3 miles from the canal to **Cooter Lake.** The Visitor Center has trail maps. Nearby is an automobile road that leads to a ¾-mile boardwalk trail with an observation tower. Along this boardwalk trail are two spur trails, and along these spur trails are four rest spots with observation towers. Keep a lookout for the Florida sandhill crane, which makes its home here.

In order to protect the swamp and its wild inhabitants, a limited number of overnight visitors are allowed into the refuge at one time. Overnight guests are allowed to travel throughout the refuge's trails, but only with a trail reservation. Obtain a permit by calling the **U.S. Fish and Wildlife Service,** Okefenokee National Wildlife Refuge (912-496-3331), but reservations can be made no more than two months in advance.

Overnight canoe trips in this section of the refuge take you through the Suwannee Canal and into the swamp's Chesser, Grand, and Mizell prairies, vast open areas of land scattered with small lakes.

What to Pack

While spring is likely to bring warm weather and sunny skies, bring appropriate gear to keep you dry, including waterproof jackets, pants, and shoes (rubber boots are fine), just in case. Bring layers as well, including a sweatshirt if it's cool, a hat for shade, and leather gloves to save your hands from calluses. Remember the bug spray. Mosquitoes are in the swamp after dark April through October. Be mindful as well of snakes, although outfitters like to use the phrase "you'll be lucky if you see them," as snakes tend to hide from people.

More Sites

The Okefenokee Swamp Park is 8 miles south of Waycross off U.S. 1; (912) 283-0583; www.okeswamp.com. This private wildlife sanctuary is on the northern end of the Okefenokee Swamp. Begin your visit with **Eye on Nature,** a chance to see some larger alligators and snakes, as well as

You never know just what you will encounter when you explore the Okefenokee National Wildlife Refuge.

otters and black bears. The **Group Boat Tour** is a twenty-minute guided tour around the Seminole Indian Waterways. There's also a one-hour tour that goes farther into the swamp, and a two-hour **Land of the Trembling Earth** tour that goes even farther in and demonstrates what they mean by "trembling earth." The **Okefenokee Railroad Tour** stops at Pioneer Island for a look at some re-created homesteads and a country store. This private business is not part of the wildlife refuge.

SIDE TRIPS

Spend some time before or after the Okefenokee in Savannah, a southern charmer of a city made for strolling. (See the Savannah chapter.) Combine a trip to the swamp with some upscale beach vacationing at Hilton Head, South Carolina. (See the Hilton Head chapter.)

SPECIAL EVENTS

For more information about these events, contact the Okefenokee National Wildlife Refuge at (912) 496-7836 or the Stephen C. Foster State Park at (912) 637-5274. All are held at the Okefenokee East Entrance, unless otherwise noted.

April. National Wildlife Week, third week in April, a chance to explore the refuge and participate in special environmental programs with the rangers.

May. Free Fishing Weekend and Youth Fishing Tournament, third Saturday in May.

October. Okefenokee Festival.

November. Okefenokee Birding and Man in the Swamp, Stephen C. Foster State Park.

WHERE TO STAY

At **Stephen C. Foster State Park,** nestled within the western side of the refuge, you can rent one of nine comfortable and inexpensive two-bedroom, two-bath cabins with a full kitchen, but you must stay at least two nights. Reserve these eleven months in advance.

There are also sixty-eight campsites with water, electrical hookups, picnic tables, and grills. Each area has a comfort station with hot showers, flush toilets, and laundry facilities. Strict regulations apply to all campers. Visitors may stay only one night at any designated site and must remain at the site from sunset until sunrise. Like the cabins, campsites fill up quickly. Reservations can be made up to ninety days before your stay. Call the Park Office at (912) 637-5274.

For those who missed out on cabin and campsite reservations or are stopping by on a day trip, motels are available in Folkston, 10 miles from the Okefenokee East Entrance, and in Fargo, 18 miles from the Stephen C. Foster State Park.

In **Folkston** try the **Daystop Tahiti,** (a Days Inn) 1201 South Second Street off U.S. 1, Folkston (912-496-2514 or 800-DAYSINN), or the **Okefenokee Motel,** U.S. 1 North, Folkston (912-496-7380). The Folkston Chamber of Commerce (912-496-2536) can supply other possibilities. In **Fargo** visitors can rest their heads at the **Gator Hotel;** (912) 637-5445.

WHERE TO EAT

Although the convenience store at the Stephen C. Foster State Park has some basic groceries and soups, the selection is minimal and the prices higher than those outside the park. Overnighters should stock up on groceries before arriving.

Okefenokee Adventures (912-496-7156) will pack a box lunch for you of barbecued hot dogs or sausage, baked beans, and coleslaw. Call ahead to be sure, or bring along your own lunch and picnic on the grounds. Snacks and drinks are also available. In Folkston, there's the **Okefenokee Restaurant,** Second and Main Streets (912-496-3263), where they serve sandwiches, salads, and buffet lunch. You can also try **Big J Deli,** U.S. 1 and 301 South (912-496-2315) for hot meals, sandwiches, and takeout, and **The Fleming House,** U.S. 1 and 301 South (912-496-7958) for Southern cooking and homemade desserts.

FOR MORE INFORMATION

For more information on the **Okefenokee National Wildlife Refuge,** write to Refuge Manager, Okefenokee National Wildlife Refuge, Route 2, Box 3330, Folkston, Georgia 31537, or call (912) 496-7836; okefenokee. fws.gov.

To get in touch with the **Stephen C. Foster State Park,** contact Stephen C. Foster State Park, Fargo, Georgia 31631; (912) 637-5274. Write or contact Okefenokee Swamp Park, Waycross, Georgia 31301 (912-283-0583), for more information. To contact the main headquarters of the refuge, write or call Refuge Manager, Okefenokee National Wildlife Refuge, Route 2, Box 3330, Folkston, Georgia 31537; (912) 496-7836.

For more information on Georgia's parks, write to Georgia Department of Natural Resources, Communications Office, 205 Butler Street, SE, Suite 1352 East, Atlanta, Georgia 30334, or call (404) 656-3530.

Emergency Numbers

Remember, a pay telephone is located at the east and west entrances only. Important phone numbers are posted next to the phones.

Charlton County Sheriff: (912) 496-2281

Clinch County Sheriff: (912) 487-5315

Clinch Memorial Hospital, 524 Carswell Street, Homerville, Georgia; (912) 487-5211 (about a 55-mile drive up Highway 441 North). In Folkston, Charlton Memorial Hospital, 1203 North Third Street, (912) 496-2531.

For twenty-four-hour emergency and pharmacy service, use the South Georgia Medical Center, Pendleton Park, Valdosta, Georgia; (912) 333-1086 (pharmacy)/333-1110 (emergency room). The Center is about 65 miles from the park.

SAVANNAH

S avannah, with its shady streets and parklike squares, is a city made for walking. As you stroll from the waterfront to Forsyth Park, you walk through part of the 2½-square-mile downtown, one of the largest urban historic districts. Laid out by General James Oglethorpe in the eighteenth century, the city's orderly pattern of shady streets and landscaped squares lends itself to leisurely strolls.

Called "the most beautiful city in North America" by *Le Monde*, the Parisian newspaper, this southern city, easy to navigate, friendly, and historic, will charm you and your kids. Saunter along the streets lined by venerable oaks draped with Spanish moss and pass the numerous graceful squares. Savannah has many sweet surprises for families.

GETTING THERE

Located 15 miles from historic Savannah, **Savannah International Airport** (912-964-0514) serves numerous national and international airlines. **Amtrak** (800-USA-RAIL or 912-234-2611) stops at the Savannah terminal, 2611 Seaboard Coastline Drive, six times daily. Trains originate from New York, Jacksonville, Miami, and St. Petersburg. **Greyhound/ Trailways,** 600 West Oglethorpe Avenue (912-233-7723), stops in Savannah as well. Located 17 miles inland from the Atlantic Ocean near the Georgia–South Carolina border, the city is accessible via I–95 north–south and I–16 east–west (via I–75 from Atlanta).

GETTING AROUND

The best way to see Savannah is by walking. **Old Town Trolley Tours** (912-233-0083; www.historictours.com), which stops at various attractions, offer a convenient way to get around. Reboarding is allowed. Old Town also offers a "Ghosts & Gravestones" tour of the city. **Grayline Red Trolley Tours/Grayline Historic Tours** (912-234-TOUR or 800-426-2318) offers a variety of specialized tours, as well as general tours of

---

Savannah

AT A GLANCE

▶ Stroll charming streets shaded by live oaks draped with Spanish moss

▶ Tour historic houses, including birthplace of Juliette Gordon Low, founder of the Girl Scouts

▶ Visit a Civil War fort and ocean beaches on nearby barrier islands

▶ Savannah Area Convention and Visitors Bureau: 877–SAVANNAH; www.savannahvisit.com

---

the city. **CAT** (Chatham Area Transit) public bus service offers routes for the downtown and south side area. The free CAT Shuttle provides shuttle service from downtown hotels, inns, and the Savannah Visitor Information Center to Savannah's historic sites, squares, and other attractions. For CAT schedules call (912) 233-5767; www.catchacat.org.

Phone **Yellow Cab** at (912) 236-1133 or **Adam Cab** at (912) 927-7466, for taxi service.

WHAT TO SEE AND DO

A good place to begin your tour is at the **Savannah History Museum** (912-238-1779; www.chsgeorgia.org)/**Savannah Visitors Center,** 301 Martin Luther King, Jr., Boulevard; (912) 944-0455. This facility, a restored 1860s railroad station, presents a short introductory film on Savannah. The museum has exhibits on coastal life and on early Savannah, plus a locomotive and lots of brochures. There's also an exhibit on the more than 170,000 African-American soldiers who fought in the Civil War. Admission.

If your family is interested in trains, be sure to visit the **Historic Railroad Shops,** 601 W. Harris adjacent to the Visitors Center (912-651-6823), the oldest and most complete existing locomotive repair shop in the country. Here you'll find a 130-ton diesel locomotive on a turntable and steam engines on display. Special programs such as a lantern Tour & Dinner and a Hobo Bonfire & Dinner are also offered. Admission.

Special Tours

- **Riverboat cruises.** See the city from the water aboard the *Savannah River Queen* and the *Georgia Queen.* The one-hour narrated cruises are just long enough to provide a relaxing interlude. Dinner and brunch cruises are available, as well as the popular Murder Afloat Cruise. Call (912) 232-6404 or (800) 786-6404; www.savannah-riverboat.com.
- **Carriage rides.** Kids love the slow pace and the Percherons. Carriage Tours of Savannah depart from the Visitors Center, 301 Martin Luther King Boulevard; (912) 236-6756. Reservations suggested.
- **Black Heritage.** Learn about pre-Civil War African-American life in Savannah by visiting several historic sites. Negro Heritage Trail Tour, 502 East Harris Street; (912) 234-8000.
- **Ghost Tours.** Find out about the city's ghosts and haunted spots. Ghost Talk Ghost Walk, 127 East Congress Street; (912) 233-3896 or (800) 563-3896.
- **Legends.** Get in on the city's gossip and lore. Companies offering tours include Historic Walking Tours, 135 Bull Street (912-233-0119); Savannah By Foot (912-238-3843); and Savannah Walks (912-238-WALK or 888-SAV-WALK).
- **Dolphins.** Watch dolphins dive through Savannah's waters with Cap'n Mike's Dolphin Tours, Lazaretto Creek Marina; (912) 786-5848 or 800-242-0166. Dolphin Magic Tours leave from the Hyatt Dock (800-721-1240).

Riverfront Attractions

The **Waving Girl Statue** on River Street commemorates Florence Martus, a city native who, from 1887 to 1931, reputedly waved at every ship entering the harbor in hopes of greeting her husband who sailed away just after their marriage, never to return. Be sure to stroll along nearby **Factors Walk.** At this historic site eighteenth-century merchants perched on the iron catwalks to judge the price of goods paraded below. The nineteenth-century riverside buildings, which once functioned as offices, now offer excellent browsing and shopping opportunities. Plan to spend some time here and along River Street looking for T-shirts and souvenirs.

Historic Sites

Take time to stroll through Savannah's historic district. The many historic squares, set up by General Oglethorpe to slow advancing troops in case of attack, offer peaceful, shady places to sit. Kids like romping through these.

Savannah's stately homes are a gift to the eye, with their archways, pillars, and fanciful iron railings, balconies, and gates. There's no shortage of historic homes in this city, but a tour of **one** or **two** of these goes a long way with kids, so don't attempt to see them all.

Juliette Gordon Low Girl Scout Center, 142 Bull Street (912-233-4501), is a must-see for any girl scout, or even boy scout, in your family. Juliette Gordon Low, founder of the Girl Scouts, was born here on Halloween night 1860. Now the 1818 Regency-style home, restored to its 1870s appearance, serves as the national center for the Girl Scouts. (The guided tour can get bogged down in boring details, but my daughter, a girl scout at the time, just liked being in Low's house.) After visiting the home, buy a merit badge in the gift shop. Admission.

The **Owens Thomas House,** 124 Abercorn Street (912-233-9743), is among the important historic houses. From a balcony at this English Regency-style mansion designed by William Jay and built between 1816 and 1819, the Marquis de Lafayette addressed the townspeople in 1825. Inside, fine antiques and *trompe l'oeil* decorations convey the ruffles and flourishes of gentrified life in this southern town.

The **Telfair Mansion,** 121 Barnard Street (912-232-1177) and the Owens-Thomas House are part of the **Telfair Museum** (www.telfair.org), which houses the **Telfair Academy of Arts & Sciences** (also known as the Telfair Museum of Art) on the west corner of Telfair Square. The oldest public art museum in the South, Telfair has a fine collection of eighteenth- and nineteenth-century American and European paintings. The museum has regularly scheduled Family Sunday events related to current exhibits, featuring music and hands-on activities, and there's a family guide available at the entrance to pique children's curiosity about what they're going to see. Admission. Museums in Savannah participate in what's called **Museum Sunday** meaning that on that day they don't charge admission.

The Gothic-style **Green-Meldrim House,** 1 West Macon Street (912-233-1251), marks ties to the Civil War. This house became General Sherman's Savannah headquarters in 1864 after his trail of destruction through the South. Pick up a brochure that details the house's sophisticated architectural features. Closed mid-December to mid-January. Admission.

Congregation Mickve Israel, 20 East Gordon Street at Monterey Square (912-233-1547), whose current building dates back to 1878, traces its congregants to the second boatload of settlers to Georgia, landing in 1733 after General Oglethorpe's English settlers. According to legend these Jews fleeing the Spanish Inquisition were allowed to take refuge in Savannah because among them was a physician whose services Oglethorpe needed for his ailing colonists. The good doctor refused to land unless all his shipmates were permitted ashore as well. The temple includes a museum with many artifacts on display, including historical books, letters from presidents Washington and Jefferson, as well as one of the oldest Torahs in the United States. This is the only Gothic-style synagogue in the U.S.

The **Davenport House Museum,** 324 East State Street (912-236-8097), was built in 1820 by Rhode Island carpenter Isaiah Davenport after a careful study of traditional Federal architecture. Older children will appreciate a tour of the home's intricate ironwork, flowing staircase, and authentic period pieces. Be sure to tour the garden afterward. The museum shop is a good place to pick out a Savannah souvenir. Admission.

At the **King-Tisdell Cottage,** 514 East Huntingdon Street (912-234-8000), an 1896 gingerbread cottage, learn about African-American history in Savannah and the Sea Islands. A tour of this quaint home reveals black life a century ago through furniture, artwork, and historical documents. Tours are by appointment only. The museum also sponsors a **Negro Heritage Trail,** 502 East Harris Street (912-234-8000), a tour of seventeen historic sites from the river docks, where the first slaves arrived, to the first Negro Baptist church.

Green Spaces

Besides romping in the twenty town squares, find time for **Forsyth Park,** twenty acres of greenery and fountains between Gaston Street and Park Avenue. This is a great place for a picnic or an impromptu game of tag. The park has a Confederate Monument to honor those killed in the Civil War and a Fragrant Garden for the Blind, as well as basketball and tennis courts and a 1-mile jogging course.

If your kids don't spook at the mere mention of cemeteries, the **Colonial Park Cemetery,** Abercorn between Oglethorpe and Perry, is an interesting stop. The weathered gravestones mark many of the Revolutionary War dead.

Forts

Fort Jackson, One Fort Jackson Road (912-232-3945; www.chsgeorgia. org), on the Savannah River, served as the headquarters of the Confederate defense during the Civil War. This fortress actually dates back to the Revolutionary War and is now the oldest existing fort in the state. There's a maritime museum to explore, and mid-June to mid-August you can witness the firing of the thirty-two-pound black powder cannon. A self-guided tour includes a fifteen-minute film on the history of the fort. There are also rooms dating from the Civil War where kids can play. In

May Scottish games are held at the fort. This is a great spot from which to watch the massive freighters coming up the Savannah River. Admission.

Fort McAllister State Historic Park, Route 2, Richmond Hill (912-727-2339; www.gastateparks.org), offers a space for a leisurely afternoon and a history lesson on the banks of the Great Ogeechee River. The fort has been called the best preserved earthwork fortification of the Confederacy, one which held up during seven Union attacks. The current museum of Civil War artifacts will be replaced with a new, expanded facility, scheduled to open in June 2001. Tours of the fort are available (call for registration), and there's a 3-mile, posted hiking trail and a picknicking area. Admission. (There's also a sixty-five-site campground where guests can rent bicycles and kayaks.)

Fort Pulaski National Monument (912-786-5787; www.nps.gov) is on Cockspur Island. This fort impresses with massive walls, a wide drawbridge, and two moats. Explore the fort outworks and surrounding nature trails; then stop by the museum and bookstore. In summertime the fort presents daily talks and demonstrations on the Civil War. The Junior Ranger program is available for children ages six to twelve, and hiking, biking, and picnicking are allowed in designated areas.

Other Attractions

Ships of the Sea Maritime Museum, 41 Martin Luther King, Jr. Boulevard (912-232-1511; www.shipsofthesea.org), is housed in Scarbrough House, a mansion built in 1819 for the owner of the *Savannah,* the first steamship to cross the Atlantic Ocean. The collection features paintings and maritime antiques, but kids will be most captivated by the intricately constructed model ships that range from minuscule to 8 feet and include a replica of the sinking *Titanic.* There are video presentations in four of the galleries and a museum search sheet for kids over eight. Admission.

The **Ralph Mark Gilbert Civil Rights Museum,** 460 Martin Luther King, Jr. Boulevard (912-231-8900), has three floors of photographs and interactive exhibits chronicling the genesis of the Civil Rights movement in Savannah. Of special interest is the video in which Savannah residents speak movingly of their roles in the movement's struggles. Admission.

For families into aviation, there's the **Mighty Eighth Air Force Heritage Museum,** on Bourne Avenue off I-95 (912-748-8888; www.mighty8thmuseum.com), with its displays of memorabilia and equipment and a simulated ride on a B-17 combat mission.

If you want to take a drive beyond Savannah's historic district, there are other interesting sites. The **Wormsloe State Historic Site,** 7601 Skidaway Road (912-353-3023; www.gastateparks.org), brings you back to Colonial times and the accomplishments of one of Georgia's first settlers—

Noble Jones. The 1½ mile drive, lined with live oaks, is impressive. Children enjoy a discovery romp through the ruins of this early estate and a nature trail. Check for schedules of a living-history demonstration of early Colonial life.

At the **Laurel Hill Wildlife Drive/Savannah National Wildlife Refuge** (912-652-4415), Highway 17 in South Carolina, about 6 miles from Savannah, pick up a brochure at the Visitors Center; then explore the wildlife refuge on a 4-mile drive. You pass dikes constructed in the late 1700s and early 1800s to retain the rice fields. The refuge is home to many of the area's marsh and saltwater birds and ducks (at certain times of the year). If you keep your eyes peeled, you might even sight an alligator.

Side Trips

- **Tybee Island,** thirty minutes outside Savannah, is a great family day trip that combines beach bathing, recreation, and maritime history. Before or after you hit the beach, check out the **Museum and Lighthouse.** The lighthouse recently underwent a major renovation. Self-guided tours include a visit to the keeper's cottage and other exhibits, as well as a 154-foot climb to the top. Admission. The museum is located in an 1898 coastal artillery battery and has displays on island life from colonial times to the Second World War. Admission. The **Tybee Island Marine Science Center** has an aquarium, a touch tank, and displays featuring sharks and shells. Call for a schedule of the early-morning guided nature tours; kids are encouraged to bring a shovel and bucket and examine marine life along the shoreline. Donations accepted. Call the Tybee Island Visitors Center (800-868-BEACH or 912-786-5444) for more information.
- On **Skidaway Island State Park** (912-598-2300; www.gastateparks. org) there are nature trails winding through marshes and an observation tower from which to spot deer, raccoon, and rare migrating birds. Rangers are available for nature tours. Of special interest is the University of Georgia Marine Extension Service Aquarium (912-598-2496), with its twelve tanks holding fifty species of fish and invertebrates. Admission.
- Georgia's **Golden Isles** are approximately 70 miles south of Savannah, or a little more than an hour away. Treat yourself to a day on the beach at one of these four barrier islands, featuring untouched beaches and resorts, with golf, tennis, fishing, sailing, and swimming.

  The islands have history as well. **Sea Island** was formerly a renowned cotton plantation, and **St. Simons Island** is home to Fort Frederica, a costly colonial British fort built by General Oglethorpe. Millionaire

American families, including the Rockefellers and the Morgans, made **Jekyll Island** their summer playground in the early part of the century. For more information contact the Brunswick and Golden Isles Visitors Bureau, 4 Glynn Avenue, Brunswick; (912) 265-0620.

■ Other day trip possibilities include the **Okefenokee Swamp** to the south. (See Okefenokee chapter for attractions.)

■ **Atlanta** is about four and a half hours away by car. (See Atlanta chapter for more information.)

SPECIAL EVENTS

For a schedule of Savannah's cultural and historical events, call (912) 233-ARTS. For a comprehensive listing of Savannah's events, call the **Savannah Waterfront Association** at (912) 234-0295 and **The Savannah Area Convention and Visitors Bureau** at (877) SAVANNAH.

January. In celebration of Martin Luther King, Jr., Day, Savannah hosts Martin Luther King, Jr., Week; a celebration offering week-long activities such as Gospelfest, jobs fair, blood drive at YMCA, parade, and dance, (912-234-5502).

February. Celebrate the past at Georgia Heritage Celebration, with lectures, tours, and a parade (912-651-2125).

February–November. The first Saturday of each month means the First Saturday Festival, a Historic Waterfront celebration complete with food, music, arts and crafts, clowns, and face painting all weekend long. Sponsored by the Savannah Waterfront Association (912-234-0295).

March. The Savannah Onstage International Arts Festival offers five days of musical performances featuring rising young stars (912-236-5745). Savannah House and Garden Tour (912-233-7787).

May. Arts on the River Festival brings together artists, food, and entertainment. Savannah Scottish Games & Highland Gathering includes sport competitions, dance, music, food, and children's activities (912-369-5203).

June. The Annual Beach Music Festival.

July. The Savannah Maritime Festival takes place at the waterfront.

September. The Savannah Jazz Festival is four days of local and national jazz musicians (912-356-2381). Three-day Folkmusic Fest (912-927-1376).

December. Christmas on the River includes a riverside parade, arts and crafts, music, food, caroling, and entertainment. Holiday Tour of Homes (912-233-0220).

WHERE TO STAY

For reservations at most of Savannah's properties, call (800) 444-CHARM. Among Savannah's newer accommodations is the **Westin Savannah Harbor Resort,** One Resort Drive (912-201-2000; www.westinsavannah. com), adjacent to the International Trade and Convention Center on Hutchinson Island, across from Savannah's Historic District. The resort has a championship 18-hole golf course, a Greenbrier Spa, two outdoor swimming pools, and water ferry and water taxi transportation to the historic district. The Westin Kids' Club provides a full day (8:30 A.M.–4:30 P.M.) of arts and crafts, swimming, and other activities for children four to twelve. Right now the only packages are for those interested in golfing or spa-ing, but that may change. Call for information.

The **Olde Harbour Inn,** 508 East Factor's Walk (912-234-4100 or 800-553-6533; www.oldeharbourinn.com), right on the river, offers twenty-four suites, each with a kitchenette. Your kids will like the extra space, the easy snacking, and the scoop of ice cream at turndown. Ask about special weekend rates.

The Mulberry Inn, 601 East Bay Street (912-238-1200 or 800-HOL-IDAY; www.savannahhotel.com), has 119 rooms. The rooftop deck offers a great view of the river by moonlight, plus there's a complimentary afternoon tea. **Presidents' Quarters,** 225 East President Street (912-233-1600 or 800-233-1776; www.presidentsquarters.com), an 1855 inn located in the historic and business district, invites you to afternoon tea, and children under ten stay for free.

Best Western-Historic District, 412 West Bay Street (912-233-1011 or 800-528-1234) is newly renovated and has reasonable rates, plus continental breakfast and an outdoor pool. Also in the historic district, **Days Inn-Days Suites,** 201 West Bay Street (912-236-4440 or 800-325-2525) has more than 200 rooms, including 57 apartment-style suites.

R.S.V.P. Georgia and Savannah Bed and Breakfast (912-232-7787 or 800-729-7787) provides a free reservation service for bed and breakfasts and guest houses in historic Savannah. Call for more information. **Savannah Historic Inns and Guest Houses Reservation Service,** 11 Silver Leaf Court (912-233-7666 or 800-262-4667), is a similar organization.

WHERE TO EAT

For an authentic Savannah tradition, be sure to line up early for lunch at **Mrs. Wilkes' Boarding House,** 107 West Jones Street, served 11:30 A.M. to 3:00 P.M. Her family-style fare, served ten guests to a table, includes fried chicken, stew, rice, beans, biscuits, collard greens, sweet potatoes, and three kinds of dessert. **The Lady & Sons,** 311 West Congress Street

(912-233-2600), serves a southern buffet from 11:00 A.M. to 3:00 P.M. **Carey Hilliard's,** with four locations including 8316 Skidaway Road (912-354-7240) and 8410 Waters Avenue, scores good marks with little kids. This family-style restaurant pampers children with crayons and a coloring place mat, plus a children's menu with chicken fingers, fries, and milkshakes.

The **Pirate's House,** 20 East Broad Street, (912-233-5757), is strewn with pirate-themed treasures or debris, depending upon your point of view. The American fare is reasonably priced, and young kids tend to like the nautical decor. Children are given a souvenir menu, which doubles as a pirate's mask. **Clary's Café,** 404 Abercorn Street (912-233-0402), has sidewalk tables and an old soda fountain. Several of the characters in *Midnight in the Garden of Good and Evil* met here. If you have teens and older children and if you plan well ahead, try **Elizabeth on 37th,** 105 East Thirty-seventh Street (912-236-5547), consistently rated as Savannah's top restaurant.

The *Savannah River Queen,* 9 East River Street (912-232-6404) does a variety of river tours, including a Sunday morning brunch.

For More Information

The Savannah Area Convention and Visitors Bureau, 222 West Oglethorpe Avenue, Suite 100, Savannah, Georgia 31401 (912-644-6400 or 800-444-2427), has informational brochures and visitor's guides. Check the Web site, www.savannahvisit.com. Other good sources of local goings-ons are the *Savannah Tourist Guide* bimonthly newspaper and the *Savannah Parent,* which lists special children's events; both are available at area stores and libraries.

Emergency Numbers

Ambulance, fire, and police: 911

Medical services: The Memorial Health University Medical Center, 4700 Waters Avenue; (912) 356-8000

Poison Control: (800) 282-5846

Twenty-four-hour pharmacy: CVS, Waters Avenue and Sixty-third Street; (912) 355-7111

11 🍨 Kentucky

LEXINGTON

L exington, Kentucky's second-largest city, is set in the heart of Bluegrass horse country. If your kids get starry-eyed watching a thoroughbred go through his paces, enjoy taking riding lessons at camp, or just like to imagine themselves astride the perfect steed, Lexington is a good place to be. Besides all that, the countryside with its white-rail fences, rolling pasturelands, and tobacco farms is picture-perfect for a Sunday drive. Added attractions include historic buildings, a thriving arts and crafts scene, several golf courses, and some interesting museums.

GETTING THERE

ASA, Delta Air Lines, Comair, Continental Express, Trans World Express, USAirways, United Express, and Northwest Airlink serve the **Blue Grass Airport;** (859) 255-7218.

   Amtrak (800-USA-RAIL) does not run direct service to Lexington, Kentucky. You could take the train to Cincinnati, where **Greyhound/ Trailways** (859-299-8804) bus service has daily routes between Cincinnati and Lexington. Flying or driving here, though, is preferable to the combined bus and train route. Lexington is easily accessible, as I-75, I-64, U.S. 60, and U.S. 68 lead to this city.

GETTING AROUND

Route 4 circles the area surrounding the city and serves as a beltway. Lexington's public bus line, **LexTran** (859-253-4936) serves the downtown area. For taxi service dial (859) 231-8294.

   Wheels offers transportation for the physically challenged. Call (859) 233-3433 twenty-four hours in advance.

Lexington

AT A GLANCE

▶ Visit the Kentucky Horse Park, the world's only park dedicated to horses

▶ Tour historic homes, including Ashland (the Henry Clay Estate) and the Mary Todd Lincoln House

▶ Drive through the scenic countryside of rolling fields and horse farms

▶ See Shaker Village of Pleasant Hill, an outdoor living history museum

▶ Lexington Convention and Visitors Bureau, (859) 233-7299 or (800) 845-3959; www.visitlex.com

WHAT TO SEE AND DO

Horse Country Attractions

Kentucky Horse Park, 4089 Iron Works Pike, exit 120 off I-75; (859) 233-4303 or 800-678-8813; www.kyhorsepark.com. The showcase of Kentucky's proud horse tradition, Kentucky Horse Park is set on more than 1,000 acres and offers an extensive look at the horse, its history, its breeding, and its importance to humans. Start at the Visitor Center, where you can book some options, including a horse-drawn carriage ride (sleigh ride in the winter months), pony ride, or horseback trail ride across the sweeping acres of bluegrass. Either of two films shown regularly should delight older children. *Thou Shalt Fly Without Wings* describes what it's like to be a jockey.

Allow time to browse the **International Museum of the Horse,** which documents the evolution of human/equine relations from prehistoric times to today. Kids like discovering that the earliest ancestor of the horse, the *Eohippus,* was no bigger than a fox. There's also an eye-catching collection of thirty horse-drawn vehicles featuring carriages, racing rigs, and commercial wagons. Admission.

On the **Walking Farm Tour,** you can review a day in the life of a racehorse and his handlers. Visit the farrier's (blacksmith's) shop, the harness maker's shop, the training track, and the horse cemetery. At the **Hall of**

Champions, take a look at some of the elite racers of yesteryear who live at the park. Among the stars are John Henry, the first horse ever to win $3 million, $5 million, and $6.5 million, and Kentucky Derby Winner Bold Forbes. The horses are presented three times daily, April through October.

Don't miss the **Parade of Breeds** or the **American Saddle Horse Museum.** The narrated parade, available April through October, presents up to ten breeds, some with costumed riders, twice daily. The **American Saddle Horse Museum** (separate admission), 4093 Iron Works Pike (859-259-2746), dedicates itself to the history and heritage of the American saddlebred horse, Kentucky's only native breed. A touch-screen video scrapbook highlights past world-champion horses.

Throughout the year the park hosts more than sixty equestrian events. Plan ahead to see if you can obtain tickets to the Rolex Kentucky Three-Day Event (the United States Olympic Equestrian Team's spring event) and the polo matches, which are held each Sunday from June through October.

The park also offers one- and two-day courses on all aspects of horse training and maintenance; early registration required. For information and registration, call (800) 568-8813, extension 206, or 895-259-4206. The park is open mid-March through October, from 9:00 A.M. to 5:00 P.M. and is closed Monday and Tuesday, November 1 to mid-March and on holidays. Admission.

A visit to Lexington wouldn't be complete without spending some time observing horses close-up at a track. At **Keeneland Race Course,** U.S. 60 west, 4201 Versailles Road (859-254-3412 or 800-456-3412), about 13 miles from Lexington, you can be railside from spring through fall while watching some of racing's best. You should arrive by 6:00 A.M. to watch these horses go through their paces until about 9:30 A.M. Afterward tour the course grounds and training facilities. Keeneland races occur in April and October, but call ahead for a schedule. Among the notable runs is the spring Blue Grass Stakes, the last of the major prep races for the Kentucky Derby. The **Red Mile Harness Track,** South Broadway and Red Mile Road (859-255-0752 or 800-354-9092), offers harness racing and welcomes the public at morning workouts. But phone ahead for rules about admitting children to facilities where betting occurs.

Horseback Riding

With all the horse talk, you'll want to ride. The Kentucky Horse Park, Lexington (859-233-4303), offers trail rides spring through fall. Also try Big Red Stables, Harrodsburg (859-734-3118); Deer Run Stables, Madison County (859-527-6339); and Wildwood Stables, Nicholasville (859-885-9359).

Lexington Area Horse Farms

Organized group tours can be three or more hours, long enough to bore and bother kids. But on your own a visit to these Bluegrass farms can be the highlight of your trip.

The advantage to a custom trip is that the guide will give you lots of local lore and likely have access to farms that don't accept walk-ins. Some companies to consider: Blue Grass Tours (859-252-5744), Karen Edelstein Private Guide (859-266-5465), Kentucky Horse Tours (800-873-7889 or 859-846-9400), and Lexington Connection (859-269-4040).

The following farms accept individual visitors, but always call first: Three Chimneys Farm, Old Frankfort Pike, West Lexington (859-873-7053); Gainesway Farm, 3750 Paris Pike, Lexington (859-293-2676); Claiborne Farm, near Paris, north of Lexington (859-233-4252).

Historic Sites

There's more to Lexington than just horses. While in town, tour **Ashland,** the Henry Clay Estate, Richmond Road at 120 Sycamore Road; (859) 266-8581; www.henryclay.org. Admission. It's closed during January, on holidays, and on Mondays from November through March. This National Historic Landmark, once an estate covering close to six hundred acres, features twenty acres of woodland and is furnished with nineteenth-century antiques. Admission. If the kids aren't that interested in period furniture, take them to the carriage house to view Clay's 1,500-pound glistening black coach. The Ginko Tree Café, located on the brick patio surrounding the smokehouse, serves snacks, lunch, afternoon tea, and desserts.

Another famous American is remembered at the **Mary Todd Lincoln House,** 578 West Main Street (859-233-9999); open April to mid-December. Built in 1803, the home was restored and opened to the public in 1977, when it became the first shrine to a first lady in America.

If you and your older children are still in the mood for more homes, visit **Hopemont,** the Hunt-Morgan House, 201 North Mill Street; (859) 253-0362 or 233-3290; www.bluegrasstrust.org. Open March to mid-December. Located in Gratz Park, the county's oldest historic district, this well-appointed Federal-style town house holds an impressive collection of porcelain and nineteenth-century Kentucky furniture. Built by Kentucky's first millionaire, John Wesley Hunt, the second floor of the house is the Alexander T. Hunt Civil War Museum, which displays swords, saddles, uniforms and other artifacts from Gen. John Hunt Morgan (Hunt's grandson) and Morgan's Men. **The Waveland State Historic Site,** 225 Higbee Mill Road (859-272-3611), is an 1847 Greek Revival house built by Joseph Bryan, a grandnephew of Daniel Boone. Kids like peeking into the brick servants' quarters, the icehouse, and the smokehouse. There are also flower and herb gardens, a short nature trail, picnic tables, and a playground. Open March to mid-December. Admission. For information on special events at Waveland, call (800) 255-PARK.

Museums

Lexington Children's Museum, 401 West Main Street, Victorian Square; (859) 258-3256; wwwlfucg.com/childrensmuseum. While not as large as some big-city museums, this could prove an entertaining respite for younger kids. At Brainzilla kids can touch a giant fabricated brain and see what their brains look like on the inside. Science Station X lets them see what it's like to stand on the Moon, weigh a dinosaur, and bend light with their eyelashes. Several other exhibits take kids through adventures in home-building and geography. In spring 2001 the museum is opening a new toddler area called Wonder Woods, with trees, animals, and water play. Free drop-in workshops are held every Saturday and Sunday, year-round, featuring arts and crafts and science projects.

At the **University of Kentucky Basketball Museum,** Civic Center complex, learn about the physics of the game, shoot "virtual hoops" against top players, and compare your skills with those of the Wildcats. Call (859) 225-5670.

See stars and planets and learn about heavenly bodies at the **Arnim D. Hummel Planetarium,** Richmond (859-622-1547; www.planetarium.eku.edu), on the campus of Eastern Kentucky University, about a half-hour drive from Lexington. Laser shows are presented throughout the year. Call ahead for program schedules.

Green Spaces and Play Spaces

Lexington's many playgrounds and community parks have trained supervisors who plan and direct activities. The playgrounds are open Monday through Friday, 11:30 A.M. to 8:30 P.M., June through August. Activities include movie nights, horseback riding, sports, and nature hikes. Call the Lexington Parks and Recreation Department (859-288-2900) for program information.

Woodland Park, off High Street on Woodland, has a swimming pool, playground, volleyball and tennis courts, and a new skateboard park that opened in 2000.

Thoroughbred Park has life-size bronze statues of horses racing and grazing. Kids can climb aboard—a good photo op and a lot of fun for younger children.

More Outdoor Fun

- **Hike** the trails at Raven Run Nature Sanctuary, Jacks Creek Pike, and sign up for "insect walks" (859-272-6105); and enjoy the walking paths at Masterson Station Park, Leestown Road.
- **Paddle** a canoe in Elkhorn Creek. Rent one at Oser Landing or Great Crossing Park or call Canoe Kentucky at (800) 522-6631.
- **Llama trek** through woods and meadows at Seldom Scene Farm; (859) 873-1622.
- **Fish** at Jacobson Park (permit required), Richmond Road. A fishing license is required for those over sixteen. There's also a Creative Playground for younger children, and in summer you can rent a paddleboat.
- **Pick Pumpkins** in fall at Double Stink Hog Farm, Newtown Pike and U.S. 460; (859) 868-9703.

Folk Art of Kentucky

- **Churchill Weavers,** 6525 Lorraine Court, Berea (800) 598-5263 or (859) 986-3127. About 38 miles south of Lexington, Berea is a small community of artisans founded in 1922. Churchill Weavers, one of the top handweaving studios in the United States, dedicates itself to quality handmade goods. Enjoy the daily tours of the loomhouse and allow time to shop for blankets, and table linens in the gift shop.
- **Berea crafts area,** contact the Berea Welcome Center, 201 North Broadway (859-986-2540) for a map and directory. Artisans at work here include potters, chair makers, stained-glass artists, leather workers, jewelers, and woodworkers.
- **Kentucky Folk Art Center,** 102 West First Street, Morehead (859-783-2204), has an extensive collection of wood carvings, furniture, and other folk art. Morehead is about zan hour's drive from Lexington.

Sometimes it rains. That's when you might take the younger ones to **Kids Place,** inside the Athletic Center, 3992 West Tiverton Court; (859) 272-5433. Kids can swing from rope bridges, shoot down slides, and climb on a variety of structures at this indoor playground. A rainy-day destination for older kids, **Laser Quest** (859-225-1742) gives them a laser gun and a vest with special sensors and sends them into a dark labyrinth to shoot it out and score points. It's located in a renovated warehouse at 224 Bolivar Street, near the University of Kentucky campus.

Tours

Maps for self-guided walking and driving tours of downtown Lexington and the horse farms are available from Lexington Convention and Visitors Bureau, 301 East Vine Street, Lexington, Kentucky 40507; (606) 233-7299 or (800) 845-3959.

For a scenic tour of downtown, call **Carriage Rides to Lexington Livery** (606-259-0000); they will take you around in a horse-drawn buggy.

Shopping

Lexington offers several shopping areas, including the following:

Clay Avenue Shops, Clay Avenue off East Main, features an eclectic group of stores in a turn-of-the-century neighborhood. Specialty stores include children's fashions, custom stationery, yarn and needlework, furniture, jewelry, antiques, collectibles, and more. **Civic Center**

Thoroughbred Park contains seven life-size bronze racehorses streaking toward the finish line, while broodmares, foals, and stallions graze in a nearby field.

Shops: This spacious shopping complex is located in the heart of downtown, adjacent to Rupp Arena and the Hyatt Regency. The mall is connected by covered pedestrian walkway to Victorian Square and other downtown buildings. The specialty boutiques and shops feature antiques, clothing, unique gifts, jewelry, Appalachian crafts, and handmade candies and toys. There's also a food court. Hours: 10:00 A.M. to 9:00 P.M. Monday to Saturday; 1:00 to 5:00 P.M. Sunday. **Victorian Square,** 401 West Main Street (859–252–7575), is a block of renovated Victorian-era buildings whose shops include Laura Ashley and Talbots. **The Kentucky**

Shaker Village of Pleasant Hill

Shaker Village of Pleasant Hill, 3501 Lexington Road, Harrodsburg; (859) 734-5411; www.shakervillageky.org. Located 25 miles from Lexington, this landmark 2,700-acre preserve has thirty-three buildings from the original Shaker settlement begun in 1805.

Costumed historians demonstrate different skills, including weaving and broom making. Shaker period furniture is displayed in the Centre Family House. The Shaker Life Exhibit in the East Family Dwelling has changing exhibits, a video viewing area, and a discover room where kids can touch exhibits and try their hand at crafts. Special activities and workshops are available, including crafts, textiles, nature walks, archeology, and even a Shaker funeral. Call (800) 734-5611 or check out the web site for schedules.

The Shaker Village Trustees' Office Inn serves breakfast and lunch as well as a family-style dinner; save room for the cakes and pies. A children's menu is available. In summer a light midday meal is also served at the Summer Kitchen. Reservations are suggested.

Catch the *Dixie Belle,* a sternwheel riverboat at Shaker Landing. Available April through October, the one-hour trip along the Kentucky River offers scenic views of limestone cliffs and green shoreline. Admission.

The village is open daily from 9:30 A.M. to 5:00 P.M. from April through late November; otherwise, hours vary. Overnight lodging is provided in fifteen restored buildings with eighty rooms. Although each room keeps to its original Shaker simplicity, telephones, televisions, and private baths help modernize your quarters. No charge for children under seventeen. Call (800) 734-5611.

Gallery of Fine Crafts & Arts, 139 West Short Street (859-281-1166), features paintings, pottery, jewelry, quilts, and furniture by 250 regional artists. At **Fayette Mall** you'll find some two hundred stores, among them The Disney Store and Natural Wonders, which sells science-oriented toys and kits.

Performing Arts

Lexington Children's Theatre, 418 West Short Street (859-254-4546 or 800-928-4545, www.lctonstage.org) presents a full season of theater for children that includes staged classics and plays from other cultures. In the summer five-day theater workshops are offered for different age groups. Each workshop ends with a performance. The **ArtsPlace,** 161

North Mill Street (859-255-2951) hosts numerous cultural events. Each Tuesday at noon there are free hour-long musical performances that in the summer are geared toward children. Call (859) 233-1469 for schedule.

Golf

For a complete listing of Lexington's public golf courses, call the Lexington Parks and Recreation Department at (859) 288-2900. Some public courses on which to enjoy the bluegrass are **the Picadome Golf Course,** 469 Parkway Drive (859-244-8454); the **Kearney Hill Links,** 3403 Kearny Road (859-253-1981); **Marriott's Griffin Gate Golf Club,** 1720 Newtown Pike (859-254-4101; and **Shady Brook Golf,** 444 Hutchinson Road (859-987-1544).

SIDE TRIPS

- **Toyota Plant Tours,** 1001 Cherry Blossom Way, Georgetown; (502) 868-3027 or 800-866-4485. What's a car assembly line really like? Travel 12 miles north of Lexington on I-75 to the Toyota Factory, and you'll find out. The tour, restricted to visitors of first grade age and above, features a one-hour tram-ride tour of the factory, a ten-minute introductory film, and the opportunity to witness the behind-the-scenes construction of a Kentucky Camry, Avalon, or mini-van. Admission is free, and reservations are strongly suggested. Tours are given Monday through Friday at 10:00 A.M., noon, and 2:00 P.M., with an additional tour on Thursday at 6:00 P.M.
- The **Nostalgia Station Toy Train Museum and Train Shop,** 279 Depot Street, Versailles (859-873-2497), is about 10 miles from Lexington. Train buffs will appreciate such items as a Lionel girl's stove and a Lionel O gauge dealer display, as well as a gift shop crammed with books and train accessories.
- **Fort Boonesborough State Park,** 4375 Boonesborough Road, Richmond (859-527-3131), is 36 miles outside Lexington and features a reconstructed fort that contains a variety of cabins, each with a craftsperson demonstrating a particular Colonial skill, including weaving, woodworking, doll making, and potting.

  An orientation film, shown in the blockhouse, introduces visitors to the frontier life of 200 years ago. In the park's museum peruse a collection of Daniel Boone's possessions. Daniel Boone's original settlement was near Fort Boonesborough.

  Save some time to hike on the Boonesborough Historic Walking Trail, which passes fourteen sites detailing stories of early Kentucky settlers' rocky relations with local Indian tribes.

The park has a campground open year-round on the banks of the Kentucky River. It offers 167 sites, with electricity and water hookups, and a central service building that has showers, rest rooms, and laundry facilities. The fort's gift shop has a nice collection of Kentucky crafts, some of them made in the fort.

Special Events

For more information about these events, contact the Lexington Convention and Visitors Bureau at (859) 233-1221 or (800) 845-3959.

April. Rolex Kentucky Three-Day Event at Kentucky Horse Park. Keeneland Thoroughbred Racing, Keeneland Race Course.

July. Mid-America Miniature Horse Show, Kentucky Horse Park. Junior League Horse Show, the largest outdoor Saddlebred Horse show in America (859-252-1893).

August. Big Hill Mountain Bluegrass Festival (VanWinkle Farm, 7 miles from Berea; 800-598-2563). Picnic with the Pops, Kentucky Horse Park. Woodland Arts Fair (859-254-7024).

September. Grand Circle Meet at the Red Mile, the final leg of harness racing's Triple Crown, is held at Red Mile in late September or October.

October. Fall Classic Saddlebred Show, Kentucky Horse Park.

December. Southern Lights: Spectacular Sights on Holiday Nights at Kentucky Horse Park, late November to December 23, seven nights a week (800-678-8813). Christmas at Waveland, with costumed interpreters and holiday fare (859-272-3611).

Where to Stay

Kentucky Horse Park Campground, Kentucky Horse Park, 4089 Iron Works Pike, Lexington, Kentucky 40511; (859) 233-4303. This facility has 260 sites, each with electrical and water hookups and picnic tables. The resortlike amenities also include a swimming pool, tennis and basketball courts, plus a recreation center, playground, grocery, and laundromat. This facility is open year-round.

Rooms at the **Best Western Regency Lexington,** 2241 Elkhorn Road, Lexington (859-293-2202 or 800-528-1234), include free continental breakfast. The **Campbell House Inn,** 1375 Harrodsburg Road, Lexington (859-255-4281), is a 300-room hotel with seventy suites, tennis courts, and golf facilities. The **Radisson Plaza Lexington,** 369 West Vine

Street, Lexington (859-231-9000 or 800-333-3333), has an indoor pool and a restaurant.

WHERE TO EAT

For family dining and American cuisine Kentucky-style—including lamb chops, veal cutlets, salmon croquettes, and country ham—head to **Rogers Restaurant** at 808 South Broadway; (859) 254-1077. The daily specials at **Ramsey's Diner,** 496 East High Street (859-259-2708), sometimes include Cajun catfish and chicken dishes. Ramsey's other locations are 4053 Tates Creek Road (859-271-2638), 43910 Harrodsburg Road, and 1660 Bryan Stations Road (859-299-9669). For leg of lamb and country ham, try **Merrick Inn,** 3380 Tates Creek Road; (859) 269-5417. For pizza and Italian food, go to **Joe Bologna's,** 120 West Maxwell; (859) 252-4933. This Lexington longtime favorite is located in a renovated church. The **Parkette Drive-In,** 1216 New Circle Road, NE (859-254-8723), is a real fifties drive-in restaurant complete with carhops and mostly original 1952 decor. Your kids will feel as though they're on a movie set. Try the Kentucky Poor Boy, a double-decker cheeseburger.

FOR MORE INFORMATION

Contact the **Lexington Convention and Visitors Bureau,** 301 East Vine Street, Lexington (859-233-7299 or 800-845-3959), for more information on Lexington, Kentucky, www.visitlex.com.

Emergency Numbers

Ambulance, fire, and police: 911

Police department (nonemergency): (859) 258-3600

Fire department (nonemergency): (859) 254-1120

Emergency medical information, poison control, and twenty-four-hour pharmacy: Central Baptist Hospital, 1794 South Limestone (859-275-6100); Lexington Clinic Immediate Care Service First Choice Walk-In Clinic, 3061 Fieldstone Way, Suite 700 (Beaumont Center), 859-296-9900

Urgent Treatment Center, 1055 Dove Run Road (859-269-4668)

Pharmacy: Hutchinson's in Victorian Square, 401 West Main Street (859-252-3554)

NEW ORLEANS

N ew Orleans is a city of contrasts. A party place and the birthplace of jazz, this city is known for wild Mardi Gras celebrations and the lively nightlife of the French Quarter. Yet New Orleans is also a terrific family destination with great museums, a world-class aquarium and zoo, and historical sights—not to mention some of the best food around. A visit to this port city on the Mississippi—a mixture of eighteenth-century charm, Old South graciousness, and lively good times —makes for a memorable family vacation. Since summers are hot and steamy, the best times to visit are March and April and October and November. Avoid February—that's Mardi Gras time, when the city is too crowded and wild to be appreciated by kids.

GETTING THERE

New Orleans International Airport, U.S. 61 in Kenner, about 12 miles west of downtown (504–464–0831), is about a half-hour drive. The **Airport Shuttle** (504–592–0555) departs every ten minutes for major downtown hotels. Purchase tickets from the Airport Shuttle Information desks. Car rentals are available.

    Greyhound (504–524–7571 or 800–231–2222) and **Amtrak** (504–528–1610 or 800–USA–RAIL) are neighbors at 1001 Loyola Avenue.

GETTING AROUND

Much of New Orleans is best seen on foot; self-guided walking tour brochures are available from the Convention and Visitors Bureau. Public bus and streetcar service is provided by the **Regional Transit Authority** (RTA), 2817 Canal Street, (504) 248–3900. New Orleans is on a 5-mile land strip between the Mississippi River and Lake Pontchartrain. Because streets twist in this crescent-shaped city, locals usually give directions indicating riverside, lakeside, uptown (or upriver), and downtown (or downriver)—which is the location of both the Central Business District (CBD), where Canal Street meets the river, and the French Quarter.

New Orleans

AT A GLANCE

▶ Stroll the French Quarter: a place to walk, watch, listen, and eat

▶ Tour the Aquarium of the Americas, the Louisiana Nature Center, and the Audubon Park and Zoo

▶ Visit Jazzland Theme Park

▶ New Orleans Metropolitan Convention and Visitors Bureau: (504) 566-5033 or (800) 672-6124; www. neworleanscvb.com

Taxis are abundant, and usually you can hail one with little difficulty in the CBD and French Quarter. The Canal Street Ferry connects Canal Street with Algiers Point several times a day, offering great skyline views. Leave from the Canal Street and Jackson Avenue docks for the twelve-minute trip. Pedestrians ride free; cars are $1.00.

If you drive, downtown has short-term metered parking, but read the signs because towing is enforced.

WHAT TO SEE AND DO

The people, sights, and sounds (there's music everywhere) are what make a visit here unique. Here are some of the attractions your family won't want to miss.

The French Quarter

The French Quarter (*Vieux Carré*), considered the heart and soul of the city, is the site of New Orleans' original settlement. The approximately 90-block area is bordered by Canal on the west, Rampart on the north, Esplanade on the east, and the Mississippi River on the south. Besides family sites, the French Quarter also has many tawdry attractions. It might be wise to talk with your children ahead of time about what they may see as they walk along—scantily clad women dancing in bar entranceways, for instance. Nevertheless, there are family attractions in the French Quarter that your whole family will enjoy.

Visit **Preservation Hall,** 726 St. Peter Street; (504) 522-2841—day or 523-8939—night. It's a great way to introduce kids to the city's incomparable jazz. No alcohol or food is served. Seating is minimal. Be

Streetcars

Transfers from the 5-mile-long St. Charles Avenue Streetcar line to public buses are available. The 1920s era Riverfront Streetcars connect the cultural and commercial developments along the riverfront. A ride along St. Charles Avenue is an easy way to get the flavor of New Orleans. The streetcars take you through the **Garden District,** near the **Tulane** and **Loyola** campuses and to **Audubon Park.** Obtain a VisiTour Pass for unlimited rides on all buses and streetcars from hotels and shopping areas. RTA's RideGuide Map is available at their office or the New Orleans Welcome Center, 529 St. Ann Street; (504) 566-5031. The "Ladies in Red" streetcars operate along the riverfront. A $14 million expansion project is now underway that will eventually extend the line along the riverfront area and create a streetcar museum. The Canal Streetcar Line is expected to be running again by 2003.

prepared to wait in line outside the door for the evening shows. Doors open at 8:00 P.M., but get in line between 7:00 and 7:30 P.M.

Jackson Square, 700 Chartres, is a lively pedestrian mall, bordered by St. Ann, St. Peter, and Decatur Streets, in the heart of the Quarter. Along with an equestrian statue of General Andrew Jackson, you'll find mimes, portrait artists, tap dancers, and reggae musicians. Some of the city's most distinguished buildings are here, including the beautiful Spanish-style **St. Louis Cathedral,** Jackson Square (504-861-9521), where tours are given daily except Sundays. Two historic buildings are the **Presbytere,** 751 Chartres Street (504-568-6968), home of the Supreme Court during Spanish colonial times, and the **Cabildo,** built in 1795 as the Spanish Governor's Palace and site of the ratification of the Louisiana Purchase. Both are part of the **Louisiana State Museum** complex (504-568-6968 or 800-568-6968), which houses its valuable historical collections in these and several other buildings. The **Old U.S. Mint,** 400 Esplanade Avenue (504-568-8213), part of the State Museum Complex, is devoted to the history of jazz. Instruments once belonging to Louis Armstrong and other famous musicians plus a Mardi Gras exhibit are on display.

Musée Conti Wax Museum, 917 Conti Street; (504) 525-2605 or (800) 233-5405. Historical, costumed Louisiana figures, ranging from Napoleon to Louis Armstrong, are re-created in wax. Give this one a chance. Young kids may find the Haunted Dungeon scary, particularly the sound effects (shrieks and wails), although older kids will like the drama.

Mardi Gras

Mardi Gras (Fat Tuesday), the day before Lent, is the culmination of at least two weeks of elaborate parades, with the largest occurring the weekend before. All along the parade route the mostly costumed, mostly rowdy crowd lives it up. Unless your kids are lively, older teens, don't visit the city during Mardi Gras. Disorderly conduct is commonplace, madness is everywhere, the streets are crowded, and hotels up their prices.

A colorful Caribbean Reef exhibit at Aquarium of the Americas features a clear, 30-foot-long tunnel.

Zoos, Aquariums, and Nature Centers

Make a day of it visiting the **Audubon Park and Zoo,** the **Louisiana Nature Center,** and the **Aquarium of the Americas,** all run by the non-profit Audubon Institute (www.auduboninstitute.org). The aquarium is located on sixteen acres along the Mississippi River in the French Quarter. After a visit to the aquarium, hop aboard the *John James Audubon* riverboat, which travels back and forth several times a day between the aquarium and the uptown zoo; (504) 586-8777 or (800) 233-BOAT. No reservations are needed. Buy tickets and board in front of the aquarium. Call the Audubon Institute (504-861-2537) for information.

Aquarium of the Americas, 1 Canal Street (504-565-3033), is an outstanding facility that re-creates the Western hemisphere's saltwater and freshwater habitats. With the world's largest collection of sharks and jellies, it features tanks of eerily beautiful pulsating and floating creatures.

The lush and misty Amazon Rainforest exhibit has cascading waterfalls, rare orchids, colorful birds, and such exotic species as poison arrow frogs, red-bellied piranha, and giant anaconda. Visit Doc's Lab for some hands-on learning about sea snails, hermit crabs, and other invertebrates. Kids will be amazed at the tiny dwarf seahorses and chunky potbelly seahorses in the new Seahorse Gallery. Also new are two young sea otters named Buck and Emma. They're fun to watch, especially when they're playing in the waves crated by a waterfall that surges 900 gallons of water. An IMAX theater adds to the fun. Admission.

The adjacent **Woldenberg Riverfront Park** (also managed by the Audubon Institute) covers sixteen landscaped acres along a river bend between Toulouse and Canal Streets. Pick a shady spot under one of the many oak, magnolia, willow, and crape myrtle trees, and watch the ships, tugboats, and paddlewheelers on the Mississippi. Call (504) 861-2537.

The **Audubon Zoo** is at 6500 Magazine Park, just south of Audubon Park, which borders the Mississippi between Exposition Boulevard, Walnut Street, and St. Charles Avenue. Acclaimed as one of the top zoos in the country, this facility displays animals in re-created natural habitats. Along with presenting animals the exhibit uses crab traps, antique boats, and other artifacts to show how the Cajuns used the land.

At the **Komodo Dragon** exhibit, two 10-foot-long lizards, the world's largest, enthrall visitors. The glass enclosure lets you get nose to nose (if the lizard's willing) to these prehistoric-looking critters. Jaguars rule at the Maya-themed **Jaguar Jungle,** a one-and-a-half-acre themed exhibit that recreates a Central American rain forest, complete with simulated Mayan ruins like those found at Copan and Chichan Itza. In 2000 two young white tiger brothers, each weighing more than 250 pounds, took up residence here.

For younger children there's a petting zoo, and everyone enjoys the live animal demonstrations. Check the day's schedule when you arrive. The zoo entrance is in the process of being refurbished; a large clock has been installed over the new front gate. Note the animal faces that appear on the hour. Costumed characters to greet visitors are among the improvements expected to be completed by spring 2001. Admission.

The **Louisiana Nature Center,** 11000 Lake Forest Boulevard, in Joe Brown Memorial Park (eastern New Orleans); (504) 246-5672. This eighty-six-acre wildlife preserve comes complete with nature trails, the Discovery Loft, hands-on teaching stations, the Nature Center Planetarium with an IMAX theater, a hands-on museum, and a greenhouse. Kids can try on a giant turtle shell for size, watch a laser beam show set to music, and follow nature trails through wetlands and forests. Check out a Discovery Kit and take a walk around the preserve. Each kit has binoculars, magnifying glasses, field guides, and an activity guide. In the summer the planetarium has several shows throughout the day and Laser Rock Concerts Friday and Saturday nights.

Open Spaces
City Park, 1 Palm Drive, at the city's northern edges (504-482-4888; www.neworleans.com/citypark), is on 1,500 acres dotted with majestic oaks draped with Spanish moss. Here you'll find tennis courts; picnic tables; four golf courses; a miniature train ride; 8 miles of lagoons with ducks, geese, pedalboat rentals; a Botanical Garden; and Storyland, a

fairy-tale-themed amusement area complete with nineteenth-century carousel and two miniature trains. (If you come during the humid summer, bring bug repellent!)

Jean Lafitte National Historical Park and Preserve (504–589–3882; www.npa.gov/jela) comprises several units throughout the city and the surrounding area. All offer ranger-led programs, tours, and exhibits. The **French Quarter Unit,** 916 North Peters (504–589-2636), has a daily (free) ranger-led French Quarter Walking Tour at 10:30 A.M. Tickets are handed out beginning at 9:00 A.M. and, especially in the summer, it's a good idea to get there early, as tickets can go fast. While waiting for the tour to begin, you can look at the exhibits on local history and culture, or you can come back at 3:00 P.M. for a daily talk given on those topics.

The **Chalmette Unit,** 8606 West St. Bernard Highway (6 miles from the French Quarter); (504) 281-0510. Take a 1½-mile self-guided tour along a road linking key positions on the field where the 1815 Battle of New Orleans took place. General Andrew Jackson and his troops triumphed over the British, thus ensuring America's claim to the Louisiana Territory. Exhibits and an audiovisual program in the visitor's center explain the city's role in the War of 1812. Daily talks are given by rangers at 11:15 A.M. and 2:45 P.M. on the battle and its impact on the city, and there is a twenty-five-minute video that is run continuously. In the fall living history demonstrations are held periodically, and there is a commemoration of the battle the weekend nearest its anniversary of January 8.

New Orleans by Ship

Anchor a New Orleans visit to a cruise. Passenger ships departing from the city include:

- **Delta Queen Steamboat Co.**'s *Delta Queen, Mississippi Queen,* and *American Queen:* (800) 543-1949); www.deltaqueen.com.
- **Carnival Cruise Lines:** (305) 599-2000 or (800) 327-7276; www.carnival.com.
- **American Canadian Caribbean Line**'s *Niagara Prince:* (800) 556-7450; www.accl-smallships.com.
- **RiverBarge Excursion Lines, Inc.**'s *R/B River Explorer:* (888) GO-BARGE; www.riverbarge.com.

The **Barataria Unit,** 7400 Highway 45, Marrero (504–589-2330), 15 miles south of town, preserves 20,000 acres of marshes and bayous. This is a good place to show your kids this part of Louisiana's landscape. You can rent a canoe by calling (504) 689-3271. Tell them when you'll be at the Visitor Center and how long you want to keep the canoe. They'll drop it off and pick it up for you. You can paddle along 20 miles of waterways through cypress swamp. Watch a film that introduces visitors to life in south Louisiana; then set out on a nature trail to see the wetlands creatures: alligators, egrets, and ibis among them. In spring, native wild irises bloom.

Saxophone solos, Cajun dancing, and crawfish dishes spice up **Jazzland Theme Park,** 12301 Lake Forest Boulevard (504–253-8100; www.jazzlandthemepark.com), which opened in May 2000. To the

Special Tours

- **Mule-drawn carriage rides.** Kids like these slow-paced, if pricey, rides through the French Quarter. Royal Carriages Inc., 1824 North Rampart Street; (504) 943-8820.
- **Kids Only City Tours.** Dependable Kid Care, 702 North Carrollton Avenue (504-486-4001 or 800-862-5806; www.dependablekidcare.com), creates customized kids' tours of the city and offers hotel child care.
- **Black Heritage.** Le Ob's Tours and Transportation Service, 4635 Touro Street (504-288-3478 or 800-827-0932), offers family, group, and children's tours of African-American heritage sites.
- **Cemetery, Ghost, Voodoo, and Vampire Tours.** Built above ground because of the high water table, the cemeteries are tourist attractions. These tours interest older children who don't mind walking for one and a half to two hours.
- On the **New Orleans Historic Voodoo Museum**'s tour, visit the grave of voodoo queen Marie Laveau at St. Louis Cemetery #1 and learn about the French Quarter's haunted houses. The museum's Tour of the Undead adds a visit to a voodoo temple. Contact the museum, 724 Rue Domaine; (504) 523-7685; www.voodoomuseum.com.
- **Magic Walking Tours** (504-588-9693) feature the cemetery and ghosts and add some vampire haunts.
- **River rides.** A relaxing narrated cruise offers history and scenic views. The *Steamboat Natchez,* 2 Canal Street, #1300, offers two-hour harbor cruises and evening jazz, dinner, and dancing cruises; (504) 586-8777 or (800) 233-BOAT; www.steamboatnatchez.com. The *Cajun Queen* riverboat and the *Creole Queen* paddlewheeler depart from the Poydras Street Wharf; (504) 529-4567 or (800) 445-4109; www.bigeasy.com.

formula of thrill rides, funnel cakes, and hot dogs, this 140-acre park adds a New Orleans sizzle of Mardi Gras–like parades, faux French Quarter architecture, and multiple stages for good-time music. Try such regional delights as seafood gumbo, jambalaya, and po'boys to the background riff of classical jazz standards. For younger children there's Kids' Carnival, where they can fly their own planes and ride on a Ferris wheel.

Museums

Enter the **Louisiana Children's Museum,** 420 Julia Street (504-523-1357; www.lcm.org), through the bright, blue doors. Inside this former 1860s warehouse are 45,000 square feet of hands-on exhibits. In the largest space the Lab, a math and science center geared for gradeschoolers, kids solve math problems to open a combination safe, hoist themselves up a wall using a 500-pound lever, and find out, by throwing balls, how radar detects speed. In the summer of 2001, the Lab will have a new exhibit called "Healthy Life Choices" that will make learning about healthy lifestyles fun and interesting. In Body Works kids test their flexibility, arm strength, and climbing skills on a Rock Wall. At the television studio kids can star as anchors. With Challenges, kids can shoot baskets from a wheelchair and try reading in Braille to better understand the everyday lives of persons with disabilities. In the Art Trek studio, open daily, kids can participate in fifteen-minute art projects that are based on a different theme every week. In March every year the museum hosts the Children's World's Fair. Admission.

The **New Orleans Museum of Art,** Lelong Drive (504-488-2631; www.noma.org), in the southern section of City Park, has painting, sculpture, photographs, and decorative pieces relating to Western civilization from the pre-Christian era to the present. Among the items with kid appeal: the bejeweled imperial eggs of Peter Carl Fabergé, Mayan artifacts in the Art of the Americas collection, and the Impressionist works of Edgar Degas. Sign up for a Sunday afternoon art workshop, where children ages five to twelve (accompanied by a parent or parents) can let loose their creativity and learn about art. Call (504) 488-2631, extension 639 for more information. Admission.

Scheduled to open in September 2001, the **Ogden Museum of Southern Art,** 615 Howard Avenue (504-539-9600), will showcase southern painting, prints, sculpture, and textiles from the 1800s to modern times. For kids who only know about D-Day from *Saving Private Ryan,* the **National D-Day Museum,** 945 Magazine Street (504-527-6012 or 877-813-3329; www.ddaymuseum.org) makes the gritty history of the great invasion come to life. In the Beaches Gallery, the heart of the museum, kids can learn how the Americans and British struggled to take the beaches at Normandy. The oral histories of paratroopers, and those of the women at home who became "Rosie the Riveters" in the factories, bring home even more strongly what it must have been like for the men and women who lived through World War II.

Theater, Music, and the Arts

For information on cultural events, see the entertainment sections of the morning and evening newspapers, *Times-Picayune* and *States-Item,* as well as tourist publications such as *Where* and *This Week in New Orleans,* available around town and at hotels. Ticketmaster (504-522-5555) supplies tickets for most events.

Among the theater troupes: **Le Petit Théâtre Du Vieux Carré,** 616 St. Peter Street (504-522-9958), has a Children's Corner with humorous and traditional plays from October through May. Musical comedies and dramas are also performed here in the city's oldest theater, built in 1797. **The Saenger Theatre,** Rampart at Canal (504-525-1052; www.saengertheatre.com), features touring Broadway shows and pop and rock shows.

Theatre of Performing Arts, North Rampart near corner of Dumaine (504-529-2278), is home to the city's opera and ballet companies. **Louisiana Philharmonic** (504-523-6530) performs at several locations, including the Orpheum Theater, 129 University Place; call for schedule.

Spectator Sports

The NFL **Saints** play at the Superdome, 5800 Airline Highway, Metairie (504-733-0255; www.nfl.com/saints), from August to December. Site of the Sugar Bowl, this stadium is one of the largest buildings in the world, spanning more than fifty-two acres and standing twenty-five stories high. Tours are offered several times daily, except when events are in progress. Website: www.saints.nfl.com.

The **New Orleans Zephyrs,** an AAA farm team of the Houston Astros, play ball at their new Zephyr Stadium, 6000 Airline Highway, Metairie; call (504) 734-5155; www.zephyrbaseball.com. The **New Orleans Brass,** a minor league hockey team, plays at the New Orleans Municipal Auditorium; call (504) 522-7825. The **New Orleans Sports** has a capacity of 20,000; It's located on Girod Street across from the Superdome. In 2002 New Orleans will host the Super Bowl.

Shopping

Canal Street is the center of a downtown shopping thoroughfare that is highlighted by **Canal Place,** 333 Canal Street (504-522-9200), with some fifty upscale shops such as Gucci, Saks, and Brooks Brothers. **Riverwalk Marketplace,** (504-522-1555; www.riverwalkmarketplace.com) between Canal and Poydras Streets, features some one hundred forty shops (including the Disney and Warner Bros. stores) and seventeen eateries along the Mississippi on the site of the 1984 World's Fair.

Antiques hunters venture down to Royal and Chartres Streets in the French Quarter to seek out remnants of the Old (and wealthy) South. In the arcades of the over 250-year-old **French Market,** (504-522-2621, www.frenchmarket.org) along Decatur Street, you'll find a variety of shops, open-air produce stands, and casual restaurants. **Jax Brewery,** 600-610 Decatur Street, across from Jackson Square (504-566-7245), has more than fifty specialty shops and restaurants. **Magazine Street** has 6 miles of boutique and antiques stores. Browse or go in style with the Windsor Court Hotel's three-hour, chauffeur-driven tour. Call (504) 897-3111; www.magazinestreet.com.

SIDE TRIPS

- The saltwater **Lake Pontchartrain,** north of town, measures 40 by 25 miles and is a popular place for water sports and sunning on the many beaches. (The water is too murky for swimming.) If you have the time, take a scenic ride over the Lake Pontchartrain Causeway, a toll road that consists of two separate, parallel 24-mile highways that connect the lake's two shores: It's the longest highway bridge in the world.

- Several area companies offer tours through the Louisiana swamplands, where visitors can observe fascinating plant and animal life. **Gray Line** (504-569-1401 or 888-802-9628; www.GrayLineNewOrleans.com) has a combination Swamp/Plantation Tour that includes marshes, swamps, and bayous and a visit to the Oak Alley Plantation, famous for its ¼-mile alley of 250-year-old oak trees.

  Cypress Swamp Tours, 501 Laroussini Street, Westwego (504-581-4501 or 800-633-0503; www.cypressswamptour.com), offers a variety of tours. Sunset in the Swamp, an evening boat ride through wooded marshes, is a good bet for preteens who like "spooky" settings. The company also has a Cajun and Plantation Stories Excursion, but at seven and a half hours, it's most likely too long for many children. If you want to zip above the marsh, try **Airboat Tours,** Bayou Gauche at Des Allemands; (504) 758-2365 or (800) 975-9345; www.airboattours. com. These lightweight, but noisy, boats zip along at 50 miles per hour, making their own trails through the dense grassy areas. You're likely to see great blue herons and alligators. The captain gives you earplugs to wear.

- A visit to a sugar cane plantation can be interesting history, revealing the genteel past of the Old South's privileged classes and the harsh realities of slavery. The closest to the city (22 miles away) is **Destrahan Plantation,** 13034 River Road, Destrahan (504-764-9315), the lower Mississippi Valley's oldest plantation house, built in 1787.

  The most impressive is **Oak Alley Plantation,** 3645 Louisiana Highway 18, Vacherie (60 miles from New Orleans, on the river's west bank); (504) 265-2151 or (800) 442-5539; www.oakalleyplantation. com. The Greek Revival–style mansion has twenty-eight white columns and, outside, twenty-eight oak trees, whose branches form an arch over the wide drive to the mansion's entrance. There's a restaurant on site.

SPECIAL EVENTS

Contact the Convention and Visitors Bureau at (504) 566-5003 for more information on the following events.

January. Sugar Bowl around New Year's Day at the Superdome.

February–March. Masquerade balls, parades, and festive music of Mardi Gras.

March. Crescent City Classic 10,000-meter race beginning at Jackson Square. Black Heritage Festival. Children's World's Fair, Louisiana Children's Museum.

April. Crescent City Classic Jr. race for ages four to twelve at East Jefferson Stadium.

April–May. New Orleans Jazz and Heritage Festival at the Fairgrounds, ten-day event. Zoo-To-Do at Audubon Zoo features live entertainment, face painters, and a petting zoo.

November–January. City Park's Celebration in the Oaks includes caroling and decorations.

WHERE TO STAY

The CVB publishes a lodging guide that indicates which hotels provide babysitting referrals. Rates are higher during Mardi Gras, the Jazz Festival, and Sugar Bowl, when it's wise to reserve up to a year in advance.

Because New Orleans hotels are pricey, bed and breakfasts are a good alternative. Call **Bed and Breakfast Inc.,** 1021 Moss Street; (504) 488-4640 or (800) 749-4640; www.historiclodging.com. This reservation service books rooms and suites in various neighborhoods; some inns welcome children. Although the French Quarter is fine for exploring, families with young kids probably are better off elsewhere: either uptown or in the city's Garden District (around St. Charles Avenue, with charming nineteenth-century homes), where the atmosphere is less intense. A good bet in the Garden District is **The Avenue Plaza Hotel and Pro Spa,** 2111 St. Charles Avenue; (800) 535-9575 or (504) 566-1212. For families seeking extra space, the junior and one-bedroom suites are good deals.

If you desire to stay in the French Quarter, however, choose a lodging in the quieter part, such as the **Chateau Hotel,** 1001 Chartres Street; (504) 524-9636 or (800) 828-1822. The property has reasonable prices, free garage, pool, and a coffee shop. Ask for a room overlooking the courtyard.

For a big splurge try one of the following. **The Pontchartrain Hotel,** 2031 St. Charles Avenue, near downtown; (504) 524-0581 or (800) 777-6193; www.pontchartrainhotel.com. It offers one hundred charming rooms and free cribs. **Windsor Court,** 300 Gravier Street (504-523-6000 or 800-262-2662; www.windsorcourthotel.com), is a 5-diamond property with rooms and suites, some with kitchenettes.

Hyatt Regency New Orleans, 500 Poydras Plaza; (504-561-1234 or 800-233-1234; www.hyatt.com). The Hyatt is connected to the New Orleans Centre mall. The hotel is big, with 1,200 rooms, and has a heated outdoor pool. Camp Hyatt kids' menus are available. The **Hampton Inn Downtown/French Quarter Area,** 226 Carondelet Street (504-529-9990 or 800-HAMPTON; www.neworleans.com/hampton), includes complimentary continental breakfast. The **Hotel Inter-Continental,** 444 St. Charles Avenue (504-525-5566, or 800-445-6563; www.inter-conti.com), offers the chain's Kids-in-Tow program. Aimed at children along on a business trip but available to all kids, the program gives kids a backpack with goodies and a kid-friendly list of attractions.

Comfort Suites, 346 Baronne Street (504-524-1140 or 800-524-1140), is an all-suite property where rooms have microwaves, refrigerators and coffeemakers. **Embassy Suites,** 315 Julia Street (504-525-1993 or 800-362-2779; www.embassy-suites.com), offers a free hot breakfast.

WHERE TO EAT

Restaurants are featured in the tabloid section of the Friday *Times-Picayune.* Louisiana cooking is a combination of the delicate Creole (French, Spanish, and African), with its subtle seasonings, and Cajun (Acadian), known for its hearty spices: hot peppers, sausage, and brown sauce. Adventurous eaters will discover some delicious dishes, and even fussy kids will usually find something on the menu to suit their tastebuds.

Ralph and Kacoos Seafood Restaurant, 519 Toulouse Street (and several suburban locations); (504) 522-5226. This place is known for its Cajun dishes, such as charcoal-broiled redfish, shrimp, crawfish, and large crab. No reservations at this popular, casual spot, so you might have to wait. **The Gumbo Shop,** 630 St. Peter Street (504-899-2460), serves Creole cuisine, including gumbo (a thick, spicy soup made with seafood, poultry, or sausage). Enjoy lunch or dinner in this casual atmosphere.

Café du Monde, 813 Decatur Street (also at Esplanade Mall, Lakeside Mall, and New Orleans Centre); (504) 587-0833. Home of beignets and café au lait, the French Market location is open twenty-four hours.

Mother's, 401 Poydras Street; (504) 523-9656. This restaurant is noted for its yummy po-boys and Creole dishes, including red beans and rice with sausage. It serves three meals daily, but expect long lines at lunch.

Two longtime New Orleans noteworthy—and expensive—restaurants are **Brennan's,** 417 Royal Street (504-525-9713), and **Commander's Palace,** 1403 Washington Avenue (504-899-8221). Older children and teens might appreciate these places. Commander's Palace, with its gardens, fountains, and courtyards, has a romantic feel. Dinner is expensive, so if you want to sample the flair and the food, try the fixed-price lunch.

Other restaurants to try include **Bubba Gump Shrimp Co.,** 429 Decatur Street (504) 522-5800; **Johnny's Po Boys,** 511 St. Louis Street, (504) 524-8129; **Central Grocery Store,** 923 Decatur Street (504) 523-1620; and **Camelia Grill,** 626 South Carrollton (504) 861-9573.

FOR MORE INFORMATION

New Orleans Metropolitan Convention & Visitors Bureau, Inc., 1520 Sugar Bowl Drive (504-566-5003 or 800-672-6124), has helpful literature. *The Big Easy For Families,* a handy guide for families, is available from them for $5.00, including shipping and handling. A **Welcome Visitor Center** at 529 St. Ann Street (504-566-5031) is open seven days. Pick up the brochure *99 Things for Kids.*

Emergency Numbers

Ambulance, fire, police: 911

Non-emergency police: (504) 821-2222

Non-emergency fire: (504) 581-3473

Hospitals with twenty-four-hour emergency rooms include Tulane University Medical Center, 1415 Tulane Avenue (504) 588-3096; and Touro Infirmary, 1401 Foucher Street (504) 897-8663

Poison Control: (800) 256-9822—Louisiana

Pharmacy: Walgreen's Pharmacy, 1429 St. Charles Avenue; (504) 561-8332, open until 11:00 P.M.

ASHEVILLE AND THE SURROUNDING REGION

While the Great Smoky Mountains National Park is the most-visited national park in the United States, nearby Madison County and Jackson County, bordered by the Great Smoky Mountains, the Balsam Mountains, and the Blue Ridge Mountains, may be North Carolina's best-kept secret. Centered around Sylva, Jackson County is 45 miles west of Asheville. Nearby Madison County calls itself "the Jewel of the Blue Ridge." Charles Frazier wrote about this scenic area in his novel *Cold Mountain*. Both counties and the other areas surrounding Asheville encompass lush mountains, valleys, and crystal-blue lakes.

GETTING THERE

Asheville Regional Airport, located 65 miles to the east of the Great Smoky Mountains (and fifteen minutes from Asheville), is served by US Airways, COMAIR, and ASA. Car rentals are available at the airport.

Asheville is accessible by **Greyhound** bus. The station is located at 2 Tunnel Road, Asheville; (828) 253-5353.

GETTING AROUND

A car is a must. If arriving by plane, rent a car at the Asheville Airport.

WHAT TO SEE AND DO

Situated in a valley surrounded by mountain peaks, Asheville has a natural beauty. Three mountain chains—the Great Smoky Mountains, the Blue Ridge Mountains, and the Black Mountains—dominate the countryside around Asheville. Asheville makes a great base for an array of outdoor activities, including white-water rafting, horseback riding, and hiking. The countryside surrounding Asheville is also home to numerous high-quality craftspeople. Visit studios and galleries offering quality blown

Asheville and the Surrounding Region

AT A GLANCE

▶ Tour Biltmore Estate, 250-room mansion set on 8,000 acres of gardens and farmland

▶ Enjoy panoramic views and kid-friendly hikes at Chimney Rock Park

▶ Go white-water rafting, hiking, canoeing, and mountain biking

▶ Asheville Convention and Visitors Bureau, (800) 257-1300; www.ashevillechamber.org

▶ Jackson County Chamber of Commerce, (800) 962-1911 or (828) 586-2155; www.mountainlovers.com

glass, pottery, quilts, handcrafted tables, beds, rockers, and other furniture as well as a variety of other craft items.

The Biltmore Estate

The number-one attraction in town is the **Biltmore Estate,** off Biltmore Avenue; (828) 274-6333 or (800) 295-4730; www.biltmore.com. Built in 1895 by George W. Vanderbilt, this 250-room mansion was modeled after a sixteenth century French château with a winery, stables converted to gift shops, a restaurant, and acres of beautiful gardens.

The **mansion** is furnished with fine antiques and art. For Vanderbilt, after all, money was no object. Truly one of America's great houses, Biltmore is beautiful, but for families, it comes with a big "beware." The mansion is best toured by teens and older (adult) children who like period furnishings and fancy look-but-don't-touch houses. To tour the property you move on your own along a more or less designated path, viewing rooms such as the impressive banquet hall, the music room, the library, and Mrs. Vanderbilt's bedroom.

Keep young kids entertained outside on the grounds (or have one adult take young kids to play at **Pack Place Education, Arts and Science Center,** while another adult and older teens visit Biltmore).

The Biltmore mansion is usually crowded. Given all the people and the roped-off rooms, young kids who aren't held will be at butt-eye-level most of the time. Stairs make it impractical to use a stroller, and the elevators are sometimes difficult to get to.

The **Stable Cafe** offers reasonably priced meals. If you eat lunch here, try to get in line early (before 11:30 A.M.) and request a table located in one of the former horse stalls. The Stables contain a **toy shop** with lots of Victorian dolls, a **Christmas Shop** and other gift shops. **Deerpark Restaurant** (open 11:00 A.M.–3:00 P.M. from late March to early January) has a luncheon buffet, and children nine and under eat free when accompanied by an adult.

Set on 8,000 acres (the estate once had 125,000), the **formal gardens,** designed by Frederick Law Olmsted of New York Central Park fame, are impressive. For kids the gardens are the best part. In late April and early May, the gardens are especially beautiful as the hundreds of azalea bushes are in bloom.

Museums

The downtown complex off Pack Square, **Pack Place Education, Arts and Science Center,** 2 South Pack Square (828-257-4500; www.main. nc.us/packplace), houses several museums, including Health Adventure, the Asheville Art Museum, and the Colburn Mineral Museum. **The Health Adventure,** (828-254-6373 or 800-935-0204; www.health-adventure. com) a small hands-on kids' museum for pre-schoolers and young kids, is a good rainy-day stop. Kids pedal an energy cycle, press buttons to light up parts of a plastic brain, and take a safety quiz on driving. Kids under age eight have their own Creative PlaySpace. Each of the eleven galleries contains hands-on activities for kids and informational exhibits for adults. Terrific Thursday is a weekly summer program that gives kids a chance to paint with mud, make daisy chains, and learn how to do bark rubbings. Although small, the **Asheville Art Museum** (828-253-3227; www.ashevilleart.org) is a pleasant stop, focusing on American art from 1866 to the present with rotating exhibits of artists such as Edward Hopper and Georgia O'Keeffe. If your kids like gems and minerals, the **Colburn Gem and Mineral Museum** (828-254-7162; www.main.nc.us/colburn) is a nice surprise. After all, North Carolina is called the "gem state." Eye-poppers include a 229-carat blue topaz and masses of glittering calcite crystals and sparkly purple quartz amethyst. The Grove Stone Earth Center, a new hands-on gallery, explores volcanoes and earthquakes and has a large-scale model of a volcano and one of the Earth. Pack Place also has **Adventure Place,** a shop with a nice collection of puppets and other hands-on kid toys. Admission.

More Asheville Attractions

The **Thomas Wolfe Memorial,** 52 North Market Street (828-253-8304), is the childhood home and the reputed boardinghouse this novelist described in *Look Homeward, Angel.* The home is currently being restored

Chimney Rock, a 1,200-foot-tall natural rock ledge, provides a panoramic view of the surrounding countryside.

Chimney Rock Park

Take your kids to **Chimney Rock Park,** Chimney Rock, N.C. (828–625-9611 or 800-277-9611; www.chimneyrockpark.com), a 1,000-acre park in the Blue Ridge foothills, about 25 miles southeast of Asheville. Trail blazers will love the challenge and the views, and little ones will like the twenty-six-story elevator that gets them to the top. To get to the elevator, you must go through a 198-foot tunnel blasted through rock, a memorable walk for most kids. The park's highlight is Chimney Rock, a 1,200-foot-tall natural rock ledge that provides a panoramic view of the lush, surrounding countryside.

Hickory Nut Falls, a 404-foot waterfall, is a good reward for a walk in the woods. Bring a snack (and lots of water). Two picnic tables at the fall's base are a favorite picnic area. Hearty hikers might try the Skyline-Cliff Trail Loop, which ascends to the top of the falls and comes down along the Cliff Trail. The Forest Stroll, a route for moderate climbers, is a one-half hour, slightly uphill walk to the lower waterfall (and one-half hour back). With young children take the Woodland Walk, a half-mile (one mile round trip) level path that leads to a waterfall.

The Four Seasons Trail is the park's newest, covering ⅜-mile. It will remain open all year long and can be hiked during the winter months. This new trail provides a route from the Meadows to the top of the mountain without having to drive.

Kiddie backpacks are available for rental at the ticket office; self-guided trail brochures are detailed, telling you where to stop and what trees and natural formations you're looking at. A cafeteria located at the top serves meals and snacks.

Hands-on craft workshops are available throughout the year (call for schedule or check the Web site), as are guided nature walks.

The Old Rock Café, just outside the entrance to the park on Highway 64/74-A (828–625-2329), offers sandwiches, snacks, and souvenirs. Picnic tables are outside.

following a fire, but the Visitor Center is open and has an audiovisual presentation on Wolfe. There's also an exterior walking tour of the property. Admission.

The **Zebulon B. Vance Birthplace State Historic Site,** 911 Reams Creek Road, Weaverville (828-645-6706, www.ah.dcr.state.nc.us/sections/hs/vance/vance.htm) is the reconstructed 1830s mountain farmstead home of North Carolina's Civil War governor. In the Visitor Center you'll find exhibits of traditional southern Appalachian crafts. In April and

The Surrounding Region

JACKSON COUNTY

- **Hiking.** The Jackson County Chamber of Commerce, 18 North Central Street, Sylva (828–586–2155 or 800–962–1911; www.mountainlovers.com), is a good source of hiking trail information. Ask about directions to several family-friendly hikes and to waterfalls.

- **White-water Rafting.** Enjoy a ride on the county's two rivers, the Tuckaseegee and the Chattooga, where the trips range from a mellow float trip on class I waters to an exhilarating class III white-water journey.

  Blue Ridge Outing Company, U.S. 74/441 between Dillsboro and Cherokee (800–572–3510; www.raftwithkids.com), offers a white-water rafting trip specifically for families with children twelve and under, plus flat-water rafting and tubing trips. Tuckaseegee Outfitters, Highway 441 and 74 near Dillsboro (828–586–5050), will equip you and your family (children must weigh at least forty pounds) for all sorts of river adventures including rafting, tubing, and canoeing. Bring old sneakers, towels, and a change of clothes.

MADISON COUNTY

- **White-water Rafting.** Enthusiasts take to the French Broad River. The French Broad Rafting Company, 376 Walnut Drive, Marshall; (800) 570–RAFT; www.frenchbroadrafting.com offers half-day or full-day trips, with an experienced guide in every raft.

- **Horseback Riding.** Check out the terrain by horse with Arrowmont Stable, Cullowhee Mountain Road, Cullowhee; (828) 743–2762. A forty-minute drive from Sylva, Arrowmont offers 6 miles of trails. Take a day trip and ride up to Trout Lake for fishing, swimming, and an evening campfire.

- **Skiing.** Sapphire Valley Resort, Cashiers; (828) 743–5022 or (800) 533–8368 for the rental management company. Snowmaking makes the cozy Sapphire Valley Resort, with four slopes and a vertical drop of 425 feet, a good beginners' mountain. The resort offers kids' programs and lessons.

September there are Spring and Fall Pioneer Living Days, with demonstrations of how people lived and worked in the mid- to late 1800s.

At the **Cradle of Forestry,** 1002 Pisgah Highway, Pisgah National Forest (828-877-3130 or 800-660-0671; www.cradleofforestry.com) kids can see old logging equipment, visit historic cabins, see craftspeople at work, and try their hand at making their own crafts. Open April to early Novem-

ber. **Sliding Rock,** a natural water slide crowded with kids in the summer, is located nearby on Highway 276.
The Botanical Gardens at Asheville, 151 W.T. Weaver Boulevard; (828) 252-5190. Take a Sunday stroll through the ten acres planted with trees, flowers, and plants, native to the Appalachian Mountains.

Outdoor Specialists

The **Nantahala Outdoor Center** takes neophyte outdoor families and teaches them mountain biking, canoeing, and kayaking. With your new-found skills, sign on for an outdoor trip with Nantahala experts and others. The package includes rental of bikes, helmets, and a guide so that you'll feel safe on the trail. Classes are offered to adults, women only, and to kids. Families can opt for private group lessons or can sign their kids up for a class and take an adult class at the same time.

Paddling is truly the Nantahala Outdoor Center's forte. For kayakers, the two- to seven-day classes are open to ages sixteen and older and private instruction is available for ages ten and older. In summer the center offers special classes for ages ten to sixteen. Two five-day canoeing classes are offered for ages sixteen and older, and private instruction is available to kids age five and older.

Nantahala Outdoor Center leads kayak and canoe trips in North Carolina and Georgia. Nantahala Outdoor Center, 13077 U.S. 19 West, Bryson City; (828) 488-2175 or (888) 662-1662; www.noc.com.

Southern Safaris aims to put together a North Carolina outdoor experience modeled after, says owner Bart Ely, an African safari. Instead of wildlife viewing you'll be hiking, biking, rafting, fishing, horseback riding, and llama trekking. You'll participate in these and other outdoor adventures during the day and come back to your base camp at night. There you'll gather around the campfire and listen to dulcimer playing or folktales before sleeping in your platform tent (solar showers and toilets outside). As the day-trip adventures are subcontracted to local outfitters, you could arrange these yourself. But what Ely is selling is not only the convenience of an all-inclusive package, but what he calls " the total experience of upscale camping." Food is provided by local caterers. Prices vary depending on your wishes as Ely customizes the tours. Half- and full-day excursions, with a catered lunch, are available. A second camp offers some activities for kids. Southern Safari, P.O. Box 8237, Asheville; (800) 454-SFRI or (828) 626-3400; www.southernsafari.com.

Other Area Attractions and Scenic Drives

The **Northwest Trading Post,** Milepost (MP) 258.6 on the **Blue Ridge Parkway,** features crafts by artisans from eleven counties in North Carolina. Trails from E. B. Jeffress Park, MP 272, lead to an old frontier cabin

Special Tours

- **Great Smoky Mountains Railway,** 119 Front Street, Dillsboro Depot, Dillsboro; (828) 586-8811 or (800) 872-4681; www.gsmr.com. Take an enchanted ride through tunnels, river gorges, and across mountains aboard a brightly colored 1942 train.

    The Tuckaseegee River Excursion follows the river on a three-and-a-half-hour route from Dillsboro to Bryson City. You'll travel through an 836-foot-long tunnel and see for yourself whether or not it's haunted by the nineteen convict laborers who died while digging it with a pickax.

    The Nantahala Gorge excursion leaves from Bryson City for a four-and-a-half-hour trip along Fontana Lake that allows for a one-hour stop in the gorge. The all-day "Raft 'n' Rail" package travels to the gorge, where you join a raft trip down the Nantahala River.

    Murder Mystery outings, dinner trains, and the Santa Express are also available. Call ahead for schedules and reservations.

- **Avalon Llama Treks.** Hike the Blue Ridge Mountains with a llama by your side. Located in Swannanoa, N.C.; call (828) 299-7155 for details.

and a church. At Moses Cone Park, MP 292 to 295, is the **Folk Art Center,** MP 382 (828-298-7928; www.southernhighlandguild.org), home of the **Southern Highland Craft Guild.** The Center showcases traditional and contemporary southern Appalachian crafts and houses the Guild's Allanstand Craft Shop, two galleries with changing exhibitions, a craft library, and a 270-seat auditorium. From April through December, craftspeople demonstrate their work, and from May to December there are special events featuring potters, fiber artists, woodturners, woodcarvers, and more. The guild's annual Holiday Celebration in December has a Childrens Handmade Holiday Festival where kids can "make and take" holiday crafts.

Mountain Heritage Center, Western Carolina University, located off highway 107 between Sylva and Cashiers, N.C., in Cullowhee; (828) 227-7129. Appreciate the history of Appalachian mountain life through exhibits on the Scotch-Irish migration to the region.

For a sample of the area's mining heritage, visit the **Museum of North Carolina,** Spruce Pine, near MP 331, Blue Ridge Parkway, and visit a mine in Emerald Village near MP 334. The Blue Ridge Parkway intersects Route 441, which leads to the Oconaluftee Visitors Center, Great Smoky Mountains National Park.

Kids and adventurous adults will love walking across the **Mile High Swinging Bridge** (elevation 5,320 feet) at **Grandfather Mountain,** Linville (828-733-2013; www.grandfather-mountain.com), the highest peak in the Blue Ridge. The bridge, built in 1952 and refurbished in 1999, continues to be one of the Blue Ridge's most popular attractions. At Grandfather Mountain you can also visit the nature museum and see original movies about the mountain.

Shopping

Western North Carolina shelters some of America's best craftspeople. Born of the mountain handmade tradition, many of these craftspeople are artists, producing first-rate work.

A brochure and a detailed guide, the *Craft Heritage Trails of Western North Carolina,* lead you to artists in twenty-one mountain counties. Browse through galleries and studios that sell carefully crafted furniture, jewelry, pottery, quilts, woven rugs, hand-blown goblets, carved bowls, and much more. Look up **HandMade In America,** www.wnccrafts.org.

Asheville has several interesting galleries. These include the **Grovewood Gallery,** on the grounds of the Grove Park Inn, 111 Grovewood Road (828-253-7651; www.grovewood.com), featuring a variety of crafts including jewelry, clothing, pottery, and a nice collection of furniture; the **Blue Spiral I,** 38 Biltmore Avenue (828-251-0202), selling sculpture, glass, and painting; and the **New Morning Gallery,** 7 Boston Way, (828-274-2831), offering a large collection of pottery and jewelry.

SPECIAL EVENTS

Information on these and other special events is available from the Asheville Convention and Visitors Bureau, (828-258-6101 or (800) 257-1300.

January. Annual All That Jazz Weekend, Grove Park Inn Resort.

February–March. Hands-On Asheville is a wonderful chance for families to enjoy learning crafts together. A series of crafts workshops is offered in a two- to four-hour session, and many are geared toward children. The sessions can be packaged, with special rates at partici-pating hotels, inns, and b&bs (888-874-7799).

April–May. Biltmore Estate Festival of Flowers, Biltmore. Appalachian Spring Celebration, Cradle of Forestry.

June. Dillsboro Heritage Food & Craft Festival, Dillsboro, features fiddling and clogging to the local music.

The Grove Park Inn

Built of granite boulders, this grand old hotel dating from 1913 has 140 mountain acres and is surrounded by Blue Ridge peaks. The hotel has many of its original Arts and Crafts and Mission style furnishings. In Asheville it's warm enough to play golf year-round, so you can share nine holes with your kids, then splash in the indoor pool, or move on to tennis. Kids ages three to twelve enjoy crafts, volleyball, and sing-alongs on Saturdays and holidays, and daily in summer. Kids' Night Out operates daily in summer and on weekends the rest of the year, providing dinner parties and outdoor activities from 6:00 to 9:00 P.M. The resort offers golf, tennis, an Indoor Sports Center, and an indoor pool. In 2001 the resort opened a 40,000-square-foot spa. Located at 290 Macon Avenue (828-252-2711 or 800-267-8413; www.groveparkinn.com).

Also on-property:

Grovewood Gallery, 111 Grovewood Road, (828-253-7651), features a broad selection of quality work by North Carolina's craftspeople.

The Estes-Winn-Blomberg Antique Car Museum, 111 Grovewood Road; (828-253-7651). Open weekends, weather permitting, January through March, and daily rest of the year.

July. Symphony Under the Stars Fourth of July, Sapphire Lake; Blue Ridge Reunion, Balsam Mountain Inn, Balsam.

August. Mountain Dance and Folk Festival, Diana Wortham Theatre.

September. Mountain Heritage Day, Mountain Heritage Center, Cullowhee.

WHERE TO STAY

Balsam Mountain Inn, Box 40, 7 Springs Road, Balsam, N.C. 28707; (828) 456-9498 or (800) 224-9498; www.balsaminn.com. This inviting turn-of-the-century mansion with a two-tier porch rests at the foot of the Smoky Mountains. Curl up in the rockers with a book. After a restful night and a hearty country breakfast, head out for such mountains treasures as Yellow Face, Licklog Gap, and Waterrock Knob. Children are welcome.

Dillsboro Inn, 2 River Road, P.O. Box 490, Dillsboro, N.C. 28725 (828-586-3898), is a family-friendly inn near the Tuckaseegee River overlooking a waterfall. Enjoy canoeing and rafting. Both the Great Smoky Mountain Railroad and the shops in Dillsboro are easily accessible, and children are welcome.

Historic Fontana Village, Fontana Dam, is in the far west of the Smoky Mountains; (800) 849-2258; www.fontanavillage,com. This low-key family-oriented resort is situated on the southwestern edge of the Great Smokies, and borders the man-made 10,000-acre Fontana Lake, where bass fishing is exceptional. Ask at the check-in office for hiking maps. Gaze upon trees older than our nation in the Joyce Kilmer Memorial Forest, and climb along the nearby Appalachian Trail to Lookout Rock for a panoramic mountain view. Smaller children are entertained by the resort's organized activities, including horseback riding, badminton, archery, and craft classes.

High Hampton Inn, P.O. Box 338, Cashiers (800-334-2551 or 828-743-2411; www.highhamptoninn.com), situated on 1,400 mountain acres, offers basic accommodations and relies on the natural beauty of the surrounding area to keep guests coming back. Boat, fish, and swim on thirty-five-acre Hampton Lake and play golf at the resort's own course. In summer the Kids' Club offers activities for ages five to eleven from 9:00 A.M. to 2:00 P.M. and from 6:00 to 9:00 P.M. The Play Group keeps kids ages two to four busy from 9:00 A.M. to 2:00 P.M. Teens have their own Gathering Place, with a pool table and Ping-Pong. Cashiers is about one and a half hours from Asheville.

Sapphire Valley Resort, 4350 Highway 64 West, Cashiers; (828) 743-1763, (800) 722-3956. Situated on 5,700 acres in Cashiers Valley, this resort offers cabins with or without kitchens or deluxe condominium suites replete with kitchen and fireplace. There's an eighteen-hole golf course carved into the valley's thick forest, and younger tots have their own miniature golf course. The resort also has tennis courts, outdoor and indoor pools, a beach, and a health club. The little ones will be entertained by the Kids Camp, a half-day or full-day camp running from June to August.

For a complete accommodations guide, including camping information, call Jackson County Chamber of Commerce at (828) 586-2155 or (800) 962-1911.

WHERE TO EAT

Asheville

In Biltmore Village **La Paz Restaurante-y-Cantina,** 10 Biltmore Plaza (828-277-8779), offers moderately priced Mexican and Southwestern fare. For German cuisine go to the **Black Forest Restaurant,** 2155 Hendersonville Highway; (828) 684-8160. Children will enjoy this Hansel-and-Gretel-style building hung with cuckoo clocks.

Two moderately priced choices: Laughing Seed Café and Salsas. Vegetarians and diners interested in light fare should try the **Laughing Seed Café,** 40 Wall Street; (828) 252-3445. Good choices include vegetarian Sloppy Joe and the Thai green curry. **Salsas,** 6 Patton Avenue (828-252-9805), serves imaginative Mexican and Caribbean cuisine. Try the taco made with smoked trout, eggplant, and a plantain.

The Surrounding Area

Balsam Mountain Inn Restaurant, Balsam (828) 456-9498, features southern dishes. House specialties include roasted leg of lamb and homemade bread. For dessert treat yourself to the hot-fudge-brownie cheesecake. Reservations recommended.

Dillsboro Smokehouse, downtown Dillsboro (828-586-9556), is for the barbecue-loving family. Try some finger-licking hickory-smoked ribs marinated in a secret sauce or a smoked turkey sandwich. There's fresh fruit cobbler with vanilla ice cream for dessert.

The Well House, among the Riverwood Shops in Dillsboro (828-586-8588), is located in the town's first home. Children can peer into the enclosed well at the front of the restaurant and imagine what it was like to live without a tap. Hot deli sandwiches are the specialty of the house.

Meatball's, in Sylva (828-586-9808), is the place to go for Italian food. There are homemade pizza and calzones for lunch and pasta and seafood for dinner. The atmosphere is relaxed and casual, and, weather permitting, there's outdoor dining.

The Jarrett House in Dillsboro (828-586-0265 or 800-972-5623), one of the oldest inns in North Carolina, has a great restaurant where children can eat for as little as $2.50 and Sunday meals are served family style. **Dillsboro Steak & Seafood House** (828-586-8934) is also a good value and has a children's menu. **Lulu's Cafe** in Sylva (828-586-8989) has fresh seafood dishes, vegetarian dinners, tofu concoctions, and homemade desserts.

For More Information

The Jackson County Chamber of Commerce, 116 North Central Street, Sylva; (828) 586-2155 or (800) 962-1911; www.mountainlovers. com. The *Sylva Herald* is published every Thursday.

　　Asheville Convention and Visitors Bureau, P.O. Box 1010, Asheville, N.C.; (828-258-6101 or 800-257-1300), has information on special events, attractions, and accommodations; www. ashevillechamber.org.

　　Contact the **Visitors Center,** 151 Haywood Street; (828) 258-6101.

　　The area paper, the *Asheville Citizen-Times,* publishes a useful weekend entertainment guide on Fridays.

　　The **Madison County Tourism Authority,** Madison County Visitors Center, South Main Street, Box 1527, Mars Hill; (828) 680-9031; www. madisoncounty.nc.com

Emergency Numbers

Ambulance, fire, and police: 911

Police department (nonemergency): (828) 586-2916

Harris Regional Hospital, Sylva; (828) 586-7000

Poison Hotline: (800) 848-6946

Prescriptions can be filled at the hospital twenty-four hours a day

THE GREAT SMOKY MOUNTAINS

Vistas from the overlooks of the Great Smoky Mountains offer a gift to the eye—a series of craggy peaks and soft ridges that roll, seemingly endlessly, into the soft, blue, smoky mist from which the chain takes its name. For 70 miles these dramatic mountains straddle the border of Tennessee and northwestern North Carolina.

The Great Smoky Mountains National Park, with more than a half million acres, offers myriad recreational opportunities. For families with young children, there are scenic drives and easy hikes. Older kids and teens appreciate the more challenging trails. The natural beauty of the waterfalls, gorges, and the mountains, plus the history of stalwart settlers and the culture of the Cherokee Indians, combine to make the Great Smoky Mountains interesting, educational, and scenic.

The Great Smoky Mountains National Park is the most-visited national park in the United States. More than ten million people come here each year. To enjoy the park—and get away from crowds—you need to get off the beaten path, at least a little bit. The best way to do this is to get out of your car and hit the trail. Even little kids can try the easy walks. For visitors with older children, take to the moderate and difficult paths. The most beautiful and, unfortunately, one of the most popular times to visit the park is when the leaves turn. Mid-October is considered the peak. From late summer throughout fall, visitors wanting to avoid crowds should not visit on weekends, when the roads are jammed with cars.

GETTING THERE

Asheville Regional Airport (828-684-2226), about 65 miles east of the Great Smoky Mountains, is served by US Airways and Delta as well as several regional airlines. Car rentals are available at the airport. From Asheville take U.S. 23/74, the Great Smoky Mountains Expressway. This

The Great Smoky Mountains
AT A GLANCE

▶ Hike and horseback ride

▶ Drive scenic park roads

▶ Enjoy a 360-degree perspective from Clingmans Dome (elevation 6,643 feet)

▶ Tour the Cherokee Botanical Gardens and the Museum of the Cherokee Indian

▶ Great Smoky Mountains National Park: (865) 436–1200; www.nps.gov

scenic, four-lane road allows you to avoid U.S. 19, which is small, curvy, and can be dangerous. From Gatlinburg, Tennessee, drive 2 miles south to the Sugarlands Visitor Center.

If driving from Virginia or northern North Carolina, try a route that includes the scenic **Blue Ridge Parkway,** which winds its way for 470 miles from Shenandoah National Park in Virginia to Great Smoky Mountains National Park in North Carolina. Take a leisurely drive, stopping for picnics, short hikes, and photographs.

The visitor's center has a map. The **Northwest Trading Post,** Milepost (MP) 258.6, features crafts by artisans from eleven counties in North Carolina. Trails from **E. B. Jeffress Park,** MP 272, lead to an old frontier cabin and a church. At **Moses Cone Park,** MP 292 to 295, there are more crafts and demonstrations of weaving and woodworking at the Southern Highland Handicraft Guild Shop, as well as scenic trails. For a sample of the area's mining heritage, visit the **Museum of North Carolina,** Spruce Pine, near MP 331. Visit a mine in Emerald Village near MP 334. The Blue Ridge Parkway intersects Route 441. Follow Route 441 north to the park's entrance at the Oconaluftee Visitors Center.

Asheville is accessible by **Greyhound** bus. The station is at 2 Tunnel Road, Asheville; (828) 253-5353.

GETTING AROUND

A car is a must for getting around. If arriving by plane, rent a car at the Asheville Airport.

WHAT TO SEE AND DO

Great Smoky Mountains National Park

Great Smoky Mountains National Park has three gateways. The two visitor's centers in Tennessee are **Sugarlands Visitors Center,** which is the park's headquarters, 2 miles south of Gatlinburg (865-436-1200), and the **Cades Cove Visitor Center,** Cable Mill, Tennessee.

The entrance in North Carolina is in **Oconaluftee,** 1194 Newfound Gap Road, Highway 441 North, about a mile north of Cherokee (828-497-1900). Be sure to obtain maps of driving tours and hiking trails and a schedule of special park activities. Have your kids ages five to twelve purchase a Junior Ranger book of activities required to obtain a **Junior Ranger badge,** a particularly nice memento of their trip.

Near the Oconaluftee entrance is the **Mountain Farm Museum** (828-497-1900). Tour these fifteen turn-of-the-century buildings—including an apple house, blacksmith's shop, hog pen, meat house, and chicken coop—and come away with a sense of the stalwart nature of the mountain people. A half mile north at the water-powered Mingus Mill are frequent demonstrations of corn being ground the old-fashioned way.

A nice thing about this park is the ease of combining a tour by car and by foot. Don't just see these mountains by zipping through in your car. Get out to enjoy the trails.

Quick Tour. If you only have time for a quick tour, drive the 32-mile **Newfound Gap Road** that bisects the park, connecting the entrance in Cherokee, North Carolina, with the one in Gatlinburg, Tennessee. When not crowded, viewing this winding road dotted with spectacular lookouts takes about sixty minutes. For a panoramic view drive on the **Clingmans Dome Road** and hike thirty minutes to the observation tower, situated atop the park's highest peak at 6,643 feet. The truly spectacular 360-degree view of the park is worth the climb.

More Driving Routes. In the western portion of the park located in Tennessee, **Cades Cove** is surrounded by an 11-mile loop road that winds around a historic community that includes a blacksmith shop, a barn, and a smokehouse. Kids can peruse these nineteenth-century buildings and easily imagine early-settler life. During summer living history is enacted by costumed interpreters at Cable Mill, which has a functioning water-powered gristmill. The Cades Cove Visitor Center, open year-round, has a bookstore.

Horseback Riding. If the kids become tired of walking and driving, consider a horseback ride through the park or a fishing expedition. Stables, usually closed during the winter months, are located at several

Great Family Hikes

With 850 miles of trails, from easy to difficult backcountry treks, there are paths for every ability and interest. Except where stated or when the trail is a loop, the distances quoted are **one-way.**

- **Quiet walkways.** These twenty-one ¼- and ½-mile trails, many of which are loops, are just off the main roads. Great for little kids and nonhikers, these paths are easy and rewarding, giving even young kids a sense of accomplishment and an appreciation of the park's natural beauty.
- **Self-guided nature trails.** Many of these are relatively easy to walk and are conveniently located off U.S. 441 or near the Oconaluftee entrance. Some favorites are: the 1½-mile Balsam Mountain trail, one of the easiest climbing trails in the park; the 4-mile Mt. Noble trail; the 3½-mile Boundary River trail; the ½-mile Collins Creek trail; and the 4-mile Kephart Prong trail.
- **Trails to waterfalls.** To see some of the Smokies' famous waterfalls, set out on one of these popular hikes. Three waterfalls are accessible from paths off Deep Creek Road. The trail to Toms Branch Falls is an easy ¼-mile hike, the path to Indian Creek Falls is a mile long, and the path to Juneywhank Falls is 1½ miles.

   The easiest waterfall hike on the Tennessee side of the park is the 1¼ mile one-way to paved trail to Laurel Falls, which has a 60-foot plunge. Accessible from the Roaring Fork Motor Nature Trail, Grotto Falls, a 2.4-mile round-trip through a hemlock forest, is fun. This is the only waterfall you can walk behind. Kids really like standing with the roaring falls in front of them.

   Three of the parks' most photogenic falls are Abrams Falls, Rainbow Falls, and Ramsay Cascades. Abrams Falls has the largest volume of water of any of the falls. It's a moderately hearty, but not excruciating, 5-mile round-trip hike from the Cades Cove loop road. Rainbow Falls drops 80 feet, making it one of the highest falls in the park, but you have to work to get here. The 5½-mile round-trip hike is strenuous. This is a good challenge for parents and teens as is the strenuous 8-mile round-trip hike from the Greenbrier area to Ramsay Cascades, which tumbles a splendid 100 feet.

   Falls easily accessible from campgrounds: From the Smokemont Campground head to Chasteen Creek Falls, a small waterfall that's a 4-mile, moderately difficult round-trip hike. From near the Cosby Campground, the 45-foot-tall Henwallow Falls is a 4.4-mile round-trip along a moderate trail.

Dollywood

Don't miss **Dollywood,** Pigeon Forge, Tennessee. This theme park, 5 miles north of the Gatlinburg entrance to the Great Smoky Mountains National Park, mixes music, native crafts, and thrill rides. Megastar and hometown gal Dolly Parton is involved in the park's planning. Not as big or glitzy as the megaparks in Orlando, Dollywood sparkles with down-home mountain magic.

Mountain heritage—crafts and music—is as important here as monster rides. Traditional handiwork takes center stage at Craftsmen's Village. Watch artisans create dulcimers, forge products from glowing bars of iron, fashion brooms, and carve faces in wood. Toe-tap through scores of live musical performances daily. In Jukebox Junction relive the fifties from rock 'n' roll songs to hula hoops. Country twangs and tunes take over in Heartsong, Dreamland Express, Paradise Road, an hour-long tribute to the life and songs of Dolly Parton.

Good as the other stuff is, the rides will still be the big draw for your kids. Thunder Road puts you in the middle of a classic movie car chase, and the Tennessee Tornado, Dollywood's newest rollercoaster, has a 128-foot drop through a mountain at 65 mph. Scheduled to open Memorial Day 2001 is a water park, with waterfalls, wading pools, and wild river rides. Little kids like the Dentzel carved carousel; the Dollywood Express, an outing on a real mountain steam train; and Imagination Station, a hands-on play area. The newest attraction for younger children is Dreamland Forest, the world's largest interactive treehouse, featuring hundreds of games and gadgets for toddlers and older children.

Dollywood, 1020 Dollywood Lane, Pigeon Forge (865-428-9488; www.dollywood.com), is open daily May through October; weekends and selected times mid-April and September–December. Call ahead for the schedule.

points. These include the **Cades Cove Riding Stables,** Cades Cove (865-448-6286), open mid-March to November 1, and the **Smokemount Riding Stables,** near the Smokemount Campground (828-497-2373), open April through October. Smokemount also offers a horseback riding trip combined with a two-and-a-half hour waterfall trip past a waterfall. **Meigs Falls,** 12.9 miles west of the Sugarlands Visitor Center, near the Townsend Wye, the only waterfall you can see without hiking.

Park Programs. Park rangers offer many programs to the public. Some teach how to spot a fox squirrel, or distinguish among some of the park's hundreds of varieties of trees. Programs are generally available June through October. **Junior Ranger** programs, open to ages five to twelve, not only provide activities that teach kids about the park's woods and wildlife, but the badges kids earn after completing a few activities often prove to be the best mementos of a park vacation. Ask about these programs at the visitors centers.

In summer the rangers present evening talks and walks at the major campgrounds; these are open to anyone, camper or not. Another favorite family activity is the evening flashlight walk. Bring your own beacon, follow the ranger through the nighttime woods, and discover what lurks in the park after dark.

Be sure to pick up a copy of the *Smokies Guide,* the park newsletter, which lists special programs and activities.

Accessible Travel

Persons with disabilities can obtain the *Access North Carolina* travel guide free of charge from the North Carolina Division of Travel and Tourism, 301 North Wiilmington Street, Raleigh, NC 27601 (919-733-4171 or 800-VISIT-NC.

Native American Culture

Cherokee Indian Reservation, Qualla Boundary, Great Smoky Mountains. Cherokee Visitors Center, U.S. 19 and Business 441 in downtown Cherokee; (828) 497-9195 or (800) 438-1601; www.cherokee-nc.com. Formerly inhabiting all of the Great Smoky Mountains, the Cherokee Indians now lay claim to a 56,000-acre reservation within the mountains. Open to the public, the reservation offers motels, campgrounds, crafts, Cherokee historical and cultural attractions, and some exceptional trout fishing, for which a Tribal Fishing Permit (not a North Carolina state fishing license) is required. In 1990 the state record for a brown trout—weighing more than fifteen pounds—was set in this area. In addition there are some wonderful and very doable hikes, such as the one from Big Cove Road (about 6 miles from downtown Cherokee) up to Mingo Falls, which takes only about ten minutes.

For younger children there's **Santa's Land Fun Park and Zoo,** on U.S. 19 toward Maggie Valley (828-497-9191), where they can enjoy a small roller coaster and Ferris wheel, a train ride, paddle boats, a petting zoo, shops, food and, of course, Santa. Admission.

Unto These Hills, Cherokee Indian Reservation, Cherokee; (828) 497-2111; www.untothesehills.com. This summertime outdoor drama depicts the history of the Eastern Band of Cherokee Indians from the arrival of the Spanish explorers in 1540 to the near extinction of the tribe on the forced march, the Trail of Tears. This visual history lesson in the Mountainside Theater is worth watching; some one hundred actors, in authentic dress, dance, sing, and act out their past. Performances are

Oconaluftee Indian Village, home of the Eastern Band of the Cherokee Indians, is an authentic re-creation of an eighteenth-century Indian community.

nightly, except Sundays, from mid-June through August. Those arriving thirty minutes before the show are treated to a preshow performance of folk and bluegrass music. Admission.

Oconaluftee Indian Village, U.S. 441 North, Cherokee; (828) 497–2315 or (828) 497–2111; www.oconalufteevillage.com. Set against the pines and peaks of the Great Smokies, Oconaluftee re-creates a 1750 Cherokee reservation. Cherokee men, wearing bear-claw necklaces, demonstrate such survival skills as hunting with a blowgun, chipping flint into arrowheads, and fashioning a dugout canoe. Women in long skirts and beaded necklaces weave baskets from river cane and white oak saplings, cook bean bread, and mold coiled ropes of clay into pottery. A

Great Smoky Mountains Railways

Great Smoky Mountains Railway, Dillsboro Depot, Dillsboro; (828) 586-8811 or (800) 872-4681; www.gsmr.com. Take an enchanted ride through tunnels, river gorges, and across mountains aboard a brightly colored 1942 train. The Great Smoky Mountains Railway offers several excursions in an open or enclosed car.

- **The Tuckaseegee River Excursion** follows the river on a three-hour-and-thirty-minute route from Dillsboro to Bryson City, with a layover in Bryson City. You'll travel through an 836-foot tunnel and see for yourself whether or not it's haunted by the nineteen convict laborers who died while digging it with a pickax.
- **The Nantahala Gorge** excursion leaves from Bryson City for a four-and-one-half-hour trip along Fontana Lake that allows for an hour's stop in the gorge. The all-day Raft 'n' Rail package travels to the gorge, where you join an 8-mile raft trip down the Nantahala River. (Or you can choose a self-guided raft trip.) Children must weigh at least sixty pounds to be allowed on rafting trips.
- **Special Events.** The Railway also offers Murder Mystery trains, dinner trains, and the Santa Express. Call ahead for reservations.

tribe elder in the seven-sided council house talks of the traditional customs and dances. It's commercial but still educational. Admission.

Then take time to smell such seasonal flowers as Indian paintbrush, Indian pipe, and sunflowers along the trails of the adjacent **Cherokee Botanical Gardens;** (828) 497-2315. (Admission is charged for the village, but entry to the gardens is free.) At the **Museum of the Cherokee Indian,** U.S. 441 at Drama Road, Cherokee (828-497-3481; www.cherokeemuseum.org) hear the Cherokee language spoken, listen to tapes that tell the ancient legends of the origins of fire and the formation of the mountains, and learn about the Trail of Tears, the 1830s forced march of the Cherokee from this area to Oklahoma.

There's more Indian lore and legends at **Kituwah,** the annual **American Indian Celebration,** sponsored by the High Country Art and Craft Guild, 46 Haywood Street, Asheville 28801; (828) 252-3880. Usually held in September at the Asheville Civic Center, this gathering brings together scores of Native American tribes. You and your kids will enjoy browsing among the arts and crafts, watching the dance demonstrations, and listening to elders at the wisdom-keeper sessions discuss customs.

SIDE TRIPS

Situated in a valley surrounded by peaks, **Asheville** has a natural beauty. The number-one attraction here is the **Biltmore Estate,** off Biltmore Avenue, Asheville (828-274-6333 or 800-295-4730; www.biltmore.com), the largest privately owned house in America. (See chapter on Asheville and the Surrounding Region.)

SPECIAL EVENTS

For more information contact the Great Smoky Mountains National Park (865-436-1200) or the Cherokee Visitors Center (828-497-9195).

The Cherokee Indian Reservation holds three Pow Wows during the year: one on Memorial Day Weekend, another over Labor Day Weekend and the third on the Fourth of July. These attract thousands of people, Native and non-Native, with their food, music, crafts, and dance competitions.

September. Mountain Life Festival at the Mountain Farm Museum, near the Oconaluftee Visitor Center, Great Smoky Mountains National Park.

October. Great leaf peeping, as the foliage colors are at their best.

WHERE TO STAY

There is only one public lodge within Great Smoky Mountains National Park: The **LeConte Lodge,** 250 Apple Valley Road, Sevierville, Tennessee 37862 (865-429-5704), is accessible only by an all-day hike. Reservations can also be made by e-mail: reservations@leconte-lodge.com. Note that the Tennessee address is a reservations address, not the address of the lodge. The lodge is open from late March to late November.

Ten campgrounds with varying facilities are scattered throughout the park. Three developed campgrounds with water, but no showers or trailer hookups, are **Cades Cove, Elkmont,** and **Smokemont;** all are open year-round and operate on a first-come basis from November through mid-May. Reservations, however, are required from mid-May through October. Call The National Park Reservations Service at (800) 365-2267, for information about availability, cost, and facilities.

WHERE TO EAT

Here are some places to eat nearby.

Balsam Mountain Inn Restaurant, Balsam (828-456-9498), has a hearty meal to take care of your fresh-air appetite. The menu features southern dishes, and house specialties include roasted leg of lamb and homemade bread. For dessert treat yourself to the hot-fudge-brownie cheesecake. Reservations are recommended.

Dillsboro Smokehouse in downtown Dillsboro (828-586-9556) is for the barbecue-loving family. Try some finger-licking hickory-smoked ribs marinated in a secret sauce or a smoked turkey sandwich. There's fresh fruit cobbler with vanilla ice cream for dessert.

Meatball's, in Sylva (828-586-9808), is the place to go for Italian food. There's homemade pizza and calzones for lunch and pasta and seafood for dinner. The atmosphere is relaxed and casual, and weather permitting, there's outdoor dining.

The Well House, among the Riverwood Shops in Dillsboro (828-586-8588), is in the town's first home. Children can peer into the enclosed well at the front of the restaurant and imagine what it was like to live without a tap. Hot deli sandwiches are the specialty of the house.

FOR MORE INFORMATION

For park information write to **Great Smoky Mountain National Park,** 107 Park Headquarters Road, Gatlinburg, Tennessee 37738; (865) 436-1200; www.nps.gov. The **Oconaluftee Visitor Center** is at the North Carolina entrance to the park, 150 Highway 441 North, Cherokee, North Carolina 28719; (828) 497-1900. The *Smokies Guide,* the park's official newspaper, is available at park visitor centers and includes good seasonal information (www.nps.gov. Click on Great Smoky Mountains National Park.)

Cherokee Visitors Center, P.O. Box 460, Cherokee, North Carolina 28719 (800-438-1601 or 828-497-9195; www.cherokee-nc.com), has information on Cherokee reservation attractions and events. Ask for an official visitor's guide and directory to the reservation.

Emergency Numbers

Ambulance, fire, and police: 911. In the Great Smoky Mountains National Park, call Smoky Mountains National Park Headquarters at (865) 436-1230

Harris Regional Hospital, Sylva: (828) 586-7000. Kel-Save Discount Drugs, 38 East Main Street, Sylva: (828-586-2213). Open 9:00 A.M. to 9:00 P.M., Monday to Friday, 9:00 A.M. to 6:00 P.M., Saturday, and 1:00 to 6:00 P.M. on Sunday.

Sylva Police: (828) 586-2916

Poison Hotline: (800) 848-6946

OKLAHOMA CITY

O klahoma City (or OKC, as it's known in these parts) went from a
frontier wilderness to a busy town of 10,000 in just one afternoon, when unassigned lands were opened to the first takers in
the Great Land Run of April 22, 1889. The legacy of the early pioneers
and an identification with Native American culture are still evident
throughout Oklahoma's capital (now a city of more than one million)
and in surrounding towns and villages. OKC is in the midst of a major
renewal, with the renovation of the historic Bricktown section (now an
entertainment, dining, and shopping center), the revamping of the State
Capitol building, a new facility for the Museum of Oklahoma History,
and a Native American Cultural Center in the works. Exploring this historic town of the past and emerging city of the future is a fascinating and
fun experience for visiting families.

GETTING THERE

Will Rogers World Airport, south of I-40 on South Meridian, is a
fifteen-minute drive 10 miles southwest of downtown. **Airport Express**
(405-681-3311 or 800-225-5652) provides transportation downtown
and to any location in the state. Car rentals and taxis are also available.

Amtrak (800-USA-RAIL) Heartland Flyer trains arrive daily at the
Sante Fe Train Depot, 100 EK Gaylord Boulevard across from the Myriad
Convention Center.

Greyhound (405-235-6425 or 800-231-2222) has a terminal at 427
West Sheridan. Interstate highways I-40, I-35, and I-44 connect Oklahoma City to the rest of the country.

GETTING AROUND

Since most of the major attractions are not within walking distance of
one another, a car is a necessity.

Metro Transit (405-235-7433) has frequent bus service Monday
through Saturday to all major attractions. More fun but less frequent is

Oklahoma City

AT A GLANCE

▶ View paintings and sculptures by noted artists at the National Cowboy Hall of Fame and Western Heritage Center

▶ See 2,000 animals at the Oklahoma City Zoo

▶ Learn about Native American culture at the Red Earth Indian Center

▶ Oklahoma City Convention and Visitors Bureau: 189 West Sheridan; (405) 297-8912 or (800) 225-5652; www.visitokc.com

the new Oklahoma Spirit Trolley Transit System, which covers a 7-mile area along two routes: one for downtown and Bricktown and one that covers the hotel-restaurant area, downtown, and Stockyards City.

WHAT TO SEE AND DO

Museums and Historical Sites

The city's museums and galleries are numerous, so we've narrowed the choices to the most appealing for kids.

Enterprise Square, USA, 2501 East Memorial Road, on the campus of Oklahoma Christian (between Broadway Extension and I-35); (405) 425-5030, currently closed for renovation, is scheduled to reopen in 2001. This Disneyesque, high-tech tribute to free enterprise is full of electronic gadgetry that will tickle your family's collective fancy.

The **National Cowboy Hall of Fame and Western Heritage Center,** 1700 N.E. Sixty-third (405-478-2250; www.cowboyhalloffame.org), is more than a Western art museum. A recent addition of 75,000 square feet has created three new galleries: Prosperity Junction, a Western town circa 1890, the American Cowboy Gallery, with its 300 saddles and other cowboy essentials; and the American Rodeo Gallery, with a replica of a 1950 rodeo arena. In the Children's Wing kids learn cowboy terms, how cowboys directed their horses on a cattle drive, and all about chuckwagons. On the fourth Saturday of each month, there's a special hands-on program for families, and in summer special Native American art and cowboy art camps for kids. Admission.

Oklahoma City Zoo

Ranked as one of the best and largest zoos in the country, the 110-acre Oklahoma City Zoo, 2101 N.E. Fiftieth Street, next to the Omniplex Center (405-424-3344; www.okczoo.com), has more than 2,000 animals. Highlights include:

- **Great EscApe,** a habitat of gorillas, orangutans, and chimps in a natural setting of cliffs, streams, pools, and clearings.
- **Aquaticus,** has dolphin and sea lion shows.
- **Children's Zoo and Discovery Area** has barnyard animals for kids to feed and pet.
- **Safari Tram** takes visitors on a narrated tour of several animal habitats.
- **Cat Forest/Lion Overlook,** a naturalistic habitat for lions, tigers, and leopards. Kids have their own "zone"—a 20-foot-

high bamboo activity maze that follows the make-believe antics of a pair of playful lion cubs.
- **Butterfly Garden** has thousands of rainbow-colored butterflies in mid-spring and early fall.

In the summers Morning Zoo Rise allows visitors entry at 7:30 a.m. to watch the zoo's permanent residents awakening and enjoying their morning feed. Friday through Sunday, Keeper Chats have keepers available at areas around the zoo to answer questions. Admission.

The **State Capitol,** N.E. Twenty-third and Lincoln Boulevard (405-521-3356), is open to the public from 8:00 A.M. to 4:00 P.M. daily. Free tours are given from 9:00 A.M. to 3:00 P.M., Monday through Friday, and you do need advance reservations. Following the tour, visit the nearby **Harn Homestead Museum,** 313 N.E. 16th Street (405-235-4058), which includes a farmhouse, the 1890 Shepherd House, the 1897 one-room school, and the 1900 working farm. Admission.

Highlights of the **Oklahoma Historical Society and State Museum of History,** 2100 Lincoln Boulevard (405-521-2491), are the exhibits on settler life during the 1890s, the Native Americans, and the oil rigs on the grounds. For more local traditions consider a visit to **Stockyards City,** 2500 Exchange Avenue (405-235-7267). Established in 1910, Stockyards City is the oldest and largest live cattle auction in the world. Stockyards City's western wear shops sell cowboy clothing and gear. Livestock auctions are held Monday and Tuesday at 8:00 A.M.

A moving tribute to the victims of the 1995 bombing of the Murrah Federal Building, the **Oklahoma City National Memorial,** N.W. Fifth and Harvey Streets (405-235-3313; www.oklahoman.net/connections/

memorial) was dedicated in April 2000. A reflecting pool, a field of empty chairs, and a children's area honor the bombing's victims, survivors, and rescuers. The Oklahoma City National Memorial Center, an interactive learning museum, is scheduled to open in late 2000.

At the **99s Museum of Women Pilots,** 4300 Amelia Earhart Lane (405-685-9990; www.ninety-nines.org/museum.html), you'll see exhibits about Amelia Earhart and other women pilots, hear the oral histories of women who were flyers in the world wars, and learn about today's female aviators in the space program. Admission.

The **Oklahoma Firefighters Museum,** 2716 N.E. 50th Street (405-424-3440), owned and operated by volunteer and paid firefighters, has some of the finest examples of antique fire wagons, tools, and machinery you'll ever see, dating back to 1736. Admission.

Parks and Zoos

Myriad Botanical Gardens, Reno and Robinson, downtown; (405) 297-3995. The garden's centerpiece is the seven-story Crystal Bridge Tropical Conservatory, a covered glass and steel greenhouse-type structure with exotic plants, palm trees, and flowers. Take the Adventure Walk under a 35-foot cascading waterfall or enjoy the view from the suspended Skywalk. The Water Stage frequently has live entertainment. Admission charged; free guided tours can be arranged in advance.

Will Rogers Park, N.W. Thirty-sixth Street and North Portland; (405) 297-2211. This 130-acre parks department facility is the city's finest for families, with grassy slopes, freshwater ponds, and a beautiful rose garden. For fun there's an olympic-size pool, Frisbee, golf course, picnic tables, and the lighted OKC Tennis Center.

Native American Festival

More than one hundred tribes from North America come together in Oklahoma City for **Red Earth,** one of the largest Native American celebrations. A parade of more than 2,000 Native Americans decked out in full regalia kicks off the festival each June.

In addition to dancing, storytellers weave tales of creation, telling of legends and heroes, and more than 250 artists present paintings, silver jewelry, beadwork, photography, and other crafts.

For more information, call the Red Earth Festival at (405) 427-5228; www.redearth.org. Nominal fee for tickets to day and evening events.

Other Attractions

Frontier City Theme Park, 11501 N.E. Expressway (7 miles north of the city); (405) 478-2412; www.sixflags.com/frontiercity. Younger children

A Native American boy in full regalia is just one of the many sights at Red Earth, America's largest Native American cultural festival.

will enjoy Paul Bunyan's Buzzsaw Company, the Moon Walk, the Flying Dragon, the O.K. Kids Corral. Older kids will head for the Hangman (a very steep free fall) and the Wild West Gunfighters Show, which features some very fancy stunts. There are twelve restaurants to choose from, with everything from basic chuckwagon fare to south-of-the-border specialities to German cuisine to cotton candy and ice cream. Admission. Open daily June to August; weekends April, May, September, and October.

White Water Bay, 3908 West Reno; (405) 943-9687, for recorded information 405-943-0392; www.whitewaterbay.com. It's wet and wild and has everything a family water park should have, with more than

Omniplex Attractions

Omniplex, 2100 N.E. Fifty-second Street; (405) 602–3770 (recording), 405–602–OMNI, or (800) 532–7652; www.omniplex.org. Seven kid-friendly museums and a new OMNIDOME theater under one roof for one reasonably priced admission. Make a day out of it, with lunch in the Garden Cafe or an outdoor picnic. Highlights include:

- **Kirkpatrick Science Museum.** Come here first, as your kids will want to spend the most time in this colorful, inviting space. FAMILYSPACE, for children in first grade and above, has twenty brainteasing activities, such as assembling giant jigsaw puzzles and solving number games. Toddlers have their own KIDSPACE and BABYSPACE has activities for children under two.
- **Oklahoma Air Space Museum** features more than 500 exhibits with memorabilia honoring famous Oklahoma pilots and astronauts are also on display.
- **Red Earth Indian Center.** (405) 427–5228. Kids are particularly interested in the Dwellings of the Earth exhibit, featuring scale replicas of early Native American homes and colorful art from Oklahoma Indian artists.
- **Kirkpatrick Galleries.** An eclectic collection of interesting objects includes a portion of the Berlin Wall, toy trains, and a fascinating collection of more than 700 hats.

- At the **Kirkpatrick Planetarium** see dazzling star shows in the Star Theater with sophisticated special effects and a state-of-the-art sound system.
- **Kirkpatrick Gardens and Greenhouse.** A perfect place to sit down and relax, this facility has six different gardens, including a miniature fruit orchard, and a children's garden. Weekend showcases and summer programs are part of the fun.
- **OMNIDOME Theater.** (405–602–DOME) The state's first 70mm IWERKS theater has a huge screen that stretches around the sides of the theater and curves over the heads of viewers.

Omniplex is among the sixty-two U.S. museums chosen as a site for public education about the International Space Station (ISS) currently under construction. Omniplex will be offering live demonstrations, activities, and events to inform visitors about the laboratory's construction as it progresses. Admission.

Bricktown

This revitalized downtown area, once a collection of warehouses and factories, has come back strong as an entertainment, dining, and sports area. Dozens of restaurants, clubs, and shops line the Bricktown Canal, and construction is underway for a twenty-one-screen movie megaplex and a large landscaped area with trails and recreational facilities at the far end of the canal. The Southwestern Bell Bricktown Ballpark houses OKC's AAA baseball club, the Oklahoma Redhawks, and Bricktown's Water Taxi system transports visitors with a cruise along the mile-long canal.

twenty-five acres of chutes, flumes, high-speed dives, and a giant wave pool. The gentler Kids Kove is for those under eight.

Theater, Music, and the Arts

Lyric Theatre (405-524-9312), a professional company, performs musicals June through August at **Kirkpatrick Fine Arts Auditorium,** 2501 North Blackwelder Avenue, on the Oklahoma City University Campus, and **Ballet Oklahoma** (405-843-9898) performs there, too. The **Oklahoma City Philharmonic Orchestra** (405-842-5387), performs at the new Rose State Performing Arts Theater. And don't forget the **Oklahoma Opry,** 404 West Commerce (405-632-8322), with weekly, Saturday night country western performances at 8:00 P.M.

Shopping

Penn Square Mall, Northwest Expressway at Pennsylvania (405-842-4424; www.pennsquaremall.com), boasts department stores, specialty shops and a large cinema complex.

SIDE TRIPS

At present, more American Indians live in Oklahoma than anywhere else: Thirty-seven federally recognized tribes maintain headquarters in the state. A wide variety of attractions, festivals, and events pay tribute to Native American culture—and many are just a day trip away from OKC.

- The town of **Anadarko,** about an hour's drive southwest, is tribal headquarters for the Apache, Wichita, and Western Delaware tribes. **Indian City U.S.A.,** 2 miles southeast of town on Highway 8 (405-247-5661; www.indiancityusa.com), is an outdoor restoration of Native American dwellings. Guides lead daily tours through seven life-size villages. Once past the gift shop, it's interesting for young kids.
- **Guthrie,** thirty-five minutes north of OKC on I-35, has retained almost all of its original nineteenth-century architecture. Along with numerous shops and galleries are a number of interesting museums and historical sites.

- **Wewoka,** the capital of the Seminole Indian tribe, is home to the **Seminole Nation Museum,** 524 South Wewoka; (405) 257-5580. The free museum is closed in January; open daily from 1:00 to 5:00 P.M. the rest of the year.
- **Seminole** is the site of the **Jasmine Moran Children's Museum,** 1714 Wrangler Boulevard (405-382-0950 or 800-259-KIDS, www. jasminemoran.mus.ok.us), where kids pretend to be doctors and fire-fighters and engage in challenging but enjoyable games. Admission.
- **Norman,** home of the University of Oklahoma, has the **Sam Noble Oklahoma Museum of Natural History,** 2401 Chautauqua Avenue (405-325-4712, www.ou.edu), with its seven galleries that examine the natural and cultural history of Oklahoma and the world. In the Pleistocene Plaza there's a monumental sculpture of Paleo-Indians crossing the path of a giant mammoth—a sure kid pleaser.

SPECIAL EVENTS

Contact the Oklahoma City Convention and Visitors Bureau (405-297-8912 or 800-225-5052) for specifics on the following annual events.

February. An Affair of the Heart, one of the country's largest arts and crafts festivals, Oklahoma State Fairgrounds (Also held in October).

March. Spring Fair & Junior Livestock Show, complete with rides, concerts, and food, Oklahoma State Fairgrounds.

May. Chuckwagon Gathering and National Children's Cowboy Festival, Cowboy Hall of Fame.

June. Stockyard Stampede, with western arts, crafts, and rodeo demonstrations, and more. Red Earth Festival and Parade

Mid-September–Early October. State Fair of Oklahoma.

November. World Championship Quarter Horse Show, state's largest out-of-state visitor attraction.

WHERE TO STAY

Consult the *Visitors Guide* for accommodations information. Lodging choices include seven **Motel 6** (800-466-8356) and four **Holiday Inns** (800-465-4329) as well as luxury hotels. There's also a selection of all-suite hotels that are ideal for families. **Embassy Suites,** 1815 South Meridian (405-682-6000 or 800-EMBASSY), has one- and two-bedroom suites and a pool. **Hawthorne Suites,** 1600 Richmond Square (405-

840–1440 or 800–843–1440), has good-size suites. **Best Value Inn,** 4800 S. I-35 (405) 670–3815, has comfortable rooms (some with kitchnettes) at reasonable prices, as does **Comfort Inn,** 6600 NW Expressway (405 722–8694 or 800–444–5133).

WHERE TO EAT

The *Visitors Guide* has a restaurant listing. Choose from a variety of eateries in **Bricktown,** the city's renovated warehouse district 1 block east of downtown's Myriad Convention Center, on Sheridan. An eatery that's fun for families: **The Spaghetti Warehouse,** 101 East Sheridan (405-235-0402), features a wide selection of Italian and American dishes. The Meridian Avenue area also has many of the city's restaurants, from fast food to fine dining.

For beef head to **Cattlemen's Steakhouse,** 2 blocks south of I-40 at 1309 South Agnew in Stockyard City; (405) 236-0416. Their specialty is tasty, reasonably priced steak with all the trimmings. **Allie's American Grille,** 3233 NW Expressway (405-842-6633), in the Oklahoma City Marriott Hotel, is a family-style restaurant. **Garfield's,** Quail Springs Mall, 2501 West Memorial Drive (405-742-7515), has a nice size children's menu, and it's open seven days a week for breakfast, lunch, and dinner. **Sub Way Deli & Grill,** OKC's oldest deli, has gourmet deli sandwiches, burgers and fries, pizza, and drive-through service (plus casual dining inside).

FOR MORE INFORMATION

Oklahoma City Convention and Visitors Bureau, 189 West Sheridan; (405) 297–8912 or (800) 225–5652; www.visitokc.com

Statewide vacation guide: **Oklahoma Tourism and Recreation Department,** 15 North Robinson; (405) 521–2409 or (800) 652–6552

State parks information: (800) 654–8240

Emergency Numbers

Ambulance, fire, police: 911

Poison Control: (800) 764–7661

Twenty-four-hour emergency room: Baptist Medical Center, 3300 Northwest Expressway; (405) 949–3011

Twenty-four-hour pharmacies: Eckerd Drugs at 6951 SE 15th Street (405-737-7886) and at 4026 N MacArthur Boulevard (405-789-0101).

16 ☀ South Carolina

HILTON HEAD

The well-heeled, well-connected, and just plain choosy have been traveling to Hilton Head for years. Why? This island off the southern coast of South Carolina does a good job of balancing beach and wildlife areas with development. The result is 12 miles of white sand barrier beach, plus twenty-two golf courses, more than 300 tennis courts, fifty racquet clubs, and numerous resorts.

This classy resort island, divided into public areas and plantations (resort and lodging sections) bars neon signs and protects trees. Despite the hearty development the island sports an underlying tastefulness. The blue beach umbrellas, available for rental, are lined up in orderly rows. The resorts are set back from the sands so that the buildings don't seem to be devouring the shore. If you know where to look, you can find wildlife and nature preserves too. It's no surprise that six of the seven South Carolina resorts that made the prestigious *Conde Nast Traveler* 1998 Gold List were located at Hilton Head.

GETTING THERE

If you choose to fly to Hilton Head, **Savannah International Airport** (912–964–0514), 45 miles south of Hilton Head Island, is the nearest major airport. Delta, COMAIR, and USAirways offer daily flights to Savannah.

Amtrak (800–USA–RAIL or 912–234–2611) offers train service to Savannah (forty-five minutes from Hilton Head), stopping at the Savannah terminal, 2611 Seaboard Coastline Drive, six times daily. Trains originate from New York, Jacksonville, Miami, and St. Petersburg.

Traveling by car to Hilton Head Island, take I–95. Hilton Head Island is 40 miles east of I–95. Highway 278 leads to the island.

GETTING AROUND

Hilton Head Island is divided into plantation and village areas, both public and private. Destination areas are often labeled according to these plantation and village boundaries.

Hilton Head

AT A GLANCE

▶ Take a boat into the Sound to look for dolphins

▶ Enjoy 12 miles of white-sand beaches for swimming and sailboarding

▶ Play at top-ranked golf courses and tennis centers

▶ Hilton Head Island Chamber of Commerce, (843) 785-3673; 800-523-3373; www.hiltonheadisland.org; or www.hiltonheadisland.com

The best way to get around the island is by car. Biking offers a practical and fun way to travel around Hilton Head. There are public bike paths and trails within each plantationline. Several places rent bikes, including: **Hilton Head Bicycle Company,** (843-686-6888), **Cycle Center Bike Rentals** (843-671-2453), and the **Fun Center** (843-785-6607).

WHAT TO SEE AND DO

The Beach

The beach is alluring, dune bordered, and wide. As a resort guest or lodging renter, you have access to the beach through the paths nearest your property. At the gates to most plantations, guards ask about your destination. Mention a resort, and some guards simply wave you in; at other gates the guards check for car passes issued by rental companies or hotels. To many visitors this system is an annoying waste of time. If you are not a renter or a resort guest, then technically you are supposed to enter the beach through the public-access areas. There are several of these, but the two with the largest parking areas are at **Coligny Circle** and **Folly Field Road.** Once you are on the beach, feel free to walk anywhere. Vendors along the beach rent chairs, umbrellas, rafts and beach trykes, and other water toys.

Don't forget the simple beach pleasures. You can practice your "porpoise" stroke by swimming alongside real pods of friendly bottle-nosed dolphins who arch through the waves close to the Atlantic shore. Enjoy kite flying, crabbing, sand-castle building, or simply relaxing in the sun to the sound of the surf.

For more information on Hilton Head Island's beaches, see the Hilton Head Island Chamber of Commerce's *Hilton Head Island Vacation Planner.*

Family and Kid Fun

- **Gregg Russell.** The Pied Piper of Hilton Head, Gregg Russell sings under the one-hundred-year-old live oak in Harbour Town. He enchants children and adults with his presence, sixties lyrics, and good-spirited fun. Don't miss this old-fashioned, small-town gathering. Your kids will be converts, chanting the "Gregg Russell Bubble Gum Kid Song," a light-hearted ditty with a refrain about "bugger in the sugar." Gradeschoolers love this stuff. The performances are free, Sunday through Friday from 8:00 to 9:00 P.M. in summer.
- **Gregg Russell's Fun for Kids.** Based in Harbour Town at the town pool, the day camp has full and half-day programs for ages four to twelve from 9:00 A.M. to 4:00 P.M. Each morning kids go on a daily outing; trips include crabbing, playing mini-golf, shrimp trawling, and searching for dolphins: Register in advance; call (843)671-3590.
- **Bubble Gum Cruise Club.** If your kids can't get enough of Hilton Head's resident troubadour, then take this hour-long scenic cruise. Gregg Russell sings onboard. Available Thursday and Friday 9:30 A.M.; (843) 842-4155. Vagabond Cruise, which offers the Bubble Gum Cruise, also offers one-and-a-half-hour ocean dolphin cruises

and in the evening, fireworks cruises and sunset trip cruises.
- **Kids' Cruise.** Designed for kids, this two-hour cruise aboard the *Gypsy* provides a hands-on Low Country experience. Kids learn how to throw a shrimp net, pull crab pots, fish for shark, and spot a dolphin; (843) 363-2900.
- **Commander Zodiac.** Zodiac raft outings take you and your kids into Calibogue Sound to get close to frolicking dolphins and maybe motor up to a shrimp boat. The trips leave from South Beach Marina, Sea Pines Plantation. Ages six to sixteen can sign up for the three-day Commander Zodiac Junior Sailing School. Kids can also take outings with Captain Zodiac's/Kids Waterfun, a day adventure of dolphin spotting, crabbing, water-balloon tossing, and face painting; (843) 671-3344.
- **Awesome Adventures Kids Camp.** Older kids, ages nine to sixteen, kayak, sail, waterski, parasail, surf, and mountain bike. Check in at Shelter Cove Marina, but call ahead (843-842-7024).
- **Kayak.** Learn kayaking with Outside Hilton Head. Make it a family outing or sign your kids up for their Kids Kayak Camp for ages seven to ten and eleven to fourteen (843-686-6996).

(continued)

Family and Kid Fun *(continued)*

- **Museum Camp.** At the Coastal Discovery Museum's ecological-oriented camps, kids learn about fish, dolphins, beach habitats, and Hilton Head's early Native Americans. The four-day sessions are available for children entering grades one through eight; call (843) 689-6767; www.coastaldiscovery.org.

- **Eco-Adventures.** The Coastal Discovery Museum offers nature-oriented outings for families and adults. Every second Thursday of each month, the museum offers SkyWatch, an astronomy program highlighting the constellations, the planets, and the moon's geography. Major celestial events, such as meteor showers, have special viewing times. Take a birding or dolphin cruise, pho-

tography class, or beach walk (843-689-6767; www.coastaldiscovery.org).

- **Sea Pines EcoTours.** Among the nine ecological outings for families and adults offered by naturalist guides are bike tours, stargazing nights, crabbing, fishing, and beach explorations (800) SEAPINES, extension 4530; www.seapines.com.

- **Shrimping.** Learn how shrimp are caught and help pull in the nets. Then enjoy your catch. One child sails free with two adults. Call (843) 384-7833.

- **Bicycling.** Pedal past lagoons and creeks and through pine and palmetto-tree woods and stands of live oaks draped with Spanish moss. The flat lowland roads make pedaling easy even for young kids using training wheels.

Golf

Ranked as one of the top golf and tennis destinations in the United States, Hilton Head lures avid sports enthusiasts who want quality facilities and pleasing views. Hilton Head sports twenty-two golf courses. These include **Robert Culpp Golf Course** at the **Palmetto Dunes Resort;** (843) 785-1138. This course uses geometric designs, including angular sand traps and square greens. Palmetto Dunes also has the **Robert Trent Jones** course (843-785-1138) and the **George Fazio Course** (843-785-1138). Among the places island regulars practice their swings is the **Harbour Town Golf Links,** Sea Pines Resort (843-363-4485), site of the annual April PGA tour event, the MCI Classic.

Other courses include the two eighteen-hole **Arthur Hills** courses—one at Palmetto Dunes (843-785-1140) and the other at Palmetto Hall (843-689-4100); **Rose Hill Country Club,** Rose Hill Plantation

(843-842-3740), and **Shipyard,** Shipyard Plantation (843-689-GOLF). For additional golf information check out www.golfisland.com.

For miniature golf excitement head to **Island Putt & Drive,** Highway 278 at Folly Field Road (843-842-9990), where they also have batting cages and a playworld with tunnels, slides, and games.

For a complete listing of Hilton Head Island's twenty-two golf courses, refer to the Hilton Head Island Chamber of Commerce's *Hilton Head Island Vacation Planner* or obtain the *Hilton Head Golf Planner.*

Tennis

To learn to lob and serve with the best, try the clinics and the private lessons at the island's posh tennis clubs. Four that often make *Tennis Magazine*'s list of the top 50 tennis clubs are **Port Royal Racquet Club,** Port Royal Resort (843-686-8803); **Sea Pines Racquet Club,** Sea Pines Resort (843-363-4495); **Palmetto Dunes Tennis Center,** Palmetto Dunes Resort (843-785-1152); and the **Van der Meer Shipyard Racquet Club,** Shipyard Plantation (843-785-8388).

For some intensive instruction for you and your children, sign on for Tennis University at the **Van der Meer Tennis Center,** Shipyard Plantation (843) 686-8804 or (800) 845-6138; www.vandermeertennis.com. Besides lessons for adults, the center offers daily and weekly programs for ages three to five, six to eight, plus clinics and advanced programs for ages nine to sixteen.

For more information on Hilton Head's tennis facilities, refer to the Hilton Head Island Chamber of Commerce's *Hilton Head Island Vacation Planner.*

Wildlife and Waters

When you want a break from such man-made pleasures as tennis and golf, sample the art of nature at Hilton Head. See deer, or possibly an alligator, as you walk along 7 miles of trails at the **Sea Pines Forest Preserve,** Sea Pines Resort; (843) 785-3333 or (800) 732-7463; www.seapines.com. The forest preserve offers visitors a taste of South Carolina wilderness. Bring along a picnic lunch and pause awhile. The preserve's two trails, the Indian Shell Ring Loop and the Waterfowl Pond Loop, are both self-guided nature walks, although during summer months an on-site naturalist leads walks and haywagon rides, a nice alternative in the heat.

Shopping

Just before the causeway to Hilton Head are more than eighty outlet stores that offer discounts of 20 percent or more. This is a good rainy-day diversion for older kids and teens. Hilton Head Factory Stores 1 & 2, 1414 Fording Island Road, Bluffton, S.C.; (843) 837-4399 or (888) SHOP-333; www.charter-oak.com/hiltonhead.

Hilton Head Island holds something special in store for every member of the family.

Walk through stands of oak, pine, bay, and sassafras trees, past a wild-flower meadow, and along the shores of two small lakes. Sometimes white herons, who nest here, dot the nearby trees. If you bring a permit (obtained from the CSA Security Office, 843-671-7170) and a pole, you can fish for crappie and bream (all released). But whatever you do, don't wade in the water, as alligators rule here. In fall the preserve is also an especially good spot to admire the thousands of migratory birds, flying in V formations, that head south along the Atlantic Flyway. A special treat for little kids are the haywagon rides. Horseback rides are also available from Lawton Stables (843-671-2586).

For more information on the Sea Pines Forest Preserve, write or call Sea Pines, 32 Greenwood Drive, Hilton Head Island, South Carolina 29938; (843) 785-3333 or (888) 807-6873.

Be sure you see the plants and birds along the paths of the **Audubon-Newhall Preserve,** Palmetto Bay Road, while touring its fifty acres of woods and wetlands. Walk through areas of saw palmetto, sapling live oak, thickets of bracken ferns, and fetterbush. Along the nature trail look for raccoon and deer prints and mole tunnels. Self-guiding brochures are available inside the park. Call (843) 785-5775.

Look for snowy egrets, blue herons, the endangered wood stork, and white ibis, as well as raccoons and deer at the **Pinckney Island Wildlife Preserve,** entrance on U.S. 278, a half-mile west of Hilton Head Island. It's the largest refuge island in the South Carolina-Georgia area. Bring

The Golden Isles of Georgia

The Golden Isles of Georgia include Jekyll Island, St. Simons Island, Sea Island, Sapelo, Blackbeard, St. Catherines, Cumberland, and Little St. Simons. Each has a different personality.

- **Jekyll Island,** with 10 miles of beach plus golf and tennis courts, is a resort area. The Jekyll Island Club Hotel (912-635-2600 or 800-535-9547; www.jekyllisland.com) offers the Club Juniors Program. Kids go on bicycle safaris, and enjoy crabbing, beach explorations, and turtle watches. Contact the Jekyll Island Welcome Center, 901 Jekyll Island Causeway (912-635-3636 or 877-453-5955), for more information.
- **St. Simons,** which was a base for English ships as early as 1736, offers visitors golf, fishing, and biking trails.
- **Cumberland,** accessible by ferry from Saint Mary's, Georgia (912-882-4335), was once the exclusive retreat of wealthy families. Along with a few remaining private estates and bed and breakfast inns, the island has more than 8,000 acres of wilderness available for day visits and camping. Kids love hiking along the trails, admiring the dunes and forests, searching for wild horses, and from April to August, seeking the loggerhead turtles who lay their eggs along the beach. For more information contact the Cumberland Island National Seashore, P.O. Box 806, Saint Mary's, Georgia 31558; (912) 882-4335.

your own drinking water to Pinckney, as there's none available on the island. Covering more than 4,000 acres of salt marsh, forestland, brushland, and freshwater ponds, Pinckney is located between Hilton Head and the South Carolina mainland. Cars are not allowed, so bring your bikes, as the 14 miles of trails make scenic bicycling and hiking paths. Pinckney Island is named after Charles Cotesworth Pinckney, who received the island from his father and lived there until 1824. C. C. Pinckney was a soldier in the Revolutionary War, a presidential candidate in 1804, and a signer of the U.S. Constitution.

More Kids Stuff

Besides EcoAdventures and Camp, the **Coastal Discovery Museum,** 100 William Hilton Parkway (843-689-6767; www.coastaldiscovery.org) is a nifty place to visit. Kids can see for themselves how heavy a loggerhead sea turtle shell is (the turtles weight around 300 pounds), follow the trails in the Butterfly Garden, or take a tour of the old Ridgeland Plantation.

The **Self Family Arts Center,** 14 Shelter Cove Lane (843-842-ARTS or 888-860-ARTS; www.artscenter-hhi.org) is a place to introduce young children to theater, with its year-round theater, dance, art, and music performances. After enjoying Gregg Russell's show at Harbour Town, kids can play at the Harbour Town playground.

The **Sea Pines Lighthouse** (843-671-0429) is open every day from 9:30 A.M. to 9:00 P.M., with a fine view of Hilton Head and gift shops on the top and at the bottom. For more information about activities for kids, call the Hilton Head Chamber of Commerce (843-785-3673 or 800-523-3373) for a copy of *The Kids Guide to Hilton Head Island.*

SIDE TRIPS

- Day trips from Hilton Head include **Savannah** (see the Savannah chapter), and the barrier islands.
- Not part of the Golden Isles, **Daufuskie,** an island 4 miles south of Hilton Head and accessible by ferry from Hilton Head, provides another interesting day trip. This is the island Pat Conroy wrote about in *The Water Is Wide.* His book depicts the rural lifestyle of this isolated island, where many inhabitants still speak Gullah, a dialect that combines Creole and English. Nonetheless, the resorts are arriving, including golf clubs at Melrose and Haig's Point. For now you can still take a walk and imagine life here in plantation days and at the turn of the century.

WHERE TO STAY

Hilton Head Island has a variety of lodgings, ranging from elegant resorts to more affordable home and villa rentals.

The tried-and-true standard for luxury is the **Westin Resort,** Port Royal Resort (843-681-4000 and 800-228-3000), the island's only 5-diamond property. Camp Wackatoo, organized activities for ages four to twelve, is available from Memorial Day through Labor Day. Awesome Adventures, available summer afternoons, is a sports-oriented fun camp for ages nine to sixteen. Teens windsurf, kayak, raft, and have lots of fun outdoors and with one another. The Westin Kids Club, an amenities program, makes family stays easier by providing, upon request, items such as a crib, bed rails, and potty seats. This beachfront hotel has indoor and outdoor pools, and the adjacent Van der Meer Tennis center is first-rate. Villas are also available. Call (800) WESTIN-1 or (843) 681-4000.

Disney's Hilton Head Island Resort, a time-share resort, offers families the convenience of studio or one-, two-, and three-bedroom villas, each complete with kitchen facilities. The lodgings, which are not beachfront, are located on a private islet, Longview Island, within Shelter Cove. The resort's beach club with outdoor pool and snack bar is 1½ miles away. Free shuttles take you there. In summer the Disney Discovery Club, the children's program for ages three to twelve, operates daily from Memorial Day to Labor Day and on weekends and holidays the rest of the year. Call (800) 453-4911 or (843) 341-4100.

The Hyatt Regency Hilton Head has children's programs for ages three to twelve in summer and during spring break. The beachfront property has an indoor and an outdoor pool, bike rentals, and a convenience shop that sells take-out sandwiches and snacks (800-233-1234 or 843-785-1234; www.hyatthotels.com. **The Hilton Head Island Hilton Resort** offers the Vacation Station children's camp for ages three to twelve from Memorial Day to Labor Day and on weekends and holidays the rest of the year. The beachfront property has an outdoor pool. Holiday carnivals and daily activities for families and teens are also available. These guest rooms, which are larger than typical rooms, come with refrigerator, coffeepot and microwave (800-221-2424 or 843-341-8056; www.hiltonheadhilton.com.

On a moderate budget? Try the **Holiday Inn Oceanfront,** Pope Avenue at Coligny Circle, 1 South Forest Beach Drive, Oceanfront; (843) 785-5126 or (800) 423-9897. This hotel has one- and two-bedroom units on the beach, a pool, and golf and tennis packages.

Sea Pines Resort, 32 Greenwood Drive (800-SEAPINE), is a villa resort complex with its own nature preserve, plus golf and tennis facilities. In addition to junior tennis, golf, and sailing clinics, Sea Pines offers a Fun For Kids program for four to twelve year olds from Memorial Day to Labor Day, plus EcoTours and scavenger hunts. Other programs for children and families are offered year-round.

Villa rentals provide families with more space for less money, especially when these homes are shared with another family. For rental information call **Adventure Inn Villa Rentals** (843-785-5151 or 800-845-9500), **Hilton Head Vacation Rentals** (843-686-3400 or 800-732-7671), or **Seacoast Homes and Villas** (843-686-6226 or 800-654-7101).

For more information on Hilton Head's child care services, lodging, and attractions, contact the Hilton Head Island Chamber of Commerce at (843) 785-3673 or (800) 523-3373; www.hiltonheadisland.org.

WHERE TO EAT

There are lots of places where it's fun to take the whole family, especially if your kids are older. The **Old Fort Pub,** 65 Skull Creek Drive (843-681-2386), is known for its low-country cuisine, especially its oyster pies. For dining with a marina view, try **Café Europa,** base of the Harbour Town Lighthouse; (843) 671-3399. This restaurant has the best sunset views. Open for breakfast, lunch, and dinner; reservations suggested for dinner. The ice-cream shop **Scoops,** also in the Lighthouse, is known for its Sweet Georgia Peach and Pecan ice cream and its mango sorbet. Older kids might like the dinner theater at the **Port Royal Clubhouse;** (843) 681-1700. Try **Crazy Crab,** Harbour Town (843-363-2722), for reasonably priced seafood and a marina view. A special treat is Crazy Crab's low-country Crazy Crab Boil (Alaskan crab legs boiled with sausage and sweet corn and served with a baked potato). For a memorable meal, suitable for well-behaved teens, try the **Barony,** at the Westin Resort; (843) 681-4000.

The Hilton Head Island Chamber of Commerce's *Hilton Head Island Vacation Planner* has an extensive listing of the island's many restaurants.

FOR MORE INFORMATION

A handy reference is the *Hilton Head Island Vacation Planner,* available from the **Hilton Head Island Chamber of Commerce,** P.O. Box 5647, Hilton Head Island, South Carolina 29938; (843) 785-3673 or (800) 523-3373; www.hiltonheadisland.org.

Emergency Numbers

Ambulance, fire, and police: 911

Parkway Medical Center and Clinics, 25 Hospital Center Boulevard: (843) 785-7515

Although Hilton Head Island does not have a twenty-four-hour pharmacy, the Parkway Medical Center's pharmacy remains open until 7:00 P.M.

Twenty-four-hour poison control: Palmetto Poison Center; (800) 922-1117

CHATTANOOGA

C hattanooga will surprise you. Downtown is no longer a down-and-out collection of empty warehouses and eyesores. The revitalized waterfront is eminently child-friendly and appealing; its gem, the Tennessee Aquarium, sparkles with river wonders. With lots of Civil War history, natural attractions such as caverns and mountaintop lookouts plus rows of outlet shops, this city offers families a manageable and affordable combination of museum and outdoor attractions.

GETTING THERE

The **Chattanooga Metropolitan Airport** (423–855–2200) is the only area airport, located about twenty minutes from the city center. The airlines that operate here are US Airways, Northwest Airlink, United Express, ComAir, and ASA. **Greyhound/Trailways** Bus Lines (423–892–1277) provides interstate service to Chattanooga.

Three interstate highways, I–59, I–75, and I–24, intersect near the greater Chattanooga area.

GETTING AROUND

Car-rental agencies are located near or at the airport.

Electric buses provide a free shuttle service in the downtown area. The shuttle, which runs along Market Street from the Chattanooga Choo Choo Holiday Inn to the Tennessee Aquarium at the waterfront, stops every five minutes on every block. The shuttle operates from 6:00 A.M. until 9:30 P.M. Monday through Friday, from 9:00 A.M. until 9:30 P.M. Saturday, and from 9:00 A.M. until 8:30 P.M. Sunday. For more information call **CARTA** (Chattanooga Area Regional Transportation Authority) at (423) 629-1473. Public buses are also available. Call (423) 629-1411 for more information.

Chattanooga

AT A GLANCE

▶ Take in the view from Lookout Mountain, the Incline Railway, and Rock City Gardens

▶ Visit the Tennessee Aquarium

▶ Explore Chickamauga and Chattanooga National Military Park

▶ Tour Lookout Mountain Caverns

▶ Chattanooga Area Convention & Visitors Bureau: (423) 756-8687 or (800) 322-3344; www.chattanoogafun.com

WHAT TO SEE AND DO

The place to start your tour of Chattanooga is at **Ross's Landing,** 100 Broad Street, the revitalized area on the downtown riverfront. What the city affectionately labels "a front porch, a quilt, a tapestry, a park" is, after millions of dollars in revitalization, a very pleasant place. Between 1990 and 1995, twenty-four acres of abandoned warehouses and buildings were transformed into a lively riverfront district complete with park, world-class aquarium, rows of outlet shops, a children's museum, and office space.

Ross's Landing Park and Plaza occupies four acres. At the **Chattanooga Visitors Center,** 2 Broad Street (423-756-8687), pick up brochures, and find out about organized tours. Allow some time to explore the plaza at Ross's Landing. Children love this imaginative outdoor, urban park. Not only is it great for running, but you can easily turn your time here into a treasure hunt in which you discover the city's history. Named for Cherokee chieftain John Ross, who established a trading post on the banks of the Tennessee River almost 200 years ago, the plaza has a wavy arch to climb and historic time bands that contain lots of interesting items.

The brochure *Discover the Legacy of Life on the River* describes the plaza's time bands, which go further back in history as you get closer to the river. Within each band landscaping features suggest parts of Chattanooga's natural history, and appropriate artifacts represent the band's time period. The plaza brochure asks children to find such items as seven

The Tennessee Aquarium

This facility, the world's largest freshwater aquarium, presents the ecology of river systems through clever exhibits that depict the changes in river water from forest to cypress swamp to the Mississippi Delta. Explanatory material, however, is sometimes sparse. Nevertheless, children grow wide-eyed at the huge, often wall-size, tanks with their interesting river inhabitants.

- Walk through two living forests and a 60-foot canyon as 9,000 animals swim, fly, crawl, and slither in their re-created natural habitats.
- See 80-pound catfish and the world's largest collection of freshwater turtles at the River Gallery.
- In Amazon River see piranha dart among anaconda and boa constrictors.
- In VENOM! Striking Beauties go face to face with some of the world's deadliest fish.

- During the winter months Dive Into Winter lets visitors watch as divers feed otters and other marine animals. Look, also, for activity carts throughout the aquarium, which have see-and-touch materials for kids.
- Watch wildlife movies at the 3-D IMAX theater with its six-story screen.

The Tennessee Aquarium, 1 Broad Street, Ross's Landing; (800) 262–0695 or (423) 266–3467; www.tnaqua.org.

arrowheads, two magnolia flowers, seven concrete snapping turtles, and the composer of "Chattanooga Choo Choo."

There's much to learn here. For example, in the children's play area, Band 126, the limestone steps are reminiscent of Chattanooga's natural limestone bluffs. The moldings of Civil War Minié balls, buckles, and canteens embedded in the steps suggest the post–Civil War era of 1875, which this time band represents. Band 123 celebrates the city's railroading past circa 1890; railroad tracks frame lyrics from "Chattanooga Choo Choo," popularized by Glenn Miller. Band 122, which represents the date 1900, contains the wavy bridge, a kid-favorite. Embedded in the bridge are bottle bottoms cast from original Coca-Cola molds; this display honors Chattanooga as the home of the world's first franchised Coca-Cola bottling plant.

All the bands are not "fun"; some of them acknowledge ignoble deeds. The events leading to the Trail of Tears, the removal of the Cherokees from this region, are represented in Band 128, year 1855. Some of the stones are cracked to symbolize the broken promises made to the Cherokees, and a quotation from a local paper circa 1838 says, "The scenes of distress exhibited at Ross's Landing defy all description."

Museums

At Ross's Landing is the **Creative Discovery Museum,** 321 Chestnut Street; (423) 756-2738; www.cdmfun.org. Admission. The Kinetic Water Sculpture, the museum's signature piece, celebrates the transforming power of ideas, setting a tone for the museum. Children push slides to change the pattern of the falling water, create clouds to strike chimes, and make bubbles. Toddlers have their own tank of floating boats, cargo ships, and blocks with which to make a splash.

In the new ZOOMzone, (from PBS show of the same name) kids can watch themselves perform scientific experiments on television or surf the web to see what's new in the world of science. In the Inventor's Workshop they can build robots and create their own inventions.

At the Artist's Studio children create prints by making rubbings from items as diverse as Mayan artifacts, sneakers, and Braille texts. Children become naturalists and scientists in the Field Scientist's Lab, dominated by a full-scale replica of *Tyrannosaurus rex.* Kids literally "dig" this exhibit by using tools such as a Plexi scraper and toothbrush to uncover buried dinosaur remains. For younger children the Little Yellow House offers many of the same activities but designed for ages four and under. Throughout the year the museum holds workshops on subjects such as weird wonders in science, while Summer Discovery Camps turn kids into time travelers or take them on science odysseys. There's also a four-day Winter Holiday Camp held between Christmas and New Year's Day.

About a ten-minute walk from the aquarium and children's museum is the **Hunter Museum of American Art,** 10 Bluff View (423-267-0968; www.huntermuseum.org), which houses one of the most complete collections (many artists from different periods are represented) of American art in the Southeast. Children are charmed by the building, a 1904 classic Southern mansion, and also by the works of such notables as Andy Warhol, Mary Cassatt, and Andrew Wyeth. Toddler Tuesdays and Wee Wednesdays encourage creativity in preschoolers. Call for schedule and program information. Admission.

War memorabilia is found at the **National Medal of Honor Museum,** Fourth and Georgia, located at the south end of Veterans Bridge; (423) 267-1737. This facility features artifacts from the Civil War, the Spanish-American War, World War I, World War II, Vietnam, Korean War, and the Persian Gulf War. The museum also houses a piece of the historic Berlin Wall.

If you like cars, trucks and wrecks, visit the **International Towing and Recovery Hall of Fame Museum,** 401 Broad Street; (423) 267-3132;

Civil War History

- **Tennessee Civil War Museum,** 3914 St. Elmo Avenue; (423) 821–4954; www. tncivilwarmuseum.com. Admission. Find out how the common soldier—Union and Confederate—lived and fought. A historian gives daily talks about uniforms, equipment, and weapons and tells real war stories. Kids can feel how much a Civil War musket weighed and touch Civil War relics in the archaeological section.

- **Battles for Chattanooga Electric Map & Museum,** 1110 East Brow Road, Lookout Mountain; (423) 821–2812. Young children like the museum's three-dimensional battle map with 5,000 miniature soldiers, 650 lights, and sound effects. The small museum displays rifles, uniforms, and other Civil War artifacts. Admission.

- **Chickamauga and Chattanooga National Military Park.** The Visitor Center is located 9 miles south of Chattanooga on U.S. 27. The 8,113-acre park, located in Georgia and Tennessee, commemorates the Civil War battles in September and November 1863 that ended with the Union forces gaining control of Chattanooga. The Visitor Center has one of the best collections of Springfield rifles.

- **Point Park,** northern crest of Lookout Mountain (reach this via the Incline Railroad). Part of the Chickamauga and Chattanooga National Military Park, Point Park commemorates the Battle of Chattanooga, "The Battle Above the Clouds," with a series of cannons. The seven-minute narration about the battle, given at the Visitor Center, is worth seeing.

www.internationaltowingmuseum.com. The brightly colored antique vehicles and tow trucks look like life-size toys, and, in fact, there's a tow truck children can ride on. Admission.

Two other museums to consider: At the **Chattanooga Regional History Museum,** two blocks from the aquarium, at 400 Chestnut Street; (423-265-3247), hands-on activities for children and adults include a touch wall, discovery boxes, and activity guides. Admission. **Chattanooga African American History Museum,** 200 East Martin Luther King Boulevard (423-266-8658), has African-American art, records, newspapers, a moving tribute to Chattanooga's African American heroes, and cultural items such as an African village with a grass hut and a replica of an Ethiopian temple. The museum's Bessie Smith Hall, named for the legendary singer, serves as a training ground for young singers and musicians.

The Lookout Mountain Area

You have to see **Lookout Mountain**. You can drive to the top, but it's much more fun to ride the **Lookout Mountain Incline Railway,** 827 East Brow Road, Lookout Mountain; (423) 821-4224; www.lookoutmtnattractions. com. The 72.7-percent grade makes chugging up this mile road memorable. The railcars, which have been taking visitors to the top of Lookout Mountain Station since 1895, make three to four trips an hour. Free parking is available at the base of the mountain. Admission.

Chattanooga is an Indian name that means "rock coming to a point." Lookout Mountain towers high above the city. A key strategic position, this mountain was the site of many battles, including the last battle of the American Revolutionary War and the Battle above the Clouds, an important Union victory over the Confederates, who had held the mountain during the Civil War. Halfway up the mountain is **Cravens House,** off State Route 148 (423-821-7786), Civil War headquarters for both Confederate and Federal troops. The building houses Civil War artifacts.

At the top of the mountain is **Rock City Gardens,** 1400 Patten Road, Lookout Mountain; (706) 820-2531; www.seerockcity.com. Frieda Carter planted ferns, shrubs, wildflowers, and native plants to make a garden out of these fourteen acres of unusual rock formations.

Paths lead you through various rock formations covered with moss. Because the narrow paths aren't suitable for strollers, kids should be old enough to feel comfortable walking. Little ones especially enjoy the deer park and the displays in Fairyland Caverns and Mother Goose Village. Paths lead by odd-shaped rocks called Tortoise Shell and Mushroom Rock, through tiny breaks in big boulders called Needle's Eye and Fat Man's Squeeze, and across a "swing-along bridge." At the pinnacle, called **Lovers' Leap,** you see a sweeping panorama of seven states.

Not too far from Lookout Mountain is **Ruby Falls,** Route 4, Scenic Highway, Lookout Mountain (423-821-2544; www.rubyfalls.com), a 145-foot underground waterfall inside the **Lookout Mountain Caverns.** To get here you descend in an elevator that takes you forty-four stories below ground level. This alone causes some children to stand in hushed awe.

Then you walk along a winding route through the caverns (bring a sweater, as it's always 60 degrees in the caverns), and signs instruct you to eye stalactite and stalagmite formations that look like "steak and eggs" or a "crystal chandelier" or the "Leaning Tower." These forced resemblances and tacky signs tend to delight elementary-age children. Finally, after a half-hour walk, you reach Ruby Falls, where music from *2001: A Space Odyssey* and multicolored lights add drama.

An important note for parents: The ⅘-mile round-trip walk takes about an hour, and there are no bathrooms in the caverns. Back above ground, the Visitors Center has these facilities.

Before you leave visit the **Ruby Falls Castle Tower** if you have preschoolers and young elementary-age kids. The Fun Forest play area has climbing equipment, the views of Chattanooga are scenic, and a refreshment stand offers burgers and hot dogs.

Parks and Green Spaces

Reflection Riding, Garden Road, off I-24, exit 175 (423-821-9582), a 300-acre botanical garden nestled between the western slope of Lookout Mountain and Lookout Creek, is a peaceful place for strolling, especially in spring. You can also drive on the 3½-mile paved route, or *riding,* an English term for "path of pleasure." Children like finding Lookout Mountain's Great Stone Face, a landmark on Lookout Mountain that can be seen from Reflection Riding. Legend has it that when a great chief, the last of his tribe, prayed that his nation wouldn't be forgotten, a great wind came and etched his face in the mountain.

At the gateway to Reflection Riding is the **Tennessee Wildlife Center,** 400 Garden Road; (423) 821-1160; www.tnwildlifecenter.org. This environmental education center hosts various interpretive activities for children and adults. Check their schedule. The Niche, a discovery room for kids, has a crawl-in beaver lodge and other hands-on items. The newly opened Discovery Forest Treehouse along the Blue Heron boardwalk is an intricate structure kids will have a ball climbing through.

Located near the Hunter Museum of Art in Chattanooga, the **River Gallery Sculpture Garden,** 214 Spring Street (423-267-7353; www.bluffviewartdistrict.com), is a two-acre oasis situated on a bluff that overlooks the river. The park is carefully landscaped and adorned with sculpture. Kids tend to appreciate both the play space and the outdoor sculpture.

Trains

What would Chattanooga be without trains? That's what one group of businesspeople thought when they established the **Tennessee Valley Railroad Museum,** 4119 Cromwell Road (423-894-8028; www.tvrail.com), and what another group thought when they renovated

Tennessee Riverpark

Tennessee Riverpark, 4301 Amnicola Highway (423-842-0177), runs for 7 miles along the Tennessee River, providing open spaces and landscaped walking and jogging trails. The riverwalk begins at Ross's Landing Park and Plaza and extends over the Walnut Street Bridge to the Bluff View Art District (www.bluffviewartdistrict.com), an enclave of inns, galleries, restaurants, and museums.

The final section of Tennessee Riverpark is Coolidge Park and the Northshore riverwalk (423-757-2143), which opened in the summer of 2000. This ten-acre park directly across from the Bluff View Art District has a fully restored antique carousel with three rows of beautifully carved animals that will delight even older children. Kids will enjoy using the two metal hopscotch courts and sitting around the fountain, where sculpted animals squirt water.

the depot for the **Chattanooga Choo Choo,** 1400 Market Street (423–266–5000). (See also Chattanooga Choo Choo Holiday Inn under Where to Stay.) At the Tennessee Valley Railroad Museum, peruse such beauties as steam locomotive 4501, built in 1911; a 1926 dining car; and a 1917 office car, complete with three bedrooms and four bathrooms. The museum offers scenic, round-trip excursions aboard steam or diesel trains into northwest Georgia. One trip from Chattanooga ascends Missionary Ridge, then skirts the Chickamauga and Chattanooga National Military Park before chugging through Rock Springs, LaFayette, and Summerville. The trips include lunch. Call (423) 894–8028. Admission.

Glenn Miller made the song "Chattanooga Choo Choo" famous in 1941, but long before that, from 1900 to 1950, the railroad heyday, trains made Chattanooga famous. Twenty-four investors restored the famous depot in 1972 and bought railroad coaches, which were turned into hotel suites. At present the complex features outdoor gardens, the world's largest HO-gauge model railroad display, and a Holiday Inn.

More Attractions

If you want to see more caverns, visit **Lost Sea,** exit 60 off Highway 68 (423–337–6616), and **Raccoon Mountain Crystal Caverns,** 319 West Hills Drive (423–821–9403). Lost Sea is an underground lake and a registered National Landmark. Children seem charmed by the anthodites, rare cave flowers, and cascades of natural formations seen from a glass-bottom boat. Bring a sweater, as Lost Sea remains a constant 58 degrees year-round. The tour of Raccoon Mountain Caverns is a forty-five-minute walk through an underground cavern past rock formations, and there's also gemstone panning.

Teens might want to sample hang gliding at the **Lookout Mountain Flight Park and Resort,** Route 2, Box 215-H, Department V, Rising Fawn, Georgia; (800) 688–5637. The launch site is fifteen minutes from Lookout Mountain in Trenton, Georgia, 1,350 feet above Lookout Valley. For those not yet ready for that big leap alone, tandem flights, in which a passenger is harnessed to an instructor, are available.

Lake Winnepesaukah Amusement Park, P.O. Box 490, Rossville, 8 miles from downtown Chattanooga (706–866–5681), offers such traditional kid-pleasers as a Ferris wheel, carousel, minitrain, and go-carts, plus the usual assortment of rides that swing and fling, and musical shows at the Jukebox Junction. Admission.

Tours

The *Southern Belle,* a 500-passenger steamboat, operated by the **Chattanooga River Boat Company,** 201 Riverfront Parkway, Pier 2 (423–266–4488 or 800–766–2784), departs from downtown Chattanooga for a variety of sight-seeing, breakfast, lunch, and dinner cruises on the Tennessee River.

The **Chattanooga Ducks,** 201 West Fifth Street (423-756-DUCK), authentic World War II amphibious landing vehicles, take families on a sixty-minute narrated tour of downtown Chattanooga and then on a trip around Maclellan Island in the Tennessee River.

The **Tennessee Valley Railroad,** 4119 Cromwell Road (423-894-8028; www.tvrail.com) offers scheduled scenic tours. "Autumn Leaf Special" steam excursions travel an 80-mile round-trip through scenic areas.

Performing Arts

Call **Allied Arts,** 20 Bluff View (423-756-2787; www.alliedartschatt. org), for a schedule of the performances and showings of the city's more than sixty cultural groups. The **Tivoli Theater and Auditorium,** 709 Broad Street (423-757-5050), built in 1921, has been expanded to seat 1,762. This facility, as well as the **Soldiers and Sailors Memorial Auditorium,** 309 McCallie Avenue (423-757-5042), hosts music concerts from the blues to classical to country to opera, as well as Broadway performances. For listings of what's playing at these venues and others, call the **Allied Arts** 24-hour hotline (423-756-ARTS). **The Bessie Smith Performance Hall,** located in Heritage Hall, 200 Martin Luther King Boulevard (423-757-0020), is a cabaret-style facility that provides practice rooms for students. Call for performance schedules.

For some local bluegrass and mountain entertainment, visit **The Mountain Opry,** Walden Ridge Civic Center, P.O. Box 651, atop Signal Mountain, Walden, Tennessee (no phone). Every Friday night at 8:00 P.M. locals play, and the music is free. Your children might like this introduction to down-home, musical mountain magic.

Shopping

Prime Outlets at **Warehouse Row,** 1110 Market Street (423-267-1129 or 888-260-7620; www.primeoutlets.com), located in downtown Chattanooga, is an upscale mall of outlet and off-price stores. More than thirty-five stores offer clothing, home furnishings, jewelry, and snacks. The shops include J. Crew, Polo/Ralph Lauren Factory Store, and a J. Peterman outlet store.

Flea Market—East Ridge, 6725 Ringgold Road (423-894-3960), is a combination indoor/outdoor market open weekends, with more than 500 vendors on an eleven-acre location.

Hamilton Place, I-75, exit 4-A or 5 (423-894-7177; www.hamiltonplace. com), is Tennessee's largest mall, with 200 shops, including Laura Ashley, the Gap, the Disney Store, and Children's Place, plus thirty eateries and seventeen theaters. **Northgate Mall,** Highway 153 North and Hixson

Pike (423-870-9521), is a more elegant mall, with one hundred shops and three department stores.

Dragon Dreams Museum & Gifts, 6724-A East Brainerd Road (423-892-2384; www.dragonvet.com), has thousands of dragon carvings in jade, ivory, metal, pewter, brass, and other materials, plus drawings and prints, furniture and toys. Seasonal hours, so call ahead.

Spectator Sports

The **Chattanooga Lookouts,** a minor league baseball team under the auspices of the Cincinnati Reds, offers baseball fun close-up in a brand new park. Call (423) 267-2208 for game times and ticket information.

SIDE TRIPS

Watts Bar Lake, in Spring City, is a 38,000-acre lake with 783 miles of shoreline. A favorite spot over the past few decades has been the **Watts Bar Resort;** (423) 365-9595.

SPECIAL EVENTS

For more information on these and other events, contact the Chattanooga Area Convention & Visitors Bureau (800) 322-3344.

February–April. CoffeeHouse Series, a concert series in downtown Miller Plaza every Tuesday evening at 7:00 P.M., offering a range of music from zydeco to jazz to blues and folk.

May. The Praters Mill Country Fair includes arts and crafts, food, and entertainment the old-fashioned way. River Roast, featuring a barbecue cooking competition, volleyball tournament, fireworks, and the Mayor's Regatta at Ross's Landing.

June. Riverbend Festival, a block party with country, jazz, blues, pop, folk, rock, and classical music.

October. Fall Color Cruise and Folk Festival, with a cruise by boat, car, or bus to view autumn in the mountains, then Southern cuisine and gospel music at the folk festival.

November–January. Rock City's Enchanted Garden of Lights, an outdoor walk through twenty-four dazzling scenes, illuminated by holiday lights, carolers, hot chocolate, cookies, and an appearance by Santa.

WHERE TO STAY

The lobby for the **Chattanooga Choo Choo/Holiday Inn,** 1400 Market Street (423–266–500 or 800–TRACK29; www.choochoo.com), is the renovated Terminal Station, which has been welcoming visitors since 1909. The thirty-acre complex features indoor/outdoor pools, rose gardens, and tennis courts. Easy access to the shuttle makes getting around town simple. Book months in advance to stay in one of the forty-eight sleeping rooms created in reconditioned railroad cars, a thrill for kids, and dine one night in the Chat Choo Choo "Dinner on the Diner."

The **Radisson Read House Hotel and Suites,** 827 Broad Street (423–266–4121 or 800–333–3333), features Victorian furnishings and is close to Chattanooga's main attractions. The lodging has an outdoor pool, two restaurants, and specialty shops on-site. Free shuttle service.

Days Inn Rivergate, 901 Carter Street (423–266–7331 or 800–329–7466), includes free continental breakfast, and has an outdoor pool and a gym.

Along I-75 there are many accommodations, including **Chattanooga Marriott,** Two Carter Plaza, at the Convention Center; (423) 756–0002 or (800) 228–9290. Located in downtown Chattanooga this facility has easy access to the area's attractions and has indoor/outdoor pools and a health club.

Comfort Suites Hotel, 7324 Shallowford Road (423–892–1500 or 800–228–5150) has an indoor pool and spa, plus free continental breakfast. **Comfort Suites/Downtown,** 2431 Williams Street (423–265–0008) has suites with microwaves and refrigerators, plus a free breakfast.

WHERE TO EAT

Sticky Fingers, Jack's Alley, 420 Broad Street; (423) 265–RIBS; www.stickyfingers.net. The locals love getting sticky fingers at this restaurant, noted for its pork and beef ribs; chicken is also available. On Tuesday nights the restaurant has a supervised playroom for children, with cartoons, coloring books, and games. At the **Big River Grill & Brewing Works,** 222 Broad Street (423–267–2739), get a home-brewed root beer with your pizza or pasta.

The **Southside Grill,** on Fourteenth and Cowart Streets (423–266–9211), has garnered praise for its imaginative interpretation of Southern staples. Try the Southside's lobster and crawfish grits and their fried green tomatoes.

The **Back Inn Café,** 412 East Second Street (423-265-5033), located in a turn-of-the-century mansion, features Italian cuisine. For more than forty years, **Town & Country Restaurant,** 110 North Market Street (423-267-8544), has been serving Southern fare and homemade soups. **The Loft,** 328 Cherokee Boulevard (423-266-3601), serves steak and seafood. A children's menu is available. **212 Market Street,** 212 Market Street (423-265-1212), offers imaginative entrees such as salmon with black bean sauce and grilled duck breast on noodle pancakes. A children's menu is available.

Some less expensive and fun places: **Cheeburger Cheeburger,** 138A Market Street (423-265-4108) has mouth-watering burgers or portabella sandwiches for vegetarians, plus a cute diner theme. **Vaudeville Cafe,** 108 Tremont (423-266-6202; www.vaudevillecafe.com), within walking distance of Coolidge Park, has servers who are paid entertainers (and prove it while serving) and a Mystery Dinner Theater every Sunday night. (Even their Web site is fun.) **Lupi's Pizza Pies,** 5506 Hixson Parkway (423-847-3700; www.lupi.com) has good pizza and a fun website.

FOR MORE INFORMATION

Contact the **Chattanooga Area Convention & Visitors Bureau,** 2 Broad Street (423-756-8687 or 800-332-3344; www.chattanoogafun.com), for a free copy of *Chattanooga Visitors Guide.* The Visitors Center is open daily from 8:30 A.M. to 5:30 P.M.

Emergency Numbers

Memorial Hospital, 2525 de Sales Avenue (423-495-2525); emergency room (423-495-8577)

Poison Hotline: Georgia (800-282-5846); Tennessee (800-288-9999)

Twenty-four-hour pharmacy: Walgreens, Ringgold Road (423-892-9511); CVS, Lee Highway (423-899-1186)

Twenty-four-hour Medical Information Line: Ask-A-Nurse (at Memorial Hospital); (423) 495-4545

NASHVILLE

Nashville is known as the home of country music but the city's sounds include rock 'n' roll, blues and soul. Come for the singing, but stay for the other attractions. Two major attractions are scheduled to open in spring 2001: the new Country Music Hall of Fame and the Frist Center for the Visual Arts, both paying homage to the creativity that sparks Nashville's musical and cultural heritage. And don't forget to pay homage to Nashville's *other* natural heritage by taking a drive through the rolling hills outside the city.

GETTING THERE

Nashville International Airport, about 8 miles from downtown (615-275-1600), serves American, American Eagle, Continental, Delta, Northwest, Southwest, TWA, United; and US Airways. **Grayline Airport Express** (615-275-1180) offers shuttle service between the airport and downtown. Rental cars are available at the airport.

Amtrak does not offer service to the Nashville area. **Greyhound Lines** (615-256-6141 or 800-231-2222) stops at their Nashville terminal, Eighth Avenue and McGavock Street.

Major roads into Nashville are I-65, which runs north–south into Kentucky and Alabama, and I-24, which runs northwest into Kentucky and Illinois and southeast into Georgia. I-40 runs east–west across the state and accesses Knoxville, Nashville, and Memphis.

Nashville is a port on the route of the **Delta Queen Steamboat Company's** historic paddlewheelers; (800) 543-1949. The ship has no special programs for kids, but older children and teens may like the river scenery and the shore stops.

GETTING AROUND

Nashville's public bus service, the **Metropolitan Transit Authority** (MTA—615-862-5950), operates buses throughout the county. For van transportation for the physically challenged, call (615) 880-3970. Try a

Nashville

AT A GLANCE

▶ See the Grand Ole Opry and *General Jackson* showboat

▶ Tour the Belle Meade Plantation, Old Hickory's The Hermitage, and the Nashville Toy Museum

▶ Ride the Tennessee Fox Trot Carousel

▶ Visit the Country Music Hall of Fame and Museum

▶ Nashville Convention and Visitors Bureau: (615) 259-4700; www.nashvillecvb.com.

downtown trolley ride with the **Nashville Trolley Company;** call (615) 862-5950. Passes are available at the Visitors Center.

Among the taxicabs available are **Yellow Cab Metro** (615-256-0101), and **Music City Taxi** (615-262-0451 or 800-359-9692). Take a **river taxi** between downtown Nashville and the Opryland area and complex. The boats cruise year-round, but schedules vary with the season; (615) 889-6611. Tickets are available at the Visitor Information Center.

WHAT TO SEE AND DO

Music Industry Attractions

Music is Nashville's lure. Use a visit to share country sounds as well as blues, gospel, bluegrass, and even alternative rock with your kids, although country predominates. The **Grand Ole Opry,** Grand Ole Opry House, 2804 Opryland Drive (615-889-3060; www.grandoleopry.com), is an American classic. Performances are broadcast Friday and Saturday nights on WSM-AM 650, and a segment is televised on TNN, The Nashville Network. Because of the show's popularity, it's best to order tickets in advance.

Opry Mills, a shopping, dining, and entertainment complex that opened in 2000, has more than 200 stores, as well as an IMAX theater, a bowling alley, a rappelling wall, and live entertainment. Call (877) SHOP FUN for more information. Opryland USA complex also has the huge **Opryland Hotel** (see Where to Stay), the broadcast studios of TNN, museums, and the *General Jackson* **Showboat,** 2812 Opryland Drive (615-871-6100), which plies the Cumberland River. The four-deck paddlewheeler appeals to kids who do best on the shorter, daytime cruises. There are midday, evening, and theme cruises, as well as holiday cruises in November and December.

The complex has three museums. Exhibits at the **Grand Ole Opry Museum,** 2802 Opryland Drive (615-889-3060; www.grandoleopry. com), honor Hall of Fame members and the Opry stars. Older children and teens into music tend to like listening to early recordings and playing with the interactive sound devices.

While you're in the neighborhood, visit **Music Valley Village,** across from Opryland Hotel; (615) 871-4005 or, outside Tennessee, (800) 847-9102. **Ernest Tubb's Record Shop** is known for its vintage record collection and for its live, country radio show, the **Midnite Jamboree,** held at the **Texas Troubadour Theater,** 2416 Music Valley Drive (615-885-0028). The **Nashville Palace,** 2400 Music Valley Drive (615-885-1540) is known for its live music—Tuesday is new talent night.

Visitors won't want to miss the city's tribute to country rhythms at the **Country Music Hall of Fame and Museum,** 4 Music Square East; (615) 256-1639 or 800-816-7652; www.country.com. If your family is really into the country music scene, ask for the Official Music Row Walking tour (or get it off the Web site), which takes you to fourteen stops between Owen Bradley Park and the old Country Music Hall of Fame. On the way you'll pass just about every major record producer in the industry, including Sony Music at 34 Music Square East.

In spring 2001 the new Country Music Hall of Fame is scheduled to open at Fifth Avenue South and Demonbreun Street, across from the Gaylord Entertainment Center and near Ryman Auditorium. The $37 million facility will house over one million artifacts, interactive displays, recordings, and films and will include a 225-seat theater, a museum store, and a restaurant. Admission.

Historical Sites

Nashville offers Southern history as well as country songs. Visit the **Belle Meade Plantation,** 5025 Harding Road; (615) 356-0501 or (800) 270-3991; www.citysearch.com/nas/plantation. Kids often have their own specially guided tour through the 1790 log cabin, the smokehouse, and the thoroughbred stables. Be sure to bring a picnic lunch so that you can enjoy the sun and the landscaped grounds, or try out the new cafe. Also new are a museum shop and an antique carriage collection. The Tennessee Jazz & Blues Concerts are held here Sundays, May through August, and the Belle Meade Fall Festival is in September. Admission.

Pay tribute to an American hero at **The Hermitage,** home of the seventh President of the United States, Andrew Jackson. It's at 4580 Rachel's

More Fun Stuff

- **The Tennessee Fox Trot Carousel.** Take a spin on this fanciful carousel whose "horses" are whimsical scenes and sculptures of famous people created by native Nashville artist Red Grooms. Located in Riverfront Park. For information call (615) 242-5546.
- **Jungle Gym.** At 66,000 square feet, this play structure is reputed to be the largest in the world; it can accommodate up to 1,000 children at a time. The Toddler Village has pint-size swings and slides. Nashville Zoo at Grassmere, 3777 Nolensville Road (615) 833-1534.
- **Horseback riding.** At Ju-Ro Stables, 735 Carver Lane, Mt. Juliet (615-449-6621; www. jurostables.com), beginners and experienced riders can enjoy one- two- or three-hour rides through open fields and wooded trails. Lessons are available, plus hayrides and cookouts.
- **Games.** Family Fun Center, 460 West Main Street, Hendersonville (615-824-5685) has ice skating, bumper cars, a virtual roller coaster, laser tag, a 3D motion theater, plus Pizza Hut and Lucy's Cafe.
- **Water park.** At Nashville Shores Outdoor Water Park, 4001 Bell Road (615-889-7050; www.nashvilleshores. com), where teens and adults will enjoy the state's four largest water slides, parasiling, jet skiing, and a thriller banana boat ride while younger kids will enjoy the interactive play boat.

Lane, Hermitage (615-889-2941; www.thehermitage.com), about 12 miles east of downtown Nashville. Peruse the Andrew Jackson Center, which acquaints you with Jackson's life through a film and exhibits. The tour also includes the Old Hermitage Church, the original 1804 cabins, an original slave cabin and garden, and Jackson's tomb and family cemetery. Admission.

Museums

If past presidents bore your young kids, then visit the **Nashville Toy Museum,** 2613 McGavock Pike (615-883-8870), instead. Kids will ogle the toy trains, ship models, fuzzy bears, Matchbox cars, and toy soldiers on parade. These are just some of the more than 1,000 antique and "old" playthings on view.

At the **Cumberland Science Museum,** 800 Fort Negley Boulevard (615-862-5160; www.csmisfun.com), children discover that science can be

At the Cumberland Science Museum's Curiosity Center, kids can really use their brains.

fun, even if they are learning something. "Sharks! Fact and Fantasy" is an interactive exhibit that helps kids understand these animals complete with underwater re-creations that let them experience what it would be like to live like sharks. The museum is currently building a new preschool area to take the place of its Curiosity Corner, where toddlers can touch, see, and smell to learn about the world around them. And a new exhibit called "Mission Possible" opens the summer of 2001. It will help visitors understand what it's like to have a disability as they try to maneuver through a wheelchair obstacle course or turn on a fan without the use of their hands.

At the **Tennessee State Museum,** Tennessee Performing Arts Center, 505 Deaderick Street (615-741-2692), legends come down to life-size through artifacts, and Tennessee pioneer history is portrayed. See Sam Houston's guitar, Davy Crockett's rifle, and Andrew Jackson's inaugural top hat, along with a gristmill, covered wagons, and a log cabin.

In April 2001 the **Frist Center for the Visual Arts** will open in the historic Art Deco-style post office building on Broadway in downtown Nashville. Rather than housing a permanent collection, the Frist will exhibit art from established museums whose works travel periodically to major cities, as well as work by local artists. There will be an Education Gallery where children (and adults), through hands-on activities, will learn about and better understand art.

Green Spaces and Parks

The world-class jungle gym is only one attraction at the **Nashville Zoo at Grassmere,** 3777 Nolensville Road (615-833-1534). In 2000 the zoo opened "Critter Encounters," a petting zoo for children that has red-ruffed lemurs, baby bison, and giant anteaters, plus some "noncontact" animals, such as a baby camel and several bird species, and the "Bobcat" exhibit, which will eventually include species from the Americas. The Zoo Tots series, for children ages two to four for an hour on Friday mornings, helps little ones learn about animal sounds, colors, and homes, and meet some of the animals in person. (Preregistration is required and there is an extra fee.) There are also special programs for families, such as Camp Ins, the Zooperbowl in January, and ZooFest in May. Admission.

At **Cheekwood, Nashville's Home of Art and Gardens,** 1200 Forrest Park Drive (615-356-8000; www.cheekwood.org) the mansion contains art and antiques, but kids like the outdoors best. The fifty-five acres have boxwood, woodlands, and seasonal gardens. Saturday mornings in the Learning Center, Cheekwood offers a chance for parents and children to work on an art project together. Admission.

Bicentennial Mall State Park, built to honor the 200th birthday of the state's founding in 1776, stretches for nineteen acres from the capital to the borders of Farmer's Market in North Nashville. Patterned after the Mall in Washington, D.C., Centennial Park enlivens the downtown area with special events and provides much-welcomed open space. For information regarding special events, call (615) 741-5280 or (888) TNPARKS.

Performing Arts

Chaffin's Barn Dinner Theater, 8204 Highway 100 (615-646-9977 or 800-282-BARN), gives you a play with your food. The **Tennessee Performing Arts Center,** at 505 Deaderick Street (615-782-4000), is a multitheatrical complex that includes the **Tennessee Repertory Theatre,** at 427 Chestnut Street (615-244-4878) and the **Nashville Symphony Orchestra** 209 Tenth Avenue South (615-225-5600). Also, be sure to check the performance schedule for the **Nashville Children's Theater** at 724 Second Avenue (615) 254-9103.

Special Tours

With **Grand Ole Opry Tours** (615-889-9490), trek down Music Row and go backstage at the Opry. Take your pick of day or evening excursions on the *General Jackson* or *Music City Queen,* which travel on the Cumberland River. For information call (615) 871-6100.

Side Trips

If your family has in interest in the Civil, War, you'll want to travel an hour from Nashville to see **Stones River National Battlefield,** 3501 Old Nashville Highway, Murfreesboro (615-893-9501; www.nps.gov). The 570-acre national battlefield includes the Stones River National Cemetery, with more than 6,000 Union graves, and the Hazen Monument, believed to be the oldest extant Civil War monument. From late May through mid-November, rangers give talks and guided walks daily, and in summer and on some weekends in the spring and fall, there are living history programs. Living history can also be found at **Cannonsburgh—A Pioneer Village,** also in Murfreesboro at 312 South Front Street (615-890-0355). The village consists of restored buildings from Rutherford and other middle Tennessee counties that have been brought together. There are historical exhibits and antique farm equipment on display. Open late April to early December.

For the Savvy Shopper

The Tennessee State Fairgrounds Flea Market (615-862-5016) is held the fourth weekend of every month except December. There are more than 1,000 dealers and admission is free.

SPECIAL EVENTS

Music City hosts a variety of festivals and special events. For updated happenings call the **Nashville Convention & Visitors Bureau** at (615) 259-4700 or check out the Web site: www.nashvillecvb.com.

February. The Annual Americana Spring Sampler Craft, Folk Art, and Antique Fair.

April. Gospel Music Week. Main Street Festival with artists, crafts-people, and food. Cheekwood Easter Art Hop, featuring egg hunts, storytelling, and hands-on activities.

May. Nashville River Stages, three days of music at Riverfront Park.

May–August. Dancin' in the District, free concerts every Thursday night, Riverfront Park.

July. Celebration of Cultures has family-oriented music, dancing, crafts, and children's activities.

November. Longhorn World Championship Rodeo at Municipal Auditorium; A Country Christmas, a more than month-long festival, at the Opryland Hotel.

WHERE TO STAY

Near the airport and Opryland & Music Valley are the **Holiday Inn Select-Opryland/Airport,** 2200 Elm Hill Pike (615-883-9770 or 800-HOLIDAY), and the **Wilson Inn,** 600 Ermac Drive (615-889-4466 or 800-333-9457), which offers a wide range of rooms, from singles to suites, and children under nineteen stay free with an adult. Suite properties include **AmeriSuites Music Valley,** 220 Rudy's Circle (615-872-0422 or 800-833-1516), and **Embassy Suites,** 10 Century Boulevard (615-871-0033 or 800-EMBASSY); both are conveniently located and offer free breakfasts.

Upscale accommodations include the 2,883-room **Opryland Hotel,** 2800 Opryland Drive (615-889-1000); the **Hermitage Hotel,** 231 Sixth Avenue North (615-244-3121); and the **Union Station Hotel,** 1001 Broadway (615-726-1001 or 800-331-2123), which has Tiffany stained-glass windows and a 65-foot, barrel-vaulted ceiling from its era as a train station.

For something different try **Nashville Shores,** 4001 Bell Road, Hermitage; (615) 889-7050. On 385 acres on J. Percy Priest Lake, 10 miles from downtown, Nashville Shores is a water recreation area that has modern and rustic **cabins, tent sites,** and 101 **RV sites.** Along with 3 miles of shoreline and sandy beaches, Nashville Shores offers a water park, paddleboat and sailboat rentals, miniature golf, a scenic lake cruise, a concession stand, and a catering service—just in case you're hosting a family reunion or party. The property also has a day admission rate.

Nashville has many **bed and breakfasts,** but not all accept children. For assistance in finding a place, call **Bed & Breakfast About Tennessee** at (615) 331-5244.

Get back to nature, or at least to basic prices, by camping at one of the Nashville area's many campgrounds. These include the **Holiday Nashville Travel Park,** 2572 Music Valley Drive (615-889-4225); and **Opryland KOA,** 2626 Music Valley Drive (615-889-0282 or 800-KOA-7789).

WHERE TO EAT

In addition to the Burger Kings, Shoney's, and Chucky Cheese's, Nashville has family restaurants that serve Southern cuisine. The biscuits at the **Loveless Restaurant,** 8400 Highway 100 (615-646-9700), are said to melt in your mouth, and the country ham is good, too.

Downtown themed eateries include the **Hard Rock Cafe,** 100 Broadway (615-742-9900), serving up great burgers and music memorabilia; and **NASCAR Cafe,** Third Avenue and Broadway (615-313-RACE), featuring race cars and related items.

For barbecue try **Jack's Barbecue,** 416 Broadway (615-254-5715), known for pork, brisket, and chicken.

The **Noshville Delicatessen,** 1918 Broadway (615-329-NOSH), offers fresh breads, deli sandwiches, and Kosher fare. **Monell's,** 1235 Sixth Avenue North (615-248-4747), serves the classic Southern "meat-and-three"—a meat entree with two or three side dishes. Food critics say come for lunch and order the fried chicken.

You may find yourself surrounded by real country music stars if you eat breakfast at the **Pancake Pantry,** 1796 Twenty-first Avenue South; (615) 383-9333.

The **Wildhorse Saloon,** 120 Second Avenue North (615) 902-8200, offers daily dance lessons and has "kickin' BBQ" and life-sized horse sculptures. If you like catfish (or have a hankering for gator tail or frog legs), head to one of **Uncle Bud's** five locations, one of which is at 714 Stewart's Ferry Pike (615) 872-7700. **O'Charley's** has seven locations and at every one of them, kids eat free all day. Try 1108 Murfreesboro Road (615) 361-3651.

FOR MORE INFORMATION

For more information on Nashville events, lodging, and restaurants, contact **Nashville Convention & Visitors Bureau,** Gaylord Entertainment Center, corner of Fifth and Broadway (615-259-4747; www.nashvillecvb.com) open weekdays from 8:00 A.M. to 5:00 P.M. Check the Web: www.nashvillecvb.com.

Emergency Numbers

Ambulance, fire, and police: 911

Baptist Hospital, 2000 Church Street: (615) 329-5555 or 329-5114 (ER)

Poison Control Center: (615) 322-6435

Twenty-four-hour pharmacy: Walgreens at one of four locations: 518 Donelson Pike (615-883-5108), 5412 Charlotte Avenue (615-298-5594), 7617 Highway 70 South (615-646-5173), and 155580 Old Hickory Boulevard (615-333-2722)

Vanderbilt University Medical Center, 1211 Twenty-Second Avenue South; (615) 322-5000 or 322-3261 (ER)

HOUSTON

H ouston offers a special vitality, friendliness, lots of cultural events, and some exceptional museums and exciting attractions, making it a wonderful vacation destination.

GETTING THERE

There are two airports. **William P. Hobby Airport** (713-643-4597) is 9 miles southeast of downtown; **George Bush Intercontinental Airport** (713-230-3000) is 15 miles north. **Express Shuttle USA** (713-523-8888) offers shuttles between Intercontinental and Hobby airports and the four downtown passenger terminals.

The **Amtrak** station (800-USA-RAIL) is at 902 Washington Avenue at Bagby. **Greyhound** (800-231-2222) is at 2121 Main. By car I-10 passes through the middle of Houston; U.S. 59 runs northeast to southwest, and I-45 runs northwest to southeast.

GETTING AROUND

A car and a map are helpful for exploring this sprawling city. Local nicknames for major freeways (such as the Katy for I-10 west of town, and the East Freeway for I-10 east of town) don't appear on maps. The **Metropolitan Transit Authority** (Metro) buses, 401 Louisiana (713-635-4000), can take you to many places on your agenda. It also has free trolleys that run daily around the downtown area.

WHAT TO SEE AND DO

Museums and Historical Sites
The Children's Museum of Houston, 1500 Binz, (713) 522-1138; www.cmhouston.org. Admission. It will be love at first sight once your kids see this $10-million facility featuring thirteen giant cut-out figures of boys and girls seemingly holding up the building. Inside, nine galleries house top-notch interactive exhibits including **The KID-TV Studio,**

Houston

AT A GLANCE

▶ Find out about astronaut training, rockets, and the universe at Space Center Houston

▶ Walk through the human body at the Museum of Health and Medical Science

▶ Try the hands-on displays at the Children's Museum of Houston

▶ Houston Convention and Visitors Bureau: (800) 4-HOUSTON; www.houston-guide.com

where youngsters create sound tracks and use video equipment to manipulate images. At the new outdoor EcoStation kids discover pond life, make plant rubbings, and watch eco-friendly puppet shows. The museum's re-creation of a Mexican Village is especially engaging with its open-air market. It also gives kids a chance to practice Spanish and Zapotec. In the outdoor courtyard, kids can play the challenging Buckminster Fuller's Junior World Game on a giant map and enjoy the outdoor waterworks in spring and summer. There is a Victorian Playhouse where kids can let their imaginations run wild in creative role-playing and fantasy games. Something special is always going on, so check the schedule. No admission charge on Thursdays from 5:00 to 9:00 P.M.

Located in the northern section of Hermann Park is the **Houston Museum of Natural Science,** 1 Hermann Circle, Hermann Park; (713) 639-4600; www.hmns.org. Admission. Each of nineteen halls involves a different natural science, and many have interactive exhibits. Yes, there are dinosaur skeletons (considered one of the best displays in the country), plus other interesting collections, including North and South American Indian artifacts (shrunken heads from Ecuador).

Kids become part of a mission control crew at the **Challenger Center** (at the George Observatory, about an hour's drive south of Houston in Brazos Bend State Park) or see models of future space vehicles at the **Arnold Hall of Space Science.** Save enough time for the daily star (or weekly laser) shows at the **Burke Baker Planetarium** (713-639-4600) and/or a giant-screen film on natural science topics at the Wortham IMAX Theatre (713-639-IMAX). Stroll through a bevy of butterflies at the **Cockrell Butterfly Center** with its 40-foot waterfall and thousands

Space Center Houston

Space Center Houston, the visitor's center for NASA/Johnson Space Center, is a mix of spacecraft, information, hands-on exhibits, and an IMAX film theater giving it the feel of a theme park.

- **Space Center Plaza.** Tour a full-scale mock-up of the space shuttle. Find out how astronauts eat, sleep, shower—and, yes, go to the bathroom—in space.
- **Kids Space Place.** Kids don't want to leave here. The seventeen activity areas feature forty interactive stations geared to intriguing and explaining space exploration to ages three to eleven. Control a rocket launch, design a spacecraft, execute tasks while being "weightless," and build moon craters with Legos.
- **Feel of Space.** Computer simulators enable you to land a shuttle or retrieve a satellite.

- **Starship Gallery.** See the largest collection of moon rocks and touch a 3.8-billion-year-old rock chip brought back by *Apollo 17*. See the original *Mercury* capsule and the *Apollo 17* command module.
- **Space Center Theater.** Watch IMAX films about space flight.
- **Tram Tour.** Take a behind-the-scenes guided tour, one lasting seventy-five minutes, the other forty-five minutes.

Space Center Houston, 1601 NASA Road One, Houston, 25 miles southeast of Houston; (281) 244–2100 or (800) 972–0369; www.spacecenter.org.

of wondrous butterflies flitting about. In the Welch Chemistry Hall, kids can touch a super-hot Space Shuttle tile without getting burned and step on a special scale that will tell how much hydrogen, helium, oxygen, and other elements make up their body chemistry.

Learn about human physiology and biology at the **Museum of Health & Medical Science,** 1515 Hermann Drive; (713) 942-7054; www.mhms.org. At the Amazing Body Pavilion, walk through a human body wired with sound effects. Walk through a 10-foot-tall brain and play memory games, check out a 22-foot-long backbone that descends from ceiling to floor, and use computers to find out such things as how long blood cells live (four months) and how far they travel (930 miles). Weird Science Saturday presentations that include storytelling, games, and special activities are held throughout the year.

The **Museum of Fine Arts,** 1001 Bissonnet; (713) 639-7300; www.mfah.org. With 27,000 outstanding works of art, this museum may be a little daunting for some kids, so be selective. Creation Station, on Sundays from 1:00 to 4:00 P.M., is a drop-in workshop with different hands-on activities each week. Storytime Sunday, at 2:30 P.M., presents stories related to works of art in various galleries and is followed by an art workshop. Postcard Tours, available every day, let families explore the museum using image cards as guides. Call (713) 639-7324 for more information about special programs.

The 1,000 acre **San Jacinto Battleground State Historical Complex,** 24 miles from Houston's downtown on Highway 225 (281-479-2431; www.tpwd.state.tx.us), commemorates the site where on April 21, 1836, Sam Houston led forces to win independence from Mexico—just weeks after the Alamo massacre. On-site is the **San Jacinto Monument and Museum of History,** 1800 Park Road 1826, La Porte; (281) 479-2421. In the base of this commemorative fifty-story masonry obelisk are exhibits on the development of Texas from Native American civilization to statehood. Take the elevator to the 489-foot Observation Floor for a great view of Houston. Right across the street is the *Battleship Texas* (281-479-4414), a dreadnought built in 1914 that saw action in both world wars. Kids enjoy scrambling around the decks.

The **Orange Show,** 2402 Munger (713-926-6368), is a change of pace from the usual. This folk-art environment dedicated to the orange amuses most kids. Open from Memorial Day to Labor Day. Weekly art workshops are held for kids.

The **Contemporary Arts Museum,** 5216 Montrose (713-284-8250; www.camh.org), is as interesting as its exhibits. Before looking at the exhibits, request a Family Guide and a Factivity Kit. The guide includes activities related to the museum's art, and the kit is filled with fun stuff for kids to help them learn about and understand art. The **Holocaust Museum Houston,** 5401 Caroline Street (713-942-8000; www.hmh. org), the third largest facility of its kind in the United States, is both an educational center and a memorial. The museum offers exhibits and a thirty-minute oral history film of Houston-area Holocaust survivors and liberators.

Parks and Zoos

Hermann Park, at the intersection of Fannin and Montrose (between downtown and the Astrodome), comprises 400 acres filled with family fun including picnic grounds, a miniature train, pedalboat rides, the beautiful **Mecom Fountain** (between Fannin and San Jacinto Streets), the **Miller Outdoor Theater,** where free concerts are held, and the **Houston Zoological Gardens** at 1513 North MacGregor (713-523-5888; www.houstonzoo.org), which locals call the Hermann Park Zoo. This appealing facility has a walk-through aviary, an aquarium, and 3,000 animals representing more than 700 species. A new, expanded children's zoo is scheduled to open at press time as are new viewing areas above the lion and tiger pavilions. Meet the Keeper sessions are held weekly in the summer. Admission is free on city holidays.

The **Children's Museum** and **Museum of Fine Arts** are within walking distance of Hermann Park. Walk through a lush rainforest habitat in Wortham World of Primates to view thirteen species of prosimians, monkeys, and apes. Other highlights: white tigers, pygmy hippos, Mexican wolves, sea lions, and koala bears.

Other Attractions
Six Flags AstroWorld, off Loop 610 at the Fannin exit; (713) 799-1234; www.sixflags.com/astroworld. Adjacent to the Astrodome, this seventy-five-acre park has something for everyone. The newest coaster is the Serial Thriller, which tears through seven inversions, including loops, spirals, and hairpin turns. There's a Looney Tunes Town for younger children. AstroWorld is open daily in the summer, and weekends mid-March to October 31. Next door, **Six Flags WaterWorld,** a fifteen-acre water park (same phone as AstroWorld), offers a children's play area and the usual wet and wonderful water rides; for preteens and teens the Edge, an 88-foot slide, offers plunging excitement.

The Kemah Boardwalk, 555 Bradford Street and Second Street, Kemah (281-334-2284; www.kemahboardwalk.com) has evolved into an old-fashioned boardwalk experience, with a Ferris wheel, rides for younger children, and a walk-through water fountain that kids enjoy. It's loaded with restaurants and shops, including The Toy Crossing store.

Theater, Music, and the Arts
Houston is rich in cultural offerings. Check the schedule of performances and gallery exhibits listed in *The Chronicle,* the city's daily newspaper, and the *Official Guide to Houston,* a free quarterly publication available around town or by calling (800) 4-HOUSTON.

The **Children's Theatre Festival** at the University of Houston presents high-quality children's theater all year. Call (713) 743-2929.

For information on some of the most popular attractions, call these numbers: the **Houston Ballet** (713-523-6300; www.houstonballet.org); the **Houston Symphony Orchestra** (713-227-ARTS); **Houston Grand Opera** (713-227-ARTS; www.hgo.com); **Theater Under the Stars,** the largest nonprofit producer of musical theater in America (713-622-1626 or 800-678-5440; www.tuts.com); **Ensemble Theatre,** the largest minority theater in the South (713-520-0055); **Alley Theater,** one of the oldest and most creative resident professional theater companies in the South (713-228-8421; www.alleytheatre.com).

In the theater district **Bayou Place,** the city's new entertainment complex, features restaurants, live music, and the eight-screen **Angelika Theater** (713) 952-1313.

Scheduled for completion in 2002, **The Hobby Center for the Performing Arts** (713-227-2001; www.thehobbycenter.org) will seat more than 3,000 theatergoers and feature major Broadway productions.

Houston Ticket Company, 2707 Chimney Rock at Westheimer (Galleria) (713-877-1555), sells tickets to concerts, theater, sports, and other events. Tickets are also available from **Ticketmaster** (713-629-3700). Free music, dance, theater, and festivals are held year-round in the **Miller Outdoor Theater,** 100 Concert Drive, Hermann Park; (713) 520-3290. Special shows are held on selected Saturdays for kids and their families.

Shopping

Houston has many shopping areas. The glass-domed, three-level **Galleria,** 5075 Westheimer (713-621-1907), has department stores, 300 shops, plus restaurants, movies, and a giant indoor ice skating rink on the ground floor. **Katy Mills** (281-644-6000) offers more than 200 stores, plus restaurants and family entertainment.

Spectator Sports

Houston Astros step up to bat in their new downtown, retractable-roof stadium, Enron Field. Call (713) 799-9555 for ticket and schedule information or check out www.astros.com. The **Houston Rockets** NBA action and the **Houston Comets** WNBA action take place at the Compaq Center, 10 Greenway Plaza; (713) 627-0600. The legendary Astrodome offers tours of the facility. Call (713) 799-9544 for information. Houston's new NFL franchise will begin play in 2002 in a new 69,000-square-foot facility (adjacent to the Astrodome) that will be the world's first retractable-roof football stadium. Call (713) 336-7700.

SIDE TRIPS

Galveston Island, 51 miles south of Houston on the Gulf of Mexico, is a leading summer resort with 32 miles of sandy beaches, fishing piers, and a variety of interesting sites. From Houston, drive via I-45 south.

Galveston hosts more than six million tourists a year, so be prepared for company. Stewart Beach (409-765-5023), Seawall Boulevard at Broadway Boulevard, at the east end of the island, is the island's most popular, with a pavilion, bathhouses, restaurants, concessions, rides, arcades, water slides, bumper boats, go-carts, and miniature golf.

A fun way to explore the island is to board the diesel and electric town trolley, which travels a 4.7-mile track from Seawall Boulevard to The Strand, the historic Victorian district. A recorded narrative details points of interest on the one-hour round-trip ride. Tickets and information are available at Moody Terminal South, 2100 Seawall (409-763-4311), and Strand Terminal North, The Strand Visitors Center, 2016 Strand (409-765-7834).

SPECIAL EVENTS

Contact the GHCVB at (800) 4-HOUSTON for more information on the following special events or visit the Web site at www.houston-guide.com.

Late February–early March. Houston Livestock Show and Rodeo, one of the largest rodeos in the world.

Spring. Houston Children's Festival, Houston's official family celebration.

July. Fourth of July Freedom Festival.

August. Museum District Day/Theater District Day, featuring free admission to theaters and museums, along with music, arts and crafts, and food.

Fall. Multicultural outdoor festivals reflecting the city's ethnic diversity including Greek Festival in October.

October. Westheimer Arts Festival; Texaco Grand Prix, International Quilt Festival.

November. Bank United Annual Thanksgiving Day Parade. The Mayor's Official Downtown Houston Holiday Celebration, with fireworks, music, and entertainment.

December. Dickens on the Strand, Victorian-style celebration, Galveston Island. Christmas Boat Lane Parade, Clear Lake. Candlelight Tour, Sam Houston Park. Miracle on Main Street, outdoor ice skating rink.

WHERE TO STAY

Official Guide to Houston has an accommodations listing. **Downtown Houston Bed and Breakfast,** 1200 Southmore Avenue (713-523-1114 or 800-553-5797; www.texasbnb.com), provides information on area inns that welcome kids. The best rates usually are offered on weekends, so book well in advance. Familiar budget and moderately priced chains are **Days Inns** (800-325-2525), **Comfort Inns** (800-228-5150), **Quality Inns** (800-228-5151), and **Super 8 Motel** (800-800-8000).

Embassy Suites Hotel, 9090 Southwest Freeway; (713) 995-0123 or (800) 362-2779; www.embassysuites.com. The two-room suites with sleeper sofa and kitchenettes are ideal for families, as are the pool and complimentary breakfast. The **Radisson Suite Hotel Astrodome Houston,** 1400 Old Spanish Trail (713-796-1000 or 800-333-3333; www. radisson.com), has separate living area with kitchenette and sleeper sofa, plus a bedroom, and free transportation to the Astrodome 5 miles away and WaterWorld.

Located in the center of downtown, the **Hyatt Regency Houston,** 1200 Louisiana (713-654-1234 or 800-233-1234; www.hyatt.com), is another good choice for families because of Hyatt's family-friendly policies. This hotel has an outdoor heated pool.

Westin has two hotels in the Galleria Mall, both on the expensive side, that have great benefits: shops, department stores, restaurants, an Olympic-size ice-skating rink, and lighted tennis right at your doorstep, plus the new Westin Kids Club. Staff are trained to be sensitive to the needs of parents and kids. Rooms, if requested, can be child safe and child friendly (already equipped with necessary cribs, etc.). Kids can enjoy programs year-round in the Kids Club. You can request such niceties as a jogging stroller, emergency diapers, potty seats, bicycle seats, refrigerators, and step stools. Call ahead about babysitting services.

Westin's **Oaks,** 5011 Westheimer Road (713-960-8100), is the older of the two, with 406 rooms and some suites in a twenty-one-story building, a pool, cafe, and free parking garage. Westin's **Galleria,** 5060 West Alabama (same phone as Oaks), has similar offerings, with 492 rooms and suites in a twenty-three-story complex.

WHERE TO EAT

Official Guide to Houston has a restaurant listing. Along with the expected Tex-Mex and Mexican fare, Houston has a surprising variety of diverse eateries—there are more than 8,000. Here are a few possibilities.

The Great Caruso, 10001 Westheimer at Briarpark in Cariloon Center; (713) 780-4900. Super service and good food abound at this establishment, where singing waiters, Broadway performers, and concert pianists entertain nightly in an opera-house setting. **Magic Island,** 2215 Southwest Freeway; (713) 526-2442. Magicians, psychics, ventriloquists, and comedians entertain at this supper club known for its Texas prime rib. Dining here could get pricey for a family.

Otto's Bar-B-Que, 5502 Memorial Drive (713-864-2573), dishes up East Texas–style ribs, brisket, sausage links, and ham, chicken, and pork for lunch and dinner. Kids' meals available. Another hot barbecue spot serving heapin' platters is **Billy Blues Bar and Grill,** 6025 Richmond; (713) 266-9294. Look for the 63-foot saxophone outside. **Good Company Bar-B-Q,** 5109 Kirby Drive (713-522-2530), is known for its mesquite-barbecued ribs, chicken, turkey, and duck. **Spanish Flowers,** 4701 North Main (713-869-1706), offers good-tasting, inexpensive Mexican fare. **Sierra,** 4704 Montrose Boulevard (713-942-7757), features imaginative Southwest fare. Teens with adventuresome palettes should like this place.

Houston This Is It, 207 Gray Street (713-659-1608), serves up chitlins, yams, meatloaf, and other soul food. Seafood lovers should head to **Landry's Seafood House,** at 8816 Westheimer Road (713-975-7873), and at other locations. At **Joe's Crab Shack,** 6218 Richmond Avenue, and other locations (713-952-5400), your kids will fit right into the lively—and noisy—atmosphere, and it includes a kids' play area and outdoor seating.

For 'tweens and teens: the **Hard Rock Cafe,** in Bayou Place in downtown Houston (713-227-1392), has rock 'n' roll memorabilia, with multiscreen images, lots of music and burgers, pastas, and salads.

For More Information

The Greater Houston Convention and Visitors Bureau: 901 Bagby (713) 437-5200 or (800) 4-HOUSTON; www.houston-guide.com. Ask for information on the Houston three-day/two-night Getaway Packages—Houston Fun and Houston Fun Plus—which feature hotel and attraction discounts.

Emergency Numbers

Ambulance, fire, police: 911

Poison control: (713) 654-1701

Hospital: The Texas Medical Center, Ben Taub General Hospital, 1502 Taub Loop; (713) 793-2000

Twenty-four-hour pharmacy: Eckerd's, 6011 Kirby Drive; (713) 522-3983

SAN ANTONIO

Y es, San Antonio is a big city—the eighth largest in the United States—but it doesn't have that hectic, congested feeling. What this town near the south central tip of Texas does have is loads of charm. The city's southwestern flair comes from mixing Hispanic heritage, Native American culture, and cowboy lore. San Antonio will open your kids' eyes to different cultures and lifestyles as well as to some significant moments in U.S. history. The city has kid-friendly markets, museums and, nearby, the largest marine mammal park in the world.

GETTING THERE

San Antonio International Airport (210-207-3411), about fifteen minutes from downtown, is served by fourteen major airlines. **The Star Shuttle** (210-341-6000; wwwstarshuttle.com) provides twenty-four-hour service to anywhere to and from the airport. Taxis and car rentals are available at the airport.

Amtrak (800-USA-RAIL) has a station at 1174 East Commerce; the local phone number is (210) 223-3226.

Greyhound/Trailways is at 500 North St. Mary's Street; (800) 231-2222.

By car you can reach San Antonio via one of three major interstates leading into it from every direction: I-35, I-10, I-37 and I-410. The city is surrounded by an outer loop; each freeway leads into the central business district.

GETTING AROUND

The Metropolitan Transit Service's 105 regular VIA bus routes and five downtown streetcar routes go to every major tourist attraction and business in the central district. Express bus routes operate from downtown to Sea World of Texas and Six Flags Fiesta Texas. The streetcars, reproductions of those used a half-century ago, are a special treat—and the fare is 50 cents. VIA's downtown information center is at 112 North Soledad; (210) 362-2020.

San Antonio

AT A GLANCE

▶ Explore SeaWorld Adventure Park

▶ See the famous Alamo

▶ Stroll the River Walk

▶ Visit the San Antonio zoo

▶ San Antonio Convention and Visitors Bureau: (800) 447-3372 or (210) 207-6748; www.sanantoniocvb.com

WHAT TO SEE AND DO

Museums and Historical Sites

The Alamo, 300 Alamo Plaza; (210) 225-1391; www.thealamo.org. Smack in the heart of the city is one of the best-known tourist sites in Texas. All of the 189 patriots who fought for Texas's independence from Mexico died here on March 6, 1836. With modern San Antonio's buildings surroundings the Alamo, it takes some imagination to envision the pioneer era. Viewing the IMAX film *Alamo: The Price of Freedom* helps. It is adjacent to Rivercenter Mall (210-247-4629). As part of the living history program every Wednesday, costumed interpreters give presentations and answer questions. Admission.

Cowboy Museum, 209 Alamo Plaza; (210) 229-1257; www.cowboymuseum.net. Wild West aficionados will like the authentic cowboy, Indian, gunfighter, and trail-driver outfits displayed at this fun museum, along other Wild West memorabilia—including a Sioux necklace made out of human finger bones (the kids will be talking about this for months). Ask for the museum information sheet for kids, which points out interesting facts and exhibits. Admission.

Hertzberg Circus Museum, 210 Market Street (corner of South Presa and West Market Streets); (210-207-7810 for recorded information or 210-207-7819; www.sat.lib.tx.us/hertzberg/hzmain.html). Appealing exhibits include a miniature model of a three-ring circus, complete with animals and performers, Tom Thumb's carriage, a priceless antique circus poster collection, plus lots of other Big Top memorabilia. Special weekend events feature workshops with puppeteers and magicians, plus performances at the Gallery Theatre, and videos of circus performances, and old classic films about the circus. Throughout the museum there are

Located on four acres in downtown San Antonio, the Alamo attracts more than 2.5 million visitors each year.

hands-on activities, such as fun mirrors and masks, face painting, and clown costumes to try on. Admission.

Institute of Texan Cultures, 801 South Bowie at Durango, HemisFair Park; (210) 458–2300; www.texancultures.utsa.edu/main). Admission. The institute, which presents Texas history and folk culture, encourages visitor participation, so don't worry if your kids head to the loom to try out weaving or climb inside the Indian tepee. Ask for a copy of "History Mystery" to help your kids learn about the ethnic groups represented in the exhibits. The Dome Theatre shows a thirty-six screen, multimedia presentation of Texas history.

San Antonio Museum of Art, 200 West Jones Avenue; (210) 978–8100; www.sa-museum.org. Admission. This castlelike structure houses a wide range of exhibits including Egyptian, Greek, and Roman antiquities and European, Japanese, and American paintings. In 2000 a new gallery dedicated to Oceanic art opened. Every Sunday afternoon families can participate in Make & Take Family Art Classes, which are free with admission, no reservation necessary. A brochure about the museum's collection written especially for families is available free with admission.

Be sure to allow time for the new **Rockefeller Center for Latin American Art,** which covers 3,000 years of art from 1000 B.C. to modern times. The orientation gallery's computer stations let visitors find out about Latin American culture and history. Kids should find much of interest, including the pre-Columbian jaguar masks taken from the tombs of

SeaWorld Adventure Park San Antonio

SeaWorld Adventure Park San Antonio packs a lot of adventure. Highlights of the world's largest marine park include:

ANIMAL ENCOUNTERS

- **Beluga Interaction Program.** Get in the tank with these gentle animals and learn about their physiology and habitat. This is the only such program in the United States.
- **Sharks/Coral Reef.** Watch hammerhead sharks, moray eels, groupers, and thousands of tropical fish in a re-created coral-reef environment.
- **Penguin Encounter.** Observe 200 penguins play and swim in their sub-Arctic environment.
- **Sea Lion Interaction Program.** Become an apprentice sea lion trainer at the Sea Lion pool.
- **Marine Mammal Pool.** Touch and feed Atlantic bottlenose dolphins.
- **Bird Adventure Tour.** Let a 6-inch-tall Indonesian parrot, perch on your hand and meet a penguin.

WATER FUN

- **Lost Lagoon Water Park.** Ride the surf in the wave pool, slide down five stories of rapids on Sky Tubin'!, and sun on the beach. In 2001 Lost Lagoon will be expanded to include a Fun House and more.
- **Lil' Gators Lagoon.** Let little kids splash in a kiddie pool and climb on a starfish in this just-for-preschoolers play area.

- **Shamu's Happy Harbor.** Wade and splash through this three-acre kids-only play area.
- **Rico Loco.** Churn down this six-person circular raft.

SHOWS

- **Shamu Visions.** Watch **Shamu,** the killer whale, and friends breech, spy hop, and show off.
- **Fools with Tools.** Laugh at the antics of Clyde and Sea-more, sea lions, at this vaudevillian show.
- **Symphony of the Sea.** Admire the agility of graceful beluga whales and Pacific dolphins.

SeaWorld offers summer Adventure Camps to junior high and high school students. Call (800) 700-7786.

The Hyatt Regency Hill Country Resort, 9800 Hyatt Resort Drive (210–647–1234 or 800–55–HYATT), located near SeaWorld, offers a Family Adventure Package in December, consisting of a three-day/two-night stay at the resort, plus a day at SeaWorld with special activities.

SeaWorld Adventure Park San Antonio, 10500 Sea World Drive; (210) 523–3611; www.seaworld.com. Admission.

kings, the folk-art collection's toys and masks, as well as the powerful modernist paintings.

The Witte Museum, 3801 Broadway (adjoining Brackenridge Park); (210) 357-1900; www.wittemuseum.org. Admission. This institution, which will celebrate its seventy-fifth anniversary in 2001 with special events and activities, is full of hands-on exhibits of Texas history, natural science, and anthropology. On the museum's grounds is the H-E-B Science Treehouse with four levels of hands-on science exhibitions. In 2000 the Witte "launched" its "Witte Explorer One," a motion-based simulated mini-shuttle with a video screen inside. The Witte Adventure Club, for ages five to ten, lets kids use their creative energies while exploring the museum's exhibits; available during spring break, summers, and winter holidays. Reservations are required; call (210) 357-1910.

San Antonio Children's Museum, 305 East Houston Street; (210) 212-4453. Designed primarily for ages two to ten, exhibits and interpretive materials which are in both Spanish and English, foster understanding of the multicultural diversity of modern urban life. On Runway Number Nine they fly and land an airplane while in communication with the control tower, and in Life on a Construction Site, they drive a tractor. Hands-on activities are offered every day from 10:00 A.M. to noon and from 1:00 to 3:00 P.M. Each week a different theme is reflected in the activities. Admission.

San Antonio has several specialized attractions of interest. At the **Air Force History and Traditions Museum,** 2051 George Avenue, Building 5206, Lackland Air Force Base (210-671-3055), peruse seventy rare and historical aircraft. The **San Antonio Missions National Historical Park,** 2202 Roosevelt Avenue, San Antonio (210-932-1001; www. nps.gov/saan), includes five missions established in the eighteenth century by the Franciscan friars eager to bring Christianity to Native Americans of the Southwest. Along the 9-mile Mission Parkway Trail, which begins at the Alamo, you'll find these other missions, all of which are active parish churches. To garner the most enthusiasm for your tour, gather materials at the **Visitor Center,** 6701 San Jose Drive, adjacent to the Mission San Jose. Kids interested in the Junior Ranger program can buy a booklet at the Visitor Center, and regularly scheduled tours, guided walks, and demonstrations are provided by rangers. Call (210) 534-8833 for more information about other special events. There's no admission charge to the missions, but donations are accepted. The Mission Trails Project will eventually link the missions along a 10-mile trail that will include a network of hiking and biking trails.

Kids may be more enthusiastic about two other specialty museums. **Ripley's Believe It or Not!** and **Plaza Wax Museum,** 301 Alamo Plaza;

Great Performances for Families and Kids

- **San Antonio Symphony Orchestra's Interactive Classics.** Five times a year, kids get hands-on with classical music. Before performances kids play instruments at conductor's clinics children learn what all that baton waving means, and for keepsakes kids can collect symphony trading cards. Performances are held at the Majestic Performing Arts Center. Call (210) 554-1010.
- **Magik Children's Theatre,** 420 South Alamo; (210) 227-2751; www.magiktheatre.org. See original productions and plays based on popular children's books and classics at San Anto-

nio's only professional family theater. Daytime performances are geared to pre-schoolers and young grade-schoolers, whereas evening shows aim at families, middle-school, and high-school students.

- **Majestic Performing Arts Center,** 224 East Houston; (210) 226-5700. Attend Broadway touring shows in a vintage, vaudeville movie palace.
- **Carver Community Cultural Center,** 226 North Hackberry; (210) 207-7211. Enjoy African dance companies, gospel singers, jazz musicians, and other artists.

(210) 224-9299, www.tourtexas.com/ripleys and www.tourtexas.com/palaceofwax. At the wax theater more than 250 lifelike characters loom in four theme sections: Hollywood, Texas History, Religion, and Horror. Ripley's exhibits include 500 one-of-a-kind oddities from around the world. **Buckhorn Saloon & Museums,** 318 East Houston Street (210-247-4000; www.buckhornmuseum.com), has its own wax museum of famous Texas pioneers; a Curio Store selling Mexican pottery and other items; the Buckhorn Arcade, with old-fashioned nickelodeons and fortunetellers; and several display halls, including the Hall of Fins and the Hall of Horns. But the big draw is the re-created 118-year-old saloon where kids can order sodas while they stare at the big mounted buck in the center of the backbar. And every Saturday and Sunday there's a gunfight at High Noon outside the saloon on Houston Street. Admission.

The **Texas Air Museum,** located on the grounds of Stinson Field on the south side of the city (210-977-9885), exhibits vintage and replicated World War I and II aircraft and artifacts, shows films on early aviation, and has a simulated cockpit exhibit where kids can pretend they're flying a vintage airplane.

More Attractions

Six Flags Fiesta Texas, at the junction of I-10 and Loop 1604, north-western San Antonio; (210) 697-5050 or (800) 473-4378; www.sixflags. com. This theme park, home to Bugs Bunny and his Looney Tunes pals, is great fun, with rides, food, performers, a water park, and themed areas. The Superman Krypton Coaster, the largest steel coaster in the Southwest, takes you through more than 4,000 feet of twists, turns, and spiral loops and corkscrews at 70 miles an hour—all without a floor underneath you. Crackaxle Canyon, a 1920s boom town, has the Rattler —one of the highest and fastest wooden roller coasters in the world. A major draw is the Joker, a steel roller coaster that runs backwards and turns riders upside down. At the fifties themed Fiesta Bay Boardwalk, walk along the boards, take time out to play at the arcade, and ride the 90-foot Ferris wheel. Admission.

Younger children and those fascinated by dinosaurs will want to visit **Dinosaur World,** 622 NW Loop 410 Central Park Mall (210-349-5566 or 800-468-0614; www.dinosaurworld.com), a store selling dinosaur toys and kits. There is also an Activity Room where kids can watch dinosaur videos or dig for "fossils" in the 12-foot Fossil Digging Pit. Little ones will also enjoy a visit to **Kiddie Park,** 3015 Broadway (210-824-4351) in Brackenridge Park, a relaxed, old-fashioned amusement park (established in 1925) that has a 1918 Herschell-Spillman Carousel with thirty-six jumping horses and two chariots.

Paseo Del Rio (River Walk), in central downtown, is San Antonio's heartbeat. A narrow slice of the San Antonio River gently winds for 2½ miles through the city some 20 feet below tree-lined cobblestone walkways lined with restaurants, galleries, and shops. Narrated tours are offered by Yanaguana Cruises (210-244-5700 or 800-417-4139; www. sarivencruise.com).

You can also take the plunge at **Splashtown,** 3600 IH 35 North (3 minutes north of downtown on I-35N); (210) 227-1400; www.splash-townsa.com. This family water park features fifty rides and attractions, the largest wave pool in south Texas, and Kids Kove for tykes.

Parks, Gardens, and Zoos

Brackenridge Park, 3910 North St. Mary's Street (main entrance); (210) 736-9534. This 343-acre park is a gem. The idyllic setting includes the San Antonio River, which originates from underground springs north of the park and then winds through groves of ancient oaks and a Japanese Tea Garden. The park is also good fun: You'll find a golf course, a polo field and a bike trail. The Brackenridge Eagle Miniature Train, at number 3810, runs on a 3-mile track through the park. Also visit the **San Anto-**

nio Zoo, 3903 North St. Mary's Street (210-734-7183), home to more than 3,400 animals representing 600 species, all displayed in barless cages and habitats. Children's Zoo highlights include a Tropical Tour boat ride and an Everglades and Rain Forest exhibit. The renovated Snow Leopard exhibit is now home to a ten-year-old male and a five-year-old female. The zoo recently acquired a nine-year-old female jaguar and by 2001 there will be a new anaconda exhibit and a new exhibit featuring gibbons.

San Antonio Botanical Gardens, 555 Funston; (210) 207-3255; www.sabot.org. Feast your eyes (and nose) on this thirty-three-acre garden of flowers found throughout the state. A third of the facility is devoted to formal gardens including an aquatic, herb, and biblical garden with fig trees, date palms, and other plant life mentioned in the Holy Book. There's also a special garden for the blind, where emphasis is placed on touch and feel. Check out the Web site for "Maja's Forest," a fun kids page that tells them how to make a terrarium and plant seeds and all about "weird" plants.

HemisFair Park, 200 South Alamo, the site of the 1968 World's Fair and located near the Alamo, offers a nice oasis of water gardens. Come here for some serendipitous fun at the children's playground. From the Tower of the Americas, you get a panoramic city view.

Theater, Music, and the Arts

Consult the Friday "Weekender" section of the *San Antonio Express News* for cultural and special events, or call the San Antonio Convention and Visitors Bureau (800-447-3372; www.sanantoniocvb.com). Tickets for a variety of major events and concerts, including those held at the Alamodome, can be obtained from Ticketmaster at (210) 224-9600.

The unique **Arneson River Theatre**, in La Villita on the River Walk (210-207-8610), has its stage on one side of the river and its audience on the other. Something entertaining is bound to be going on during

Ranching Texas-Style

Three nearby ranches (all less than forty-five minutes from San Antonio) offer a chance to experience ranch life: Diamond W. Longhorn Ranch (210-695-4888; www.wildwestsanantonio.com), offers a chuck wagon supper and a cowboy show with a trick steer act and some fancy ropin' and shootin'. Lightning Ranch (830-510-4136; www.lightningranch.com) offers one- or two-hour, half-day and overnight trail rides through Texas Hill Country, plus hayrides, roping demonstrations, and guest lodges for overnights. Natural Bridge Wildlife Ranch (830-438-7400; www.nbwildliferanchtx.com) has something a little different—a safari in your car through more than 200 acres of ranchland stocked with African animals. Also available are a petting zoo, gift shop, and snack bar.

your stay: Fiesta Noche del Rio and Fiesta Flamenco are two popular shows that are being performed regularly.

Spectator Sports
For information on schedules and tickets, contact the following: **San Antonio Missions** baseball, April through August (210-675-7275); **San Antonio Spurs** basketball (NBA), November through April (210-554-7787); and the **San Antonio Dragons** (Central Hockey League), October through March (210-737-7825). The **Alamodome** is the site of the **Alamo Bowl,** featuring major college football at the end of December; call (210) 207-3651. Guided tours of the Alamodome are conducted Tuesday through Saturday; call (210) 207-3601.

Shopping
Market Square is a Mexican-style market that comprises two square blocks downtown at IH-35 and Commerce Street; (210) 207-8600. The indoor market, **El Mercado,** features more than thirty-five specialty shops selling locally made arts and crafts; jewelry; and Mexican, South American, and Southwestern Indian products. Restaurants and shops line the plazas outside El Mercado, and major festivals are held here in April, May, September, and December.

Another appealing shopping area is **La Villita,** a historic district on the east bank of the River Walk. Visitors can browse through shops of twenty-five artists and craftspeople and watch many of them at their work. For more information, call (210) 207-8610.

SIDE TRIPS

- Fredericksburg and Kerrville are two historic German communities north of San Antonio. Kerrville, 65 miles away, is an arts and crafts mecca and home of the **Cowboy Artists of America Museum,** 1550 Bandera Highway, (830-896-2553; www.caamuseum.com), with exhibits of paintings, drawings, and sculpture by members of the Cowboy Artists of America. Fredericksburg, 71 miles from San Antonio and settled in 1846, has wide streets lined with century-old gingerbread houses and many antiques shops. **The National Museum of the Pacific War,** 340 East Main Street, (830-997-4379; www.tpwd.state.texas.us), is dedicated to those who served in World War II with Fleet Admiral Chester W. Nimitz. It has a Japanese Garden of Peace and an outdoor exhibit area featuring guns, tanks, and planes.
- You won't be far from the **LBJ Ranch,** 75 miles from San Antonio on U.S. 290. Former president Lyndon B. Johnson and his wife, Lady Bird,

donated 200 acres of their ranch to the National Park Service. The ranch is located 15 miles west of Johnson City on Highway 290 near the town of Stonewall. This is also where LBJ State Park is located (830-644-2252; www.tpwd.state.texas.us), with the museum and visitor's center. Bus tours to the ranch (you can't go on your own) from the visitor's center are run by the LBJ National Historical Park; call (830) 868-7128 for tour information.

- A quick trip to **Mexico** is another possibility. **Nuevo Laredo** is only 150 miles south of San Antonio and features colorful shops.

A statement to Mexican customs that you intend to visit only the border city is all that is required. If you are driving, it's also recommended you purchase short-term Mexican auto insurance that's available from several agencies and travel services on the U.S. side of the border. Most U.S. car insurance is not valid in Mexico.

Note: When only one parent (whether that parent is married or divorced) is entering Mexico with a child or children, Mexico requires a notarized statement from the other, nontraveling parent indicating that the traveling parent has permission to take the child into Mexico for a specified amount of time. Obtain a similar letter when you are traveling with children who have a different last name from yours.

SPECIAL EVENTS

It seems there's always a fiesta or two going on in San Antonio. Contact the SACVB for more information on the following events, (210-207-6700).

February. Stock Show and Rodeo.

March. Alamo Memorial Day.

April. Fiesta San Antonio, the biggest of the year, features ten days of parades, festivals, sporting events, music, arts shows, and other events.

Late April–early May. Cinco De Mayo festival at Market Square.

October. Oktoberfest.

November. River Parade & Lighting Ceremony.

December. Christmas festivities include Rivercenter Pageant; Fiesta De Las Luminarias, thousands of candles illuminate the River Walk; Fiestas Navideñas, with piñata parties, blessing of the animals, and a visit from Pancho Claus in Market Square; and Las Posadas, with singers moving along the River Walk.

WHERE TO STAY

The SACVB publishes a lodging guide and map. A lodging reservation line (800-858-4303) gives you information about the hotels they service. The city has accommodations in all prices. For bed and breakfasts, contact **Bed and Breakfast Hosts of San Antonio** reservation service; (210) 479-1155 or (800) 356-1605.

The ideal location to be, of course, is along the River Walk. Here are a few selections in this area.

If you're looking for charm versus chain hotels, here are two hotels that exude personality. **La Mansion Del Rio,** 112 College; (210) 518-1000 or (800) 292-7300. This hotel (a law school in another incarnation) overlooks the River Walk and is tastefully decorated with a Spanish Colonial flair. There's an excellent on-site restaurant and lovely garden courtyards. **The Fairmount Hotel,** 401 South Alamo (210-224-8800 or 800-642-3363), has only thirty-seven rooms, but its reputation is large.

The city's largest hotel, the **Marriott Rivercenter,** 101 Bowie (210-223-1000 or 800-648-4462), offers 1,000 rooms, plus an indoor/outdoor pool, a health club, and a full-service restaurant. The hotel is connected to the Rivercenter Mall. **The Hampton Inn River Walk,** 414 Bowie (210-225-8500 or 800-426-7866), offers good value and includes a free continental breakfast. **The Westin River Walk,** a 474-room hotel, opened in 1999. With the WestinKids' Club, parents can ask for child-safe rooms and kid equipment, and kids receive a welcome amenity (210-224-6500 or 800-WESTIN-1).

Embassy Suites (www.embassy-suites.com) has two locations. One is at the airport, **Embassy Suites Hotel-Airport,** 10110 Highway 281 North (210-525-9999); and the other is **Embassy Suites Northwest,** 7750 Briaridge (210-340-5421 or 800-362-2779).

Don't forget the Hyatt, with two area locations. **Hyatt Regency San Antonio,** 123 Losoya (210-222-1234 or 800-233-1234), built over an extension of the San Antonio River, has 631 rooms and water cascading through the lobby, linking the river and the Alamo. Kids get a Welcome Kit and specially priced menus. The **Hyatt Regency Hill Country Resort,** 9800 Resort Drive, is located 20 miles north of town; phone (210) 647-1234 or (800) 55-HYATT. The 500-room luxury hotel features a four-acre water park with two swimming pools separated by a waterfall—plus Camp Hyatt children's program for ages three to twelve during holidays, weekends, and daily throughout summer.

WHERE TO EAT

The Friday "Weekender" section of the *San Antonio Express News* contains a dining guide; the Convention and Visitors Bureau also provides a listing of restaurants. It's most fun to eat along the River Walk; many eateries here are fine for families and relatively inexpensive. **Kangaroo Court Restaurant,** 512 River Walk (210-224-6821), serves American fare (burgers, fries) and is known for its yummy cheesecake. Try Texan favorites (BBQ, chicken-fried steak) at **Republic of Texas,** 526 Riverwalk; (210) 226-6256. Sample Tex-Mex food at **Rio Rio,** 421 Commerce; (210) 226-8462. **Boudro's,** 421 East Commerce Street (210-224-8484), features good Southwestern and Creole cuisine, but it is not inexpensive.

At Market Square, **Mi Tierra Cafe y Panaderia,** 218 Produce Row, (210) 225-1262, is a local institution with a bakery in the lobby and a dining room where tamales and tacos are served to a constant flow of appreciative diners twenty-four hours a day. And if you're in the mood for deli, **Jason's Deli** has three locations: 25 NE Loop 410 (210-524-9288); 9933 IH-10 West (210-690-3354; and 5819 NW Loop 410 (210-647-5000).

FOR MORE INFORMATION

The **Convention and Visitors Bureau** operates several information sites. The main center at 317 Alamo Plaza (directly across from the Alamo), is open every day (except Thanksgiving, Christmas, and New Year's Day) 8:30 A.M. to 6:00 P.M.; (210) 207-6748 or (800) 447-3372; www.sanantoniocvb. com. There are information kiosks at Terminals One and Two at the airport.

Several helpful brochures are available from the Convention and Visitors Bureau:

- *A Guide to Puro San Antonio,* a guide to the city's Latino cultural sites
- *San Antonio, Just for Kids* guide
- *San Antonio, African American Cultural Guide*
- *S.A.V.E.,* a forty-page coupon book of savings for more than fifty-two hotels, twenty restaurants, and twenty attractions.

VIA Metropolitan Transit provides transportation for the handicapped. Call their VIA TRANS line at (210) 362-2020 or TDD 362-2019. Most San Antonio attractions are wheelchair accessible. The River Walk, however, has only limited accessibility.

Our Kids Magazine, 8400 Blanco Road (210-349-6667), features a monthly calendar of events for families and other interesting news; it's free at various locations throughout town, or call for a sample copy. Web site: www.sanantoniocvb.com

Emergency Numbers

Ambulance, fire, police: 911

Poison Control: (800) 764-7661

Twenty-four-hour pharmacies: Eckerd's Drug Stores at 6900 San Pedro Avenue (210-824-3237), and 9832 Wurzbach (210-690-1616)

Twenty-four-hour clinic: Nix River Walk Clinic, 408 Navaro; (210) 271-1841

CHINCOTEAGUE AND ASSATEAGUE ISLANDS

Although Misty, the pint-size pony, may have made the Chincoteague/Assateague area famous, there's a lot more than wild ponies here. There are shops, restaurants, camping areas, and hotels; Chincoteague also provides the only Virginia access to Assateague Island, much of which is an unspoiled national wildlife refuge, with beaches, sand dunes, scrub thickets, and forests.

Assateague Island is a narrow, 37-mile barrier strand that stretches between the Atlantic Ocean and Chincoteague Island. The southern section of Assateague Island is in Virginia and has portions of the Chincoteague National Wildlife Refuge, which is managed by the U.S. Fish and Wildlife Service. This refuge ends at the Virginia/Maryland border, where Assateague National Seashore begins. The National Seashore is in Maryland and is managed by the National Park Service. Assateague State Park, managed by Maryland's Department of Natural Resources, is in Maryland and stretches between the popular beach resort of Ocean City to the north and the National Seashore to the south.

Each region of Assateague Island contains about 9,000 acres. The Maryland side offers more beach and primitive camping facilities, and the Virginia side more migratory birds, denser pine forests, more wildlife viewing, and such delights as Assateague Lighthouse. The Chincoteague National Wildlife Refuge, located at the southern tip of Assateague Island in Virginia, is a national wildlife refuge, whose ecosystems include forests, dunes, and wetlands.

GETTING THERE

You need a car to get here and may want one to drive along some of the scenic roads, especially if you don't plan on bicycling. From Virginia's eastern shore take Route 13 to 175, which leads across Wallops Island to Chincoteague. From Baltimore and Washington take Route 50 East. To

Chincoteague and Assateague Islands

AT A GLANCE

▶ Enjoy the unspoiled beauty of beaches, sand dunes, scrub thickets, and forests

▶ Explore 18,000 acres of natural landscape on Assateague Island

▶ See the wild ponies on Chincoteague Island

▶ Take advantage of excellent birding opportunities

▶ Virginia's Eastern Shore Tourism Commission, (757) 787-2460; www.esva.net/~esvachamber

▶ Chincoteague Chamber of Commerce (757) 336-6161; www.chincoteaguechamber.com

enter from the Maryland side, continue on 50 East to 611 to Assateague State Park. Note that there is no road access through the refuge from the Maryland side to the Virginia side or vice versa. Only over-sand vehicles with special permits are allowed to drive along the shoreline between Virginia's Chincoteague National Wildlife Refuge and Maryland's Assateague State Park. To visit both sections, you must either hike on the beach route or drive on a 50-mile land route (allow 1½ hours) outside the park. To drive from Chincoteague National Wildlife Refuge to the Maryland side, take Route 175 from Chincoteague to Route 679 North, which leads into Route 12 North, which changes into Route 113 North to Route 376 East to Route 611 Southeast to the Barrier Island Visitor Center.

GETTING AROUND

The 37-mile-long island's only inhabitants include 316 different species of birds, the endangered Delmarva fox squirrel, white-tail deer, Sika (oriental elk), and wild ponies. Since cars are allowed only in limited areas, your best bet for enjoying the wildlife and undeveloped beaches is to hike or bike, although bikes are not allowed on the refuge beach.

The Virginia end of Assateague features more than 15 miles of winding trails through marshes and forests. If you didn't bring your own bicycle, several places in Chincoteague (the town) rent them, including **Piney Island Country Store,** 7085 Maddox Boulevard (757-336-6212), and **Jus' Bikes,**

6527 Maddox Blvd. (757-336-6700), both of which rent helmets and provide maps, and **The Bike Depot,** 7058 Maddox Blvd. (757-336-5511), which provides helmets and maps for free.

WHAT TO SEE AND DO

The first thing to do is stop by the **Chincoteague National Wildlife Refuge Visitor Center,** Maddox Boulevard, the first left after you turn into the refuge (757-336-6122; http://chinco.fws.gov). Here you can pick up maps and background information about the refuge, as well as find out about scheduled guided hikes and lectures. Ask about the Junior Refuge Manager and the Junior Birder Programs for kids. The **Toms Cove Visitor Center,** at the end of Beach Road near the beach parking lot (757-336-6577; www.nps.gov), which is operated by the National Park Service, offers information on naturalist programs and beach activities. If time permits, try to sign up for a guided walk through the beaches, the salt marsh, or the dunes. Children like these as well as the surf rescue demonstrations. NPS's program for kids is called the Junior Ranger Program.

A new National Wildlife Refuge Visitor Center is scheduled to open in 2003, with expanded exhibits, a wet lab, and an auditorium for presentations.

Beaches

Most people visit Chincoteague National Wildlife Refuge in summer, and many visit for the spring and fall bird migrations. Be sure to cool off at **Toms Cove** beach, located at the end of Chincoteague Wildlife Refuge. In season this recreational beach, located on the ocean side of the island, has lifeguards, making this a good choice if you have young children who want to swim. You can drive or bicycle (bring your own bikes) along **Beach Road,** the auto route that leads from refuge headquarters to Toms Cove. This route is a prime spot for sighting the wild ponies, especially in winter. Then you pass Swan Cove, a great place to view birds, on your way to the beach parking lot. Toms Cove offers relatively calm waters for swimming.

Less visited is the entire north side of the refuge, which has 10 miles of wild dune-laden sands that lead to the Virginia/Maryland border. Swimming is not encouraged here—there are no lifeguards on patrol. But even if you walk just a little bit north, the crowds thin out (yes, even Assateague beaches can be crowded in summer). Take water bottles with you and try to make it a mile or so into the Inner Dune path. The reward: a vital seascape of dunes, sea grasses, and surf.

Birding

More than 316 types of birds make their home within the refuge's wetlands and dunes. In fall Chincoteague National Wildlife Refuge is part of the Atlantic Flyway, a series of islands used by thousands of migrating birds. **Wildlife Loop,** (open to cars after 3:00 P.M.), a 3.5 mile loop around Snow Goose Pond, is a pretty tour and a good spot for birding. In fall and into winter, you'll see scores of migrating geese, and tundra swans. No matter what season you visit, the refuge has many birds, including mute swans, black vultures, terns, blue herons, surf scoters, and great horned owls. Even if you can't recognize these feathered beings well enough to identify them on the checklists available from the Visitor Center, you and your children will enjoy the specter of ducks flying in military formation above the marshy wetlands as well as the songs and twitters of the thousands of birds that make the refuge their home.

Trails

Trails around the town of Chincoteague provide great biking and hiking paths (mostly flat with a few gentle rises). Summer is certainly the prime time for families to visit Assateague, but do consider a spring or winter visit. In winter Assateague Island offers you a world of peaceful contrasts. Here the crisp, clear air vibrates with strange sounds, like the high-pitched honk of thousands of snow geese and the throaty duck calls that carry from marsh to marsh. You can walk along the miles of wild beaches bordered by dunes, hike through the loblolly pine forests populated by white-tail deer and Sika, bike through the acres of marshlands, or observe wintering ducks, geese, and swans. Almost anywhere in winter—along the roadsides, near the marshes, and especially along the **Woodland Trail** in both summer and winter, a 1.6-mile walking and biking loop through a forest—you will meet the island's famous wild ponies, which roam freely on Assateague.

The brown, white, or dappled **Chincoteague ponies,** twelve to fourteen hands tall, are stockier than other breeds. Although wild, they are accustomed to people; still it's not a good idea to get too close or to try and pet them.

No one knows how the ponies arrived. Legends abound, including speculation that the first ponies swam ashore from wrecked Spanish galleons or were driven to the barrier island in the 1680s by Colonists avoiding livestock taxes and the cost of fencing.

Tours

Assateague Wildlife Tours (757-336-3443, or 757-336-6154 after 5:00 P.M.), offers two tours. One is the Assateauge Wildlife Tour, a 1½-hour narrated tram ride that familiarizes you with the island. It's a good begin-

Great Family Hikes

- **Assateague Lighthouse.** It's an easy, ¼-mile walk to this historic lighthouse. Built in 1867, it's one of many operated by the U.S. Coast Guard to warn ships as they approach the barrier islands of the East Coast.
- **Woodland Trail.** This is a beautiful 1.6-mile trip through a shaded loblolly pine forest. If you're hiking in spring or fall, listen for songbirds along the way. This trail also leads to an overlook where, with luck, you'll catch sight of the wild ponies and, in fall and winter, see waterfowl. Another good pony-spotting point is in **Black Duck Marsh** along Beach Road.
- **Wildlife Loop.** Wildlife Loop is open only to bikers and hikers until 3:00 P.M. Walk or bike ride along the 3.5-mile trail.

ning for an extended stay or a quick way to catch a glimpse of Assateague's diverse wildlife if you're short on time. This is the easy way to explore, especially if you have children too young to bike for very long. The tram travels 7½ miles into the northern portions of the refuge and a dike-maintained freshwater system, which are otherwise accessible only by foot. Here you're likely to see eagles, hawks, herons, and herds of ponies. From April to Memorial Day, one tour departs daily; from Memorial Day to Labor Day, there are two tours daily. From Labor Day through October, tours generally operate once a day on Wednesdays, Saturdays, and Sundays. Call ahead to be sure. The second tour is Assateague Cruises Aboard the *Misty,* an ecological boat tour around the island with an onboard aquarium (kids can learn the difference between male and female crabs) and crab pots pulled from the water. This tour is available at 5:00 P.M. and 7:00 P.M. daily from May to September.

Tidewater Expeditions (757–336–6811) offers sunrise and sunset sea kayak tours by a local artist whose grandfather was one of the original carvers on the island. This ecological tour, where you'll see eagles, ponies, osprey, and other wildlife, can be geared to families and include anyone age four to ninety-four. (Kayak child seats are available for very young children.) Kayak instruction and rentals are also available.

Museums

In the town of Chincoteague, visit the **Oyster and Maritime Museum,** 7125 Maddox Boulevard (757–336–6117; www.chincoteaguechamber. com/oyster/omm.html), where exhibits detail the local oyster industry from harvesting and shucking through shipping and eating. Other highlights include walrus jaws, Native American artifacts, shipwreck relics, and an exhibit that shows the variety of places that oysters will colonize—bottles, pipes, and even inner tubes. There's an aquarium where kids can see fish from the bay close-up, as well as hands-on exhibits that include turtle shells and fish vertebrae, and the First-Order Fresnel Lens (manufactured in 1886) from the Assateague Lighthouse. Admission.

Another uniquely Chincoteague place is the **Refuge Waterfowl Museum,** 7059 Maddox Boulevard (757-336-5800). Here your children learn even more about Assateague as an established wintering site for migratory waterfowl. Along with rotating exhibits, the museum houses artwork inspired by these winter birds, as well as weapons, boats, traps, and decoys. Open weekdays, March through December. Admission.

To find out about man-made flight, visit the **NASA Wallops Flight Facility Visitors Center,** State Highway 175, Wallops Island (757-824-1344 or 757-824-2298; www.wff.nasa.gov), 5 miles from Chincoteague. Kids enjoy the life-size models of planes, probes, and rockets. Try to make it for the model rocket demonstrations on the first Saturday of each month, plus the third Saturday of June, July, and August. Kids five to ten years old can earn a "Space Ace" certificate and a lithograph by completing an activity sheet. Free, and open daily in summer and Thursday through Monday at other times. Closed to the public in December, January, and February. The Center's Web site has a terrific kids' page, with information about earth science, the space station, and more.

At the **Island Aquarium,** 8162 Landmark Plaza, Chincoteague (757-336-2212; www.assateague.com/aquarium.html), visitors can experience local marine life up close. The aquarium pipes its water directly from the Chincoteague Channel, and its guest residents are only temporary—caught and released on a regular basis. The touch tank has horseshoe crabs, starfish, whelks, and other marine animals. There's also a shark tank, with some of the smaller varieties on view. Admission.

Outdoor Recreation

Besides swimming and beachcombing, try such shore staples as surf fishing, clamming, and crabbing. At the southernmost tip of Toms Cove, just beyond the public beach, is a fishing area especially popular in late fall and early winter. You're most likely to find amberjacks, striped bass, drum fish, gray trout, and king mackerel. No special license is required, but remember, if you're there after hours, a permit is required. Check with refuge rangers for the schedule of interpretive programs and wildlife photography sessions.

Swan Cove is another popular spot for clam diggers. Generally you don't need a permit for these activities, but you should obtain information at one of the visitor centers. Other good crabbing places in the late summer and early fall months are the **Town Dock,** located on Main

Street across from the firehouse, and the **Harbor,** located on the southern end of Main Street. Assateague State Park is also a prime spot for crabbing and clamming. **South Point** and **Barrier Island,** where the Visitor's Center is just across the bay from Assateague Island, are both good local spots. The **Old Ferry Landing** is also a good spot for crabbing.

Surfside Golf, 6557 Maddox Boulevard (757-336-GOLF) has a nifty miniature golf course, plus batting cages, water games, and a snack bar. Open from 9:00 A.M. to 10:00 P.M. in the summer. Admission. For a loftier view of things, try **Capt. Mike's Parasailing** (757-336-2760), where even younger children can experience the thrill of flying. Summers only, four times a day.

SIDE TRIPS

Visit the rest of Virginia's eastern shore. Travel on Route 13 south, but be sure to take the turnoffs to visit some typically Eastern Shore towns of **Wachapreague, Onancock,** and **Nassawadox.** Then, continue on Route 13 and cross the **Chesapeake Bay Bridge Tunnel,** itself something of an attraction. The other side brings you to Virginia Beach. (See Coastal Virginia.)

SPECIAL EVENTS

Information about all of these events can be obtained from the Chincoteague Chamber of Commerce at (757) 336-6161.

May. The International Migratory Bird Celebration.

July. Annual Pony Swim and Auction, the wild ponies from Assateague Island are rounded up for their swim to Chincoteague for a foal auction.

October. The Oyster Festival, an all-you-can-eat seafood fête of oysters, crabs, and clam fritters. National Wildlife Refuge Week has family activities.

Thanksgiving Week. Refuge Waterfowl Week, when Chincoteague National Wildlife Refuge invites visitors to tour the northern part of the refuge. Annual Deborah Waterfowl Show.

WHERE TO STAY

Stay at one of the island's bed and breakfast inns for a cozy getaway. Keep in mind that most of them close for the winter and not all of them welcome children. A good one to try is the **Year of the Horse Inn,** 3583

Main Street (757-336-3221 or 800-680-0090), a sprawling white stucco house, with three bed and breakfast rooms and a two-bedroom apartment. The apartment sleeps five. Continental breakfast included. Children are welcome.

Of the several motels on Chincoteague, here are some that remain open year-round: **Driftwood Motor Lodge,** 7105 Maddox Boulevard (757-336-6557 or 800-553-6117), overlooks the wildlife refuge. **Waterside Motor Inn,** 3761 Main Street (757-336-3434), offers rooms on the waterfront and has a pool, fishing and crabbing pier, and a tennis court.

The **Lighthouse Inn,** 4218 Main Street (757-336-5091 or 800-505-5257) is a very basic, affordable, comfortable motel, with refrigerators in the rooms and a pool. **Comfort Suites,** 4195 Main Street (757-336-3700; www.chincoteaguechamber.com/comfortsuites) is a bit fancier, with suites providing a refrigerator, microwave, dataports, and voice mail. Also provided are free deluxe continental breakfast buffet, pool, fitness center, and laundry. **Heron Woods Vacation Cottages** (888-491-2941; www.heronwoods.com) have fully equipped kitchens, cable TV, and laundry facilities. Children over six who are intrigued by Marguerite Henry's *Misty of Chincoteague* will want to stay at **Miss Molly's Inn,** 4141 Main Street (757-336-6686 or 800-221-5620; www.missmollys-inn.com), where Henry stayed while writing her book. Full breakfast and afternoon tea provided.

Camping

No camping is allowed on the Virginia side of Assateague, not even backcountry camping. It's a 10-mile hike from Virginia over to Maryland, where backcountry camping is allowed, but this is too long a trek for most families. The Maryland side of the island offers some established camping areas. Contact the **Assateague Island National Seashore** (410-641-3030 or 410-336-6577) and **Assateague State Park** (410-641-2120) for more information about Maryland camping.

The **Maddox Family Campground,** 6742 Maddox Boulevard (757-336-3111 or 757-336-6648), is close to Assateague and still near the shops and restaurants of Chincoteague. The camp has a pool, playground, grocery and RV store, laundry room, and modern bathhouses. The campground has an arcade and offers such activities as shuffleboard, horseshoes, crabbing, and bird-watching, as well as a propane filling station.

Tom's Cove Family Campground, 8128 Beebe Road (757-336-6498), offers waterfront camping plus a boat ramp and marina. Sites have hookups for water and electricity.

There are also a variety of vacation houses and cottages available for rent, mostly in the summertime. Contact the Chincoteague Chamber of

Commerce, P.O. Box 258, Chincoteague, VA 23336 (757-336-6161; www.chincoteaguechamber.com), for a complete listing.

WHERE TO EAT

Etta's Family Restaurant, 7452 Eastside Road (757-336-5644), a waterfront eatery that overlooks the Assateague Lighthouse and the channel where the ponies swim, specializes in local seafood, steak, and, of course, crab cakes. The children's menu includes such favorites as shrimp, clams, chicken, and chopped steak. The restaurant is open daily from April to December

For jumbo flounder and other seafood, try **Bill's Seafood Restaurant,** 4040 Main Street (757-336-5831), open for breakfast, lunch, and dinner. A children's menu is available. Another restaurant that specializes in seafood for the family is **Steamers Seafood Restaurant,** 6251 Maddox Boulevard (757-336-6236), with a children's menu and all-you-can-eat steamed crabs and shrimp. For dessert indulge in ice cream and frozen yogurt at **Island Creamery, Ice Cream and Yogurt,** 6243 Maddox Boulevard (757-336-6236), or at **Muller's Old-Fashioned Ice Cream Parlour,** 4034 Main Street, next to the firehouse (757-336-5894).

FOR MORE INFORMATION

Call or write **Virginia's Eastern Shore Tourism Commission,** P.O. Box 460, Melfa, VA 23410; (757) 787-2460; www.esva.net/esvatourism; Chincoteague Chamber of Commerce, P.O. Box 258, Chincoteague, VA 23336; (757) 336-6161; www.chincoteaguechamber.com. The office, located at 6733 Maddox Boulevard, is open year-round, Monday through Saturday from 9:00 A.M. to 4:30 P.M., and Sundays from 12:30 to 4:30 P.M. from Memorial Day to Labor Day.

Emergency Numbers

Ambulance, fire, and police: 911

Two hospitals are located 40 miles from Chincoteague and Assateague: to the north—Shore Memorial Hospital, Hospital Drive, Nassawadox, Virginia (emergency room: 757-414-8777); to the south—Peninsula Regional Medical Center, 100 East Carroll Street, Salisbury, Maryland (410-546-6400)

A twenty-four-hour pharmacy is located in Shore Memorial Hospital: (757) 442-8781

Chincoteague police (non-emergency): (757) 336-3155

COLONIAL WILLIAMSBURG AND JAMESTOWN

C olonial Williamsburg is America's best-known living-history museum. The area served as the capital of Virginia, England's oldest, largest, most populous, and richest colony from 1699 to 1776. Colonial Williamsburg and the historic Virginia triangle of Jamestown and Yorktown offer hands-on history that makes learning about Colonial life fun.

GETTING THERE

Williamsburg is midway between Richmond and Norfolk, Virginia. I-64 leads into town, which is easily accessible via car, plane, train, and bus.

Three airports will get you to the city of Williamsburg, which contains more than just Colonial Williamsburg, the historic area. The **Newport News/Williamsburg International Airport** (757-877-0221) offers only limited service. The **Richmond** airport, about 40 miles east of Williamsburg, and the **Norfolk** airport, 55 miles south of Williamsburg, offer frequent domestic and international service and also have car-rental facilities.

Amtrak trains (800-USA-RAIL) stop in Williamsburg, 468 North Boundary Street, on northeast routes that also stop in Boston, New York, Philadelphia, Baltimore, Washington, and other major East Coast cities. **Greyhound/Trailways** 468 North Boundary Street (757-229-1460), offers direct service to Williamsburg. For Colonial Williamsburg travel assistance and information, call 800-HISTORY.

GETTING AROUND

Once you reach Colonial Williamsburg, the best way to experience the ambience is to travel around town the way most colonists did—on foot. As cars are not allowed on historic site streets, visitors should park at the

Colonial Williamsburg and Jamestown

AT A GLANCE

▶ Explore Colonial Williamsburg: A living-history community re-creating life in Virginia's 1770s capital

▶ See Jamestown, the first permanent English settlement in America, and the Yorktown Victory Center

▶ Ride the roller coasters at Busch Gardens Williamsburg, and get wet at Water Country U.S.A.

▶ Colonial Williamsburg Foundation: 800–HISTORY; www. history.org or www.colonialwilliamsburg.org

▶ Williamsburg Area Convention and Visitors Bureau: (800) 368-6511 or (757) 253-0192; www.visitwilliamsburg.com

Visitor Center. From here a free shuttle bus service takes ticket holders to the Historic Area. To travel to Jamestown and other attractions in the area, a car is a necessity.

WHAT TO SEE AND DO

Colonial Williamsburg

This living-history community re-creates life in Virginia's capital as it existed in the 1770s just before the Revolutionary War. In a decade of visits to Colonial Williamsburg, we have found this 173-acre living-history museum to be a delightful evergreen. Visitors mingle with actors in period costume who roam the streets, tend the hundreds of shops, and demonstrate trade skills and other mainstays of eighteenth-century life. Also open for exploration are government buildings, such as the Capitol (where Colonial lawmakers met) and the Governor's Palace (bedecked with bayonets, muskets, and rifles) proclaiming the power of the British crown. Two on-site museums provide glimpses of the era's decorative and folk arts.

Whatever age kids you have, don't miss walking through the Historic Area at night. In the lamplight it's easy to imagine that inside the frame and brick houses women are stirring kettles over open-hearth fireplaces and schoolchildren are puzzling out their 'rithmetic by candlelight.

Colonial Williamsburg is the kind of place you can visit many times because what you do depends on the season and the age and interests of your children.

Dress a child in a tri-cornered hat or a Colonial gown at Colonial Williamsburg and amazing things happen: They're hooked, and history lessons are never the same!

Tickets. What you see depends on what you pay, and your plans. Williamsburg has more than 500 buildings, including eighty-eight original homes, shops, public buildings, and taverns. To see it all—the ninety acres of gardens, the exceptional museums (the **DeWitt Wallace Decorative Arts Gallery** and the **Abby Aldrich Rockefeller Folk Art Center**), plus the nearby **Carter's Grove** plantation—a multiday stay is recommended. A General Admission Pass is for one day and gains you entrance to the Historic Area buildings, Carter's Grove Plantation and the Orientation Walking Tour. A Value Pass is for two days and adds to the basic package a 5 percent discount on any of the Shops of Williamsburg. A Colonial Pass is for up to five days and adds to the basic package free parking, a 10 percent discount on shopping, and evening program admission, and a souvenir postcard packet. If you plan on returning to Williamsburg within a year, then consider the most expensive (but practical) Liberty Pass, which gives you unlimited admission to all major exhibits, homes, and museums for one year and adds to the basic package a Special Focus Walking Tour and higher discounts at more attractions, plus a subscription to Williamsburg's quarterly newsletter. Children's tickets for six to seventeen year olds are comparable (though less expensive), and children under six are free.

Tickets are sold at the Visitor Center and at various locations in the Historic Area. Although you may roam through the Historic Area for free, you need a ticket to enter any of the buildings and to use the public shuttles.

Great Things to Do in Colonial Williamsburg

The key to making the most of the colonial experience and to see beyond the area's commercialism is to get involved. The daytime special programs, most of which don't cost extra, bring the region's history and culture to life. Meet a printer, listen to a grandmother tell stories about her life, and a soldier talk about encampment. The evening programs, most of which do cost extra, provide good fun as well. Check the *Visitor's Companion*. Some of our favorite programs are:

- **Welcome, Little Stranger,** Milliner's. When James Slate, a tailor at the Milliner's discusses children's clothing, kids make those "I-can't-believe-it" faces as they learn that in the eighteenth century even tots wore "stays," those corsetlike contraptions; little boys sported dresses until about age five; and girls never, not ever, had buttons, except on riding habits.

- **The Geddy House.** A visit to the Geddy House provides insight into the lives of Williamsburg's slaves. On a rare break from cooking, weeding, scrubbing, washing, and spinning, Grace, one of Miz Elizabeth's slaves, chats. When we ask about her husband, Grace says, "Will and I jumped the broom but he ran away out west because the master was going to sell him south." When we inquire about her children, she replies that she worries the master might sell Christopher, nine. Her dearest wish is to convince Mr. Geddy of Christopher's usefulness in Geddy's foundry. Then Grace leans

toward me, telling me that Miz Elizabeth demands that rosemary be sprinkled on the floors to get rid of odors. "But that's a waste of good rosemary," confides Grace, smiling, "so after I sweeps up the floor, I use the rosemary to make Miz Elizabeth's tea." That story still makes my family laugh.

- **Order in the Court,** Courthouse. With kids of middle-school age or older, this is a good choice. When the clerk at the courthouse calls for jurors, if you are, as required by law, a man, over twenty-one, Protestant, white, and a land-owner, you can serve. Others can be plaintiffs, defendants, and witnesses.

- **Felicity in Williamsburg**. If you have a daughter enamored of Felicity, the doll in the American Girls Collection, book the tour and see the Colonial area from Felicity's point of view. The tour, available on weekends and also during the week in summer, is charming. Girls, some dressed identically to the dolls they clutch (bring your own) and

(continued)

Great Things to Do in Colonial Williamsburg *(continued)*

their accompanying moms learn "courtesies" (curtsies), wave to Penny, Felicity's horse, and scout a home for such everyday staples as buckles, plate warmers, and fancy parlor chairs. The pièce de résistance is the afternoon visit to Miss Manderly, Felicity's teacher, for sewing, dancing lessons, and tea. Children must be accompanied by an adult. Recommended for ages seven and older. The Colonial Williamsburg hotels all have "Felicity" packages including tickets.

- **Legends of the Past Tour,** Historic Area at night. Lanterns light the way on tours of historic taverns and houses at night. Meet Mrs. Jonathan Edwards, a merchant's wife, who relates a Cherokee legend of how the Milky Way came to be; a tipsy sailor who tells a tall tale of Blackbeard, booty, and pirates; and Emma Johnston, who gossips about a woman who puts on airs by wearing French fashions.

- **Military Encampment,** summer. Sign up with the Second Virginia Regiment and practice drills, learn the bayonet lunge,

present arms (using sticks instead of loaded muskets), and assist with cleaning and firing a cannon.

- **Young Recruits and Good Girls,** summer. Boys ages six to fourteen can sign up for the Young Recruit Program, and girls can be Good Girls, providing entertaining ways for young kids to experience Colonial life as they tour with their parents. Children receive a period costume to wear and a list of tasks that takes them around the Historic Area. Boys sign up for duty under Colonel Woodford, who sends them to inspect the powder kegs in the magazine, report needed repairs and new orders to the cooper, and deliver a bill to the post office and an urgent message to the Colonel. Girls help Mistress Grimes with her errands by going to the Geddy House for a recipe, the post office for a letter, the Powell house to borrow some lye soap, and the general store for yarn samples.

For program information, call (800) 246-2099.

Visitor Center. Colonial Williamsburg is big and can be overwhelming, so take some time to plan. Start off early at the Visitor Center. First make reservations for lunch and dinner if you have not already booked them before your arrival, especially if you plan to dine at one of the historic taverns. Then get oriented by viewing the introductory thirty-five-minute movie, *Williamsburg—The Story of a Patriot.* Pick up a copy of the *Visitor's Companion,* a weekly newsletter, for a listing of specific events that may interest your family.

Family Life and Black History. The visitor center can direct you to specific exhibits about Colonial life. At the **Benjamin Powell House,** you may come upon the teenage daughters weeding the garden, practicing their cross-stitch with their mother, or doing their lessons with their music teacher. You may also meet Benjamin and Sarah, children of Mrs. Powell's personal slave, Rose. Listen to the boys speak in eighteenth-century dialect as they help with the house laundry.

Colonial Williamsburg is also a good place to talk to your kids about slavery. **The Other Half Tour,** highlights sites important to blacks and talks about their lives. Programs throughout the day and special evening programs present reenactments of the discussions, fears, and relationships of Williamsburg's African American slaves and freepersons, and its white residents. Some of these are very realistic (you hear the sound of whipping and a slave patrol rounding up rebellious slaves) and may be too much for very young children. But the tour does present the raw truth about slavery then and the issues that resonate with us today. New programs are added each year. The evening program "Remember Me, When Freedom Comes" is particularly moving and is an excellent basis for a discussion about slavery for parents and their children, as Paris, an enslaved man, tells of his experiences in Africa and Williamsburg and his community brings his memories to life through spirituals and work songs. In February, Black History Month, Colonial Williamsburg hosts additional lectures, storytellers, and activities.

For another side of family life, a program explores the lives of another often forgotten group—women. The **Widows of Williamsburg Tour** discusses the ironic benefits of eighteenth-century widowhood and is told from the perspective of five widows of the era who represent different social classes. In March, in celebration of Women's History Month, the Historic Area offers more programs.

Check for tickets and admission policies to these tours and special programs.

More Tour Highlights. Stroll along the main road, the **Duke of Gloucester Street,** which extends from the Wren Building to the Capitol. Side streets lead to museums, private homes, shops, and to the Governor's Palace. While walking throughout the Historic Area, children often have the most fun engaging in spirited conversations with costumed interpreters on their way to the wig maker, the apothecary, or the tavern. Encourage your kids to talk to these "characters," who speak as if they are living in the eighteenth century. They'll tell you about running low on candles and how their children play quoits (the Colonial version of horseshoes), but not about electricity or Nintendo. Kids find out what a cooper is and what a milliner does, and they witness a shoemaker and blacksmith at work.

At the **Governor's Palace** view Colonial artifacts, including some 800 guns and swords. Touring this gracious mansion instills a sense of English power, and a stroll by the Palace Green might get your kids to join in a game of quoits, hoop rolling, lawn bowling, or stilt walking.

In winter, a less popular but extremely pretty time for a family visit, enjoy the festivities and natural decorations. Yes, Virginia, there is a holiday beyond neon, flashing red and green lights, and glad-handing Santas. Dance the minuet at a candlelight ball (great for teens who have learned their rhythms with hard rock), enjoy the carolers, visit tastefully decorated homes, and gaze at the moonlight reflecting on the icicles.

Museums. Don't miss the **Abby Aldrich Rockefeller Folk Art Museum,** 307 South England Street (757-220-7698). Kids are intrigued by the folk art, with its unusual perspective; they comment on the lack of proportion and like the easily recognizable figures. With more than 400 paintings and objects, including old-fashioned toys, plus a schedule of temporary exhibits, the center is definitely worth a stop. You will be surprised at how much your kids like the art.

The **DeWitt Wallace Decorative Arts Gallery,** 325 Francis Street in the Public Hospital (757-220-7724), is home to Colonial Williamsburg's art masterworks. More than 8,000 seventeenth- through early nineteenth-century decorative delights, from silver and ceramics to linen and lace, are presented here. Although the gallery may cater more to older children, don't avoid the place; instead find something to catch your child's interest. Go on a treasure hunt here; let your kids follow their fancies through a door and see what they find. These exceptional galleries unfold like boxes within boxes from the central masterworks gallery, which features exquisite Colonial furnishings. Browse through the gallery of hand-colored Colonial maps, where the pink for Virginia bleeds all the way past the Mississippi River, and Indian names mark the territories of Michigan. Kids who see the world only through television and computer screens can find out how people used to view the world in the exhibit "PEEP SHOW! Panoramas of the Past," a display of viewing devices used in the eighteenth and early-nineteenth centuries that made flat prints three-dimensional and provided perspective to landscapes. At the museum through December 9, 2002. Admission.

Carter's Grove Plantation. **Carter's Grove,** U.S. 60 (757-229-1000), is a manor house sited on a former seventeenth-century plantation 8 miles from the Historic Area. The house tour bored us, but the re-created slave quarters, while small, gave us insight. The interpreters spoke of crowding, cold, and dawn-to-dark backbreaking work, but they also wove in tales of wily resistance.

Also on the plantation you'll find the **Winthrop Rockefeller Archaeological Museum,** where artifacts discovered on the property reveal a seventeenth-century village, **Wolstenholme Towne,** which was destroyed by Indians in 1622, just three years after its founding. Some of the partially re-created buildings are nearby. In the summer there's a Kid's Dig Archaeological Camp where kids (ages eight to twelve) are introduced to archeological methods. The 1¼-hour program only involves about fifteen minutes of actual digging, and kids enjoy the detective work too. Separate fee.

The plantation is closed in January, February, and the first two weeks of March.

Colonial National Historical Park: Jamestown and Yorktown

Jamestown. From Williamsburg the **Colonial Parkway** leads to Jamestown. While it's only about a 10-mile drive, you "go back" to 1607, when the first permanent English settlement in the New World was established.

The Colonial National Historical Park encompasses 9,000 acres of land on the peninsula between the York and James rivers, and includes Jamestown Island, Colonial Parkway, Yorktown Battlefield, and the Cape Henry Memorial.

Jamestown Island, the westernmost point of Colonial Parkway (757-229-1733; www.nps.gov/colo), is the original site of the Jamestown settlement, the first permanent English settlement, established in 1607, thirteen years before the pilgrims landed in Massachusetts. The colonists suffered severe hardships. Two years after the settlement was founded, 440 of the original 500 inhabitants had died from starvation and disease. Today the only remaining structure among the ruins is the **Old Church Tower**.

The visitor center displays pottery shards, bits of buckles, and other period artifacts, and the rangers lead interpretive programs.

Begin your tour at the visitor center by watching an audiovisual presentation of the colony's tragic story.

Water Country USA

Cool off at Water Country USA, a forty-acre water park. Highlights:

- **Meltdown.** A high-speed toboggan race that propels you at a rate of 22 feet per second down into a surfer's splash pool.
- **Aquazoid.** The thrills of an enclosed water slide are enhanced by laser light flashes and eerie howls.
- **Big Daddy Falls.** Families float together on this four-person river-rafting adventure through a 670-foot series of twists and turns.
- **Cow-A-Bunga.** Kids get happily soaked with slides, fountains, and a kids' pool.
- **Kids' Kingdom.** Little kids splash and scamper on scaled-down play equipment.

Water Country USA, 176 Water Country Parkway (State Highway 199), (757) 253-3350 or (800) 343-SWIM; www.watercountryusa.com or www.buschgardens.com.

The mile-long self-guided tour of the ruins of New Towne lets you imagine the colonists' life here nearly 400 years ago. For a more extensive exploration of the island, take the 5-mile loop drive to witness the wilderness that these first colonists encountered. There are also Living History Character tours and year-round ranger-guided tours. Inquire at the visitor center for schedule, and ask about the Junior Ranger program. One admission covers both Jamestown Island and Yorktown Battlefield.

Those interested in archaeology might want to visit an ongoing excavation of James Fort. It is open to the public, and, depending on the activities of the day, excavators will answer questions about the dig. More than 160,000 artifacts dating to the first half of the seventeenth century have been found along the James River. The processing lab is also open to the public.

Jamestown Settlement, next to Jamestown Island (757-253-4838 or 888-593-4682; www.historyisfun.org), re-creates the story of the colonists' struggle as well as the lifestyle of the Native Americans whom the settlers encountered. An indoor museum features three permanent galleries, and the history continues outdoors in three re-created settings: a Powhatan Indian hamlet, James Fort, and full-scale replicas of the three ships that landed in 1607.

Begin your tour with a dramatic twenty-minute film, *Jamestown: The Beginning,* for an overview. The English Gallery outlines the events in England that led to the colonization of Jamestown and includes an examination of ship designs, navigational tools, and maps. In the Powhatan Gallery contrast the British way of life with that of the Powhatan Indians. The Jamestown Gallery traces the development of the Jamestown Colony from the colonists' landing to the 1699 movement of the Virginia capital from Jamestown to Williamsburg.

Kids like the outdoor living-history area best. At the **Powhatan Indian Village,** families can explore the Powhatan houses, called *yehakins,* and watch and even help the Native Americans grow and prepare food, tan animal hides, and make pottery or tools from antlers and bones.

Follow a path from the Indian hamlet and arrive at a pier on the James River, where full-size replicas of the three ships that sailed to Jamestown are docked. Board one of the ships, climb the ladders, and experiment with the navigational tools and equipment. Costumed performers recount the four-and-a-half-month voyage, demonstrate piloting and navigation, and even set the sails.

At **Fort James** help build and defend Jamestown, a re-created colony of homes, a church, a storehouse, and a guardhouse built in seventeenth-century style. Children can tend the gardens, play in games with the

Busch Gardens Williamsburg

Take a break from history and visit **Busch Gardens Williamsburg,** a theme park where you get twirled, tossed, drenched and still come away giggling for more. "America's Most Beautiful Theme Park," features roller coasters, rides, and live entertainment in its themed German, French, and Italian villages. And, of course, the Clydesdales are here for your kids to admire. New in 2001 will be Ireland, with an Irish festival marketplace, a 3-D simulator journey through a land of giants, and an authentic Irish pub.

COASTERS

- **Apollo's Chariot.** With plunges up to 210 feet, this "hypercoaster" gives riders the sensation of flying.
- **Alpengeist.** Billed as the world's tallest, fastest, and most-twisted inverted steel coaster, this monster ride hurtles riders at 67 mph, flipping them six times, and dropping them a dizzying 170 feet.
- **Big Bad Wolf.** This coaster whizzes through an ersatz alpine village at a top clip of 48 mph before descending a stomach-wrenching 76 feet.
- **Drachen Fire.** A multiple-looping steel roller coaster, Drachen Fire twists through corkscrew-shaped turns, drops riders 150 feet, and hurls along at speeds up to 60 mph.
- **Loch Ness Monster**. "Nessie," a steel coaster, features a 114-foot drop, two upside-down loops, and top speeds of 60 mph.
- **Wilde Maus.** At a top speed of 22 mph, the Maus is the perfect beginner's coaster.

MORE ATTRACTIONS

- **The Battering Ram.** An enormous pendulum that swings to great heights.
- **Rockin' the Boat.** To calm down after the coasters, take in a show. Rockin' The Boat is a clever medley of show tunes and rock with enough scene changes and surprises, including a chorus line of dancing skeletons, to please kids as well as adults.
- **Jack Hanna's Wild Reserve.** Close-up encounters with gray wolves and other exotic and endangered animals.

JUST FOR LITTLE KIDS

- **Land of the Dragons.** Preschoolers climb treehouses, cross rope bridges, and get happily squirted by purple sea serpents.

Busch Gardens Williamsburg, One Busch Gardens Boulevard; (757) 253-3350; www. buschgardens.com costumed colonists, and even be called to duty as part of the colony's militia. The Settlement has an inexpensive snack shop that serves sandwiches, burgers, and snacks. Admission.

Located on the Parkway between Williamsburg and Yorktown is the **Yorktown Battlefield** (757-898-2410; www.nps.gov/colo), the site of the final, determining battle of the Revolutionary War and the surrender of British forces to George Washington and his troops. The battlefield includes Washington's headquarters, the spot where the surrender took place, and the Yorktown Victory Monument. Also here is the Yorktown National Cemetery of the Civil War. The Visitor Center has a short film on the siege of Yorktown and Junior Ranger program materials.

Inquire at the Visitor Center for directions to the **Cape Henry Memorial** (near Virginia Beach), the approximate site where the Jamestown settlers first landed in April 1607. From here there's a wonderful view of the Chesapeake Bay and the Atlantic Ocean.

Yorktown. At the other end of the Colonial Parkway, 23 miles away, the **Yorktown Victory Center,** (757-253-4838 or 888-593-4682; www.historyisfun.org), commemorates the 1781 defeat of the British along the banks of the York River. Amid the static displays of maps and timelines, **Witness to the Revolution** captures kids' interest with its real war stories. Listen to Jeremiah Greenman, a Rhode Island American soldier, complain about the deep snow and the constant hunger and to Tigoransera, a Mohawk chief, counsel his people to stay out of this white man's war. Outside in an encampment, history comes to life with costumed interpreters demonstrating wartime activities from musketry and field medicine to farming and cooking. In the Children's Kaleidoscope Room, kids can try on period costumes, copy from a horn book, play the African game Mancala, and examine reproduction artifacts. Admission.

More Area Attractions

In Williamsburg several other attractions are worth a look. At the **Williamsburg Doll Factory,** 7441 Richmond Road (757-564-9703). Visitors watch porcelain Lady Anne dolls being made and also can shop for dollhouse furnishings and stuffed animals.

Kids who are curious about how things are made will enjoy the movie about soap and candle making at the **Williamsburg Soap and Candle Company,** Route 60 West; (757) 564-3354. Then watch production firsthand from the factory's observation booth.

Special Tours

For a broad overview or a higher perspective on the area's geographical layout, try **Historic Air Tours;** (757) 253-8185 or (757) 229-7330. They'll fly you over Colonial Williamsburg, the Jamestown and Yorktown settlements, and the James River plantations.

SIDE TRIPS

- In **Newport News** visit the **Mariners' Museum** (757-596-2222 or 800-581-SAIL; www.mariner.org), with its extensive collection of ship and maritime artifacts, and the **Virginia Living Museum** (757-595-1900 or 888-4WE-RFUN; www.valivingmuseum.org), which features such native wildlife as otters and bobcats. (See Coastal Virginia.)
- **Paramount's King's Dominion,** Doswell (804-876-5000; www. kingsdominion.com), yet another family theme park, has recently added the razzle-dazzle of movies to the thrills of roller coasters, water rides, and a wild animal park. The Days of Thunder ride puts you in the driver's seat for a simulated stock-car race. Volcano shoots you straight out of a raging volcano at more than 70 miles per hour and then takes you on a 80-foot plummet. Admission. Coming in 2001 is the Hyper-Sonic XLC, the world's first compressed-air launch coaster, combining zero-gravity airtime and free-fall sensations.
- The **plantations along the James River** give a glimpse into the pomp and pleasures of prosperous life in the New World. From the drawing rooms of Shirley and Berkeley Plantations, the lawns sweep to the river, and the antiques trace an ancestry that dates back to Queen Elizabeth I.

  Some of the lesser-known plantations offer a more personal view of history, fewer crowds, and more space to enjoy the sweeping views of the James River. **Shirley Plantation,** 35 miles west of Williamsburg on Route 5, Charles City (800-232-1613; www.shirleyplantation.com), is Virginia's oldest. This imposing brick Queen Anne manor house, built in 1723, sits like a crown jewel, flanked by its dependencies. Shirley exudes a genteel hospitality and a lived-in practicality; it is still a working plantation and home to the ninth generation of Hill Carters, whose scion may often be seen out the windows overseeing farm chores in his blue jeans.

  At **Berkeley,** 2 miles down the road, Route 5, Charles City (804-829-6018; www.berkeleyplantation.com), you'll discover a site of unusual historic firsts. Birthplace of Benjamin Harrison, a signer of the Declaration of Independence, and William Henry Harrison, ninth President of the United States, this Georgian brick manor house was built in 1726. It was the site of the first "Thanksgiving" in 1619 and witnessed the composition of "Taps" during a Civil War encampment.

If children don't appreciate the Virginia antiques and landscaped terraces, their curiosity will be piqued by the story of the plantation's thirty-year restoration from its 1907 condition, when sheep inhabited the manure-covered basement and pigs ate out of the dining room windows. For more information contact the **James River Plantations,** Petersburg Visitor Center, 4250 Cockade Alley, Petersburg (804-733-2400 or 800-368-3595) or Hopewell Visitor Center, 41 Oaklawn Street, Hopewell (804-541-2462).

SPECIAL EVENTS

For more information call Colonial Williamsburg at (800) HISTORY or the Williamsburg Area Convention & Visitors Bureau at (800) 368-6511.

February. Washington's Birthday Weekend.

March. In honor of Women's History Month, Colonial Williamsburg focuses on the contributions of eighteenth-century women.

May. Celebrate the 1607 landing of the Jamestown Settlers with the fanfare on Jamestown Landing Day, Memorial Day ceremonies at Yorktown Cemetery.

June. Virginia Indian Heritage Festival, Jamestown, which includes storytelling, dance, and demonstrations.

July. Independence Day celebrations at Colonial Williamsburg, Yorktown Battlefield, and Jamestown Island.

September. Publick Times celebration, Colonial Williamsburg. Kids and parents alike enjoy the dances, games, auctions, horse races, barbecues, magic shows, and military events.

November. Annual holiday exhibit of antique toys at the Abby Aldrich Rockefeller Folk Art Center.

December. Grand Illumination of the City, Colonial Williamsburg. Celebrate Christmas the seventeenth-century way.

WHERE TO STAY

Colonial Williamsburg offers a number of accommodations in the historical area and nearby, with a wide range of amenities and prices. The luxurious **Williamsburg Inn** has world-class golf courses, a fitness center with an indoor pool, outdoor tennis courts, nature walks, and the Regency Dining Room, plus themed programs and seasonal festivities.

The deluxe **Providence Wings** are separate areas adjacent to the Inn that share many of its amenities. Staying at the **Colonial Houses and Taverns** in and around the Historic Area is a great way to immerse your family in the Williamsburg experience. The **Williamsburg Lodge,** the **Williamsburg Woodlands,** and the **Governor's Inn** all offer modest accommodations, pools, and some recreational activities. In the summer children (ages five to twelve) staying at any of these hotels can take part in the Young Colonials' Club (extra fee), with daytime and evening programs, tours, and activities. There are also children's programs at other times of the year. For further information about programs and reservations, call (800) HISTORY.

Many bed and breakfasts welcome families. The **War Hill Inn,** 4 miles from Colonial Williamsburg, 4560 Longhill Road (757-565-0248 or 800-743-0248), is decorated with comfortable country furnishings and offers thirty-five acres of fields to roam and black Angus cattle to watch. The property has a separate, two-bedroom cottage that works well for families. The **Williamsburg Cottage,** a 1,300-square-foot house less than a mile from the Historic Area, has a bedroom, parlor with pull-out sofa, and kitchenette for snacks. Contact Bensonhouse, 2036 Monument Avenue, Richmond (804-353-6900), for more information on Williamsburg Cottage.

A Virginia historian hosts guests at the **Newport House** (757-229-1775), five minutes by foot from Colonial Williamsburg. **Fox & Grape B&B,** 701 Monumental Avenue (757-229-6914 or 800-292-3699) provides a full country breakfast and displays a collection of Noah's Arks made by the host.

The following campgrounds offer discounts: **Jamestown Beach Campsites,** (757) 229-7609 or (800) 446-9228 (reservations only), across the street from the Jamestown Settlement, and **Williamsburg KOA Resort** (757-565-2907 or 800-KOA-1733), which also has a complimentary shuttle service to Colonial Williamsburg in spring and fall, and a children's fishing area.

Call the Williamsburg Area Convention and Visitor's Bureau (757-253-0192) for a free brochure on accommodation packages. The

Kingsmill Resort

Kingsmill Resort, 1010 Kingsmill Road, Williamsburg; (757) 253-1703 or (800) 832-5665; www.kingsmill.com. Situated on the banks of the James River, this conveniently located, upscale property offers a respite for kids and adults. Besides an eighteen-hole golf course, tennis courts, outdoor and indoor swimming pools, racquetball, and a fitness center, in summer the property offers a supervised, half-day or full-day children's program, the Kingsmill Kampers, for ages five to twelve. The health and sports center has an indoor pool, a gathering room with billiards and arcade games, and a moderately priced restaurant. Guests can choose to stay in hotel rooms or condominiums with kitchens.

Williamsburg Hotel and Motel Association (800–899–9462; www. williamsburghotel.com) offers a complimentary reservation service.

WHERE TO EAT

In Colonial Williamsburg try the four local taverns. With waiters and waitresses in period costumes and balladeers strolling through, dining is fun, and the food is okay. As these places are popular, book your meal reservations when you make your room reservations. Each tavern serves a different cuisine and some Colonial dishes. **Christiana Campbell's Tavern,** 120 Waller Street, offers seafood. Campbell's most noteworthy plates include clam chowder, jambalaya, and lobster. Try the spoon bread here. **Josiah Chowning's Tavern,** 100 East Duke of Gloucester Street, serves up meat—pork chops, prime rib, pork rib, and steak—and is known for its Brunswick stew. The **King's Arms Tavern,** 409 East Duke of Gloucester Street, has Southern dishes such as Virginia Baked Ham, fried chicken, and peanut soup. **Shield's Tavern,** 417 East Duke of Gloucester Street, is a fowl place—in the sense of winged fare—and also serves a modest seafood menu, including crayfish soup. At Shield's try such Colonial desserts as Indian pudding or syllabub—a whipping cream and lemon juice dessert. Call (757) 229–2141 to make reservations for all the Williamsburg taverns.

Adjacent to the Historic Area, Merchants Square offers a few cafes, many shops, and one really good restaurant, **The Trellis Restaurant,** 403 Duke of Gloucester Street, Williamsburg; (757) 229–8610. Award-winning chef Marcel Desaulniers is known for his creative cooking. At lunch a variety of affordable salads, sandwiches, and light fare is served. Dinner can be pricey, but the food is wonderful. Children will feel more comfortable at lunch, but the restaurant welcomes well-behaved children. (There is no children's menu.) Save room for the chef's desserts, especially his signature Death by Chocolate, a rich, cakelike concoction that chocoholics "die for."

La Tolteca, 135 Second Street (757–253–0598), offers Mexican cuisine. **Capital Pancake & Waffle House,** 800 Capitol Landing Road (757–564–1238), serves nineteen varieties of pancakes and waffles for breakfast and lunch. **Pierce's Pitt Bar-B-Que,** 477 East Rochambeau Drive (757–565–2955), offers hand-pulled shredded pork barbeque in a casual setting at breakfast, lunch, and dinner. For seafood try **The Whaling Company,** 494 McLaws Circle (757–229–0275), which will delight younger children with its old New England fishing village decor. And for a quick bite, try **A Good Place To Eat,** 410 Duke of Gloucester Street (757–229–4370), which serves breakfast, lunch, and dinner, plus good desserts.

For More Information

For more tourist information concerning Colonial Williamsburg, contact (800) HISTORY; www.colonialwilliamsburg.org. For information about Williamsburg, Jamestown, and Yorktown, call the **Williamsburg Area Convention and Visitors Bureau,** P.O. Box 3585, Williamsburg, Virginia 23187; (757) 253-0192 or (800) 368-6511; www.visitwilliamsburg.com.

Emergency Numbers

Ambulance, fire, and police: 911

Poison Control: (800) 552-6337

There are no twenty-four-hour pharmacies in the Williamsburg area. In the event of a pharmaceutical emergency, try contacting Williamsburg Community Hospital's emergency room. For normal pharmaceutical service try the Williamsburg Drug Company, Duke of Gloucester Street in Merchants Square, Williamsburg, Virginia; (757) 229-1041.

Williamsburg Community Hospital Emergency Room, 301 Monticello Avenue, Williamsburg, Virginia; (757) 259-6000

THE SHENANDOAH VALLEY

T he **Shenandoah Valley** stretches for some 200 miles between the Blue Ridge and Allegheny mountain ranges in the northwestern part of Virginia. The mountains and valleys make this region one of the most beautiful in the east. *Shenandoah* is believed to mean either "daughter of the stars" or "river of high mountains." Whatever the real meaning, the area's beauty is legendary, and it is best preserved in **Shenandoah National Park,** whose 195,000 acres contain forests, mountains, rivers, and streams.

The Shenandoah National Park offers families miles of hiking trails, many of which lead to waterfalls and sweeping views. With young children it's easy to sample the park's beauty by driving along scenic routes, taking quick stops for easy strolls to dramatic overlooks. The renowned **Skyline Drive** snakes for 105 miles along the mountain crests of Shenandoah National Park, offering pastoral views of ridges and hollows. In the valley towns enjoy an array of country culture that is as down-home as apple-blossom festivals, bluegrass concerts, and square dances and as unique as Staunton's living-history farmsteads.

The towns of **Front Royal, New Market, Luray,** and **Staunton,** each near various sections of Shenandoah National Park, offer several opportunities for exploring.

GETTING THERE

Roanoke Regional Airport, 5202 Aviation Drive Northwest (540–362-1999), is accessible via I–581, which is 3 miles from downtown Roanoke, Virginia. The airport serves USAir, USAir Express, The Delta Connection, Northwest Air, and the Delta Connection/Atlantic Southeast Airlines (ASA).

Coming from the north take I–81 into the Shenandoah Valley. Exit 315 provides easy access into Winchester, and exits 217 and 225 lead to

The Shenandoah Valley

AT A GLANCE

▶ Enjoy the legendary beauty of forests, mountains, rivers, and streams

▶ Motor along 105 miles of scenic mountain crests in Shenandoah National Park

▶ Explore underground caverns

▶ Shenandoah National Park: (540) 999-3500; www.nps.gov/shen

▶ Shenandoah Valley Travel Association: (540) 740-3132 or 877-VISITSV;www.shenandoah.org

Staunton. Coming from the east or west, take I-66. From the Washington, D.C., area take I-66 to exit 6, Front Royal.

GETTING AROUND

Roanoke Regional Airport has car rental agencies.

WHAT TO SEE AND DO

Shenandoah National Park

The park, located at 3655 U.S. Highway 211 East, Luray (540-999-3500), offers families wonders that are literally as big as all outdoors, plus various ways to enjoy them.

The town of Front Royal is the gateway to the Shenandoah National Park and to Skyline Drive. Stock up on brochures at the renovated train depot, **Main Street Station,** 414 East Main Street, Front Royal (540-635-3185 or 800-338-2576; wwwfrontroyalchamber.com) which houses the Front Royal/Warren County Visitor Center and Chamber of Commerce offices.

Near the Front Royal Entrance Station, the **Dickey Ridge Visitor Center** at milepost (MP) 4.6 is open daily in season from 9:00 A.M. to 5:00 P.M. but is closed from late November to early April. A film orients you to the park's offerings, and some exhibits depict the park's flora and fauna. Be sure to pick up a copy of the *Shenandoah Overlook,* the park's visitor

Entrance Fees

In 1998 Congress mandated that Shenandoah National Park is a U.S. Recreation Fee Area, which means you have to pay a fee to enter the park. The noncommercial entrance fee is $10.00 per vehicle and $5.00 per bicyclist or hiker (age seventeen or older) and is valid for seven consecutive days. There are other fee options, such as the Shenandoah Annual Pass ($20.00) and the Golden Passport ($50.00 for entry to all national parks). The NPS Web site (www.nps.gov) has more detailed information.

guide. Along with listing the hours of the visitor centers, the *Shenandoah Overlook,* as well as park bulletin boards, contain listings of the park's numerous ranger-led activities for adults and kids, which take place in and around visitor centers and campgrounds. A valuable aid: the free brochures on short hikes throughout the park, which you can obtain at the visitor centers.

The **Byrd Visitor Center** (MP 51), which is open daily from April through November, offers interpretive exhibits plus a good selection of books and information. **Big Meadows,** the adjacent field and largest meadow in the park, is a popular park hub and also has a lodge.

The park is unofficially divided into three main sections: The northern area, just 72 miles from Washington, D.C., receives the most visitors; the central section features the park's main overnight lodging, which, park officials say, attracts more long-term visitors than overnighters; and the southern section features gorgeous backcountry and wilderness with fewer facilities. Loft Mountain Campground campstore and the Information Center are open late May through October. The northern park entrance is easily accessible, as it's 1 mile south of Front Royal, close to the junction of I-81 and I-66 and accessible via U.S. 340 and VA Highway 55.

There are special activities for families and children, most of which operate in the summer months only. Adults and kids enjoy the ranger programs. At the visitor centers and gift shops, pick up a Junior Ranger Program activity booklet (cost is $2.50). After children complete the activities (two of which include attending a ranger-led program), they receive official Junior Ranger badges, a nice reward and worthwhile keepsake.

The *Shenandoah Overlook* also lists information about special events and educational programs.

Scenic Drives. If you have only one day to spend in the park, officials recommend driving along **Skyline Drive,** which runs for 105 miles along the mountain crests the entire length of Shenandoah National Park, where it joins the **Blue Ridge Parkway,** another famed drive, which leads from Virginia's Shenandoah National Park 470 miles to North Carolina's Great Smoky Mountains.

Don't do it all, however tempting it seems, as an hour or two of slow, snaking, scenic roads is a long way with kids, particularly young ones. But

Great Family Hikes in Shenandoah National Park

All of these self-guided nature trails are easy enough for families with young kids. Pick up brochures at the visitor centers.

- **Fox Hollow nature trail** (MP 4.6) is a 1.2-mile circuit hike with a 310-foot elevation gain. Allow about one and a quarter hours. It leads past old farm fences and a cemetery, one of the many remnants of the mountaineers who lived here decades ago.
- **Story of the Forest Nature Trail** (MP 51), a 1.8-mile route with a 90-foot elevation gain, gives visitors a sense of the history of the forest and swamp. Along the way (allow about one and a half hours), you may see deer, chipmunks, and birds, and the occasional bear at a distance. (Do *not* leave your car if you see a bear.)
- **Little Stony Man Cliffs** (MP 39.1), a 0.9-mile, one-hour round-trip has a 300-foot elevation gain.
- **Blackrock Summit** (MP 84.8), a 2-mile round-trip, which takes about two and half hours, has a 75-foot elevation gain.
- Other recommended walking trails that take less than an hour or two to cover are the Stony Man Nature Trail, Dark Hollow Falls; Frazier Discovery Trail, in the southern district of the park. The Big Meadows, across from the Visitor Center, has a nearby lodge, which is a popular place to

start and has many trails leading off into its wooded surroundings. For a map and more information on these trails, contact the Shenandoah National Park.
- For the more advanced hiker, try a segment of the Appalachian Trail, 101 miles of which cut through the park. For more information, contact the Potomac Appalachian Trail Club, 118 Park Street Southeast, Vienna, VA 22180.

GREAT VIEWS
The park delights with more than sixty-five scenic overlooks, all located along Skyline Drive.
- **Shenandoah Valley Overlook** (MP 2.8). Children especially like Signal Knob, used by Confederate troops in the Civil War to convey semaphore signals.
- **Range View Overlook** (MP 17.1), boasts the best view in the northern region. At 2,800 feet this spot provides views of the Blue Ridge, Massanutten, and Allegheny mountains.
- **Stony Man Overlook** (MP 38.6), offers views of cliffs and the surrounding valley.
- **Thoroughfare Mountain Overlook** (MP 40.5). At about 3,600 feet this overlook is one of the highest, with views of Old Rag Mountain.

do drive on some of this renowned route, being sure to get out of your car to stroll along a nature trail or two. (Just driving through would mean missing out on the real beauties of the park.) Check the park brochures to see which of the short trails are nearby. As Skyline Drive remains open year-round, weather permitting, don't rule out a winter visit. With fewer crowds the park seems to open up. If there's some snow or even mud, have fun looking for animal tracks. When there's lots of snow, cross-country skiers head off into the woods along the hiking trails and the fire roads, but you must bring your own skis, as the park has no rental facilities. In winter all services are closed, so be sure you have snacks, water, and a full tank of gas.

Skyline Drive can be accessed from all four park entrances. Once on this road, use the mile markers on the west side of the drive to find your locale, as well as the nearest facilities, services, and areas of interest. The countdown for the milepost markers starts at the Front Royal Entrance Station in the north (MP 4.6) and ends at the Rockfish Gap Entrance Station in the south (MP 105). Other entrances to Skyline Drive are at **Thornton Gap** (MP 31.5, accessible via U.S. 211) and at **Swift Run Gap** (MP 65.7, accessible via U.S. 33). There is a 35-mph speed limit on Skyline Drive, as the road has many curves, as well as crowds and many cars, particularly in leaf-peeping season. (You also need to watch out for wildlife, especially in the mornings and evenings. Bear sightings are not unusual. If you see a bear, be sure to remain in your car, no matter how tempting it is to get a closer look.) As a result, plan ahead and allow more time than usual when calculating driving distances.

Hiking. This is a great park in which to introduce your children to the joys of hiking. There are a variety of trails from easy to moderate to challenging. To encourage families to get out and hike, the park rents explorer backpacks, which include a field guide, binoculars, hand lenses, and other items that turn your walk into an environmental treasure hunt.

More Outdoor Activities. A great way to enjoy the trails is from atop a horse. **Skyland Stables,** located at Skyland (MP 41.7), offers guided trail rides from April through October; call (540) 999–2210 for information. To ride, children must be at least 4'10" tall. For smaller children the stables have pony rides. Your best bet is to reserve ahead, either through the lodge or by calling the stables.

Fishing enthusiasts can try their luck in some thirty streams. Anyone between sixteen and sixty-five must have a valid license, and all ages must use only artificial lures with a single hook.

Caverns
Skyline Caverns, ½ mile from Front Royal on Route 340 South, just

beyond Shenandoah National Park (540-635-4545 or 800-296-4545; www.skylinecaverns.com), is notable for being one of the only places in the world that has caverns with clusters of unique, shimmering, white calcium-carbonate crystals called anthodites. So rare, these formations, nicknamed "the orchids of the mineral kingdom," are also slow-growing, gaining only 1 inch every 7,000 years compared with the 120 to 125 years required for similar growth in stalagmites and stalactites.

Remember to bring along a sweater for these caverns, as no matter how hot the surface temperature, the underground rooms are cool. On the guided hour-long tour, the twelve stairs going down and the forty-eight going up are "doable" by younger kids—just don't attempt this sin-glehandedly before a tot's nap time, as carrying a child up the steps can be hard and slippery work.

Kids like Rainbow Waterfall, which plunges more than 37 feet from one of three underground streams that flow through the caverns, as well as the 1-mile miniature train ride of the grounds, a special delight for wee tots. This is offered daily, weather permitting. For refreshments there's a snack bar, and the gift shop has lots of trinkets. Admission.

For more underground delights visit **Luray Caverns,** 9 miles west of Skyline Drive on Route 22, (540-743-6551; www.luraycaverns.com) the largest caverns in Virginia and the most popular in the East. The subter-ranean chambers range from 30 to 140 feet high and feature thousands of colored formations. Even the most blasé of teens will want to listen to chords played on the Great Stalactite Organ, billed as the world's largest natural musical instrument.

One-hour cavern tours begin every twenty minutes, and the admission fee also includes a self-guided tour of the on-premises **Car and Carriage Caravan Museum of Luray Caverns,** whose one hundred vehicles include such finds as an 1892 Benz and early model Fords. There's also a Singing Tower carillon, with free recitals throughout the spring, summer, and fall. New in 2000 is the Garden Maze, a one-acre ornamental garden with more than 1,500 Dark American Arborvitae (trees), each 8 feet tall and 4 feet wide. There is an admission fee to Luray Caverns and a sepa-rate fee for the Garden Maze.

No charge for ages six and under. Opens daily at 9:00 A.M.; closing hours vary seasonally. For more information, as well as for reservations for the motel accommodations on the property, call (540) 743-6551.

Museums
Staunton (pronounced Stanton), 42 miles south of New Market and 11 miles west of the southern end of Skyline Drive at Waynesboro, is the birthplace of Woodrow Wilson and one of the oldest cities west of the Blue Ridge mountains. Since Staunton survived the Civil War intact, the

town boasts some splendid nineteenth-century buildings. This is a pleasant place to take a stroll, and walking tour maps are available weekdays from the Staunton–Augusta Chamber of Commerce, 511 Thornrose Street; (540) 886-2351.

Staunton, a prominent stop for pioneers on their journey west, pays tribute to this heritage at the **Frontier Culture Museum,** U.S. 250, 1250 Richmond Road; (540) 332-7850; wwwfrontiermuseum.org. Plan to spend several hours at this living-history museum; your kids will love it.

On a trail formerly used by Native Americans, pioneer farmsteading becomes as real as the pigs in the pen and the plow horses in the paddock. Although you can still hear the cars on this 185-acre complex, which is not too distant from the highway, the four seventeenth-, eighteenth-, and nineteenth-century homes transport you to a rural time. The buildings, laced along a ⅝-mile dirt loop, illustrate the hopes and the customs that these hardy immigrants from Germany, Scotland, Ireland, and England brought with them and planted in the fertile Virginia soil.

The interpretive guides and the hands-on history lessons make learning fun. A bonneted matron at the eighteenth-century German home sits in the *stube* (the family room) carding wool. She carefully teaches kids to pick the straw and hay from the fibers. Outside, another *hausfrau* knits fingerless gloves, which kept workers' hands warm while still enabling them to toss grain to the animals.

The stone fence, thatched roof, and Prudence the Pig rooting in the mud endear the Scotch-Irish farm to city kids. In this proverbial cottage of yore, circa eighteenth–nineteenth century, pull up a "creepie" stool (because you crept closer to the fire as the night wore on) and learn how to cook Donegal pie in the open-hearth fireplace.

At the seventeenth–eighteenth-century English farm, a poor man's one-room abode with a cattail roof and mud cob walls, practice your darning. At the log American house, with its double-pen log barn, flail wheat on the central threshing floor; then try your hand at the "new-fangled" fanning mill, which cleaned a bushel a minute. On the first Friday of June, July, and August, the museum is open in the evening for hands-on activities with featured entertainment. There are also Family Nights in the summer that include dinner, dancing, and music. From January through March there are no costumed interpreters, but personally guided tours that focus on your family's interests and children's ages are available. Admission.

Other Attractions

While it's just as well that the nearby **Guilford Ridge Vineyard,** Route 5, Box 148, Luray (540-778-3853), doesn't offer tours (crushers, metal tanks, and rack rooms bore most kids), the winery is a worthy stop dur-

The German farm at the Frontier Culture Museum includes a peasant farmhouse that dates to 1688 and came from the Rhineland-Palantinate region of Germany.

ing its August Fête Champêtre, when the grounds come alive with theater, music, and grape stamping.

For slithery things visit the **Luray Reptile Center, Dinosaur Park, and Petting Zoo,** 1087 U.S. Highway 211 West (540-743-4113; www.lurayzoo.com), where the gliders include huge pythons and alligators, along with rattlesnakes and cobras. The Petting Zoo has ringtail monkeys, Sicilian donkeys, llamas, sheep, and exotic birds. Admission.

The town of **New Market,** just off I-81 and 12 miles west of Luray on Route 211, has the **New Market Battlefield State Historical Park,** off Route 305 (George Collins Parkway); (540) 740-3102. School-age children interested in the Civil War connect with this park, as it commemorates the corps of 257 Virginia Military Institute students, some as young as fifteen (though the average age was eighteen), who were called to active duty during the 1864 Battle of New Market. Although the cadets were supposed to be kept in reserve until needed to fill a gap in the advancing line of badly outnumbered Confederate troops, these schoolboys were accidentally put on the front lines to face the Union soldiers. The cadets managed to hold the line for thirty minutes, forcing the Union troops to retreat. Ten VMI students were killed, and their troop's heroism is honored here. The **Hall of Valor Museum** (540-740-3101; www.vmi.edu/museum.nm) shows a film about the battle and another about Stonewall Jackson's Shenandoah campaign. Models and dioramas also detail the

Civil War. A self-guided, 1-mile battlefield tour features the **Bushong Farm** (open periodically throughout the summer), where some of the fiercest fighting took place. There are also staff-guided, forty-five-minute tours daily during the summer. When paying admission at the museum, be sure and ask for the handout for children, who can get a sticker if they complete the scavenger hunt or play the matching games. Also ask about the Ghost Cadet Tours, available on selected summer evenings. A reenactment of the battle, sponsored by the Chamber of Commerce, takes place here every May.

The **New Market Battlefield Military Museum,** Route 305 (9500 Collins Drive) (540-740-8065), on the battlefield, is a separate, privately run entity that requires additional admission. In this replica of Gen. Robert E. Lee's home, more than 3,000 military artifacts from American wars, beginning with the Revolutionary War up through Desert Storm, are displayed. A thirty-five-minute film about the battlefield is intriguing. Fourteen markers on the grounds denote Union and Confederate troop positions. Open mid-March to December 1. Admission.

Tours

From April to October splash along the river with the **Shenandoah River Outfitters,** 6502 South Page Valley Road, Luray (540-743-4159 or 800-622-6632; www.shenandoahriver.com), whose canoeing and tubing trips on the Shenandoah River provide a playful and pleasing outing, especially in the heat of summer. They have six-person rafts and two-person kayaks, both of which are good for families, especially those with younger children. **Shenandoah Canoe & Tube Voyagers,** Route 2, Box 1130, McGaheysville (540-289-WILD; www.massanutten.com), also offers canoe and tube trips, with reservations strongly encouraged. Canoe and picnic packages are available. Children under twelve must be accompanied by an adult.

Shopping

A good place to shop right in the heart of the Shenandoah Valley is the **Waynesboro Village and Factory Outlets,** 601 Shenandoah Valley Drive, Box 1B, Waynesboro (540-949-5000), whose shops are open seven days a week. There are some designer and sportswear shops plus stores that sell housewares and specialty items, as well as restaurants.

SIDE TRIPS

The **Blue Ridge Parkway,** which starts in Waynesboro, Virginia, at MP 0 and ends in Cherokee, North Carolina, at MP 469, connects the Shenandoah National Park (Skyline Drive) to the Great Smoky Mountains National Park. The Blue Ridge Parkway affords a number of scenic overlooks and hiking trails, some of them easy enough for young children. For a complete list of the trails and their difficulty levels, as well as attractions, obtain the *Blue Ridge Parkway Information Guide* from the visitor centers. **Humpback Rocks Visitor Center** (MP 5.8), 6 miles southeast of Afton, maintains a reconstructed pioneer mountain farmstead accessible via an easy, 0.25-mile self-guided trail. Although the Parkway is open all year, winter may bring icy conditions that temporarily close the roads. For general parkway information call (704) 298-0398.

SPECIAL EVENTS

Check with the *Shenandoah Overlook,* which lists information about seasonal special events in Shenandoah National Park, or call (540) 999-3500.

May. Wildflower Weekend.

July. The North American Butterfly Association Annual Count, with volunteers counting butterflies in a 15-mile-diameter circle as a way to identify population trends and habitat preferences.

WHERE TO STAY

Shenandoah National Park

Park lodges don't charge for cribs or for children under sixteen who share a room with parents. Reserve ahead for the following **park lodgings** by calling (540) 743-5108 or (800) 999-4717.

Skyland Lodge (MP 41.7) offers 186 modernized lodge rooms (the lodge was built in 1894) and rustic cabins; open from the end of March to early December. Facilities include a restaurant, a craft shop, naturalist program, horseback activities, a playground, TVs in most rooms, and nightly entertainment.

Big Meadows Lodge (MP 51.3), the largest in the park, offers great views of wildflowers and often of deer, particularly in the evening and early morning. Accommodations range from twenty-one rooms in the main lodge to eighty-one rustic cabins and multi-unit lodges with modern suites. Open from early May to the end of October, the facility has a playground, and naturalist programs.

Lewis Mountain (MP 57.3) features cabins with private baths and heat; linens are provided. Cooking facilities include a fireplace, grills, and a picnic table in the connecting outdoor area. A coin laundry is nearby. Open mid-May to October.

The **Potomac Appalachian Trail Club,** 118 Park Street Southeast,

Vienna, VA 22180 (703-242-0693), operates six trail cabins for hikers and publishes trail maps. A new campground, **Mathews Arm** (MP 22.2), for tents and trailers, has 178 sites and sewage disposal but no showers or laundry facilities. A camp store is located about 2 miles south of the campground on Skyline Drive.

Campgrounds are available on a first-come basis, except for **Big Meadows,** which strongly encourages reservations from Memorial Day weekend until the end of October. Big Meadows (MP 51.3) has forty tent sites and 167 trailer sites, flush toilets, and showers. **Lewis Mountain** (MP 57.6) has sixteen tent sites and sixteen trailer sites, flush toilets, showers, a coin laundry, and a general store. **Loft Mountain** (MP 79.5) has fifty-four tent sites and 167 trailer sites, flush toilets, and showers. There's an Information Station at Loft Mountain.

Two ATM machines are available in the park: at Skyland's registration building (MP 41.7) and at Big Meadows Wayside (MP 51.2).

Front Royal

Front Royal has the **Woodward House on Manor Grade Bed and Breakfast,** at the intersection of Routes 55 and 340, ¼ mile north of Skyline Drive (540-635-7010 or 800-635-7011; www.acountryhome.com). This three-room, five-suite property has limited accommodations (one suite) for families. Well-behaved children of any age are welcome. The family suite is on the first floor and features a pull-out couch. All rooms have private bath and cable television. The suites also have telephones. Rates include a full breakfast. Front Royal also has a host of motels, including the **Super 8 Motel,** at the junction of Routes 55 and 340; (800) 800-8000; www.super8.com.

In nearby Strasburg is **The Hotel Strasburg,** 213 South Holliday Street (800-348-8327 or 540-465-9191), an elegant Victorian hotel and dining room in downtown Strasburg, near most of the town's antiques shops.

Luray

A different option, near Luray, is the **Jordan Hollow Farm Inn,** Route 2, Stanley, 6 miles south of Luray (540-778-2285 or 888-418-7000; www.jordanhollow.com), a combination horse farm and inn on 150 acres. The farm and inn buildings form a cozy complex: Choose to stay in Mare Meadow Lodge, a modern, hand-hewn log building, where all the rooms have gas fireplaces and whirlpool jets in oversize tubs, or the vine covered Arbor View Lodge, whose sixteen motel-style rooms are furnished in Victorian decor. Breakfast is included in the room rate, and breakfast and dinner are served in a wood-paneled dining room.

New Market

New Market has several motels, including the **Quality Inn–Shenandoah Valley,** I–81 at exit 264 (800-221-2222; or 540-740-3141), and the **Days Inn-New Market,** off I-81 (800-325-2525 or 540-740-4100). In addition to a **Holiday Inn,** I-81, exit 225, and Woodrow Wilson Parkway (800-932-9061 or 540-248-6020), and a **Comfort Inn,** I-81 at exit 222 (540-886-5000 or 800-228-5150), the **Staunton** area has the **River Ridge Guest Ranch** (540-996-4148; www.ridetheridge.com), which offers lodging, haywagon dinner rides, fishing, and horseback riding on its 330 mountaintop acres. Riders from beginning to advanced levels can enjoy rides of one hour, two hours, a half-day, or a half-day with lunch, and nonriding children can see colts being trained and perhaps even witness the arrival of a foal.

WHERE TO EAT

Shenandoah National Park

The easiest way to eat in the park is al fresco—pack your own picnic, stop where you like, and enjoy the food and the scenery. Park restaurants cook basic fare. **Panorama** (MP 31.5) serves three meals daily, featuring traditional Virginia country dishes. The dining rooms at **Skyland Lodge** (MP 41.7) and **Big Meadows Lodge** (MP 51.3, 1 mile off Skyline Drive) serve local specialties such as fried chicken and mountain trout. Let your kids try the special dessert: blackberry ice-cream pie topped with blackberry syrup. Skyland is open from late March to December, whereas Big Meadows opens from early May to late October.

Waysides along Skyline Drive also feature lunch counters, snack bars, stores, and souvenirs. These include **Elkswallow Wayside** (MP 24.1), open mid-April to November; **Big Meadows Wayside** (MP 51.2), open late March to November; **Lewis Mountain Wayside** (MP 57.5); and **Loft Mountain Wayside** (MP 79.5), open late March to October.

Front Royal

Front Royal is the place to go for fast food. Among the eateries are **Burger King,** John Marshall Highway (540-635-3326). For a little more variety, check out **Guiseppe's Italian Restaurant,** 865 John Marshall Highway (540-636-2000), **China Jade Restaurant,** 239 South Street (540-635-9161), **L Dee's Pancake House,** 522 East Main Street (540-635-3791), or **Dad's Family Restaurant,** 10 South Commerce Avenue (540-622-2768).

Luray

If your children insist, **McDonald's** is here, on East Main Street; (540) 743-6667. **The Parkhurst Restaurant,** on U.S. 211, 2 miles west of Luray Caverns, offers steaks, seafood, chicken, and pasta dishes (540-743-6009). The **Brookside Restaurant,** U.S. 211, east of Luray, offers country-style home cooking (540-743-5698 or 800-299-2655).

New Market

Three of the several down-home, "country cooking" restaurants here are **Congress Street Public House Restaurant,** U.S. 11 (540-740-3664), **Southern Kitchen,** U.S. 11 (540-740-3514), and **Johnny Appleseed,** U.S. 211 West (540-740-3141), at the Quality Inn.

Staunton

Rowe's Family Restaurant, Route 250, off I-64 and I-81 (540-886-1833), a casual eatery with booths, serves good home cooking such as Virginia ham, chicken, steak, and homemade pies. Open daily for breakfast, lunch, and dinner. **The Belle Grae Inn and Restaurant,** 515 West Frederick Street (540-886-5151), offers an informal lunch and more formal dinners of "regional cuisine with a southern flair."

FOR MORE INFORMATION

For more information on **Shenandoah National Park,** contact the **Park Superintendent,** 3655 U.S. Highway 211 East, Luray, VA 22835; (540) 999-3500; www.nps.gov/shen. For more information about Shenandoah Valley attractions, services, accommodations, and restaurants, contact **Shenandoah Valley Travel Association,** P.O. Box, 1040, New Market (540-740-3132; www.shenandoah.org), or the **Virginia Tourism Corporation,** 1021 East Cary Street, 14th Floor, Richmond (804-786-2051 or 800-VISIT-VA). Maps and other geographical materials can be obtained by contacting Geological Survey Map Distribution, Federal Center, Building 41, Box 25286, Denver, CO; (303) 202-4700.

Contact the **Blue Ridge Parkway Association,** P.O. Box 453, Asheville, NC 28802, or call Virginia Tourism at (800) 258-4748. For general parkway information call (704) 298-0398.

Emergency Numbers

Ambulance, fire, and police: 911

For emergencies in Shenandoah National Park: (800) 732-0911

Warren Memorial Hospital, 1000 North Shenandoah Avenue, Front Royal (540-636-0300), has a twenty-four-hour emergency room service.

Shenandoah County Memorial Hospital, 955 South Main Street, Woodstock (540-459-4021), has a twenty-four-hour emergency room service.

Waynesboro County Hospital, 501 Oak Avenue (540-942-6416), has a twenty-four-hour emergency room service.

COASTAL VIRGINIA

I t was to Virginia's shores that the first New World adventurers were lured. The area still beckons the curious and the fun-loving. There are miles of sandy beaches, plus museums that provide off-the-beach fun. Take the family to the "Kid's Corner" of Virginia, a string of attractions that start at Williamsburg, stretch through Newport News, Hampton, Norfolk, and Portsmouth, and end at Virginia Beach.

GETTING THERE

Two airports provide service. The **Norfolk International Airport** (757-857-3200) has more than 200 flights daily, featuring most major national and regional airlines, and is about a twenty-minute drive from the ocean. The **Newport News/Williamsburg International Airport** (757-877-0221) offers nonstop, jet, and hub service; it's about a forty-five-minute drive from the ocean.

Several major highways lead to the area. From the west take I-64, I-295, U.S. 460, or U.S. 58; from the north or south, I-85, I-95, U.S. 13 via the 17.6-mile Chesapeake Bay Bridge Tunnel (an experience in itself), or U.S. 17. These routes connect with I-264, which leads directly to the Virginia Beach visitor information center and the oceanfront area.

Amtrak trains stop in Newport News, at 9304 Warwick Boulevard; call (800) USA-RAIL. From the train station a bus goes to and from Norfolk and Virginia Beach, about twenty and thirty minutes away, respectively, without rush-hour traffic. The **Greyhound/Trailways** bus station is at 1017 Laskin Road in Virginia Beach (757-422-2998) and at Brambleton and Monticello Avenues in Norfolk.

GETTING AROUND

In Virginia Beach, take a tour on the Beach Trolley (757-640-6300) and use it as a convenient method of transportation since parking a car can be a hassle. In summer the trolley operates from the north end of the beach to The Virginia Marine Science Museum in the south. The **Hampton Trolley** (757-826-6351 or 757-222-6100), a green shuttle trolley,

Coastal Virginia

AT A GLANCE

▶ Drive the 17.6-mile Chesapeake Bay Bridge Tunnel

▶ Hike the unspoiled beaches of Back Bay National Wildlife Refuge and False Cape State Park

▶ Go on dolphin-watch trips and get hands-on learning at the kid-friendly Virginia Marine Science Museum

▶ Swim and sun on 35 miles of ocean beaches at Virginia Beach

▶ Virginia Beach Information; (800) VA-BEACH; www.vbfun.com

▶ Virginia Waterfront Information: (800) FUN-IN-VA; www.thevirginiawaterfront.com; (800) VA-TRIPS; www.coastalvirginia.com

connects the waterfront downtown to Coliseum Central (a hotel and shopping mall area). A second trolley connects hotels to nearby shopping centers. **Harborlink Passenger Ferry** (888-722-7817 or 888-722-9400; www.harborlink.com) provides an alternative to driving the bridge tunnel. Ferries connect Norfolk and Hampton downtowns. **Hampton Roads Transit** (HRT) provides the area's bus and trolley service; call (757) 222-6100. Pickups near the oceanfront are on Nineteenth and Pacific Streets. A Museum Express bus goes to the Virginia Marine Science Museum.

Rent bicycles (or bring your own) and use the bicycle paths near the oceanfront. And, of course, strolling along the boardwalk is a time-honored sport. The newly renovated boardwalk, from First to Fortieth Streets, has larger-than-life sculptures and landscaped park areas, plus intermittent stage areas featuring live performances during the summer months.

WHAT TO SEE AND DO

Virginia Beach
Virginia Beach lives up to its motto of "all kinds of fun," offering 35 miles of sandy, though often crowded, ocean beaches. The highest concentration of boom box, bikini, and college crowds are usually found in

Wilderness Refuge and Wild Beach

Near Virginia Beach's see-and-be-seen strip of sand, you can still view the land as it was seen by America's first settlers. Located at the southeastern end of Virginia Beach, **Back Bay National Wildlife Refuge** and **False Cape State Park** share similar topography but have different functions. Back Bay is mostly a wildlife refuge, whereas False Cape is primarily a rustic beach area. Both serve as havens for nature lovers.

It used to be that only the hearty who could hike or bike in for 5 miles could experience the refuge, but an electric tram service, begun in spring 1998, makes seeing these 8,000 unspoiled acres feasible even for families with young children. Plan some time to visit this ocean-to-freshwater habitat, one of the few undeveloped areas along the Atlantic Coast. There's also a beachmobile called the Terragator that provides daily transportation between the refuge and the park from October through late March (800–933–7275).

Back Bay's more than 8,000 acres are a managed area created as a waterfowl refuge. Along the 9 miles of dikes built to separate the man-made, freshwater impoundments from the saltwater Chesapeake Bay, egrets and herons dance on the water, and turtles dive into pools. In the thousands of acres of marshlands and woods, white-tail deer, red fox, and feral pigs dart through the thickets.

The tram stops at False Cape State Park, an extension of the refuge's ocean-to-bay habitat. Take the Barbour Hill trail 0.7 miles to the oceanfront, graced by dunes, gulls, and sandpipers. The unspoiled arc of beach stretches for miles. From the tram stop you can also hike westward on the South Inlet Trail, 0.7 miles through loblolly pine forests rising above tiers of blueberry patch and through marshes speckled with white hibiscus and sprays of gold asters.

The round-trip excursion, including the stopover at False Cape, takes four hours. Tours depart from Little Island at 9:00 A.M. April 1 through October 31. Carry-on gear is limited to one bag or day pack. For tram reservations call (757) 498–BIRD.

Back Bay National Wildlife Refuge, P.O. Box 6286, 4005 Sandpiper Road, Virginia Beach; (757) 721–2412. False Cape State Park, 4001 Sandpiper Road, just 5 miles south of the Back Bay refuge, Virginia Beach; for camping and other information, call (757) 426–7128 or (800) 933–7275. Admission is $5 per vehicle or $2 per family on foot or bicycles.

the resort area. Although Virginia Beach is bustling in summer, there are some relatively quiet spots for families. These include the strip of sand along the **North End,** from Forty-third Street north toward Fort Story. The southern end of town, the **Sandbridge** area, has lifeguards and a quieter pace than the hubbub in the heart of town. For something different try the beach at **Fort Story,** the army base, which is open to the public.

Whatever stretch of sand you pick, you can enjoy swimming, sunning, and bodysurfing. Ever swish along on roller blades? Rent some in-line skates from the vendors along the boardwalk on Atlantic Avenue, where you can skate in the rink, or glide down the boardwalk with the sea breeze blowing in your hair. There are also two- and four-person surries available for rent along the boardwalk.

Parks. **First Landing State Park,** U.S. 60 at Cape Henry (2500 Shore Drive), Virginia Beach; (757) 412-2320 or (757) 412-2331. This park, with its 19 miles of hiking trails, offers a pleasant respite. Paths lead you by freshwater ponds and through thickets of large cypress trees draped with Spanish moss. There is a special bicycle trail (bring your own bike), and bikes are permitted on park roads. A boat ramp offers access to Broad Bay. **The Chesapeake Bay Center,** an environmentally focused, interactive visitor center, features outdoor aquariums, a touch tank, and exhibits developed by the Virginia Marine Science Museum.

Virginia Beach offers the usual array of amusements and T-shirt shops. **Ocean Breeze Waterpark,** 849 General Booth Boulevard (757-422-4444; www.oceanbreezewaterpark.com) was completely renovated in 2000 and now has a Caribbean theme. For older kids and adults, try Bahama Mamma, the high-speed water slide, Kool Runnings, and Toucan Tunnel. For younger children check out Kiddie Caverns, Loony Lagoon, which includes a splashing fire engine, and South Seas Silly Slides with three pint-sized water slides. At **Motorworld** (757-422-4444) you can zoom along a track in three-quarter-scale Grand Prix cars or play slugger by batting home runs at the Strike Zone. New rollercoasters and rides will be opening in 2001.

Museums. **Virginia Marine Science Museum,** 717 General Booth Boulevard, Virginia Beach (757) 437-4949 or (757) 425-FISH for recorded information; www.vmsm.com. Admission.

The Virginia Marine Science Museum is a must-see. The **wall-size tank** of deep-sea denizens and sharks is dramatic. A ⅓-mile path through a salt marsh connects the main building with the newer **Owls Creek Marsh Pavilion.** On this walk sweet gum and maples offer shade, and circular loops jut out into the water, providing clear views of the gulls and great blue herons swooping down for fish.

Visitors view sand tiger, brown, and nurse sharks inside the 300,000-gallon Norfolk Canyon Aquarium at the Virginia Marine Science Museum.

The exhibits inside are equally clever, with kid-friendly touch-screen computers. In the whimsical **Macro Marsh** gallery, the "grass" is ten times larger than real life and visitors feel as tiny as hermit crabs; little things, such as a mosquito's head, come into view via microscopes.

In summer and on weekends in the fall, the museum offers two-hour **dolphin-watching trips,** and from January through mid-March the museum offers **whale-watching trips.** Sleep-Overs give families an opportunity to enjoy hands-on activities and get a closer look at the museum. Bay Lab Family Programs, at the museum's off-site facility at First Landing State Park on the Chesapeake Bay along Shore Drive, are held on Thursday evenings. Here kids can learn about the fish and invertebrates that live in the bay. There are also hour-and-a-half programs for children throughout the summer and one- and two-day mini-camps. Call (757) 437-6007 for special programs.

The **Old Coast Guard Station,** Twenty-fourth Street and Atlantic Avenue; (757) 422-1587; www.va-beach.com/old_coast. Learn about life-saving techniques from the early days of shipwrecks through submarine-mined waters during both world wars. An interactive exhibit, TowerCAM, lets you scan the sea for ships in distress. Closed Mondays. Admission.

More Attractions. **Cape Henry Lighthouse,** at the northeastern tip of Virginia Beach, on the grounds of the U.S. Army's Fort Story. Open mid-March through October. This lighthouse, built in 1791, marked the entrance to the Chesapeake Bay until 1881. In summer the lighthouse is open for tours and climbs to the top (757) 422-9421; www.us-lighthouses.org/oldcape.htm. Admission.

Association for Research and Enlightenment, Sixty-seventh Street and Atlantic Avenue, Virginia Beach; (757) 428-3588; www.are-cayce.com. Free. Dive into the world of parapsychology and psychical research. Turn-of-the-century seer Edgar Cayce obeyed instructions he received in a trance to move to Virginia Beach in 1925 to establish a hospital. Cayce, frequently called the "sleeping prophet," garnered his information from higher states of consciousness and gave "readings" in which he diagnosed people's illnesses and prescribed cures—skills he never possessed in his waking state. Visitors can browse the library, which contains Cayce's transcribed readings. Expand your beach reading with tomes on holistic health, numerology, dream interpretation, meditation, and channeling available at the bookstore.

Norfolk

Norfolk is home to the world's largest naval installation, and its history is tied to the sea. The renovated downtown harbor has many attractions, shops, and a friendly family feel, especially at Waterside Festival Marketplace, a collection of shops and eateries. The city's charms are not confined to port. Good bets to visit include the first-class botanical garden and the Chrysler Museum of Art. Just twenty minutes west of Virginia Beach, Norfolk is a good stop for families en route to the beach or those taking in Tidewater's attractions.

Norfolk Convention and Visitor's Bureau, 232 East Main Street, Norfolk 23510; (757) 664-6620; www.norfolk.va.us. For a visitor guide call (800) 368-3097.

Norfolk Trolley offers one-hour tours of downtown during the summer months. The trolley starts at the Waterside and allows visitors to get off to explore sites and then reboard.

Museums. **The Chrysler Museum of Art,** 245 West Olney Road; (757) 664-6200 or (757) 622-ARTS; www.chrysler.org. Admission. The museum's vast collection includes textiles, ceramics, bronzes, and paintings from pre-Columbian, African, and Asian artists, plus an array of European paintings and American art from the eighteenth century to the twentieth century. A highlight of the museum's notable glass collection is the many Tiffany items, whose colorful, elaborate designs dazzle. Kids

Water Fun

- **Cruise:** Blue Moon Cruises, 600 Laskin Road, Virginia Beach; (757) 422-2900. Cruise on an 80-foot luxury yacht. The boat leaves from Brownings Landing.
- **Fish:** the Virginia Beach Fishing Center, 200 Winston Salem Avenue at the Rudee Inlet Bridge; (757) 422-5700. Book a day of deep-sea fishing or a sightseeing cruise of the oceanfront.
- **Boats:** Sandbridge Boat Rentals, 3713 Sandpiper Road (757-721-6210), rents boats and canoes.

A Great Drive: the Chesapeake Bay Bridge Tunnel

Even if it costs $10 each way to cross the 17.6-mile Chesapeake Bay Bridge Tunnel, the fee is worth it, at least once. As the structure loops over and under the bay, it's easy to savor the sense of space and joy common to open roads, panoramic water views, and sea breezes.

also appreciate the prints of Norfolk by such famous photographers as Ansel Adams and Alfred Stieglitz. Family programs and special Family Days are scheduled throughout the year; call for a schedule. A restaurant and a cafe are on-site.

Parks and Gardens. **Norfolk Botanical Garden,** 6700 Azalea Garden Road, located near the airport; (757) 441-5830. This don't-miss spot outside downtown Norfolk has **155 acres** of garden blooms in season with one of the East Coast's largest collections of azaleas, camellias, roses, and rhododendrons. Stroll along 12 miles of garden pathways through more than twenty theme gardens. Kids, especially preschool ones, enjoy the **canal boat or the tram tours,** both of which save little feet from lots of walking.

The **Virginia Zoological Park,** 3500 Granby Street; (757) 441-2706; www.communitylinks.org/vazoo. Admission. Not large compared with some big city zoos, the Virginia Zoological Park offers a nice outing for families with little kids. The zoo features more than 300 animals, including the diamondback terrapin, the two-toed sloth, the Baird's tapir, which resembles a miniature elephant, Bengal tigers, a clouded leopard, and a white rhinoceros. The Xaxaba African Village is home to two male gelada baboons who enjoy the comforts of a night house, a spacious play area, a waterfall, and a small splashing pool. In 2001 the Okavango Delta exhibit is scheduled to open, with lions and giraffes in residence.

Spectator Sports. **Harbor Park Stadium,** 150 Park Avenue; (757) 622-2222. This park is home to the Norfolk Tides, an AAA team for the New York Mets. In addition to baseball games, the 12,000-seat stadium hosts concerts and other events.

Shopping. **The Waterside Festival Marketplace,** 333 Waterside Drive, on the Norfolk waterfront. This shopping mall has become an attraction and gathering place for locals. Overlooking the Elizabeth River, the facility houses more than one hundred shops, stalls, restaurants, and eateries. In season several boat tours and a tour of the Norfolk Naval Base leave from here. Your kids will undoubtedly want to come here to shop for take-home treasures. In 2000 the MacArthur Center opened, with more than one hundred fifty stores, an eighteen-screen movie theater, and nine restaurants. It's located at 300 Monticello Avenue, (757) 627-6000; www.shopmacarthurmall.com.

Ships and the Sea in Norfolk

- **Nauticus, the National Maritime Center,** 1 Waterside Drive; (757-664-1000 or 800-664-1080; www.nauticus.org) is devoted to exploring the sea's importance and power as a commercial and military force using more than 150 hands-on exhibits. Land a navy warplane on an aircraft carrier, design a seaworthy ship, and discover how an octopus travels. At the Aegis Theater live actors and video involve the audience in a high-tech naval battle aboard a destroyer. By crewing aboard Virtual Adventures, a 3-D virtual reality ride, your maneuvers can foil sea creatures in this simulated underwater environment. Recommended for ages six and older.

  Kids can also stand atop a real ship's bridge in the Exploratorium gallery, pet sharks in Aquaria, and tape their own weather forecast in Environment. Hands-on activities are scheduled regularly such as Shark Encounters (kids can touch a shark), and there's a kiddie tidepool for younger children. The battleship *Wisconsin* (www.battleshipwisconsin.org) opened in early 2001. Nauticus also houses the Hampton Roads Naval Museum (757-444-8971), one of the U.S. Navy's ten official museums. This one highlights naval battles and events in the Norfolk area through detailed ship models, naval artwork, and underwater artifacts. Admission is free.

- **The Norfolk Naval Base,** 9809 Hampton Boulevard; (757) 640-6300 for TRT bus service or (757) 444-7637 for the Naval Base. Norfolk, home port to more than a hundred ships of the Atlantic fleet, is the world's largest naval installation. Forty-five-minute bus tours go past fleet training centers, the Jamestown Exposition, a group of restored, 1907 structures now used as homes, and aircraft carriers. Two ships are open for free tours every weekend.

- **The Tugboat Museum,** docked beside Nauticus; (757) 627-4884. Looking like a storybook vessel with its red paint, the tug *Huntington is a* restored 1933 working boat turned into a dockside museum. Aboard you can tour the engine room, visit the crew's quarters and the galley and view photographs of tugboat life. Admission.

Newport News

Located along the James River near Virginia Beach, Norfolk, and Williams-burg, Newport News is home to the world's largest privately owned ship-yard and Virginia's largest employer, the Newport News Shipbuilding and Dry Dock Company. Newport News has some family-friendly attractions of its own. **Newport News Visitor Information Center,** 13560 Jefferson Avenue; (757) 886-7787 or (800) 493-7386; www.newport-news.org.

Museums and Galleries. **The Mariners' Museum,** 100 Museum Drive, (757) 596-2222 or (800) 581-SAIL; www.mariner.org. This museum explores the sea's use for transportation, warfare, food, and pleasure. Examine miniature and handcrafted ship models, carved fig-ureheads, scrimshaw, maritime paintings, and working steam engines. The museum features several galleries. Favorites with kids include the **Age of Exploration Gallery,** with its hands-on replicas of early maps and navigational tools and its fifteen short videos; the **Crabtree Collection of Miniature Ships** has sixteen detailed miniatures; the **Great Hall of Steam**'s history of steamships; the **Chesapeake Bay Gallery,** which details this body of water's development and has an exhibit on ship-building; as well as **Defending the Seas,** the newest permanent exhibit, where kids can board a replica of an eighteenth-century frigate and take the helm of a nuclear submarine. Opening in spring 2002 will be an exhibit focusing on the transatlantic slave trade in the eighteenth cen-tury. Allow time to enjoy the museum's parklike setting on 550 acres. You can rent boats, picnic, and walk a 5-mile trail that surrounds Lake Maury. Admission.

At the indoor/outdoor **Virginia Living Museum,** 524 J. Clyde Morris Boulevard (757-595-1900; www.valivingmuseum.org), the exhibits look back at you. Outdoor paths lead you by raccoons, beavers, river otters, foxes, bobcats, deer, a bald eagle, forty species of birds, and many other animals in their natural habitats. Indoor highlights include a living replica of the **James River,** a touch tank where kids handle sea stars and horseshoe crabs, an authentic dinosaur footprint made by *Kayentapus* (measure your foot size against his), plus a planetarium and observatory. The museum is beginning a major expansion in 2000, with the addition of an outdoor aviary featuring more than thirty species of native wetland birds. Admission.

Peninsula Fine Arts Center's Children's Interactive Gallery, 101 Museum Drive; (757) 596-8175. Little ones especially like the children's interactive gallery, Hands-On For Kids, a place to create art geared just for them. Kids can color, paint, and craft collages and other artistic works. Check the calendar for the facility's special classes. Admission.

Green Spaces. Take time to play at the 8,065-acre **Newport News Regional Park,** 13564 Jefferson Avenue, the second-largest municipal park in the United States. Enjoy boating, canoeing, mountain biking, paddleboats, and fishing on the lake. Rent bicycles to pedal the 10 miles of bike trails. A Discovery Center with lots of family activities is open on weekends year-round. Camping is allowed; call (757) 886-7912; www. newport-news.va.us/parks.

Hampton

Hampton, an interesting city with much history, is home to Hampton University. The area is part of **Hampton Roads,** a southeastern section of Virginia that stretches from Williamsburg to Virginia Beach to the Chesapeake. **Hampton Visitor Center,** 710 Settlers Landing Road; (757) 727-1102 or (800) 800-2202; www.hampton.va.us/tourism. Pick up brochures and city information at this conveniently located center. Most of the kid-pleasing attractions are located on the waterfront, and the most notable is the Virginia Air and Space Center.

Museums and History. **The Virginia Air and Space Center,** 600 Settlers Landing Road; (757) 727-0900 or (800) 296-0900; www.vasc.org. Admission. The Virginia Air and Space Center is not nearly as elaborate as Washington, D.C.'s National Air and Space Museum, but it isn't as crowded, either. You don't have to stand in line to see the moon rock or wait to get close enough to the copper-colored *Apollo 12* command module to read the astronauts' inscription "Yankee Clipper sailed with Intrepid to the Ocean of Storms, Moon. November 14, 1969." The facility has an IMAX theater, and in the atrium there's an impressive array of fifteen planes suspended as if in mid-flight. The photographic exhibit on the first black aviators, the Tuskegee Airmen, is informative. At Astronaut-for-a-Minute, kids can see what they'd look like as astronauts. At Launch-a-Rocket they learn about preparation for launch and then send a simulated rocket into orbit. Call (757) 727-0900, extension 780, for information about Summer Science Camps for Kids.

The **Hampton Roads History Center** is located inside the Virginia Air and Space Museum. This one-room exhibit takes you back to the Colonial past and forward to the 1960s, the days of the Mercury astronauts. View artifacts from a pirate skeleton to a reproduction of the USS *Monitor.* **Fort Monroe and the Casemate Museum,** P.O. Box 341, Fort Monroe; (804) 727-3391. This facility portrays another view of Hampton's military history. Fort Monroe, the largest stone fort ever built in the United States, is currently the only moat-encircled fort still in active use. A tour includes the Chapel of the Centurion, Cannon Park, and the army quarters of **General Robert E. Lee.** In a network of caverns once filled with Fort Monroe's massive guns, the Casemate Museum traces the history of the Civil War and the U.S. Coast Artillery Corps; the museum includes the cell in which **Confederate President Jefferson Davis** was held after the war. This fort now serves as the headquarters for the Army's Training and Doctrine Command.

Other Attractions. The **Hampton Carousel,** 602 Settlers Landing Road; (757) 727-6347 or (757) 727-6381. While you're at the waterfront, take little ones to the restored 1920s merry-go-round with forty-eight prancing steeds.

SPECIAL EVENTS

January. Wildlife Festival, Newport News.

April. Historic Garden Week House and Garden Tour

April–May. Virginia Waterfront International Beach Music Weekend, and Big Band Weekend Arts Festival.

May. Annual Children's Festival of Friends, Newport News, with hands-on activities, food, and entertainment.

June. Jazz Festival attracts national headliners to Hampton.

August. Hampton Cup Regatta powerboat race.

September. Hampton Bay Days is a tribute featuring Chesapeake Bay seafood, lots of children's entertainment, and fireworks.

November–January. Holiday Lights at the Beach (the only time vehicles are permitted to drive on the boardwalk) with more than 400,000 lights.

WHERE TO STAY

For reservations and information contact the **Virginia Beach Visitor Information Center;** (800) VA-BEACH; www.vbfun.com or www.vabeach-hotels.com.

There are many hotels in the Virginia Beach area. Decide if you want to be beachfront in the heart of the action or on the sand but in the quieter northern area or a few blocks from the water. Here are some family-friendly suggestions. Visitors planning on a longer stay should consider real estate rentals. Several rental agencies are available: **Affordable Properties** (757-428-0432) and **Siebert Realty-Sandbridge Beach** (757-426-6200 or 800-231-3037).

The **Ramada Plaza Resort,** Oceanfront at Fifty-seventh Street, Virginia Beach; (800) 365-3032 or (757) 428-7025. This beachfront property is a good choice for the quieter, north end of town. The facility has an indoor and an outdoor pool, and supervised kids' activities in season. **The Holiday Inn SunSpree Resort,** Thirty-ninth and Oceanfront, Virginia Beach; (757) 428-1711 or (800) 94-BEACH. This property has an outdoor pool and, in season, a children's activity program, Kidzone.

The Holiday Inn Surfside Hotel & Suites, 2607 Atlantic Avenue, Virginia Beach; (757) 491-6900 or (800) 810-2400. In the heart of the "action," this property offers rooms and suites plus an indoor pool. **The Barclay Towers,** 809 Atlantic Avenue, Virginia Beach; (757) 491-2700 or (800) 344-4473. This is an all-suite hotel whose rooms have kitchenettes. Three-, five-, and seven-night package plans are available. **The Days Inn Oceanfront,** at Thirty-second Street, Virginia Beach; (757) 428-7233 or (800) 292-3297. This is right on the beach and has an indoor pool, plus it offers whale-watching packages.

The Belvedere Motel, Oceanfront at Thirty-sixth Street, Virginia Beach; (757) 425-0612 or (800) 425-0612. This lodging offers families motel rooms and efficiencies. **The Cavalier Hotel,** Forty-second and Oceanfront, Virginia Beach; (757) 425-8555 or (888) SINCE27; www.cavalierhotel.com. This property has two locations, one on the beach and one nearby. At both sites there are balconies, and children under eighteen stay free. **The Hilton Resort,** Oceanfront at Eighth Street, Virginia Beach; (757) 428-8935 or (800) HILTONS. This resort has refrigerators in every room, a heated indoor and outdoor pool, and children under twelve stay free.

Norfolk provides a toll-free hotel reservations service; call (800) 368-3097.

WHERE TO EAT

Virginia Beach offers the usual array of cheap eats plus some good restaurants. Some good picks: **Pasta e Pani,** 1069 Laskin Road (757-428-2299), where the bread is legendary; or try the **Lucky Star,** 1608 Pleasure House Road (757-363-8410), where the imaginative entrees may include mahi-mahi with sautéed bananas and rum. Try **Coastal Grill,** 1427 North Great Neck Road (757-496-3348), another nouvelle American restaurant that offers good seafood and tasty black bean soup. **The Jewish Mother,** 3108 Pacific Avenue (757-422-5430), is an informal restaurant that offers deli sandwiches with enough variety for even the most finicky kid. Breakfast is served all day, and some evenings there is live music. **Mahi Mah's Seafood Restaurant & Sushi Saloon,** 615 Atlantic Avenue (757-437-8030), in the Ramada Inn offers sushi and seafood.

Treat your family to the homemade crab cakes and dinner buffet at the **Duck-In,** 3324 Shore Drive at Lynnhaven Inlet Bridge; (757) 481-0201. Looking for the best cheesecake in town and some good seafood, too? Stop by **King of the Sea,** Twenty-seventh Street and Atlantic Avenue; (757) 428-7983. Seafood and chicken plus the house specialty—She-Crab Soup—can be had at the **Lighthouse Oceanfront,**

First Street and Atlantic Avenue; (757) 428-7974. There's a kid's menu.

In Newport News there's the **Rocky Mountain Bar B Q House,** 10113 Jefferson Avenue (757) 596-0243, **Bill's Seafood House,** 10900 Warwick Boulevard (757) 595-4320, **Don Pablo's Mexican Kitchen,** 12150 Jefferson Avenue (757) 249-8411, and the **Old Country Buffet,** 14346 Warwick Boulevard (757) 874-2385.

FOR MORE INFORMATION

Virginia Beach
In Virginia Beach contact the Visitor Information Center at (800) VA-BEACH.

Hampton
Hampton Conventions and Tourism is at 2 Eaton Street; (757) 722-1222 or (800) 487-8778. There's a Visitor Center at 710 Settlers Landing Road (757) 727-1102 or (800) 800-2002.

Norfolk
The Norfolk Convention and Visitors Bureau, 232 East Main Street; (757) 664-6620. The toll-free hotel reservations number is (800) 368-3097. For a visitor's guide or information, call (800) FUN-IN-VA; www.norfolk.va.us.

Newport News
The Newport News Tourism Development office; (757) 926-3561. Contact the Visitors Center, 13560 Jefferson Avenue; (888) 4-WE-R-FUN or (757) 886-7777; www.newport-news.org.

Emergency Numbers
Ambulance, fire, and police: 911

Beach Police: (757) 427-4377

Norfolk Police: (757) 441-5610

Poison Control Center: (757) 480-5288

Sentara Bayside Hospital: (757) 460-8000

Sentara Norfolk General Hospital: (757) 668-3201

Sentara Hampton General Hospital, 3120 Victoria Boulevard; (757) 727-7000

Twenty-four-hour pharmacy: Eckerd Drug Store at Wards Corner, Norfolk; (757) 583-0515

Virginia Beach General Hospital: (757) 481-8000

THE HARPERS FERRY AREA

O n the night of October 16, 1859, John Brown led his band of twenty-one men on an abolitionist-inspired raid of Harpers Ferry. Hoping to gain access to the munitions, he envisioned the raid as the event that would spark a nationwide abolitionist movement. Although John Brown and some of his band were captured by Robert E. Lee, convicted of murder, treason, and conspiracy and hanged, this small group's actions had an impact: The raiders' abolitionist efforts, and their trial and punishment by their countrymen, foreshadowed the bloodiest years in the history of the United States. Sixteen months after John Brown's arrest and execution, the Civil War broke out. For its historical significance the lower part of town has been preserved as a living-history park, the **Harpers Ferry National Historical Park.**

The surrounding area, at the confluence of the Potomac and the Shenandoah Rivers, affords scenic countryside and miles of hiking, including the Appalachian Trail. A visit to Harpers Ferry puts you near a Civil War battle site, natural springs, and enjoyable white-water rafting rides.

GETTING THERE

By car take I-81 to exit 12 and follow Route 340 to Harpers Ferry. The park is approximately 65 miles northwest of Washington, D.C. Follow the brown-and-white signs to the main entrance of **Harpers Ferry National Historical Park Visitors Center,** where there is a parking lot. A shuttle service operates between here and town. The park remains open every day of the year except Thanksgiving Day and Christmas Day.

Amtrak (800-USA-RAIL) stops in Harpers Ferry. **MARC** (Maryland Area Rail Commuter) (800-325-RAIL) is a commuter train line to Harpers Ferry operating weekdays during rush hours. Both rail services use the Harpers Ferry train station (304-535-6346) on Potomac Street.

Harpers Ferry

AT A GLANCE

▶ Raft the Shenandoah and Potomac Rivers

▶ Tour the John Brown Museum

▶ Hike the Appalachian Trail and paths near the Shenandoah and Potomac Rivers

▶ Harpers Ferry National Historical Park: (304) 535-6298; www.nps.gov/hafe/home.htm

▶ Jefferson County Convention and Visitor Bureau: (800) 848-TOUR; www.jeffersoncountycvb.com

GETTING AROUND

Walking is the best way to see Harpers Ferry National Historical Park. Since the park occupies the lower portion of Harpers Ferry, which has only a few main streets, directions are easy to follow. The shuttle stop for the parking and visitors' center and the information center is on **Shenandoah Street.** Two of the town's other important streets, **High** and **Potomac,** run perpendicular to Shenandoah Street. As street addresses are not easily visible, and not frequently used, find your way around town with a map obtained from the visitors' center, the information center on Shenandoah Street, or by writing to Harpers Ferry National Historical Park, P.O. Box 65, Harpers Ferry, West Virginia 25425.

Physically challenged travelers will find limited accessibility to some of the buildings and exhibits. Also, note that many of Harpers Ferry's sidewalks and steps are fashioned from cobblestone and brick; the uneven nature of these surfaces could pose a problem for some visitors and prove a difficult obstacle for a baby stroller or wheelchair. For information on physically challenged accessibility, call the Harpers Ferry National Historical Park at (304) 535-6223.

WHAT TO SEE AND DO

Harpers Ferry National Historic Park

Harpers Ferry National Historical Park, Harpers Ferry, West Virginia; (304) 535-6223. Encompassing all of Harpers Ferry's lower, downtown district (as well as land in three states—West Virginia, Virginia, and Mary-

Outdoor Adventures

- **Hiking.** The famed Appalachian Trail has 25 miles of scenic trails in the Harpers Ferry area. Check with the Appalachian Trail Conference Visitors Center, Washington and Jackson Streets; (304) 535-6331; www.atconf.org. Pick up the trail at the Stone Steps off High Street.

- **White-water rafting.** Raft the Shenandoah and Potomac Rivers in Class II-III rapids. Call Blue Ridge Outfitters (304-725-3444; www.broraft.com); River Riders (304-535-2663 or 800-326-7238; www.riverriders.com); Historical River Tours (304-535-2663); River and Trail Outfitters (301-695-5177; www.rivertrail.com).

- **Horseback riding.** Elk Mountain Trails (301-834-8882 or 301-986-8483) takes families on guided horseback riding trips on weekends, March to December. Special four-hour lunch and dinner rides are available as well.

land), the National Historical Park has restored buildings to appear as they did in 1859, when John Brown and his group attempted their raid. Imagination is necessary because while the park exhibits convey the era, many of the town's stores have been turned into souvenir and craft shops. Some are interesting, and some are kitschy. You have to get beyond the commercialism to envision the nineteenth century, the era of slavery, and John Brown's bold attempt.

To help transport you back to the nineteenth century, some park rangers, dressed in period costumes, take part in living-history demonstrations. More of these occur in summer than at other times. Depending upon the availability of park rangers, interpreters may be in the dry goods store, the blacksmith's shop, the tavern, the confectionery, and the marshal/provost office. Historical tours and guided walks of the nature trails in the 2,300 acres are available from Memorial Day through Labor Day. Tours focus on such topics as John Brown's raid, the Civil War in Harpers Ferry, and camp life during the war, and there are also marsh walks. Each tour is approximately one hour long, and many are wheelchair accessible. Call for further information or inquire at the visitor center.

Among the most interesting exhibits and museums in town are the John Brown Museum, John Brown's fort, the Industry Museums, the Civil War Museums, and Black Voices from Harpers Ferry.

After visiting the Information Center, start at the **John Brown Museum,** at the opposite end of Shenandoah Street. The exhibits set the stage by explaining the complexity of the economic, cultural, and political

John Brown's Fort is one of the many nineteenth-century buildings you can tour in Harpers Ferry National Historical Park.

issues of the era, as well as the events of the raid and the aftermath.

The armory that John Brown and his men seized was destroyed in 1861 to prevent its falling into Confederate hands. **John Brown's Fort,** Old Arsenal Square, at the intersection of Shenandoah and Potomac Streets, is actually the firehouse where John Brown and his men barricaded themselves from the authorities. Col. Robert E. Lee and Lt. J.E.B. Stuart captured Brown and his "army of liberation" here on the morning of October 18.

Civil War Museums, High Street, document life in Harpers Ferry during the Civil War years. Exhibits emphasize the small, quiet town's transition to a war-torn village. Some of the documents, letters, and photographs of Harpers Ferry's citizens are moving testaments to the disruption of war.

Black Voices from Harpers Ferry, High Street, chronicles 250 years of African-American heritage through the diaries and letters of Harpers Ferry's African-American community. Many exhibits feature audio stations, which hold kids' interest.

Along the footpath of the **Appalachian Trail,** which extends behind the Black Voices from Harpers Ferry museum, explore **St. Peter's Catholic Church,** built in the 1830s. Don't miss the oldest structure in Harpers Ferry, **Harper House.** Built in 1782, it is decorated with nineteenth-century furniture. Continue along the path away from town to the ruins of **St. John's Episcopal Church,** before reaching historic

Ghost Tours

Call **Ghost Tours** at (304) 725-8019 and, with a local guide, stalk the streets in search of one of Harpers Ferry's many ghosts. The guides for this privately operated tour prefer customers at least eighteen years old, but call and discuss the issue if you think your slightly younger teen would be interested.

Winding through town, this one-hour tour has you looking for the ghost of Dangerfield Newby, a fellow raider and the first man killed in the botched John Brown Raid. Newby's body was mutilated by townsfolk, then left in an alley (Hogs Alley), where hogs feasted upon his corpse. Other ghosts who are presumed to haunt the town, though in a friendly manner, are the departed spirits of spies, soldiers, and a priest. Some date back to the Revolutionary era.

If interested, meet at the Back Street Cafe, Potomac Street, at 8:00 P.M. on Saturday nights in April and at 8:00 P.M. on Friday, Saturday, and Sunday nights from May through early November. Reservations required in October and November. Admission.

Jefferson Rock. Stand where, in 1783, the former president proclaimed the view to be "stupendous."

John Brown Wax Museum, Shenandoah Street; (304) 535-6342. Depending upon how you feel about wax museums, this one can add to your understanding of John Brown and his importance. Through dioramas and exhibits, the museum helps capture the spirit of John Brown's raid. The museum is open daily mid-March to mid-December and on weekends from December 15 to March 15. The wax museum is a private enterprise and at press time was up for sale. Admission.

Ridgefield Farm & Orchard, Kidwiler Road, Route 3, Box 840, near Harpers Ferry (304-876-3687; www.ridgefieldfarm.com) might be called a museum of the American farm. A family farm since the 1890s, Ridgefield has year-round programs that let children be part of the harvest experience and teach them about growing crops. Call ahead to see what's going to be happening when your family is in the area.

Shopping

Harpers Ferry has lots of shops, from quaint to kitschy. The bookstore at the Information Center offers some of the best buys—good reads and picture books on the era, especially helpful for children. But the shop-till-you-drop set can take heart; the surrounding area has lots of possibilities. (See Side Trips.)

SIDE TRIPS

- **Antietam National Battlefield,** Sharpsburg, Maryland; (301) 432-5124; www.nps.gov/anti. This 960-acre park, about 18 miles from Harpers Ferry, is one of the best-preserved, least commercial, and most moving of all the Civil War battlefields. The September 17, 1862, battle fought here, an important Union victory was known as one of the most bloody battles of the war. On certain weekends from June to October, costumed interpreters talk about life for the Civil War soldier. Maps, markers, and self-guided tours are available. Also visit the **Antietam National Cemetery,** established in 1865. The Antietam Visitors Center, a mile north of Sharpsburg on I-65, has murals depicting the battle scene, a movie, and information about the park.

- **Berkeley Springs, West Virginia,** is about 45 miles from Harpers Ferry. At the **Berkeley Springs State Park** (304-258-2711; www. wvparks.com/berkeleysprings), visit the site where George Washington bathed as a young surveyor. The springs also served as the hallowed waters of local Native American Indian tribes. Founded in 1776, Berkeley Springs calls itself the "country's first spa." Today the area is known for its affordable "tub and rub"—a soak in the mineral waters and a massage—available from the state park facility at the town square. You can enjoy the same mineral waters in more upscale surroundings at the **Renaissance Spa** behind the Country Inn (800-822-6630 or 304-258-2210; www.countryinnwv.com). **The Coolfont Resort** (800-888-8768 or 304-258-4500, www.coolfont.com) features a snow-tubing park, which is open to the public, with eleven 800-foot tubing runs. The resort has snowmaking capabilities. (For information on both, see Where to Stay.)

  Each winter, starting in January, the town hosts a Festival of the Waters and in February adds an international water-tasting competition. For information on the area, call (800) 447-8797 or (304) 258-9147. Hiking, swimming, horseback riding, tennis, and volleyball are nearby at **Cacapon State Park** (304-258-1022; cacaponresort.com).

- The **Tanger Factory Outlet Center,** I-81, exit 13, King Street, Martinsburg (304-262-6300 or 800-409-0810; www.tangeroutlet.com) isn't one of the larger outlet centers, but it offers discount prices on such name brands as **Bass, Hap-E-Toys,** and **Liz Claiborne. Panhandle Pottery and Design,** I-81, exit 13, 615 West King Street, Martinsburg (304-264-0478), offers discounted pottery.

- **Shepherdstown, West Virginia,** about 12 miles from Harpers Ferry, is one of the oldest towns in West Virginia, originally settled by German and English farmers around 1730. Thomas Shepherd purchased the town in 1732. The steamboat had its first successful run here,

Shenandoah National Park

From Harpers Ferry, follow U.S. 340 south 60 miles to the Shenandoah National Park's closest entrance, Skyline Drive in Front Royal, Virginia. This park rides along the Blue Ridge Mountains and extends from Front Royal in the north 80 miles to Waynesboro in the south. The Shenandoah reaches a variety of different peaks from 600 feet at the north entrance to 4,050 feet at the summit of Hawksbill Peak. Outdoor families enjoy the horseback riding, the scenic views, and the hiking trails. A 94-mile stretch of the Appalachian Trail crosses the park. Trail maps are available at park headquarters, visitor centers, and concession stands. Horses are available from April through October at Skyland (MP 41.7). Check with the rangers for free guided hikes, nature walks, and slide presentations. The Harry F. Byrd, Sr. Visitor Center (MP 51) at Big Meadows is open daily April through November. The Dickey Ridge Visitor Center (MP 4.6) is open April through late November. Write to Shenandoah National Park, 3655 U.S. Highway 211 East, Luray, VA 22835 (540-999-3500; www.nps.gov/shen). (See Shenandoah Valley chapter.)

thanks to inventor James Rumsey. A stroll through town offers a look (from the outside mostly, except for commercial shops) of well-preserved late eighteenth- and early nineteenth-century buildings. The **Historic Shepherdstown Museum** (304-876-0910) has Civil War antiques and a half-size replica of Rumsey's steamboat. For more information on Shepherdstown, contact the Welcome Center, King Street (304-876-2786) or call the West Virginia Division of Tourism and Parks (800-CALL-WVA).

SPECIAL EVENTS

The following includes events for Harpers Ferry and the surrounding towns. The most popular festivals in Harpers Ferry are the **October 1860 Election Celebration,** where visitors interact with interpreters who stump nineteenth-century style, and the **December Old Tyme Christmas Celebration,** featuring street carolers and nineteenth-century entertainers in period dress.

January–March. Winter Festival of the Waters.

May. Potomac Eagle Scenic Rail Excursions begin and continue through fall in Romney.

June. Charles Town Spring Mountain Heritage Arts and Crafts Festival.

June-August. Harpers Ferry National Historic Park Summer Military Band Concert Series.

August-October. Apple Harvest at Ridgefield Farm & Orchard.

August. Jefferson County African American Cultural & Heritage Festival, Charlestown.

September. Annual Fall Mountain Heritage Arts & Crafts Festival at Sam Michael's Park, over two hundred craftspeople and bluegrass music.

October. Election of 1860 celebration. Annual Apple Butter Festival, Berkeley Springs. Pumpkin Fest at Ridgefield Farm & Orchard.

December. Harpers Ferry Old Tyme Christmas celebration. Annual Harpers Ferry Christmas Arts & Crafts Show, Hillton House Hotel (304–876–6030).

WHERE TO STAY

Harpers Ferry, West Virginia
Cliffside Inn, U.S. 340 West, Harpers Ferry; (304) 535-6302 or 800-782-8437. This hotel has an indoor and an outdoor pool, tennis courts, and a restaurant. The **Comfort Inn,** U.S. 340 and Union Street, Harpers Ferry (800–228-5150 or 304–535-6391), offers free continental breakfast, a convenient location, and affordable prices. The **Hilltop House Hotel,** 400 East Ridge Street, Harpers Ferry (304–535-2132 or 800-338-8319; www.hilltophousehotel.com), a 112-year-old hotel and restaurant, sits on a bluff overlooking the Potomac and Shenandoah Rivers. Its casual atmosphere and home-style meals are welcoming to families, and it has Murder Mystery weekends throughout the year.

Berkeley Springs, West Virginia
The Country Inn offers seventy rooms and suites in the historic hotel, which are appointed with antiques, or updated motel-style rooms, plus two restaurants and an English country garden (304–258-2210 or 800–822-6630; www.countryinnwv.com).

Cacapon Resort State Park has golf, horseback riding, swimming, 6,000 acres to explore, and a variety of accommodations. **Cacapon Resort** has thirteen standard, eleven modern, and six efficiency cabins, all completely furnished. **Cacapon Lodge** is a fifty-room facility with a nice restaurant, a recreation room, and a craft shop featuring West Virginia crafts. **The Old Inn,** built in the 1930s by the Civilian Conservation Corps, has eleven rooms, interior hand-hewn log beams, stone chimneys, and a kitchen that accommodates up to twenty-five guests. Call (304) 258-1022 or check online at www. capaconresort.com.

Coolfont Resort and Conference Center. Not far from the town of Berkeley Springs, Coolfont offers 1,200 acres of woods. The A-frame chalets are especially nice for families, since the accommodations include kitchen facilities and often two bedrooms. Guests enjoy the lake and lap pool, and, in winter, a snow-tubing park. But most come here to walk in the woods. Call (800) 888-8768 or (304) 258-4500; www.coolfont.com.

Sharpsburg, Maryland

The **Inn at Antietam,** 220 East Main Street, P.O. Box 119, Sharpsburg, MD 21782; (301-432-6601), offers friendly hosts and a charming inn with comfortable Victorian pieces. The inn welcomes well-mannered children over six. All of its rooms are suites, each with a sitting room and private bath. This former farmhouse is surrounded by the Antietam battlefield.

Shepherdstown, West Virginia

Bavarian Inn and Lodge, Route 3, Box 30, Shepherdstown; (304) 876-2551. Shepherdstown is about 12 miles outside Harpers Ferry. Set along the banks of the Potomac, the Bavarian Inn offers seventy-three rooms, forty-two of which overlook the Potomac. The Bavarian Inn's restaurant emphasizes German cuisine. Each fall the inn hosts Oktoberfest. The **Clarion Hotel,** 17 Lowe Drive (304-876-7000), has 168 rooms, plus a spa, sauna, pool, restaurant, and pub.

WHERE TO EAT

Harpers Ferry

Try the **Mountain House Cafe,** 179 High Street, Harpers Ferry; (304) 535-2339. The Mountain House offers sandwiches and salads. **The Anvil Restaurant,** 1270 Washington Street (304-535-2582), offers American fare and a children's menu. It's located within the historic area. **Yesterday's,** 152A High Street (304-535-2738), has tasty, fresh-baked cinnamon rolls and several types of homemade fudge.

Berkeley Springs

Maria's Garden Restaurant, 201 Independence Street (304-258-2021), offers good, basic Italian fare. **Tari's Premier Cafe,** 123 North Washington Street (304-258-1196), features creative and low-fat fare.

Shepherdstown

Try the **Yellow Brick Bank Restaurant,** corner of Princess and West German Streets (304-876-2208), where the interesting cuisine mixes American and Continental touches. **Sebastian's American Grille** in the Clarion Hotel (see above) serves classic American cuisine for breakfast, lunch, and dinner.

Charlestown

Towne House Restaurant, 549 East Washington Street (304-725-3037), is a good choice for family dining in a casual atmosphere.

FOR MORE INFORMATION

For more information on the Harpers Ferry area, contact the Jefferson County Convention and Visitor Bureau, P.O. Box A, Harpers Ferry, West Virginia 25425; (800) 848-TOUR or (304) 535-2627; www.jeffersoncountyvb.com. Harpers Ferry National Historical Park, P.O. Box 65, Harpers Ferry, WV 25425; (304-535-6298; www.nps.gov/hafe/home.htm). The West Virginia Welcome Center is located off Route 340 in Harpers Ferry (304-535-2782 or 800-CALL-WVA) and has information on attractions, as well as a free reservation service. Other sources of information: Jefferson County Chamber of Commerce (304-725-2055 or 800-624-0577), Martinsburg-Berkeley Country Convention and Visitor Bureau (304-264-8801 or 800-498-2386), and Welcome to Washington County, Maryland (301-791-3246 or 888-257-2600).

Emergency Numbers

Ambulance, fire, and police: 911

Jefferson County State Police (nonemergency): (304) 725-8484

Jefferson Memorial Hospital, 300 South Preston Street, Ranson, West Virginia; (304) 728-1600

Twenty-four-hour pharmaceutical needs and poison control: City Hospital, Dry Run and Tavern Roads, Martinsburg, West Virginia; (304) 264-1000

Index